Iustitia Dei

IUSTITIA DEI

A HISTORY OF
THE CHRISTIAN DOCTRINE OF
JUSTIFICATION

VOLUME II
FROM 1500 TO THE PRESENT DAY

ALISTER E. McGRATH

**LECTURER IN CHRISTIAN DOCTRINE AND ETHICS
WYCLIFFE HALL, OXFORD**

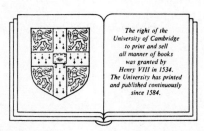

*The right of the
University of Cambridge
to print and sell
all manner of books
was granted by
Henry VIII in 1534.
The University has printed
and published continuously
since 1584.*

CAMBRIDGE UNIVERSITY PRESS

CAMBRIDGE

NEW YORK   PORT CHESTER

MELBOURNE   SYDNEY

Published by the Press Syndicate of the University of Cambridge
The Pitt Building, Trumpington Street, Cambridge CB2 1RP
40 West 20th Street, New York, NY 10011-4211, USA
10 Stamford Road, Oakleigh, Melbourne 3166, Australia

First published 1986
Reprinted 1991

Printed in Great Britain at
the University Press, Cambridge

British Library cataloguing in publication data
McGrath, Alister E.
Iustitia Dei: a history of the Christian
doctrine of justification.
Vol. 2: From 1500 to the present day
1. Justification – History of doctrines
I. Title
234'.7'09   BT764.2

Library of Congress cataloguing in publication data
McGrath, Alister E., 1953–
Iustitia Dei: a history of the Christian doctrine of
justification.
Bibliography.
Includes indexes.
Contents: v. 1. From the beginnings to 1500 – v. 2.
From 1500 to the present day.
1. Justification – History of doctrines. I. Title.
BT764.M43   1986   234'.7'09   85-31339

ISBN 0 521 32274 X

Contents

Contents

Preface

The present volume documents the development of the doctrine of justification within the western Christian tradition from 1500 to the present day. This period has witnessed the emergence of a remarkable diversity of opinions on this matter as a result of the Reformation and the subsequent divisions within a tradition hitherto characterised by relative homogeneity and continuity. Whereas it was possible, in the first volume of this work, to deal with the development of the doctrine in a broadly thematic manner, this approach cannot be sustained in the present volume. It is now necessary to deal with the subject at least in part along confessional lines, with increased attention being directed towards inter- and intraconfessional debates. The necessity of examining certain significant historical questions, such as the identity of the theological schools represented at the Council of Trent, adds further to the difficulties attending a thematic approach. It is, however, hoped that the scope of the present volume will permit the reader to discern the main lines of development of the doctrine since the Reformation, even if pressure upon space has occasionally prevented detailed doctrinal exposition where it is clearly merited.

Thanks are due to the publishers of *Theologische Zeitschrift*, *Kerygma und Dogma* and the *Churchman* for permission to reproduce material originally published in those journals, now to be found in §§31, 33 and 37.

6. The development of the doctrine in the Reformation period

Introduction

The leading principle of the Reformation is generally considered to be its doctrine of justification.[1] This is not, in fact, correct. It is certainly true that the *articulus iustificationis* is the leading feature of the theology of Martin Luther,[2] and that his enormous influence over the evangelical faction within Germany and elsewhere inevitably led to this high estimation being reflected elsewhere. Thus by the beginning of the seventeenth century the *articulus iustificationis* appears to have been generally regarded as the *articulus stantis et cadentis ecclesiae*, the 'article by which the church stands or falls'.[3] Nevertheless, as will become clear in the present study, the origins of the Reformed church owe little, if anything, to Luther's insights into justification. The relation between Luther's own theological insights and the dawn of the Reformation itself is now appreciated to be an historical question of the utmost complexity,[4] and it must be emphasised that it is no longer possible to assert with any degree of certainty that the Reformation began as a consequence of Luther's new insights into man's justification *coram Deo*, although it is unquestionably true that Luther's own personal theological preoccupations centred upon this matter. The present chapter is concerned with the documentation and critical analysis of the understandings of justification associated with the Reformation in Germany and Switzerland – in other words, with the origins and subsequent development of the Lutheran and Reformed churches. In view of the crucial importance of the development of Martin Luther's theological insights to any account of the origins of the Reformation, we begin by considering his break with the theology of the medieval period associated with his 'discovery of the righteousness of God', and the leading features of his doctrine of justification.

The Reformation is often portrayed as a rediscovery of the Bible, particularly of the Pauline corpus. Although there is undoubtedly

I

truth in this description, it is considerably more accurate to portray it as a rediscovery of Augustine's doctrine of grace, with a subsequent critique of his doctrine of the church.[5] In an age which witnessed a general revival of Augustinian studies,[6] this new interest in Augustine must be regarded as an aspect of the Renaissance in general, rather than a feature peculiar to the Reformers. What was unquestionably new, however, is the use to which the Reformers put Augustine. The most accurate description of the doctrines of justification associated with the Reformed and Lutheran churches from 1530 onwards is that they represent a radically new interpretation of the Pauline concept of 'imputed righteousness' set within an Augustinian soteriological framework. The leading primary characteristics of Protestant doctrines of justification, as established from the literary output of the theologians of the Lutheran and Reformed churches over the period 1530–1700, may be summarised as follows:

1. Justification is defined as the forensic *declaration* that the believer is righteous, rather than the process by which he is *made* righteous, involving a change in his *status* rather than his *nature*.

2. A deliberate and systematic distinction is made between *justification* (the external act by which God declares the sinner to be righteous) and *sanctification* or *regeneration* (the internal process of renewal within man). Although the two are treated as inseparable, a notional distinction is thus drawn where none was conceded before.

3. Justifying righteousness, or the formal cause of justification, is defined as the alien righteousness of Christ, external to man and imputed to him, rather than a righteousness which is inherent to him, located within him, or which in any sense may be said to belong to him. God's judgement in justification is therefore *synthetic* rather than *analytic*, in that there is no righteousness within man which can be considered to be the basis of the divine verdict of justification; the righteousness upon which such a judgement is necessarily based is external to man.

It is clearly of importance to account for this new understanding of the nature of justifying righteousness, with its associated conceptual distinction between justification and sanctification. Attempts on the part of an earlier generation of Protestant apologists to defend this innovation as a recovery of the authentic teaching of Augustine, and of their Catholic opponents to demonstrate that it constituted a vestige of a discredited and ossified Ockhamism, can no longer be taken seriously. It is the task of the historian to account for this new development, which marks a complete break with the tradition up to this point.[7]

It must be made clear that it is quite inadequate to attempt to characterise the doctrines of justification associated with the Reformation by referring merely to their anti-Pelagian structure. Such doctrines of justification can be adduced from practically every period in the history of doctrine, particularly in the later medieval period (such as within the *schola Augustiniana moderna*). The notional distinction, necessitated by a forensic understanding of justification, between the external act of God in pronouncing sentence, and the internal process of regeneration, along with the associated insistence upon the alien and external nature of justifying righteousness, must be considered to be the most reliable *historical* characterisation of Protestant doctrines of justification. As the Osiandrist controversy made clear, an anti-Pelagian doctrine of justification could still be rejected as unrepresentative of the Reformation *if justifying righteousness was conceived intrinsically*. Indeed, precisely this controversy may be considered to have exercised a decisive influence in establishing the concept of forensic justification as characteristic of the Reformation. As the history of the Reformation itself demonstrates, the criterion employed at the time to determine whether a given doctrine of justification was Protestant or not was whether justifying righteousness was conceived extrinsically. This criterion served to distinguish the doctrines of justification associated with the magisterial Reformation from those of Catholicism on the one hand, and the radical Reformation on the other.[8]

In view of the significance of the concept of the imputation of righteousness both as an idea itself, and as a criterion of the Protestant character of a doctrine of justification, much of the present chapter is concerned with documenting its development within the churches of the Reformation. The importance of the concept is also reflected in other parts of the present volume, particularly in the attention paid to the late sixteenth- and early seventeenth-century disputes over the formal cause of justification.

The present chapter begins by documenting Martin Luther's break with the soteriology of the *via moderna*, traditionally regarded as marking a pivotal point in the history of the Reformation.

§20 Luther's discovery of the 'righteousness of God'

In an earlier section (§6), we drew attention to the fact that in the period 1508–14 the young Luther appears to have adopted an understanding of the 'righteousness of God' essentially identical to that of the *via moderna*. The continuities between the young Luther and late medieval theology over the period 1509–14 include several matters of significance to his understanding of justification. Thus the young Luther rejected the implication of supernatural habits in justification,[1] following both the *via moderna* and the *schola Augustiniana moderna* in doing so (see §13). Of particular importance is the observation that in this period he developed an understanding of man's involvement in justification which is clearly based upon the *pactum*-theology of the *via moderna*,[2] and the interpretation of the axiom *facienti quod in se est Deus non denegat gratiam* characteristic of this school of thought.[3] Over the period 1514–19, however, Luther's understanding of justification underwent a radical alteration. The nature and date of this alteration have remained a matter of controversy within contemporary Luther scholarship, justifying extensive discussion of the question in the present section.

One of the most important sources for our understanding of this radical alteration in Luther's doctrine of justification is the 1545 autobiographical fragment,[4] in which Luther records his intense personal difficulties over the concept of the 'righteousness of God'.

Interim eo anno [1519] iam redieram ad Psalterium denuo interpretandum, fretus eo, quod exercitatior essem, postquam S. Pauli Epistolas ad Romanos, ad Galatas, et eam, quae est ad Ebraeos, tractassem in scholis. Miro certe ardore captus fueram cognoscendi Pauli in epistola ad Rom., sed obstiterat hactenus non frigidus circum praecordia sanguis, sed unicum vocabulum, quod est Cap. 1: Iustitia Dei revelatur in illo. Oderam enim vocabulum istud 'Iustitia Dei', quod usu et consuetudine omnium doctorum doctus eram philosophice intelligere de iustitia (ut vocant) formali seu activa, qua Deus est iustus, et peccatores iniustosque punit.[5]

The modern preoccupation of scholars with this autobiographical fragment dates from 1904, when the distinguished Catholic historian Heinrich Denifle argued that Luther's discussion of the term *iustitia Dei* indicated a near-total theological ignorance and incompetence.[6] In a remarkable appendix to his intensely hostile study of the development of Lutheranism, Denifle produced a detailed analysis of the exposition of Romans 1.16–17 by some sixty doctors of the western church, indicating that not one of them, from Ambrosiaster onwards, understood *iustitia Dei* in the sense Luther notes in the above citation.[7] However, the conclusion which Denifle drew from this demonstration – that Luther was either ignorant of the Catholic tradition, or else deliberately perverted it – was clearly unjustified.

Luther made no global reference to the tradition of the western church upon the matter, but referred specifically to the doctors who taught *him* – an unequivocal reference to the *moderni* at Erfurt, under whom he received his initial theological education. There is every indication that Luther is referring to the specific concept of *iustitia Dei* associated with the *via moderna*: God is *iustus*, in the sense that he rewards the man who does *quod in se est* with grace, and punishes the man who does not. In view of Gabriel Biel's unequivocal assertion that man cannot know for certain whether he has, in fact, done *quod in se est*,[8] there is clearly every reason to state that Luther's early concept of *iustitia Dei* was that of the righteousness of an utterly scrupulous and impartial judge, who rewarded or punished man on the basis of an ultimately unknown quality. The autobiographical fragment clearly indicates that Luther's difficulties over the concept of the 'righteousness of God' were resolved *by* (although not necessarily *in*) the year 1519.[9] An analysis of Luther's lectures on the Psalter (1513–15), on Romans (1515–16), and on Galatians (1516–17)[10] indicates that Luther's understanding of this theologoumenon in particular, and his theology of justification in general, appears to have undergone a significant alteration over the period 1514–15, with the crucial step apparently dating from 1515.

Luther's early understanding of justification (1513–14) may be summarised as follows: man must recognise his spiritual weakness and inadequacy, and turn in humility from his attempts at self-justification to ask God for his grace. God treats this humility of faith (*humilitas fidei*)[11] as the precondition necessary for justification under the terms of the *pactum* (that is, as man's *quod in se est*), and thus fulfils his obligations under the *pactum*, by bestowing grace upon him.[12] It is clear that Luther understands man to be capable of making a response towards God without the assistance of special grace, and that this response of *iustitia fidei* is the necessary precondition (*quod in se est*) for the bestowal of justifying grace.[13] Although some Luther scholars have argued that Luther's understanding of the term *iustitia Dei* appears to have undergone a significant alteration during the course of his exposition of Psalms 70 and 71,[14] it is clear that Luther has merely clarified the terminology within his *existing* theological framework, so that the precise relationship of the various *iustitiae* (specifically, the *iustitia* which man must possess if he is to be justified (that is, *iustitia fidei*) and the *iustitia* by which God is obliged to reward this righteousness with grace (that is, *iustitia Dei*)) implied in the process of justification is clarified.[15]

5

Luther still expounds with some brilliance the *pactum*-theology of the *via moderna*.

A decisive break with this theology of justification is evident in the Romans lectures of 1515–16. Three major alterations may be noted, leading to this break. First, Luther insists that man is *passive* towards his own justification.[16] Although not denying that man has *any* rôle in his justification, Luther clearly states that man is not capable of initiating the process leading to justification. Whereas in the *Dictata super Psalterium*, man was understood to be *active* in the process of his justification (in that he was able to turn to God in humility and faith, and cry out for grace), Luther now unequivocally states that it is God who turns man towards him.[17] Second, he insists that man's will is held captive by grace, and is incapable of attaining righteousness unaided by divine grace.[18] One should speak of *servum potius quam liberum arbitrium*, as Augustine reminded Julian of Eclanum (§§4, 7). Third, and perhaps most significant of all, Luther states that the idea that man can do *quod in se est* is nothing more and nothing less than Pelagian, even though he once held this position himself.[19] Despite the fact that his theology of justification up to this point was based upon the explicitly stated presupposition that man was capable of doing *quod in se est*, he now concedes the Pelagianism of the opinion that salvation is dependent upon a decision of the human will.[20] Even though he continues to identify *fides* and *humilitas* for some time to come, it is clear that a genuine and radical alteration in his theology of justification has taken place. Although he may not have arrived at any dramatically new understanding of the *nature* of faith, he has certainly arrived at a radically new understanding of *how faith comes about in the first place*.

The recognition that God bestows the precondition of justification upon man inevitably involves the abandonment of the soteriological framework underlying the *pactum*-theology of the *via moderna*. Luther's early interpretation of *iustitia Dei* was based upon the presupposition that God, in his equity (*equitas*) rewarded the man who had done *quod in se est* with justifying grace, *sine acceptione personarum*. The divine judgement is based solely upon the divine recognition of an individual's possessing a quality which God is under an obligation to reward. If God himself bestows this quality upon man, the framework of *equitas* and *iustitia* essential to the *pactum*-theology of the *via moderna* and the young Luther can no longer be sustained, in that God is open to the charge of *inequitas, iniustitia*, and *acceptio personarum*. The essential feature of Luther's theological breakthrough is thus the destruction of the framework upon which his early soteriology was based, and *thence* the necessity of reinterpretation of the concept of *iustitia Dei*. It is therefore clear that an important change in Luther's understanding of justification took place at some time in the year 1515.

How, then, does this relate to the experience described in the autobiographical fragment of 1545? The first point which should be noted is that the fragment does not state that Luther's discovery *took place* in 1519, or that it was essentially the recognition that *iustitia Dei* was none other than *iustitia qua nos Deus induit, dum nos iustificat*, as some more superficial discussions appear to suggest; if this were the case, we should be forced to conclude that Luther merely came to a conclusion identical to that already reached by Karlstadt in 1517, in a work known to have been read by Luther (see §22). Rather, the fragment states that his theological insights were *complete* by 1519, and also that these insights involved not merely the rethinking of the specific *theologoumenon* of *iustitia Dei*, but also *sapientia Dei*, *fortitudo Dei* and *gloria Dei*. Second, it is clear that the concept of *iustitia Dei* as *iustitia activa* which Luther describes in the fragment is that associated with the soteriology of the *via moderna*.[21] As we suggest elsewhere, however, Luther's discovery of the 'wonderful new definition of righteousness'[22] is essentially programmatic, and capable of being applied to other divine attributes, such as those referred to in the autobiographical fragment, leading ultimately to the *theologia crucis*, the 'theology of the cross',[23] in which there is currently such considerable interest in systematic theological circles.

Although Luther indeed recognises that *iustitia Dei* is not to be understood as the righteousness by which God is himself just, but the righteousness by which he justifies the ungodly, this does not exhaust his understanding of the concept, nor is it sufficient to characterise it adequately. Indeed, Luther's unique interpretation of the 'righteousness of God' could not be distinguished from Augustine's interpretation of the same concept if it were. The following characteristics of Luther's concept of *iustitia Dei* may be established on the basis of an analysis of the later portions of the *Dictata super Psalterium* (1513–15), and the Romans lectures (1515–16). *Iustitia Dei* is:

1. A righteousness which is a gift from God, rather than a righteousness which belongs to God.
2. A righteousness which is revealed in the cross of Christ.
3. A righteousness which contradicts human preconceptions.

While the first of these three elements unquestionably corresponds to an important aspect of Augustine's concept of *iustitia Dei*, the remaining two serve to distinguish Luther and Augustine on this point. For Luther, the 'righteousness of God' is revealed exclusively in the cross, contradicting human preconceptions and expectations of the form that revelation should take. This insight is essentially methodological, as the autobiographical fragment indicates, and is capable of being extended to the remaining divine attributes – such as the 'glory of God', the 'wisdom of God', and the 'strength of God'. All are revealed in the cross, and all are revealed *sub contrariis*, contradicting human expectations. It is this understanding of the nature of the revelation of the divine attributes which underlies Luther's *theologia crucis*, and which distinguishes the 'theologian of glory' from the 'theologian of the cross'.

Initially, Luther could not understand how the concept of a 'righteous God' was gospel, in that it appeared to offer nothing other than condemnation for sinful man. On the basis of the Ciceronian concept of *iustitia* as *reddens unicuique quod suum est*, underlying the concept of *iustitia Dei* associated with the *via moderna*, the man who failed to do *quod in se est* was condemned. The fundamental presupposition at the heart of this soteriology is that man is indeed capable of *quod in se est* – in other words, that man is capable of meeting the fundamental precondition of justification through his own unaided faculties. The essential insight encapsulated in Luther's breakthrough of 1515 is that God himself meets a precondition which man cannot fulfil – in other words, that God himself bestows upon man the gift of *fides Christi*. It is this insight which underlies Luther's remarks of 1517, paralleling the statements of the 1545 fragment: 'Mira et nova diffinitio iusticie, cum usitate sic describatur: "Iusticia est virtus reddens unicuique, quod suum est." Hic vero dicit: "Iusticia est fides Ihesu Christi."'[24] We shall return to consider Luther's concept of *fides Christi* in the following section.

In turning to assess the *significance* of Luther's 'discovery', we are confronted with what appears to be a paradox. Luther's most important insight, judged in terms of its perceived significance to him in his autobiographical reflections, actually has relatively little, if anything, to do with the origins of the Reformation. The Reformed wing of the Reformation was not initially concerned with the general question of man's justification, let alone the particular question of the proper interpretation of the 'righteousness of God'. As we shall indicate later (§22), the Reformation within the Wittenberg theological faculty was based upon essentially Augustinian insights similar to the three we noted in the Romans lectures of 1515–16. Although these insights lay behind Luther's changing conception of the 'righteousness of God', the early Lutheran Reformation did not perceive the two matters to be so intimately related, or that their relation was theologically significant. Indeed, it is clear that many of the Reformers (such as Melanchthon and Calvin) actually reverted to concepts of the 'righteousness of God' which were remarkably similar, if not identical, to that rejected by Luther. Furthermore, the historical origins of the Lutheran Reformation do not appear to have been related primarily to the theologoumenon of *iustitia Dei*. In terms of its historical and theological dimensions, therefore, the Reformation cannot be considered to be closely linked with Luther's discovery. This is not to say that the 'discovery' was of no significance, in that it appears to have been the catalyst for the development of Luther's *theologia crucis*, perhaps one of the most powerful and important understandings of the nature of Christianity ever to have been formulated – but not an understanding which was taken up and developed in the sixteenth century, even within the evangelical faction at Wittenberg itself. The origins of the Reformation at Wittenberg are more complex than might be imagined, and there are excellent reasons for suggesting that it was initially based directly upon Augustine, rather than Luther's interpretation of him.

The importance of Luther's 'theological breakthrough' – a term which, incidentally, is greatly to be preferred to the inappropriate 'Turmerlebnis' or 'reformatorische Entdeckung'[25] – thus relates to Luther's personal theological development, over which it may easily be shown to have exerted an influence which was nothing less than decisive. It is all too easy, however, to equate Luther's personal preoccupations and beliefs with those which would initially lead to, and subsequently shape the thought of, the Reformation as a whole. As noted in the introduction to the present chapter, the relationship between *initia theologiae Lutheri* and *initia Reformationis* is now appreciated to be far too complex to permit the conclusion that Luther's discovery of the 'righteousness of God' *initiated* the Reformation. To illustrate this point, we must consider the remarkable doctrines of justification associated with the early Reformed theologians, such as Zwingli, over which Luther's influence appears to have been minimal.[26] In the following section, however, we are concerned with the broad features of Luther's doctrine of justification

9

from 1515 onwards, particularly as it functions as a point of transition from late medieval thought to Protestantism.

§21 Martin Luther on justification

'Alas, gone is the horseman and the chariots of Israel!' With these words, Melanchthon broke the news of Luther's death in 1546 to the assembled students at Wittenberg. In view of the considerable influence which Melanchthon subsequently came to exercise over the Lutheran church, one may wonder whether he consciously saw himself as playing Elisha to Luther's Elijah. For reasons which will become clear, however, Luther's mantle would fit no man – neither Melanchthon nor Amsdorf.

It was Luther above all who saw the *articulus iustificationis* as *the* word of the gospel, to which all else was subordinate. The doctrine of justification which he propounded was to cause him to reject the papacy and the church of his day, not on the basis of any *direct* ecclesiological argument, but upon the basis of his conviction that the church of his day was committed to doctrines of justification which were nothing less than Pelagian.[1] The priority of his soteriology over his ecclesiology is particularly evident in his remarkable statement of 1535, to the effect that he will concede the Pope his authority if the latter concedes the free justification of sinners in Christ.[2] The cornerstone both of Luther's theological breakthrough and his subsequent controversy with the church of his day appears to have been based upon his insight that man cannot initiate the process of justification, and his conviction that the church of his day had, by affirming the direct opposite, fallen into the Pelagian error. It is, of course, obvious that this was not the case: he appears to have been familiar with the academic theology of the *via moderna* at first hand, and does not appear to have known any of the rival soteriologies – such as that of the *schola Augustiniana moderna* (despite his being a member of the Augustinian Order).[3] In view of the fact that the soteriology of certain Reformed theologians (such as Peter Martyr Vermigli and John Calvin) may reflect precisely this soteriology,[4] it is necessary to treat Luther's inadequate and ill-informed generalisations concerning the theology (especially the *pastoral* theology) of the late medieval church with considerable caution.

Following his decisive break with the soteriology of the *via moderna* in 1515, the general lines of the development of Luther's theology are clear. The important concept of *iustitia Christi aliena*, the 'commerce of exchange' between Christ and the sinner, and the *totus homo* theology all make their appearance in the Romans lectures of 1515–16; the *theologia crucis* emerges over the period 1516–19; the place of good works in justification is clarified in the 1520 *Sermo von den guten Werken*; and the crucial distinction between forgiving grace and the gift of the Holy Spirit is made clear in what is perhaps the most impressive of Luther's early works, *Rationis Latomianae confutatio* (1521). We shall consider these points individually.

It is important to appreciate that Luther's theology of justification cannot be characterised solely with reference to the strongly anti-Pelagian cast which that theology increasingly assumed from 1515 onwards. One of its most distinctive features is its explicit criticism of Augustine, evident from the same period. This point was raised by Karl Holl's interpretation of Luther's understanding of justification as a progressive *reale Gerechtmachung*.[5] For Holl, the solution to *das eigentliche Rätsel von Luthers Rechtfertigungslehre* lay not in a doctrine of double justification,[6] nor in a juxtaposition of *Rechtfertigung* and *Gerechtmachung*,[7] but in a proleptic understanding of the basis of the analytic divine judgement implicit in the process of justification. Holl illustrated this concept with reference to the analogy of a sculptor and his vision of the final product which motivates and guides him as he begins work on a block of crude marble;[8] similarly, God's present justification of the sinner is based upon his anticipation of his final sanctification, in that man's present justification takes place on the basis of his foreseen future righteousness. This influential interpretation of Luther was, according to some critics, actually a confusion of Luther's views with those of early Lutheran Orthodoxy,[9] requiring modification on the basis of the 1521 treatise *Rationis Latomianae confutatio*, to which we shall shortly return. Nevertheless, Holl's exposition of the dialectic between the sinner's state *in re* and *in spe* does indeed correspond closely to the sanative concept of justification, frequently employed by Luther in the 1515–16 Romans lectures. This clearly raises the question of precisely what *was* distinctive about Luther's early teaching on justification.

The key to Luther's distinctive early understanding of the process of justification, particularly his difference with Augustine, lies in his anthropology.[10] Departing radically from Augustine's neo-Platonist anthropology, Luther insists that the Pauline antithesis between *caro* and *spiritus* must be understood theologically, rather than anthropologically. On an anthropological approach to the antithesis, *caro* is the 'fleshly', sensual or worldly side of man, whilst *spiritus* represents man's higher nature, orientated towards striving towards God. For Luther, it is the whole man (*totus homo*) who serves the law of God and the law of sin at one and the same time, and who thus exists under a double servitude.[11] The one and the same man is spiritual and carnal, righteous and a sinner, good and evil.[12] It is on the basis of this anthropology that Luther bases his famous assertion that the believer is *iustus et peccator simul*.[13] How, then, may the believer be distinguished from the unbeliever on the basis of this anthropology? The answer lies in the frame of reference from which the *totus homo* is viewed – *coram Deo* or *coram hominibus*. For Luther, the believer is righteous *coram Deo*, whereas the unbeliever is righteous *coram hominibus*:

Sancti Intrinsece sunt peccatores semper, ideo extrinsece Iustificantur semper. Hypocrite autem intrinsece sunt Iusti semper, ideo extrinsece sunt peccatores semper. Intrinsece dico, i.e. quomodo in nobis, in nostris oculis, in nostra estimatione sumus, Extrinsece autem, quomodo apud Deum et in reputatione eius sumus. Igitur extrinsece sumus Iusti, quando non ex nobis nec ex operibus, Sed ex sola Dei reputatione Iusti sumus.[14]

The believer is thus *iustus apud Deum et in reputatione eius*, but not *iustus coram hominibus*. The justified sinner is, and will remain, *semper peccator, semper penitens, semper iustus*.[15] This point is important, on account of the evident divergence from Augustine. For Augustine, the righteousness bestowed upon man by God in his justification was recognisable as such by man – in other words, the justified sinner was *iustus coram Deo et coram hominibus*.[16] It will therefore be clear that Luther was obliged to develop a radically different understanding of the nature of justifying righteousness if he was to avoid contradicting the basic presuppositions implicit in his *totus homo* anthropology. This new understanding is to be found in the concept of *iustitia Christi aliena*, which is perhaps the most characteristic feature of his early understanding of justification.

For Luther, the gospel destroys all human righteousness,[17] in that man is forced to recognise that he is totally devoid of soteriological resources, and thus turn to receive these resources *ab extra*. Man is justified by laying hold of a righteousness which is not, and can never be, his own – the *iustitia Christi aliena*, which God mercifully 'reckons' to man. 'The Christ who is grasped by faith and lives in the heart is the true Christian righteousness, on account of which God counts us righteous and grants us eternal life.'[18] The essence of justifying faith is that it is *fides apprehensiva* – a faith which seizes Christ, and holds him fast, in order that his righteousness may be ours, and our sin his. This *commercium admirabile* is explained by Luther on the basis of the analogy of a human marriage: *sponsus et sponsa fiunt una caro*.[19] For Luther, man may thus only progress in the spiritual life by continually returning to Christ, *semper a novo incipere*.[20] Thus Luther interprets *semper iustificandus* as 'ever to be justified anew', while Augustine treats it as meaning 'ever to be made more and more righteous'.[21] Luther does not make the distinction between justification and sanctification associated with later Protestantism, treating justification as a process of becoming: *fieri est iustificatio*.[22] Justification is thus a 'sort of beginning of God's creation', *initium aliquod creaturae eius*, by which the Christian waits in hope for the consummation of his righteousness: 'sicut nondum sumus iustificati, et tamen sumus iustificati, sed iustitia nostra pendet adhuc in spe'.[23] Like a sick man under the care of a doctor, who is ill *in re* yet healthy *in spe*,[24] the Christian awaits in hope the final resolution of the dialectic between righteousness and sin. This sanative aspect of his early teaching on justification corresponds closely to the teaching of Augustine on the matter. Justification is regarded as a healing process which permits God to overlook the remaining sin on account of its pending eradication. There is thus clearly a proleptic element in this understanding of justification, as Holl suggests. However, Luther's equation of *iustitia* and *fides Christi* – foreshadowed in the concept of *iustitia fidei* in the *Dictata super Psalterium* – is potentially misleading on this point. The distinction between Luther and Augustine on this aspect of justification is best seen from Luther's discussion of the relation between grace and faith.

Luther's concept of faith represents a significant departure from Augustine's rather intellectualist counterpart. The strongly existentialist dimension of faith is brought out with particular clarity in the 1517 Hebrews lectures. Whereas a purely human faith acknowledges that God exists,[25] or – in a speculative manner – that 'Christ appears before the face of God for others', a true justifying faith recognises, in a practical manner, that 'Christ appears before the face of God for us' (*Christus apparuit vultui Dei pro nobis*).[26] Only this latter faith can resist the assaults of *Anfechtung*.[27] Whereas *fides informis* is like a candle, all too easily exstinguished by the winds of *Anfechtung*, true justifying faith is like the sun itself – unaffected by even the most tempestuous of winds.[28]

The most significant discussion of faith, however, may be found in the 1521 treatise *Rationis Latomianae confutatio*, in which, on the basis of an exegesis of John 1.17, *gratia* is identified with *favor Dei*, and *veritas* with *iustitia seu fides Christi* – both of which are given in Christ. Gratiam accipio hic proprie pro favore Dei, sicut debet, non pro qualitate animi, ut nostri recentiores docuerunt, atque haec gratia tandem vere pacem cordis operatur, ut homo a corruptione sua sanatus.[29] For Luther, the grace of God is always something external to man, and an absolute, rather than a partial, quality. Man is either totally under grace or totally under wrath. In contrast to this, faith (and its antithesis, sin) are seen as internal and partial, in that the man under grace may be partially faithful and partially sinful. Faith is thus seen as the means by which the man under grace may depend and grow in his spiritual life.[30] Luther thus abandons the traditional understanding of the rôle of grace in justification (see §9) by interpreting it as the absolute favour of God towards an individual, rather than a quality, or a series of qualities, at work within man's soul. Grace is no longer understood as a new nature within man. This latter rôle is now allocated to *fides Christi*.

It is important to appreciate that Luther insists that the distinguishing mark of faith is the real and redeeming presence of Christ. Faith is *fides apprehensiva*, a faith which 'grasps' Christ and makes him present. By arguing that grace and faith are given in Christ, Luther is able to assert at one and the same time that the righteousness of the believer is, and will remain, extrinsic to him,[31] whilst Christ is nonetheless really present within the believer, effecting his renovation and regeneration. Furthermore, by insisting that faith is given to man *in* justification, Luther avoids any suggestion that man is justified *on account of* his faith: justification is *propter Christum*, and not *propter fidem*. The reinterpretation of grace as an absolute external, and faith as a partial internal, quality permits Luther to maintain what is otherwise clearly a contradiction within his theology of justification – his simultaneous insistence upon the external nature of the righteousness of Christ, and the real presence of Christ in the believer. The divine *reputatio iustitiae* does not, therefore, imply that man can be said to *possess* righteousness: sola autem reputatione miserentis Dei per fidem verbi eius iusti sumus.[32] Although Luther does not develop a theology of *iustitia imputata* at this point, it is clear that his anthropological presuppositions dictate that justifying righteousness be conceived extrinsically, thus laying the foundations for the Melanchthonian doctrine of the imputation of the righteousness of Christ to the believer (see §22). The origins of the concept of 'imputed righteousness', so characteristic of Protestant theologies of justification after the year 1530, may therefore be considered to lie with Luther.

One of the most significant aspects of Luther's break with the soteriology of the *via moderna* lies in his doctrine of the *servum arbitrium*.[33] The 1517 *Disputatio contra scholasticam theologiam* asserted that the unjustified sinner can only will and perform evil.[34] The Heidelberg disputation of the following year included the assertion: liberum arbitrium post peccatum res est de solo titulo, et dum facit quod in se est, peccat mortaliter.[35] It is difficult, at this stage, to draw any clear distinction between Augustine and Luther on the powers of the *liberum arbitrium post peccatum*, partially because it is not clear precisely what Luther understands by the term *liberum arbitrium* (for example, if it is assumed that he is referring to Augustine's *liberum arbitrium captivatum*, the proposition is clearly Augustinian). It is therefore important to observe that the condemnation of Luther's teaching in the papal bull *Exsurge Domine* of 15 June 1520 is curiously phrased, and should probably be interpreted to mean that the condemned forty-one propositions are *variously* heretical *or* scandalous *or* false *or* offensive to pious ears *or* misleading to simple minds, rather than that each and every proposition is to be condemned on all five grounds.[36] The thirty-sixth proposition, which appears to affirm an essentially Augustinian doctrine, may therefore be regarded as having been condemned for stating an orthodox Catholic dogma in an offensive or potentially misleading manner.

In his subsequent pronouncements upon free will, however, Luther appears to move increasingly away from Augustine. Both in his defence of the thirty-sixth proposition and the anti-Erasmian *de servo arbitrio* of 1525, Luther appears to adopt a form of necessitarianism, either as the main substance of his defence of the *servum arbitrium*, or at least as an important supporting argument. His assertions that Wycliffe was correct to maintain that all things happen by absolute necessity,[37] and that God is the author of all man's evil deeds,[38] have proved serious obstacles to those who wish to suggest that Luther was merely restating an Augustinian or scriptural position. In particular, three significant points of difference between Augustine and Luther should be noted in this respect:

1. For Luther, it is God who is the author of sin: Deus operatur et mala opera in impiis.[39] For Augustine, it is man who is the author of sin.

2. The slavery of man's will is understood by Luther to be a consequence of his creatureliness, rather than his sin (the affinities with Thomas Bradwardine here are evident).[40]

3.   Luther explicitly teaches a doctrine of double predestination, whereas Augustine was reluctant to acknowledge such a doctrine, no matter how logically appropriate it might appear.

Some scholars have argued that Luther's doctrine of justification and of the *servum arbitrium* are related as the two sides of a coin,[41] so that a statement of the one amounts to a statement of the other. It must, however, be pointed out that Luther's doctrine of justification is not exhausted or adequately characterised by a statement of the doctrine of the *servum arbitrium*. Essential to his understanding of justification is the concept of *iustitia Christi aliena*, which is not necessarily implied by the doctrine of the unfree will. If man's free will is enslaved, it is certainly true that he cannot justify himself – but this does not place God under any obligation to justify him by means of an extrinsic righteousness, provided the source of justifying righteousness is conceded to be none other than God himself. That man's will is enslaved is one matter; that God should choose to justify him in one specific manner as a result is quite another. As we shall indicate, the history of Lutheran theology indicates that a wedge was driven between the concepts of an alien justifying righteousness and an enslaved will at a comparatively early stage, the former being consistently maintained as *de fide*, the latter being abandoned or reduced to the mere assertion that man cannot justify himself – a far cry from its original meaning. This implicit criticism of Luther by Lutheranism may be taken as demonstrating that there is no fundamental theological connection between the two concepts. They are two essentially independent statements about justification, related only by the personality of Luther. With his death, that relation ceased to exist within Lutheranism.

A point upon which Luther has been consistently misunderstood concerns the relationship between faith and works in justification. Luther's theological breakthrough was intimately linked with the realisation that man was not justified upon the basis of any human work, but through the work of God within man.[42] Luther's intense hostility towards anyone who wished *per legem iustificari*,[43] thus compromising the *virginitas fidei*,[44] led him to develop an understanding of the relationship between law and gospel which allocated the former a specific, but strictly circumscribed, rôle in the Christian life.[45] Luther does not, as he is frequently represented, reject the necessity of good works in justification: *opera sunt necessaria ad salutem, sed non causant salutem, quia fides sola dat vitam*.[46] He frequently appeals to the biblical image of the good tree which bears good fruit, thus testifying to, rather than causing, its good nature.

Estque necessario effectus fidei et fructus et fit ad salutem, non meretur salutem. Estque necessario effectus in christiano, qui iam salvus est in fide et spe et tamen tendit in ista spe ad salutem revelandam.[47]

In his later period, particularly in those writings dating from 1534–5, Luther distinguished two dimensions to justification: Duplex in scripturis traditur iustificatio, altera fidei coram Deo, altera operum coram mundo.[48] It is clear that he is not developing a doctrine of 'double justification' (see §25) at this point, but merely identifying one element of the *usus legis in loco iustificationis*. The good works of the justified demonstrate the believer's justification *by God*, and cannot be considered to cause it:

Tamen non sequitur, quod opera ideo salvant, nisi valde necesse intelligamus, quod oporteat esse internam et externam salutem sive iustitiam. Opera salvant externe, hoc est, testantur nos esse iustos, et fidem esse in homine, quae interne salvat, ut Paulus inquit: Corde creditur ad iustitiam, ore fit confessio ad salutem. Externa salvatio ut fructus ostendit arborem bonam, ostendit fidem adesse.[49]

Before documenting the manner in which Luther's doctrine of justification was appropriated or modified within the early Reformation, it is important that we should attempt to establish the points of contact with the earlier medieval tradition. Luther represents a figure of theological transition, standing between two eras, and it is clearly of some interest to characterise the modifications which took place. In view of the fact that he knew little at first hand of the early Dominican school, or the early or later Franciscan schools, and of the restricted influence of both German mysticism and the *schola Augustiniana moderna*,[50] we are particularly concerned with his relation to Augustine and the *via moderna*.

It is possible to characterise the relation between Luther and Augustine on justification as follows:

1. Luther and Augustine both interpret *iustitia Dei* as the righteousness by which God justifies sinners, rather than as the abstract divine attribute which stands over and against mankind, judging on the basis of merit. In this respect, Luther is closer to Augustine than the *via moderna*, although the nature of Luther's understanding of *iustitia Dei* is more complex than is usually appreciated.[51]

2. Augustine understands *iustitia Dei* to be contiguous with *iustitia hominum*, in that it underlies human concepts of *iustitia*. For Luther, *iustitia Dei* is revealed only in the cross of Christ, and, if anything, contradicts human conceptions of *iustitia*.

3. Whereas Luther's doctrine of justification is based upon the concept of *servum arbitrium*, Augustine's is based upon that of *liberum arbitrium captivatum*, which becomes *liberum arbitrium liberatum* through the action of *gratia sanans*. Luther does not appear to envisage a liberation of *servum arbitrium* after justification, in that the servitude of man's will is seen as a consequence of his creatureliness, rather than his sinfulness. The differences between Luther and Augustine on predestination, noted above, also reflect this point. Although the phrase *servum arbitrium* derives from Augustine, it is not typical of his thought (see §§4, 7).

4. Luther and Augustine concur in understanding justification as an all-embracing process, subsuming the beginning, development and subsequent perfection of the Christian life. This is one of the clearest *differentiae* between Luther and later Protestantism, and places Luther closer to the position of the Council of Trent than is generally realised.

5. Whereas Augustine understands the believer to become righteous in justification, participating in the divine life and being, Luther is reluctant to admit that man becomes righteous in justification. If anything, man becomes more and more aware of his sinfulness, and of his need for the alien righteousness of Christ. Intrinsically man is, and will remain, a sinner, despite being extrinsically righteous. Luther explicitly criticises Augustine on this point. Although Luther makes frequent reference to the righteousness of believers, his equation of *iustitia* and *fides Christi* makes it clear that he is not referring to the morality of believers, but to the real and redeeming presence of Christ. The strongly Christological orientation of Luther's concept of the righteousness of believers sets him apart from Augustine on this point.

6. Luther and Augustine work with quite different anthropological presuppositions, with important consequences for their understandings of faith and sin.

It will therefore be clear that Luther's relation to Augustine is ambivalent. While one can point to elements in his thought which are clearly Augustinian, there are points – particularly his doctrine of *iustitia Christia aliena* – where he diverges significantly from Augustine.

Luther's relation to the *via moderna* is more complex, and remains the subject of investigation. There can be no doubt that Luther's early theology, up to the year 1514, as well as some elements which persist until 1515, is essentially that of the *via moderna*. This is particularly evident in the case of his understanding of the covenantal foundations of justification, his interpretation of the axiom *facienti quod in se est Deus non denegat gratiam*, his understanding of the theologoumenon *iustitia Dei*, and his critique of the implication of created habits in justification. It is also clear that Luther's 1517 dispute against 'scholastic theology' is actually directed specifically against Gabriel Biel. The question which remains to be answered, however, is whether Luther appropriated any elements of the theology of the *via moderna* in his *later* theology of justification.

At one stage, it was considered that Luther's doctrine of the imputation of righteousness and the non-imputation of sin represented one such element. Thus de Lagarde suggested that the background to Luther's doctrine was to be found in the dialectic between the two powers of God.[52] *De potentia sua absoluta*, God may accept a man without the grace of justification. Thus Luther may be regarded as stating *de potentia ordinata* what Biel stated *de potentia absoluta* concerning divine acceptation. It may, however, be pointed out that where Biel and Ockham understand the *locus* of the doctrine of the *acceptatio divina* to be the divine will, Luther actually locates it Christologically. A similar argument was advanced by Feckes, based upon the presupposition that Biel actually states *de potentia absoluta* what he would like to have stated *de potentia ordinata*, but could not on account of possible criticism from the ecclesiastical authorities.[53] As Feckes' attempt to relate Biel and Luther is based upon this discredited understanding of Biel,[54] it cannot be sustained. Furthermore, as Vignaux has pointed out, this possibility is excluded by Luther himself, particularly by theses 56 and 57 of the *Disputatio contra scholasticam theologiam*.[55] Neither Biel nor Ockham, of course, develops a doctrine of the imputation of righteousness, which enormously weakens the case for any putative positive influence from the *via moderna* in this respect. We must look elsewhere for the origins of Luther's understanding of the *reputatio* of the *iustitia Christi aliena* to believers.

The influence of the *schola Augustiniana moderna* upon Luther is much more difficult to assess. It is clear that there are excellent reasons for believing that Luther did not encounter this school, even in the person of Johannes von Staupitz, during his theological education.[56] Furthermore, Luther does not appear to have encountered Gregory of Rimini's writings until 1519.[57] It is therefore impossible to maintain that his distinctive views on justification derive from this school. Thus Luther and Staupitz, although having a common Augustinian soteriological framework, differ totally on the question of the nature of justifying righteousness: for Staupitz, justifying righteousness is *iustitia in nobis*, whereas for Luther it is *iustitia extra nos*.[58]

The influence of mysticism upon Luther's theology of justification has been difficult to ascertain. Several scholars have identified elements of his thought on justification in the teachings of the later German mystics, such as Tauler, and have suggested that these should be regarded as 'Forerunners of the Reformation'.[59] There can be no doubt that Luther was familiar with such writings, in that he edited *Eyn theologia deutsch* in 1516 and 1518, and appears to have annotated Tauler's sermons extensively in 1519. Tauler's discussion of fallen human nature demonstrates an anthropological pessimism paralleling that of Luther: man is fallen, poisoned and introverted.[60] The possibility of man attaining salvation unaided is, however, upheld by Tauler. Furthermore, salvation is understood in terms of a direct, unbroken and unmediated mystical fellowship with God: the Christological concentration evident in Luther's concept of the *commercium admirabile* is quite absent. Tauler's essentially neo-Platonist anthropological and theological presuppositions lead to his conceiving salvation in terms of a substantive union between God and man. Luther's insistence upon the exclusive location of all soteriological resources outside man stands in diametrical opposition to Tauler's concern to promote the *Seelengrund*, and Gerson's concern to enhance the soteriological possibilities of *synteresis*.[61] While it is quite possible that Luther may have derived his concept of *Anfechtung* from late medieval mysticism,[62] it is impossible to argue that any of the crucial elements in his early theology of justification (such as the concept of *iustitia Christi aliena*) derive from such a source.

Whatever the origins of Luther's distinctive ideas on justification, it is clear that they exercised an immediate influence upon the development of the Lutheran Reformation at Wittenberg. Nevertheless, Luther's ideas were not universally accepted, and were subjected to a gradual process of modification in the years leading up to the Formula of Concord. In the following section, we shall consider the origins and subsequent development of this process of modification of Luther by Lutheranism.

§22 Justification in early Lutheranism 1516–80

The year 1516 witnessed considerable discussion within the theological faculty at the University of Wittenberg concerning the nature of Augustine's teaching on justification. In a disputation of 25 September 1516, Luther had suggested that Karlstadt should check the teachings of the *scholasticos doctores* against the writings of Augustine to discover the extent to which they diverged from him.[1] Setting off for Leipzig on 13 January 1517, Karlstadt managed to equip himself with a copy of the works of Augustine, and hence realised the radical discrepancy between his own position and that of Augustine.[2] As a result, Karlstadt was moved to arrange a public disputation on 26 April 1517, in which, to Luther's delight, he defended 151 Augustinian theses.[3] His particular attraction to Augustine's strongly anti-Pelagian *de spiritu et litera* led to his lecturing, and subsequently publishing a commentary, upon this important work. The result of Karlstadt's conversion to the *vera theologia* in 1517 was that the Wittenberg theological faculty was committed to a programme of theological reform by the year 1518, based extensively upon the anti-Pelagian writings of Augustine.

It is at this point that differences between Luther and Karlstadt are clearly discernible. In his works dating from this early period, Karlstadt appears as a remarkably faithful interpreter of Augustine, where Luther often appears as his critic. Thus Karlstadt follows Augustine in developing an antithesis between law and *grace*,[4] rather than *gospel*, and emphasises the priority of *grace*,[5] rather than *faith*. Most significantly of all, the Augustinian understanding of the *nature* of justification is faithfully reproduced. Of particular importance is his unequivocal assertion that justifying righteousness is inherent to man, and that it *makes* him righteous:

Non est sensus, quod illa iusticia dei sit per legem testificata, qua deus in se iustus est, sed illa, qua iustificat impium, qua induit hominem, qua instaurat imaginem dei in homine; de hac iusticia, qua deus suos electos iustos et pios efficit, tractamus.[6]

It is clear that Karlstadt follows Staupitz in this understanding of the nature of justifying righteousness,[7] and knows nothing of Luther's concept of justifying righteousness as *iustitia Christi aliena*. Indeed, the Christological emphasis evident in Luther's theology of justification by this stage is quite absent from Karlstadt's theology of justification,[8] which continues to be primarily a theology of the *grace of God*. It will also be clear that this passage calls into question the suggestion that Luther discovered an essentially *Augustinian* concept of *iustitia Dei* in late 1518 or early 1519 (see §20): precisely this concept of *iustitia Dei* is faithfully reproduced in Karlstadt's lectures and published commentary on Augustine. Similarly, Karlstadt follows Augustine in defining justification in terms of the non-imputation of sin, rather than the imputation of righteousness. In his writings for the period 1519–21, Karlstadt faithfully reproduces the Augustinian concept of justification as the non-imputation of sin and the impartation of righteousness, and does not develop Luther's extrinsic concept of justifying righteousness.[9] As we indicated earlier, Luther's extrinsic conception of justifying righteousness is partly a consequence of his *totus homo* anthropology, which differs significantly from Augustine's neo-Platonist understanding of man. Karlstadt adopts an essentially Augustinian anthropology, in which justification is conceived as a renewal of man's nature through a gradual eradication of sin. *Iustus ergo simul est bonus et malus, filius dei et seculi.*[10] Although this is clearly similar to Luther's assertion that the justified believer is *simul iustus et peccator*, it is clear that the two theologians interpret the phrase differently. For Luther, what is being stated is that the believer is *extrinsically righteous* and *intrinsically sinful*; for Karlstadt, what is being stated is precisely what Augustine intended when he stated that the justified sinner is *partly* righteous and *partly* sinful (*ex quadam parte iustus, ex quadam parte peccator*).[11]

There are therefore excellent reasons for suggesting that Karlstadt's doctrine of justification over the period 1517–21 is essentially Augustinian, lacking the novel elements which distinguish Luther's teaching of the time from that of the African bishop. A similar conclusion must be drawn concerning the theology of Johann Bugenhagen over the period 1521–5. In his 1525 lectures on Romans, Bugenhagen identifies the three elements of justification as *remissio peccatorum*, *donatio spiritus* and *non-imputatio peccati*.[12] Even when commenting on Romans 4.5–6, where Erasmus had retranslated the Vulgate reference to *reputatio iustitiae* as *imputatio iustitiae*, Bugenhagen still interprets the text as referring to the *non-imputation of sin* rather than the *imputation of an alien righteousness*.[13] Where Bugenhagen speaks of *imputatio* in a specifically *Christological* context, he is referring to the fact that the sin of the believer is not imputed to him on account of Christ: *iusti non imputante deo propter Christum peccatum*.[14] More generally, however, his concept of the non-imputation of sin is discussed in a pneumatological context; the renewing work of the Holy Spirit within man permits God not to impute his sin: *quod non imputetur reliquum ... quia spiritu contranitimur peccato*.[15] Although Bugenhagen thus develops a doctrine of justification which is essentially Augustinian, omitting any reference to the imputation of the alien righteousness of Christ, it is clear that he has moved away from Augustine on points of significance. In particular, grace is conceived extrinsically, as *favor Dei*:

Praeterea in hoc loco vides quam insipienter errent, qui gratiam dei, de qua loquuntur scripturae per quam solam salvamur, describunt esse habitum in hominem sive qualitatem, cum sit favor potius in deo bene volente nobis ut filiis.[16]

In this, Bugenhagen is clearly dependent upon Melanchthon's 1521 *Loci*.[17] In view of Melanchthon's importance in establishing a forensic concept of justification as normative within Protestantism, it is appropriate to consider his contribution at this point.

Although an Erasmian on his arrival at Wittenberg in 1518, Melanchthon appears to have adopted Luther's *totus homo* anthropology at an early stage,[18] regarding sin as permeating even man's higher faculties. While his baccalaureate theses of September 1519 appear to develop a theology of justification which parallels that of Luther rather than Karlstadt,[19] it is clear from his writings of the period 1519–20 that he still tends to conceive justification ethically at points, as 'mortification of the flesh and our affections'.[20] Nevertheless, by 1521 Melanchthon appears to have grasped much of Luther's distinctive understanding of justification, and incorporated it into the first edition of the *Loci communes* of that year. This is particularly clear in the *locus de gratia*, in which grace is unequivocally defined extrinsically as *favor Dei*: non aliud enim est gratia, si exactissime describenda sit, nisi dei benevolentia erga nos.[21] Nevertheless, in his early works, Melanchthon still tends to conceive justification in factitive, rather than declarative, terms.[22] Thus a conspicuous feature of these works is his emphasis upon the rôle of the *person* of Christ in justification; for example, the 1523 *Annotationes in Evangelium Iohannis* develops the idea that justification involves a personal union between Christ and the believer.[23] This contrasts significantly with his later emphasis upon the more abstract concept of the *work* of Christ associated with his doctrine of forensic justification, which becomes particularly evident from his writings dating from after 1530.

In his writings subsequent to 1530, Melanchthon increasingly emphasises the notion of *iustitia aliena* – an alien righteousness, which is imputed to the believer. Justification is then interpreted as *Gerecht-*

sprechung, being 'pronounced righteous' or 'accepted as righteous'. A sharp distinction thus comes to be drawn between justification, as the external act in which God pronounces or declares the believer to be righteous, and regeneration, as the internal process of renewal in which the believer is regenerated through the work of the Holy Spirit. Whereas Luther consistently employed images and categories of personal relationship to describe the union of the believer and Christ (such as the *commercium admirabile* of a human marriage paralleling that between the soul and Christ), Melanchthon increasingly employed images and categories drawn from the sphere of Roman law. Thus Melanchthon illustrates the concept of forensic justification with reference to a classical analogy: just as the people of Rome declared Scipio to be a free man *in foro*, so God declares the sinner to be righteous *in foro divino*.

Iustificatio significat remissionem peccatorum et reconciliationem seu acceptationem personae ad vitam aeternam. Nam Hebraeis iustificare est forense verbum; ut si dicam, populus Romanus iustificavit Scipionem accusatum a tribunis, id est, absolvit seu iustum pronuntiavit. Sumpsit igitur Paulis verbum iustificandi ex consuetudine Hebraici sermonis pro acceptatione, id est, pro reconciliatione et remissione peccatorum.[24]

Significantly, Erasmus uses the forensic concept of *acceptilatio* (the purely verbal remission of a debt without payment) in the 1516 *Novum instrumentum omne* of 1516 as an illustration of the meaning of the verb *imputare*. We shall return to this point towards the end of the present section.

The Augsburg Confession (1530) contains a brief statement on justification in its fourth article, which does not refer to the imputation of the alien righteousness of Christ, but merely restates the Pauline idea (Romans 4.5) of 'faith being reckoned as righteousness':

Item docent, quod homines non possint iustificari coram Deo propriis viribus, meritis aut operibus, sed gratis iustificentur propter Christum per fidem, cum credunt se in gratiam recipi et peccata remitti propter Christum, qui sua morte pro nostris peccatis satisfecit. Hanc fidem imputat Deus pro iustitia coram ipso.[25]

The formula *propter Christum per fidem* is significant, in that it defines the correct understanding of the formula 'justification *sola fide*'. The sole grounds for man's justification lie, not in man himself or in anything which he can do, but in Christ and his work alone. Man is not justified on account of his faith (which would be justification *propter fidem*), nor must faith be seen as a human work or achieve-

24

ment: strictly speaking, faith is a reception by man of the gracious deed of God in Christ.

In the *Apologia* (1530) for the Confession, Melanchthon develops the concept of imputation – hinted at in the above article – in a significant direction. Just as a man might pay the debt of a friend, even though it is not his own, so the believer may be reckoned as righteous on account of the alien merit of Christ.[26] Making Luther's critique of Augustine's concept of justifying righteousness explicit, Melanchthon states that justification is to be understood forensically, as the declaration that the believer is righteous on account of the alien righteousness of Christ: iustificare vero hoc loco forensi consuetudine significat reum absolvere et pronuntiare iustum, sed propter alienam iustitiam, videlicet Christi, quae aliena iustitia communicatur nobis per fidem.[27] Thus justification does not signify 'making righteous', but 'pronouncing righteous'.[28] There is no righteousness within man, or inherent to him, which can be regarded as the basis of his justification: man is justified on the basis of an external and alien righteousness, which is 'reputed' or 'imputed' to him. Propter Christum coram Deum [sic] iusti reputemur.[29] It will be clear that these statements of the imputation of righteousness go far beyond the traditional Augustinian statements concerning justification as the non-imputation of sin, and contradict such statements which define justification as 'making righteous'. It might, therefore, appear reasonable to conclude that the teaching of the Lutheran church with respect to justification had been defined and distinguished from that of Augustine at this point. In fact, this is not the case.

Alongside statements which explicitly define the forensic character of justification, and which clearly *exclude* a factitive interpretation of justification, we find statements which explicitly define justification in factitive terms. Significantly, such statements tend to be found near the beginning of the *Apologia* for the fourth article, whereas those denying the factitive character of justification tend to be found towards its end. For example, an early paragraph defends the forensic dimension of justification by appealing to its factitive aspect: et quia iustificari significat ex iniustis iustos effici seu regenerari, significat et iustos pronuntiari seu reputari.[30] This ambiguity on the part of Melanchthon has led to considerable confusion among his modern interpreters.[31]

The subsequent history of the evangelical faction within Germany, particularly in the aftermath of Luther's death (1546), the defeat of the Smalkadic League (1547) and the imposition of the Augsburg

Interim (1548) is that of controversy over the doctrine of justification. These controversies related to three main areas of the doctrine: the objective grounds of justification (the Osiandrist and Stancarist controversies); the necessity of good works after justification (the Antinomian and Majorist controversies); and the subjective appropriation of justification (the Synergist and Monergist controversies). We shall consider these areas individually.

1 The Objective Grounds of Justification: The Osiandrist and Stancarist Controversies

Among Melanchthon's contemporary critics was Andreas Osiander, leader of the evangelical faction in Nuremburg from 1522 to 1547. For Osiander, the Melanchthonian concept of justification as *Gerechtsprechung* was totally unacceptable: saving righteousness was none other than the essential indwelling righteousness of Christ, arising from his divinity, rather than his humanity.[32] Justification must therefore be understood to consist of the infusion of the essential righteousness of Christ. Although some of his critics, such as Martin Chemnitz, argued that this made justification dependent upon sanctification, it is clear that this is not the case. Osiander merely reacted against what he regarded as the unacceptably extrinsic conception of justification in the *Apologia* by emphasising those scriptural passages which speak of Christ indwelling within the believer.[33] Furthermore, Osiander claimed, with some reason, the support of Luther in his views on the significance of the indwelling of Christ: the increasing emphasis within the German evangelical faction upon the work of Christ imputed to man inevitably led to a reduction in interest in the rôle of the person of Christ within man, and thus to a certain indifference to Luther's high estimation of this aspect of man's justification. Osiander's views merely served to harden German Protestant opinion against the concept of justification by inherent righteousness, and it was left to Calvin (§23) to demonstrate how Osiander's legitimate protest against the externalisation of Christ might be appropriated while maintaining a *forensic* doctrine of justification.

Francesco Stancari maintained a totally antithetical position, and cited Melanchthon in his support (to the latter's horror). Whereas Osiander maintained that Christ's *divinity* was the ground of man's justification, Stancari argued that the implication of Christ's divinity in man's justification was quite unthinkable, involving logical contradiction (such as the fact that Christ's divine nature had to function both as mediator and offended party). The objective basis of man's justification was therefore Christ's *human* nature alone. On account of Christ's obedient suffering upon the cross in his human nature, his *acquired* (not *essential!*) righteousness was imputed to man as the basis of his justification.[34]

These controversies thus identified the need for clarification of the Augsburg Confession's unclear statements on the nature of justifying righteousness and the person of the Redeemer.

2 The Role of Works in Justification: The Antinomian and Majorist Controversies

Perhaps through his emphasis on the priority of faith in justification, Luther had often seemed to imply that good works were of no significance in the Christian life (see §21). His position on this matter was clarified in his later writings, and may be stated as follows: works are a condition, but not a cause, of salvation.[35] Luther is prepared to concede that if no works follow faith, it is certain that the faith in question is dead, and not a living faith in Christ.[36] The 1520 sermon on good works states that 'faith in Christ is the first, highest and most sublime good work', adding that 'works are not pleasing on their own account, but on account of faith'.[37] Melanchthon, however, always entertained a much more positive understanding of the rôle of the law in the Christian life. In his *Annotationes in Evangelium Matthaei*, justification is understood as a new capacity to fulfil the law,[38] and the 1521 *Loci* defined Christian freedom as a new freedom to fulfil the law spontaneously.[39] The 1527 *Articuli de quibus egerunt per visitatores* reproduced these views, and placed the preaching of the law as the heart of Christian instruction, insisting that without the law, both repentance and faith were impossible. These views outraged Johann Agricola, who argued that repentance was a consequence of the gospel, not the law. Although Agricola was restrained in his antinomianism, he would unquestionably have agreed with Jakob Schenk's suggestion that Moses ought to be hanged.

The Majorist controversy initially concerned Georg Major's justification of the failure of the Leipzig Interim to stress the exclusive rôle of faith in justification. Although it is clear from his 1552 tract *Auf des ehrwürdigen Herrn Nikolaus von Amsdorfs Schrift Antwort* that Major was totally committed to the principle of justification *sola fide*, he nevertheless stated his conviction that Luther taught that good works were necessary for salvation. Flacius immediately pointed out that this excluded both infants and the dying from being saved. Nikolaus von Amsdorf replied to Major initially with the assertion that the law had no rôle in justification whatsoever, and subsequently with the suggestion that good works were positively detrimental to salvation.[40] The related dispute *de tertio usus legis* arose over similar views expressed by Luther's pupils Andreas Poach and Anton Otho.[41] By 1560, it was clear to all that the sixth article of the Augsburg Confession required clarification if serious internal disunity on this point was to be brought to an end.

3 The Subjective Appropriation of Justification: The Synergist and Monergist Controversies

Luther's insistence upon man's utter passivity in justification, especially evident in his defence of the thirty-sixth proposition and *de servo arbitrio*, remained characteristic of his teaching on justification throughout his life. It is therefore important to note Melanchthon's growing unease concerning this aspect of Luther's theology. The 1535 edition of the *Loci* suggested, and the 1543 edition made explicit, that Melanchthon no longer agreed with Luther on this point: justification was now to be attributed to three contributing factors – the Word of God, the Holy Spirit, and the faculty of the human will. For Melanchthon, man possesses the *facultas applicandi se ad gratiam* prior to justification. As a result, nobody is drawn to God unless he wishes to be drawn.[42] Similarly, Melanchthon's early commitment to the doctrine of predestination *ante praevisa merita* in the 1521 *Loci* is replaced by that of predestination *post praevisa merita* by 1535.[43] It is possibly this change of heart which underlies the omission of an *articulus de praedestinatione* in the Augsburg Confession.[44] Melanchthon's views were defended by Strigel,[45] and subjected to heavy criticism by Amsdorf and Flacius. The occasion of the synergist controversy was the publication of Johann Pfeffinger's *Propositiones de libero arbitio* (1555), which asserted that the reason why some responded to the gospel and others not, was to be found within man himself, rather than in an extrinsic prior divine decision. Thus the ultimate difference between David and Saul, or between Peter and Judas, must lie in their respective free wills. Although Pfeffinger was careful to insist that God retains the initiative (and, indeed, the upper hand) in justification, he nevertheless stated that it is the human free will which decides whether or not the Holy Spirit enters into an individual's life. This concept of *liberum arbitrium in spiritualibus* was violently opposed by the monergists Amsdorf and Flacius,[46] with the result that the matter came to a head at the Weimar Colloquy (1560). In this dispute, Strigel suggested that the human free will was injured and weakened through original sin, although not completely destroyed. He illustrated this Augustinian position (see §§4, 7) by comparing the effect of sin upon the free will with that of garlic juice upon a magnet: once the obstruction has been removed, the power of the magnet is restored. Flacius replied by accusing Strigel of externalising sin and proceeded to develop Luther's analogy of the passivity of man in justification in a manner which seemed Manichaean to those observing the debate. Nevertheless, it was once more clear that clarification of man's rôle in his own justification was required if further internal dissent was to be avoided.

Clarification of these three areas would be provided by the Formula of Concord, drawn up in March 1577. Before considering the manner in which the Formula settled these disputes, it is necessary to return to the question of the nature of justification and justifying righteousness, in order to note that substantial internal agreement had been reached within Lutheranism and the Reformed church on this matter in the intervening period. This is best illustrated from Martin Chemnitz' *Examen Concilii Tridentini* (1563–73), an authoritative work which clearly established the difference between the Lutheran church and Augustine on these points. Chemnitz notes that there are two approaches to the term 'justification': the Latin approach, which interprets justification as *iustum facere*, and the Hebrew approach, which interprets it as *absolutio a peccato seu remissio peccatorum et imputatio iustitiae Christi*.[47] The former corresponds to that of Augustine and subsequently the Roman Catholic approach, and the latter to the Lutheran. The Latin approach involves the interpretation of justification as the infusion of righteousness,[48] whereas Chemnitz argues, on the basis of an analysis of secular Greek sources, that the verb δικαιοῦν must be interpreted as *verbum forense*: Germani *Rechtfertigen* plane Graeco more in significatione forensi usurpant.[49] Augustine is guilty of misrepresenting Paul,[50] particularly in relation to the matter of imputation.[51]

This position was endorsed by the third article of the Formula of Concord.[52] Justification is defined in forensic terms, and it is made clear that it is not faith which is reckoned as justifying righteousness, but the righteousness of Christ imputed to us.[53] Vocabulum igitur *iustificationis* in hoc negotio significat iustum pronuntiare, a peccatis et aeternis peccatorum suppliciis absolvere, propter iustitiam Christi, quae a Deo fidei imputatur.[54] The individual teachings of both Osiander and Stancari are rejected,[55] in favour of justification by the mediatorial righteousness of Christ as both God and man.[56] The Majorist controversy was ended through the fourth article of the Formula, which asserted that good works were obligatory, in that they are commanded, as well as being an appropriate expression of faith and gratitude to God;[57] they are not, however, mandatory or necessary *for salvation*.[58] Works are and remain the effects of justifying faith, and must not be confused with the cause of that faith. The synergist and monergist controversies were ended with the explicit condemnation of the synergist position.[59] Strigel's analogy of the magnet and garlic juice is explicitly rejected.[60] The text (John 6.44) which Melanchthon had interpreted (with the aid of Chrysostom) to mean that God only drew to himself those who wished to be drawn, is now interpreted in an anti-Melanchthonian sense, meaning that the free will is totally impotent and dependent upon grace. Whereas, since 1535, Melanchthon had recognised three concurrent causes of justification (the Word, the Holy Spirit, and man's will), thus permitting man a say in his own justification, the Formula recognised only one such cause – the Holy Spirit.[61]

It might therefore be thought that the Formula endorses the monergist position. In fact, it does not, as may be seen from its statements on predestination. The doctrine of double predestination – so important a feature of Luther's *de servo arbitrio* (see §21) – is explicitly rejected in favour of a doctrine of predestination based upon the *benevolentia Dei universalis*. A careful distinction is made between *praedestinatio* and *praescientia*: the former extends only to the children of God,[62] whereas the latter extends to all creatures as such.[63] The *causa perditionis* is defined to be man, rather than God[64] – a conclusion, incidentally, which stands in contrast to Luther's 1525 assertion that the only centre of freedom which cannot be said to be necessitated by another is God himself. Furthermore, Luther's doctrine of the *servum arbitrium* is radically undermined by the assertion that the free will may, under the influence of grace, assent to faith.[65] Although the Formula specifically rejects any suggestion of cooperation between man's will and the Holy Spirit,[66] it is clear that this is directed against Melanchthon's opinion that man can cooperate with God *apart from grace*. The Formula envisages the human *liberum arbitrium* as being liberated by grace, whereas Luther regarded it as being permanently enslaved through human creatureliness (see §21).

The emphasis upon the concept of forensic justification in both the Formula of Concord and Melanchthon's *Apologia* of 1530 raises the question of the origins of the concept. It is clear that the extrinsic conception of justifying righteousness which is fundamental to the notion of forensic justification is due to Luther (see §21). Although Luther incorporates traces of legal terminology into his discussion of justification,[67] it seems that the origins of the concept lie with Erasmus' 1516 translation of the New Testament. The concept of forensic justification is particularly well illustrated by the analogical concept of *acceptilatio* – indeed, this latter concept was frequently employed by the theologians of later Orthodoxy in their discussion of the nature of forensic justification. 'Acceptilation' is a Roman legal term, referring to the purely verbal remission of a debt, as if the debt has been paid – whereas, in fact, it has not. As we have noted, Melanchthon frequently uses classical legal analogies and categories in his discussion of theological concepts, and it is therefore important to note that Erasmus' *Novum instrumentum omne* of 1516 provided not merely a new Latin translation of the Greek text of the New Testament, but also extensive notes justifying departure from the Vulgate text, which often appeal to similar classical antecedents. Of particular interest are his alterations to Romans 4.5. Where the Vulgate read 'Credidit Abraham deo et reputatum est illi ad iusti-tiam', Erasmus altered the translation to 'Credidit aut Abraham deo et imputatum est ei ad iustitiam.' The potentially forensic impli-cations of this new translation of the Greek verb λογίζηται were pointed out by Erasmus himself: the basic concept underlying 'imputation' was termed 'acceptilation' by the jurisconsults.[68] In view of the fact that Melanchthon knew and used this New Tes-tament text – the best of its age – he could hardly have failed to notice the forensic implications of the concept of 'imputation' as the purely verbal remission of sin, *without* – as with Augustine, Karlstadt and Bugenhagen – the prior or concomitant renewal of the sinner. It would therefore have been a remarkable coincidence, to say the least, that Erasmus should choose to illustrate the meaning of the term 'imputation' with a classical analogy which would later become normative within Protestant Orthodoxy in the definition of the concept of forensic justification – although the concepts of *acceptatio* and *acceptilatio* were frequently confused! – if his original use of the analogy had not been taken up and developed by Melanchthon. A forensic doctrine of justification, in the proper sense of the term, would result from linking Erasmus' interpretation of the concept of imputation with Luther's concept of an extrinsic justifying righteousness – and it seems that Melanchthon took precisely this step.

It will therefore be clear that the Formula of Concord marked not only the ending of an important series of controversies in the Lutheran church immediately after Luther's death; it also marked the victory and consolidation of the critique of Luther from within Lutheranism itself. Luther's concept of justification, his concept of the presence of Christ within the believer, his doctrine of double predestination, his doctrine of *servum arbitrium* – all were rejected or radically modified by those who followed him. It would be improper to inquire as to whether this critique and modification was justified; it is, however, right and proper to note that it took place, as it is only on the basis of this recognition that the full significance of the contribution of Lutheran Orthodoxy to the development of our doctrine may be appreciated.

§23 Reformed doctrines of justification 1519–60

It is a fact, the significance of which is all too easily overlooked, that most of the major Reformers, with the notable exception of Luther, were humanists. In the case of the Reformed church, the influence of humanism was decisive.[1] Although Erasmus' interest in the doctrine of justification appears to have been minimal, it is clear that it is strongly (though not exclusively) moralist in tone.[2] Although it is possible to describe Erasmus' thought as 'Christocentric', this should be understood to refer to the centrality of the *lex Christi* to his ethics.[3] Erasmus thus emphasises the tropological sense of scripture, by which he is able to demonstrate the continuity of the *lex evangelica* from the Old Testament to the New.[4]

The influence of Erasmus over both Zwingli and Bucer appears to have been considerable,[5] and may go some way towards explaining the strongly moralist doctrines of justification associated with these two key theologians of the early Reformed church. Zwingli's theological development appears to have been decisively influenced by his near-fatal illness during an outbreak of the plague at Zurich in August 1519. During the course of this illness, Zwingli appears to have realised that he was nothing but a plaything in the hands of the Almighty; whether he was saved or not was a matter of the divine good pleasure:

Wilt du dann glych
tod haben mich
in mitz der tagen min,
so sol es willig sin.[6]

The strongly determinist cast to Zwingli's thought – probably owing more to Seneca than to St Paul – which is reflected in his emphasis upon an omnipotent and sovereign God contrasts with Luther's quest for a gracious God. In his understanding of justification, Zwingli departs considerably from Luther. In his early humanist period, Zwingli's understanding of justification appears to have been primarily ethical. His contemporaries within the *Christianismus renascens* movement regarded him as a fine exponent of the *philosophia Christi*,[7] with its emphasis upon moral integrity.[8] Zwingli's statements concerning the 'law of the living spirit' are of particular importance in this connection: he defines this law as the 'leading and instructing which God offers to us out of a true understanding of his word'.[9] For Zwingli, the 'righteousness of faith',[10] based upon obedience to God, must be contrasted with 'self-righteousness', based upon self-confidence. The similarities between Erasmus and Zwingli on the *lex evangelica* are evident, particularly in their subordination of justification to regeneration. In fact, Zwingli rarely uses the term 'justification' or 'justified', tending to use the term *rechtglöbig* ('right-believing') instead. Thus he indicates that *der rechtglöbige mensch* submits himself to the law willingly, in contrast to the unbeliever.[11] Zwingli's emphasis upon the moral character of the 'new man' (*wiedergeborene und neue Menschen*)[12] leads him to understand justification to be based upon an *analytic*, rather than a *synthetic*, divine judgement. It is this aspect of Zwingli's theology which led Melanchthon to hint darkly at Marburg of the works-righteousness of the Swiss Reformers: incommode enim loquuntur et scribunt de hominis iustificatione coram Deo, et doctrinam de fide non satis inculcant, sed ita de iustificatione loquuntur, quasi opera, quae fidem sequuntur, sint iustitia hominis.[13]

A similarly moralist approach to justification may be found in the writings of Johannes Oecolampadius, whose strong emphasis upon the importance of regeneration in the Christian life inevitably led to man's justification being subordinated to his regeneration. As Oecolampadius remarks in the course of his comments on Hebrews 10.24, the Christian must continually examine himself to see if the faith which he professes is manifested in good works. As Strohl has noted, Oecolampadius' chief concern appears to have been the ethical dimension of faith.[14] Similarly, Christ's death upon the cross exemplifies the divine love for man, which is intended to move man to moral excellence.[15] Here, as with Zwingli, we find the moral protests of the early Swiss Reformers passing into their theology: the man who has true faith is the man of moral integrity – whose faith may be proved by precisely that integrity. Similarly, Heinrich Bullinger insisted that justification did not mean the imputation of righteousness, but the actualisation of righteousness.[16] As with later Pietism, man's justification is confirmed by moral action.

The most significant exposition of the doctrine of justification within the early Reformed church is due to Martin Bucer, and it is here that we find the still-inchoate moralism of Zwingli being developed into a strongly Erasmian doctrine of justification. Even from his earliest period, Bucer was strongly inclined towards Erasmianism.[17] Although Bucer was clearly influenced by Luther, following their meeting at Heidelberg in 1518, it is significant that Bucer tended to interpret much of Luther's teaching in Erasmian terms, and to pass over many of his more distinctive ideas altogether.[18] Bucer's preoccupations are clearly moralist, as may be seen from his reduction of 'doctrine' to 'ethics' on the basis of his philological exegesis of the concept of *torah*: for Bucer, the whole of scripture is thus *lex*.[19] This moralist approach to scripture is reflected in his doctrine of justification, which represents a significant modification of that of Luther.

Bucer develops a doctrine of *double* justification: after a 'primary justification', in which man's sins are forgiven and righteousness imputed to him, there follows a 'secondary justification', in which man is *made* righteous: the *iustificatio impii*, expounded by Bucer on the basis of St Paul, is followed by the *iustificatio pii*, expounded on the basis of St James.[20] While Bucer is concerned to maintain a forensic concept of primary justification, he stresses the need for this to be manifested as good works in the secondary justification. Although man's primary justification takes place on the basis of faith alone (*sola fide*), his secondary justification takes place on the basis of his works. While Bucer maintains the forensic nature of the primary justification, he stresses the need for this to be manifested in good works. Although this secondary justification appears to be equivalent, in respects, to the later concept of sanctification, it is still conceived in primarily moralist terms.

The question which necessarily follows from this analysis is this: did Bucer actually teach a doctrine of double justification *stricto sensu*

– in other words, that the formal cause of justification is both imputed and inherent righteousness? Bucer's involvement in the drawing up of the 'Regensburg Book' (*Liber Ratisboniensis*), with its important article on justification, is certainly highly suggestive in this respect.[21] The most adequate answer to this question appears to be that Bucer did not intend his doctrine of justification to be an eirenicon, as did Gropper and Pighius (see §25), but rather intended to forge a secure theological link between the totally gratuitous justification of the sinner and the moral obligations which this subsequently placed upon him. The righteousness and good works which are effected by the Holy Spirit are to be seen as the visible evidence of man's unmerited acceptance in the sight of God. Just as a good tree produces good fruit, so the justified sinner must produce good works.[22] It is on account of his preoccupation with the ethical dimensions of the apparently anti-moral doctrine of justification *sola fide* that Bucer has been styled 'the Pietist among the Reformers'.[23] Bucer clearly considers the rôle of piety in the Christian life to be of sufficient importance to require explicit incorporation into a doctrine of justification. Faith must produce 'die ganze Frommheit und Seligkeit', and Bucer ensures this by establishing the following *ordo salutis*:[24]

praedestinatio → *electio* → *vocatio* → *iustificatio* → *glorificatio*

in which *iustificatio* is understood to have two elements: an initial justification by faith, and a subsequent justification by works.

The important point we wish to emphasise is that Bucer implicates human moral action under the aegis of justification, whereas others (such as Melanchthon) implicated them under the aegis of regeneration or sanctification, which was understood to be a quite distinct element in the *ordo salutis*. Bucer does not, as one of his recent interpreters suggests, include sanctification in the *ordo salutis*:[25] what was later termed *sanctificatio* by Calvin is termed 'secondary justification' or *iustificatio pii* by Bucer.

An important element of the theology of justification of later Reformed Orthodoxy (see §24) can be detected in the writings of the Zurich Reformers dating from the third decade of the sixteenth century.[26] The notion of a 'covenant' or 'testament', an important element of the soteriology of the *via moderna* (§§11, 17) and the young Luther (§20), is evident in that of Zwingli and Bullinger.[27] The concept of a 'covenant' between God and man served two purposes:

the *hermeneutical* function of establishing a basis upon which the unity of the Old and New Testaments might be defended;[28] and the *soteriological* function of establishing the basis upon which man might be justified.[29]

The most significant contribution to the development of the early Reformed doctrine of justification was due to John Calvin.[30] Although the 1536 edition of the *Christianae religionis institutio* contains a few scant lines on justification, that of 1539 and subsequent editions describe the doctrine of justification as the 'main hinge upon which religion turns', and the 'sum of all piety'. The terse statements of that first edition concerning justification are, however, significant:

Saepe de fidei iustitia disputatur, pauci assequuntur, quomodo fiamus iusti fide. Addamus hanc esse Christi iustitiam, non nostram, in ipso, non in nobis sitam, sed imputatione nostram fieri, quoniam accepta nobis fertur. Ita non vere nos esse iustos sed imputative, vel non esse iustos, sed pro iustis imputatione haberi, quatenus Christi iustitiam per fidem possidemus, res plana erit et expedita.[31]

This brief statement makes explicit a concept of forensic justification, which is developed in subsequent editions. Man is not made righteous in justification, but is accepted as righteous, not on account of his own righteousness, but on account of the righteousness of Christ located outside of man. Calvin's brief discussion of the nature of imputation parallels that of Erasmus' *Novum instrumentum omne* (1516), noted above. In later editions, this understanding of justification is developed (and never, apparently, modified).

For Calvin, a man may be said to be justified when he is accepted by God as if he were righteous:

Ita nos iustificationem simpliciter interpretamur acceptionem qua nos Deus in gratiam receptos pro iustis habet. Eamque in peccatorum remissione ac iustitiae Christi imputatione positam esse dicimus.[32]

Calvin himself has no hesitation in acknowledging the strongly forensic character of this concept of justification, particularly in his polemic against Osiander.[33] It will also be clear that the emphasis placed by Calvin upon the *acceptatio divina* parallels that of the *via moderna* and the *schola Augustiniana moderna* (§§13, 17, 18), suggesting an affinity with the voluntarism and extrinsicism of these late medieval movements.[34] As there is no basis in man for his divine acceptation, his righteousness in justification is always *extra seipsum*; our righteousness is always *non in nobis sed in Christo*.[35] Although Calvin may be regarded as following Melanchthon in this respect,[36]

he nevertheless preserves an important aspect of Luther's understanding of justification which Melanchthon abandoned – the personal union of Christ and the believer in justification. Calvin speaks of
the believer being 'grafted into Christ', so that the concept of
incorporation becomes central to his understanding of justification.
The *iustitia Christi*, on the basis of which man is justified, is treated as
if it were man's within the context of the intimate personal relationship of Christ and the believer.

Non ergo [Christum] extra nos procul speculamur, ut nobis imputetur eius
iustitia: sed quia ipsum induimus, et insiti sumus in eius corpus, unum
denique nos secum efficere dignatus est: ideo iustitiae societatem nobis cum
eo esse gloriamur. Ita refellitur Osiandri calumnia, fidem a nobis censeri
iustitiam; quasi Christum spoliemus iure suo, quum dicimus fidei nos ad eum
vacuous accedere, ut eius gratiae locum demus, quo nos ipse solus impleat.
Sed Osiander hac spirituali coniunctione spreta, crassam mixturam Christi
cum fidelibus urget.[37]

Calvin's polemic against Osiander concerns the nature, rather than
the existence, of the union of Christ and the believer; Osiander
understands the union to be physical, where Calvin regards it as
purely spiritual.[38] The two consequences of the believer's incorporation into Christ are *iustificatio* and *sanctificatio*, which are distinct and
inseparable.[39] Thus where Bucer speaks of *iustificatio pii* or 'secondary justification', Calvin speaks of *sanctificatio*; where Bucer links the
first and second justifications on the basis of the regenerating activity
of the Holy Spirit, Calvin relates them on the basis of the believer's
insitio in Christum. Justification and sanctification are aspects of the
believer's new life in Christ, and just as one receives the whole Christ,
and not part of him, through faith, so any separation of these two
soteriological elements – which Calvin refers to as *les deux principales
grâces*[40] – is inconceivable. It is instructive to compare Bucer and
Calvin on the *ordo salutis*:

Bucer: *electio* → *iustificatio impii* → *iustificatio pii* → *glorificatio*

Calvin: *electio* → *unio mystica* $\begin{cases} iustificatio \\ sanctificatio \end{cases}$ → *glorificatio*

The strength of Calvin's understanding of justification thus becomes
apparent, in that it is evident that justification is now conceived
Christologically, thus permitting the essentially moral conception of
justification associated with Zwingli and Bucer to be discarded.
Where Zwingli and Bucer tended to make justification dependent

upon the believer's regeneration through the renewing work of the Holy Spirit, which enabled him to keep the law and imitate the (external) example of Christ, Calvin understands both justification and sanctification to be the chief *beneficia Christi*, bestowed simultaneously and inseparably upon the believer as a consequence of his *insitio in Christum*. Calvin thus implicates Christ *intrinsically*, where Zwingli and Bucer implicated him *extrinsically*, in the *ordo salutis*. This new approach to justification may be regarded as a recovery – whether conscious or unconscious – of Luther's realist conception of justification as the personal encounter of the believer with God in Christ, while simultaneously the extrinsicism of the Melanchthonian concept of justification is retained. Like Luther, Calvin stresses that faith is only implicated in justification to the extent that it grasps and appropriates Christ.[41] Indeed, faith may be said to play its part in justification by insisting that it does *not* justify, attributing all to Christ.[42] In other words, the possibility that the slogan 'justification *sola fide*' will be understood as 'justification *propter fidem*' is excluded from the outset: justification can only be *propter Christum*. Faith is but the vessel which receives Christ – and the vessel cannot be compared in value with the treasure which it contains.[43] Faith may thus be said to be the instrumental cause of justification.[44] It will, however, be clear that Calvin is actually concerned not so much with justification, as with incorporation into Christ (which has, as one of its necessary consequences, justification). It is this point which goes some considerable way towards explaining the lack of importance which Calvin appears to attach to justification in the 1559 *Institutio*.

It is a well-known fact that, in the 1559 edition of this work, Calvin defers his discussion of justification until Book III, and it is then found only after a detailed exposition of sanctification. This has proved a serious embarrassment to those who project Luther's concern with the *articulus iustificationis* on to Calvin, asserting that justification is the 'focal centre' of the *Institutio*.[45] In fact, Calvin's concern is with the manner in which the individual is incorporated into Christ, and the personal and corporate consequences of this *insitio in Christum* – of which justification is but one. Calvin thus expresses systematically what Luther grasped intuitively – the recognition that the question of justification was essentially an aspect of the greater question of man's relation to God in Christ, which need not be discussed exclusively in terms of the category of justification.[46] In effect, all the watchwords of the Reformation relating to this theme – *sola fide*, *sola gratia*, and even *sola scriptura* – may be reduced to their common denominator: justification is *through Christ alone*.

Calvin may be regarded as establishing the framework within which subsequent discussion of justification within the Reformed school would proceed, as well as exemplifying a trend which becomes increasingly evident in the Protestantism of the following century – the increasing diminution of the perceived significance of the *locus iustificationis*. Calvin did not, however, initiate this trend: as we have argued in the present section, the early Reformed church never attached the same importance to the *articulus iustificationis* as did the early evangelical faction within Germany (apparently on account of the personal influence of Luther). Zwingli's early concern with *Christianismus renascens* and Bucer's Erasmian concept of *lex Christi* had little bearing on the doctrine of justification, and, if anything, appear to have exercised a negative influence upon its evaluation. The supposition that the Reformation was homogeneously concerned with the *articulus iustificationis*, even in its initial phase, cannot be sustained on the basis of the evidence available, in that this evidence indicates that the high estimation of and concern for this article was restricted to the initial phase of the German Reformation.

With the death of Calvin, a new phase in the development of Reformed theology took place, which resulted in the emphasis shifting still further away from justification. The rise of Reformed scholasticism led to the recognition of predestination as the central dogma of the Reformed church,[47] even though this emphasis is absent from Calvin's 1559 *Institutio*. Whereas the Lutheran church was initially faced with a series of controversies relating to justi- fication (§21), those now facing the Reformed church would concern predestination. In the following section, we shall consider the devel- opment of the doctrine of justification within Lutheran and Refor- med Orthodoxy, and establish their points of convergence and divergence.

§24 Justification in Protestant Orthodoxy

The remarkable ease with which a new scholasticism established itself within the churches of the Reformation is one of the more significant aspects of the intellectual history of that period.[1] The need to systematise both Reformed and Lutheran dogmatics was partly a consequence of the perceived need to defend such theologies, and to distinguish them not merely from that of the Council of Trent, but also from one another. The rise of Confessionalism led to a new emphasis upon doctrinal orthodoxy as conformity to the confessional documents of Protestantism, and the use of increasingly subtle and refined concepts in order to defend their theological coherence. This is particularly evident in the case of the doctrine of justification, in which the differences between the two chief Protestant confessions were well established by the year 1620.

Reformed theology was quicker to develop a new scholasticism than its Lutheran counterpart. The general drift of Reformed theology into a form of Aristotelian scholasticism is generally thought to have begun with Beza,[2] and represents a significant shift from Calvin's position on a number of matters of importance. The tendency to base theology upon the basis of deductive reasoning from given principles to yield a rationally coherent system had three significant consequences for the development of the doctrine of justification in Reformed theology:[3]

1. The Christological emphasis evident in Calvin's soteriology is replaced by a theocentric emphasis, as the basis of theological speculation shifts from an inductive method based upon the Christ-event to a deductive method based upon the divine decrees of election.[4]
2. A doctrine of limited atonement is unequivocally stated. Although it may be argued that this doctrine is merely the logical conclusion of Calvin's soteriology, the fact remains that Calvin chose not to draw that conclusion.[5]
3. Predestination is considered as an aspect of the doctrine *of God*, rather than as an aspect of the doctrine *of salvation*.

This process of modification of Calvin under Bezan inspiration culminated in the Five Articles of the Synod of Dort (1619). The English-speaking world has paid a curious tribute to the bulb-growers of the Netherlands in the TULIP mnenomic for these five soteriological points summed up in the doctrines of: (T) total depravity; (U) unconditional election; (L) limited atonement; (I) irresistible grace; (P) perseverance of the elect.[6] Against this, the Remonstrants argued that Christ was the saviour of the world, not merely of the elect, having died for each and every man, and obtained for them remission of sins.[7]

One of the most significant features of the doctrines of justification associated with Reformed Orthodoxy, distinguishing them from both that of Calvin on the one hand, and those of Lutheranism on the other, is that of the covenant between God and man. This development can be traced to the Zurich reforming theology of the 1520s (§23), but was restated in terms of a *double* covenant by Gomarus, Polanus and Wollebius.[8] It is this later form of the concept which would become normative within later Reformed Orthodoxy and Puritanism (see §32). So significant a rôle did the federal foundations of justification assume within the Reformed theological tradition that the covenant-concept was frequently defined as the 'marrow (*medula*) of divinity'. The essential features of the concept may be found outlined in the works of Ursinus, who distinguished between the *foedus naturae*, known naturally to man and offering salvation upon condition of absolute obedience to God, and the *foedus gratiae*, known to man by revelation and offering salvation upon condition that he believe in Jesus Christ.[9] Polanus, by redefining Ursinus' *foedus naturae* as the *foedus operum*, established the general outlines of the theology which would become normative within the early Reformed school. The concept of the covenant between God and man eventually came to replace Calvin's Christological solution to the problem of the relationship between the totally gratuitous justification of the sinner and the demands of obedience subsequently laid upon him, without resorting to the moralist solution associated with Zwingli and Bucer. The *foedus gratiae* was grounded Christologically, with Christ as *testator*, thus retaining the emphasis, if not the substance, of Calvin's position.

The general outlines of the pre-Cocceian theology of the double covenant may be studied from Wollebius' *Christianae theologiae compendium* (1626). A fundamental distinction is drawn between God's dealings with man in his innocent and lapsed states. In the former, God entered of his own free and sovereign decision into a covenant of works with man, which promised him eternal life upon condition that he was obedient to God.[10] Man's fall led to a new covenant being established with him, as an expression of the divine graciousness. The *foedus gratiae* must be distinguished from the universal covenant made by God with all creatures, and the *foedus operum* made with Adam: it is the covenant established between God and his elect, by which God promises himself as their father in Christ, provided that they live in filial obedience to him. Although the *foedus gratiae* is offered to all men, the explicit particularism of the later Reformed soteriology permits only the elect to enjoy its benefits.

It is important to appeciate that the *foedus gratiae* is understood to have operated throughout the period of both the Old and the New Testaments. The Old Testament may be considered as the covenant of grace, as it was administered until the time of Christ, and may be divided into three periods. Between Adam and Abraham, the covenant was expressed simply in terms of the promises of God made to all men, unsupported in any external manner, and marked by the ritual of sacrifice. Between Abraham and Moses, the covenant was expressed in terms of the promises of God to the children of Abraham, supplemented by demands of obedience and the ritual of circumcision. Between Moses and Christ, the covenant assumed a more testamentary character, being marked by the ritual of Passover and other types of the death of Christ, who may be regarded as the testator of the *foedus gratiae*, and hence of both the Old and New Testaments. In effect, both the Old and New Testaments may be regarded as the same in substance, in that both contain the promise of grace linked with the demand of obedience: their difference lies primarily in the manner in which the covenant is administered.[11] The dialectic between law and gospel, so characteristic of contemporary Lutheranism, is thus conspicuously absent.

The covenant-theology of Reformed Orthodoxy received a significant development through Cocceius, who emphasised the potential theological significance of the term *testamentum*, which tended to be used interchangeably with *foedus*. Defining the *testamentum Dei* as *libera dispositio Dei Salvatoris de bonis suis ab haerede suo*,[12] Cocceius located the difference between the *foedus operum* and *foedus gratiae* by affirming that the latter alone may be allowed the character of a divine testament (in the sense of a 'will'), ratified beforehand by God to Christ, by which God appointed a heavenly inheritance for his children, to be acquired through the intervening death of Jesus Christ. The contracting parties to this testament are God as Redeemer, man as sinner, and Christ as the federal mediator between them. The testament is actually contracted in eternity between God and Christ, in which God exacted from Christ the condition of perfect obedience to the law in return for the elect as his own inheritance.[13] This development served to distinguish the covenant of works from that of grace, emphasising the novel character of the latter, in that it alone has the status of a testament. Furthermore, the existence of the intratrinitarian pact between Father and Son was held to justify the doctrine of limited atonement, thus further increasing its influence within later Reformed Orthodoxy.

The doctrine of a three-fold covenant between God and man is particularly associated with the Salmurian Academy. In April 1608, John Cameron published *De triplici Dei cum homine foedere theses*,[14] in which he developed an analysis of salvation history based upon three distinct covenants between God and man: the *foedus naturae, foedus gratiae subserviens* and *foedus gratiae*. The *foedus gratiae subserviens* was regarded by Cameron as a preparation for the *foedus gratiae*, and appears to have represented an attempt to incorporate the Lutheran distinction between law and gospel within the context of a federal scheme. Cameron seems to have regarded the harmonisation of law and gospel implicit in the Orthodox Reformed two-fold covenant scheme as compromising the doctrine of justification *sola fide*.[15] The importance of this three-fold scheme derives from its adoption by Moses Amyraut as the basis of his distinctive theology.[16]

Amyraut's 'hypothetical universalism' and his doctrine of the triple covenant between God and man is unquestionably a direct consequence of his emphasis upon the priority of justification over other Christian doctrines.[17] The Pauline dialectic between law and gospel, underlying Cameron's covenant scheme, causes Amyraut to revise the traditional *foedus operum* or *foedus legale* by interpreting the term *lex* in a radically restricted sense. In his disputation *De tribus foederibus divinis*, Amyraut developed a theory of progressive revelation, culminating in the period of the covenant of grace:

Memorantur autem iustismodi *divina foedera tria* in scripturis, *Primum* quod contractum fuit in Paradiso terrestri, et *Naturale* dici solet, *Secundum*, quod Deus pepigit peculiari ratione cum Israelo, et appellatur *Legale*. *Tertium* denique quod *Gratiae* dicitur, et patefactum est in Evangelio.[18]

It is possible to confuse the Cocceian and Salmurian interpretations of the federal foundations of justification if it is not realised that the Salmurian academicians recognised the three covenants *to be actualised in time*. The Cocceian covenant theology may be restated in the form of three covenants, of which one is made in eternity: the eternal intratrinitarian covenant between Father and Son precedes the temporal covenants of works and grace. The Salmurian academicians recognised no such eternal intratrinitarian covenant, regarding all three covenants as pertaining to human history. The *foedus naturale* was made directly – without a mediator – between God and Adam, promising a continued blessed existence in Eden upon condition of perfect obedience to the law of nature. The *foedus legale* was made through Moses between God and Israel, and promised a blessed existence in the promised land of Canaan upon condition of perfect obedience to the law of nature *as clarified by the written law and ceremonies*. The *foedus gratiae* was made through Christ between God and all mankind, promising salvation and eternal life upon condition of faith. It is at this point that Amyraut's 'hypothetical universalism' becomes evident: Amyraut states that *Christ intended to die for all men*, although he concedes that the will of God which desires universal salvation also specifies that the condition of faith must be met before this is possible.[19]

Seventeenth-century Lutheran Orthodoxy was primarily concerned with the elucidation and defence of the doctrine of justification to be found in the Formula of Concord (§22). Although the concept of forensic justification was maintained with the utmost rigour, attention shifted to the question of the subjective appropriation of justification. As with Reformed Orthodoxy, so Lutheranism came to adopt scholastic terminology and categories in discussions of justification, although the increasing emphasis upon the practical aspect of justification led to its being discussed as a matter of practical theology (*gratia applicatrix*). Although the extrinsic and forensic aspect of justification was thus maintained formally, it is clear that interest in this aspect of the concept was now overshadowed – particularly as the threat posed by Pietism loomed large – by the practical and experiential dimensions of conversion.[20]

The distinctive positions of Lutheran and Reformed Orthodoxy on justification are most easily expounded and compared when considered under three headings: the nature of justification; the objective grounds of justification; the subjective appropriation of justification. We shall consider each of these points individually.

1 The Nature of Justification

Both confessions understand justification to be the forensic declaratory act of God (*actus Dei forensis in foro coeli*), subsequent to vocation and prior to sanctification.[21] Justification consists of two elements: the remission of sins (or the non-imputation of sin, which is treated as identical with the remission of sins), and the imputation of the obedience of Christ. The Augustinian concept of justification as both event and process, still evident in Luther (§20), is rejected by later Lutheranism. Thus the divine judgement implicit in justification is understood to be *synthetic*, rather than *analytic*. The Reformed school are able to justify their emphasis upon the *iudicium Dei secundum veritatem* through the application of the principle of the *unio mystica* between Christ and the believer, as well as the federal relationship between them, so that the alien righteousness of the former may be imputed to the latter.[22] The absence of a corresponding principle or federal basis within Lutheranism leads to a corresponding weakness at this point, with justification tending to be treated as a legal fiction.

The forensic dimension of justification is emphasised by the use of the term *acceptilation* (see §22 for its use in Erasmus). This concept is taken from Roman private law, and refers to the dissolution of an obligation (such as a debt) by a verbal decree on the part of the one to whom the debt was due, without any form of payment having taken place or necessarily being envisaged as taking place in the future. Justification is thus conceived analogically, as the remission of sins and imputation of righteousness by a purely verbal decree *in foro divino*, without any change in the sinner having taken place with reference to which this verdict could be supported. The term *acceptilation*, so frequently used in this context, appears to be misunderstood by several Reformed theologians, such as Alsted, who confuses it with the Scotist concept of *acceptation* (see §§9, 11, 13, 16).

An important distinction is made by the Reformed theologians between active and passive justification. The distinction refers to the act of God by which the sinner is justified (active justification), and the subjective feeling of grace subsequently evoked in the conscience of the justified sinner. God *acts* to justify, and man is *passive* in receiving this justification. The importance of the distinction lies in the fact that God's act of justification, in which the sinner is declared righteous, is perfect, accomplished once and for all, whereas man's realisation of this state of justification is imperfect, in so far as it is based upon the *feeling* of grace evoked in his conscience. While the two coexist simultaneously in the formal act of justification, the extent of the consciousness of justification may vary from one individual to another. The absence of a corresponding distinction within Lutheranism led to considerable confusion concerning the precise causal relationship of faith and justification, whereas the Reformed theologians were able to state that faith was posterior to objective, and prior to subjective, justification.

2 *The Objective Grounds of Justification*

Both confessions agree that the objective grounds of justification are to be located in the satisfaction offered by Christ as virtue of his fulfilment of the law and his passion. A distinction was drawn between the *obedientia activa Christi* (his obedience to and fulfilment of the law in his life) and the *obedientia Christi passiva* (his obedience in his suffering and death upon the cross). Both Lutheran and Reformed thinking on this question was stimulated by the controversies surrounding the views of Piscator and Socinus. In his *Theses theologicae*, Piscator developed the views of the Lutheran Parsimonius, who had hindered the Stancarist cause somewhat (see §22) by arguing that if man's obedience to the law was still necessary, it followed that the *obedientia activa* had no substitutionary value. Piscator observed that as believers are clearly still under an obligation to fulfil the law, Christ's active obedience cannot be directly imputed to them.[23] *Remissio peccatorum* and *imputatio iustitia* alike are based upon the *iustitia Christi passiva*.

Piscator was refuted in a variety of manners. The Lutheran Johann Gerhard argued that, as justification included both *remissio peccatorum* and *imputatio iustitiae*, the former could be held to be based upon the *obedientia passiva* and the latter upon the *obedientia activa*.[24] However, Gerhard conceded that this suggestion was only valid *secundum rationem*, and did not reflect a theological relationship between the concepts;[25] as Baier pointed out, this would imply – *secundum rationem* – the priority of *imputatio iustitiae* over *remissio peccatorum*.[26] The Reformed reply to Piscator was somewhat different, and requires careful analysis. According to the Lutheran understanding of the *communicatio idiomatum*, the incarnation of the Word may be said to result in the humanity of Christ participating in *all* the divine attributes, including that of superiority to the law (the so-called *exlex*). Thus Christ, as man, is under no positive obligation to fulfil the law, and his subsequent fulfilment of the law must be seen as a vicarious act of exinanition on his part. If this act of exinanition is to have any value, that value must relate to others, rather than to Christ himself. Thus the *obedientia activa* is of purely vicarious satisfactory value.

While insisting that the *obedientia activa* is vicarious (in other words, of value to those for whom Christ became incarnate), the Reformed theologians operated with a significantly different understanding of the *communicatio idiomatum*: the Lutheran understanding of the principle is rejected as practically dissipating the humanity of Christ. The Reformed Christology attempted to preserve the distinction between the human and divine natures at this point, and replaced the Lutheran understanding of the *communicatio idiomatum* with the quite distinct principle of the *unctio spiritus sancti*. The incarnation itself must be seen as an act of exinanition, involving the setting aside of certain divine attributes – including the so-called *exlex* – as a result of which the manhood of Christ retains its primary characteristics, with the exception of its innate sinfulness. Thus Christ, as man, is under obligation to the law,[27] so that the *obedientia activa* is not necessarily vicarious. The vicarious character of the *obedientia activa* arises through the profoundly Christological conception of justification associated with Reformed Orthodoxy, expressed in the doctrine of Christ as *caput et sponsor electorum*, by which the elect may be said to participate in all the benefits of Christ as if they had obtained them through their own efforts. The *obedientia activa*, in that it is of benefit to Christ, is also of benefit to the elect. It is this concept of Christ as *caput et sponsor electorum* – ultimately representing a central element of Luther's soteriology which Lutheranism failed to appropriate – which underlies the Reformed insistence that the verdict of justification is *iudicium Dei secundum veritatem*, and has misled many into concluding that later Reformed Orthodoxy is based upon an *analytical* understanding of the divine judgement in justification. It could thus be argued that the Reformed understanding of the *obedientia activa* involves a concept of derivative or transferred vicariousness.

The two confessions concur in their understanding of the priestly office of Christ, by which he made satisfaction for the sins of mankind, and their mutual opposition to Socinianism. Socinus had denied that God required any form of satisfaction in order to remit sin: God is to be conceived as a private creditor, able to remit debts due to him without the necessity of the imposition of any penalty.[28] Although Socinus retains the traditional three-fold office of Christ as prophet, priest and king, he restricts the office of priest to that of intercession (whereas it had traditionally included satisfaction),[29] shifting the emphasis to the prophetic office, by which Christ revealed the will of God to man. A general statement of the common Protestant understanding of the satisfaction of Christ takes the following form.[30] Man, having fallen into sin, is liable to death, because God, the righteous judge, is under obligation to punish sin. As man cannot provide the necessary satisfaction for sin, this satisfaction is provided by God himself in the form of the God-man, whose sinlessness absolves him from the common human lot of suffering and death. Christ was obedient to the law in his suffering and death on the cross, and this obedience was adequate as a satisfaction for man's sin. The strongly Anselmian basis of this scheme will be evident, although Anselm did not envisage the merit of Christ functioning as a basis for the imputation of righteousness.[31] Both confessions assert the theanthropic nature of the mediation of Christ[32] – in other words, that Christ is mediator as the God-man, and not either as God or as man separately.

The confessions diverge dramatically over the question of the extent of the redeeming work of Christ. The Lutherans asserted that Christ's merit, won by his obedience, was sufficient for all men, although only efficacious in the case of those who, after their regeneration, respond to the Word and are thus justified. The *errores Calvinianorum* are located by Gerhard in their concept of predestination, which underlies their teaching on justification.[33] In effect, Lutheran Orthodoxy interpreted the concept of election as God's affirmation of that which he foreknows will occur within the sphere of his ordained will – in other words, election takes place on the basis of *fides praevisa*. Through man's regeneration, his *liberum arbitrium* is restored, enabling him to respond freely to the Word of the gospel – whether he accepts it or not is up to the individual. This affirmation that *vocatio* is *resistibilis et universalis* is characteristic of later Lutheran Orthodoxy, and raises significant questions to which we shall return in our discussion of the subjective appropriation of justification.

The Reformed divines, while conceding the universal sufficiency of the work of Christ, emphasised the particularity of its efficacy. This opinion represents a development of the views of Calvin, who did not teach limited atonement, but affirmed that the gospel was offered by God for all mankind. Hence, in his critical discussion of the Tridentine decree on justification, Calvin raised no objections to the explicit statement that Christ died for all men.[34] Beza, however, explicitly stated that Christ died only for the elect, and not for all men.[35] As later Orthodoxy would put it, Christ died *sufficienter* for all men, but *efficienter* only for the elect.[36] As Rijssen remarked, a distinction must be drawn between God's general love, exercised towards all men, and his saving love, by which he wills to redeem them.[37] There is thus a clear distinction between the Lutheran concept of the general divine intention to save all, actualised in the case of those who believe, and the Reformed doctrine of an efficacious individual election.

3 The Subjective Appropriation of Justification

One of the most significant developments in seventeenth-century Lutheran dogmatics was the affirmation that faith was itself a cause of justification. Although it was emphasised that faith was a *causa impulsiva minus principalis iustificationis*, it was clearly stated that faith was logically prior to justification in the *ordo salutis*. This affirmation was interpreted to mean that justification was dependent upon a change in man, and resulted in justification being placed towards the end of an *ordo salutis* which included elements such as *illuminatio*, *regeneratio* and *conversio*. Although justification is still defined *forensically*, it is understood to be predicated upon a prior alteration within man – namely, that he believes. Where Luther had understood justification to concern the *unbelieving sinner*, Orthodoxy revised this view, referring justification to the *believing sinner*. Thus Calov and Quenstedt defend the following *ordo salutis*:

vocatio → *illuminatio* → *regeneratio* → *conversio* → *iustificatio*

The final Lutheran doctrine of justification, as stated by Hollaz, has the following form: man, in his natural state, is spiritually dead. By the means of grace, especially through the agency of the Word, man receives new powers, the illumination of his understanding, and the excitement of good desires. This brings about the restoration of the *liberum arbitrium*, so that the *arbitrium liberatum* is now enabled, should the individual so wish, to believe. Man thus possesses the *facultas applicandi se ad gratiam* before his justification, and his justification is contingent upon precisely such *applicatio gratiae*. If the individual chooses to do so, he may, although he need not, use these powers consequent to his regeneration to repent and believe, and as a result to be justified.[38] It will be clear that there are thus considerable affinities between later Orthodoxy and Pietism on the relationship between faith and justification.

In part, the later Lutheran insistence on the priority of regeneration and conversion over justification represents a reaction against the Reformed doctrine of irresistible grace, a leading feature of Reformed spirituality in the post-Dort period. In order to avoid such a teaching, it is necessary to develop a theology of justification which simultaneously asserts the inability of man to justify himself *sine gratia* and his ability to reject the possibility of justification once this arises. The assertion of the priority of regeneration over justification thus permits the later Lutheran divines to assert the necessity of grace in justification (in that it is necessary for man's regeneration), while restricting its efficacy (in that man's regeneration is understood to involve the repristination of his volitional faculties, by which he is able to determine whether or not to respond to his call). It will, however, be clear that the result is a theology which places regeneration prior to faith, and faith prior to justification.

The Reformed understanding of the matter is much simpler and more coherent. Man's justification is the temporal execution of the decree of election, effected through grace. The fact that this proceeds through a complex causal sequence does not alter the fact that the entire sequence of events is directly to be attributed to God. Thus Wendelin draws up the following chart for the assistance of his readers.[39]

$$
Acceptatio,\ cuius\ \begin{cases} causa\ instrumentalis = fides\ iustificans \\[6pt] effectus\ isque\ triplex \begin{cases} iustificatio \\ sanctificatio \\ glorificatio \end{cases} \end{cases}
$$

Faith is a divine gift effected within man, functioning as the instrument by which the Holy Spirit may establish the *unio mystica* between Christ and the believer, whose three-fold effect is justification, sanctification and glorification (note how Wendelin includes glorification as an effect of the *insitio in Christum*, where Calvin deferred it within the *ordo salutis*). Man's rôle at each and every stage of the *ordo salutis* is purely passive, in that the elect are called and accepted *efficaciter*. This observation goes some considerable way towards explaining the low status accorded to justification within Reformed dogmatics: justification is merely an aspect of the temporal execution of the eternal decree of election. God exercises his providential rule over creation through the efficacious justification of the elect. It is interesting to observe that although the objective grounds of justification fall under the aegis of the priestly office of Christ in Reformed dogmatics, the subjective appropriation of justification is dealt with under the aegis of the kingly office.

It will be clear that the Lutheran and Reformed understandings of the *nature* of justification are similar, the chief differences between them emerging in relation to the question of the objective grounds and subjective appropriation of justification. The Reformed doctrines of absolute and unconditional predestination and limited atonement, linked with the federal understanding of the basis of justification, distinguish the doctrines of justification associated with that school from those of Lutheranism. Significantly, the Reformed school is considerably closer to Luther (especially the 1525 Luther) than Lutheranism. Given that both confessions adopted a strongly forensic concept of justification, which set them apart from Luther on this point, the strongly predestinarian cast of Reformed theology approximates to that of Luther to a far greater extent than Lutheran Orthodoxy. Similarly, the strongly Christological conception of justification to be found in Luther's writings is carried over into Reformed theology, particularly in the image of Christ as *caput et sponsor electorum*, where it is so evidently lacking in Lutheran Orthodoxy. Both in terms of its substance and emphasis, the teaching of later Lutheran Orthodoxy bears little relation to that of Luther.

The period of Lutheran Orthodoxy was marked by considerable opposition from the increasingly influential Pietist movement, particularly associated with the university of Halle.[40] At its best, the Pietist movement may be regarded as a reaction on the part of a living faith against the empty formulae of a dead Orthodoxy. The term 'Pietism' is particularly applied to the movement within Lutheranism associated with Philipp Jakob Spener, characterised by its insistence upon the active nature of faith, and its critique of the Orthodox doctrine of forensic justification. Such criticism was foreshadowed in many quarters, including sections of the Radical Reformation.[41] The English Quaker Robert Barclay taught that justification is identical with regeneration, whose formal cause is 'the revelation of God in the soul, changing, altering and renewing the mind'.[42] On account of his being made a partaker of the divine nature, man is *made* righteous.[43] A similar, although more extended, critique of the Orthodox doctrine of justification is to be found in the writings of Jakob Böhme.[44]

As Ritschl has observed,[45] Pietism maintained the doctrine of *reconciliation* in a thoroughly orthodox form (in other words, man was understood to be alienated from God through original sin), while subjecting the doctrine of *justification* to extensive modification on the basis of the pastoral concern for personal holiness and devotion.[46] The concept of participation in the divine nature, usually expounded on the basis of 2 Peter 1.4,[47] appears to have become characteristic of Pietist understandings of the nature of justification at an early stage. Five important modifications were made by the Pietists to the Orthodox doctrine of justification.

1. Faith is understood to be active, rather than passive, in justification. The Pietist assertion of the activity of faith in justification was particularly criticised by the Lutheran Valentin Löscher, who appealed to Luther's insistence upon the passivity of justifying

faith.[48] Löscher's criticisms were rejected by Anton and Lange, who argued that faith must be active if it is to lay hold of Christ. Francke himself argued that the activity of faith in justification was not inconsistent with God's being the author of justification.[49]

2. The intense emphasis placed by Pietism upon the necessity for personal piety led to the articulation of the doctrine of Christian perfection, a concept without any counterpart within – indeed, which was excluded by – Orthodoxy.[50]

3. The concept of vicarious satisfaction is rejected as detrimental to personal piety. This criticism of the Orthodox understanding of the objective foundations of justification can be instanced from the writings of Spener, although it is particularly associated with John Wesley.[51] To Wesley, the assertion that Christ had fulfilled the law on man's behalf appeared to imply that man was no longer under any obligation to fulfil it. It is this consideration which underlies Wesley's discussion of the law *sub loco sanctificationis*.

4. The concept of imputed righteousness, which is an essential feature of the Orthodox understanding of justification, is rejected as being destructive of piety.[52] Thus in his *Theses credendorum*, Breithaupt argued for the necessary implication of inherent righteousness in justification.[53] In his sermon *A Blow at the Root, or Christ stabbed in the House of his Friends*, Wesley described the teaching 'that Christ had done as well as suffered all; that his righteousness being imputed to us, we need none of our own' as 'a blow at the root of all holiness, all true religion ... for wherever this doctrine is cordially received, it leaves no place for holiness'.[54] This criticism was expanded in the Standard Sermon *Justification by Faith*:

Least of all does justification imply that God is deceived in those whom he justifies; that he thinks them to be what, in fact, they are not; that he accounts them to be otherwise than they are. It does by no means imply that God judges concerning us contrary to the real nature of things; that he esteems us better than we really are, or believes us righteous when we are unrighteous ... [or] ... judges that I am righteous, because another is so.[55]

5. The Pietist emphasis upon the need for personal holiness appeared to be threatened by the Orthodox doctrine that man might repent at any time of his choosing, which frequently led to 'death-bed conversions' on the part of notorious sinners who had evidently chosen to postpone their conversion until the last possible moment. It was this pastoral consideration which led to the Terminist controversy, particularly associated with Böse's *Terminus peremptorius salutis hominis* (1698).[56] The course of this controversy does not concern us; its

significance lies in its illustrating the Pietist willingness to develop theologies of justification of such a character as to maximise personal piety. In that the Orthodox doctrine of repentance was held to compromise this, it was subjected to modification along the lines indicated. It was for reasons such as this that many regarded Pietists as having *de*formed, rather than *re*formed, the Lutheran church of their day.

Although the early Pietists such as Spener or Francke were more concerned with the promotion of personal piety than with the restructuring of Christian doctrine, it is an inescapable fact that the Pietist emphasis upon regeneration led to a re-evaluation of the received teachings of Lutheran Orthodoxy in terms of their promotion of piety. The emphasis upon the necessity of regeneration led to the assertion of the priority of regeneration over justification – a tendency already evident within Lutheran Orthodoxy itself, which was thus ill prepared to meet this development. The Pietist emphasis upon the priority and necessity of piety, virtue and obedience on the part of believers is significant for another reason, in that it provides a direct link with the moralism of the *Aufklärung*. If an 'active faith' is to be accepted as the arbiter and criterion of justification, in the quasi-Arminian sense often found in the writings of the Pietists, it may be concluded that the practice of piety by an individual is an adequate demonstration of his faith. In other words, the ethical renewal of the individual both causes and demonstrates his justification. This important observation goes some considerable way towards explaining the rise of legalism within the Pietist theological faculty at Halle towards the end of the eighteenth century, and also points to a fundamental affinity with the moralism of the theologians of the *Aufklärung*.

7. The Tridentine decree on justification

Introduction

The Catholic church was ill prepared to meet the challenge posed by the rise of the evangelical faction within Germany and elsewhere in the 1520s and 1530s.[1] Luther's doctrine of justification attracted considerable attention in the 1520s, not all of it unsympathetic. According to Schmidt, three reasons may be suggested to explain the remarkable importance which came to be attached within contemporary Catholicism to the doctrine of justification *sola fide*.[2] First, it required an internalisation of the religious life, thus sharply contrasting with the prevailing external forms of Christian existence.[3] Second, it restored an emphasis upon the priority of the divine rôle in justification, against the prevailing tendency to concentrate upon the human rôle. Third, it amounted to an implicit declaration of war upon the Roman curia. Relatively few works dealing with the doctrine of justification were published within Catholicism in the period 1520–45, with notable exceptions such as Tommaso de Vio Cajetan's *De fide et operibus* (1532).[4] A survey of such works suggests that the Lutheran doctrine of justification was simply not understood by the early opponents of the Reformation,[5] although the rise of polemical theology in the 1530s served to clarify points of importance. Early anti-Lutheran polemic tended to fasten upon points which Luther regarded as trivial – such as Luther's views on the papacy, indulgences or the sacraments, while failing to deal with such crucial questions as the concept of *servum arbitrium* or the nature of justifying righteousness. Indeed, Luther singled out Erasmus alone as identifying the real theological issues involved in his protest.[6]

The task facing the theologians assembled at Trent was thus not merely the clarification of Catholic teaching on justification, but also the definition of Catholic dogma in relation to the perceived errors of Protestantism. In fact, however, views on justification remarkably

54

similar to those associated with the northern European Reformers penetrated deep into the hierarchy of the Italian church in the period 1520–45, and are widely thought to have been espoused by several of those present during the Tridentine debate on justification. What those views were, and whence they originated, are the subject of the following section.

§25 Developments within Catholicism 1490–1545

The late fifteenth and early sixteenth centuries saw the emergence of numerous groups agitating for reform within the church, frequently adopting theologies of justification which foreshadowed the Augustinianism of the Wittenberg Reformation. In the present section, we are particularly concerned with developments in Italy, and the origins and significance of the doctrines of justification associated with Gropper and Contarini, which exercised some influence over evangelical–Catholic attempts at reconciliation in the period 1536–41 and emerged as an issue at the Council of Trent.

The rise of Augustinianism in the late fifteenth and early sixteenth centuries is perhaps best illustrated from developments within Spain.[1] The rise of the *alumbrados* is one of the more remarkable features of the period,[2] and the records of the Spanish Inquisition indicate that radically theocentric views on justification were in circulation within the movement by 1511.[3] Although the marked individualism characteristic of *alumbramiento* distinguishes it from Protestantism,[4] the recognition of affinities between certain *alumbrados* and Luther led to the suppression of the movement in the 1520s.

The most significant figure of the Spanish religious renaissance for our purposes is Juan de Valdés, whose *Diálogo de doctrina cristiana* (1529) developed a radically theocentric doctrine of justification which came to serve as a model for Italian Evangelism in the 1530s.[5] The central problem posed by the doctrine of justification is identified by Valdés in *Las ciento diez divinas consideraciones* as follows:

es útil al honbre que Dios sea omnipotente, liberal, sabio, fiel, vegnino, misericordioso y piadoso, mas no parece que le sea útil que él sea justo: porque, siendo Dios justo y el honbre ynjusto, no alla cómo poderse salvar en el juizio de Dios.[6]

Valdés develops a concept of *la justicia de Dios* based upon the principle 'once in jeopardy' which is markedly different from that of Augustine and the Wittenberg Reformers: God, having punished

Christ, and hence man, for the sins of mankind, may be relied upon
not to punish twice for the same offence:

determinando de executar en el su proprio Hijo todoel rigor de la justicia qua
avía de executar contra todos los honbres por todas sus ynpiedades y pecados
. . . Creamos al Evangelio qual nos certifica que en Christo fuimos castigados,
y en esto nos aseguramos, sabiendo que Dios es justo e que fuimos castigados
ya en la cruz de Iezu Christo nuestro Señor.[7]

It is therefore necessary for the believer to recognise that he is
righteous in Christ, although he is a sinner in himself, in that the
penalty for sin has been laid upon Christ:

De manera que, o me debo yo conoscer justo en Christo, bein que yo me
conosco pecador en mí; o debo negar aquello que afirmo el Evangelio, que en
Christo Dios a castigado las eniquidades y los pecados de todos los honbres y
los míos con ellos.[8]

This marks a significant departure from the Erasmian anthropology,
although it must be noted that Valdés' statement of the principle
simul iustus et peccator does not parallel that of either Augustine or
Luther exactly.[9] Valdés' arrival in Italy in 1531 led to his considerable
influence being subsequently exercised over Italian reforming circles,
to which we now turn.

The last fifteenth and early sixteenth centuries witnessed a revival
in interest in the theology of Augustine, accompanying extensive
publication of editions of his works.[10] In Italy, this Augustinian
renaissance was accompanied by a new interest on the part of Italian
humanists in the Pauline corpus of the New Testament.[11] It is against
this background that the conversion experience of Gasparo Contarini
must be seen. A member of a group of Paduan-educated humanists
which included Paolo Giustiniani,[12] Contarini shared their common
difficulty concerning the means by which salvation might be attained.
The contemporary confusion within the Catholic church concerning
the doctrine of justification was reflected within this group: some
chose to enter a hermitage as the only possible means for expiating
their sins, while others – including Contarini – chose to remain in the
world. The correspondence between Contarini and Giustiniani indicates the former's concern with problems remarkably similar to those
which so preoccupied Luther at the same time.[13] For Contarini, the
sacrifice of Christ upon the cross was more than adequate as a
satisfaction for human sin, in which man must learn to trust utterly.[14]
It is utterly impossible for man to be justified on the basis of his
works: man is justified through faith in Christ, as a result of which the

righteousness of Christ is made ours.[15] Contarini's theological break-through may be dated in the first half of 1511, thus placing it before that of Luther and even before the alleged 'discovery' by Pietro Speziali of the doctrine of justification by faith in 1512.[16]

The Contarini–Giustiniani correspondence is of importance in that it illustrates the doctrinal confusion of the immediate pre-Tridentine period in relation to the doctrine of justification. Giustiniani was convinced that it was necessary to withdraw from the world and lead a life of the utmost austerity in order to be saved, whereas Contarini came to believe that it was possible to lead a normal life in the world, trusting in the merits of Christ for salvation. But which of these positions represented, or approximated most closely to, the teaching of the Catholic church? The simple fact is that this question could not be answered with any degree of confidence. This doctrinal confusion concerning precisely the issue over which the Reformation was widely held to have begun inevitably meant that the Catholic church was in no position to attempt a coherent systematic refutation of the teaching of the evangelical faction in its crucial initial phase.

The dialectic between *iustitia Christi* and *iustitia hominis* points to an important difference between Luther and Contarini. Although both emphasise the rôle of faith and the 'alien' righteousness of Christ, the exclusivity of Luther's solafideism and extrinsicism is not to be found with Contarini. Contarini's primary concern appears to have been the elimination of human self-confidence, which he regarded as an impediment to justification; he does not exclude the possibility of human cooperation with God, nor does he consider the proper emphasis upon faith to entail the elimination of *caritas* from justi-fication. Nevertheless, Contarini concedes the truth of Luther's insights: pero il fondamento dello aedificio de Luterani e verissimo, ne per alcun modo devemo dirli contra, ma accettarlo come vero et catholico, immo come fondamento della religione christiana.[17]

In respects, Contarini's later views on justification – particularly those dating from 1541 – parallel those of the Cologne theologian Johannes Gropper, whose *Enchiridion* was published in 1538. This work has often been regarded as developing a doctrine of double justification, based on the concept of *duplex iustitia*.[18] In fact, this view appears to rest upon a serious misunderstanding of Gropper's views. It is possible that this misunderstanding derives from Bellarm-ine's attempt to discredit those present at Regensburg:

Bucerus in libro Concordiae, ut fortasse Catholicos aliquos seduceret, ut fecit, duplicem iustitiam excogitavit, a qua formaliter iustificaremur; unam imperfectam, quae in virtutibus in nobis inhaerentibus sita sit, alteram perfectam, quae est ipsa Christi iustitia nobis imputata. Quoniam enim iustitia nostra nunquam talis esse potest, ut iudicium Dei sustineat, ut ipse dicit, ideo necessarium esse imputationem iustitia Christi, ut illa induti, et quodammodo tecti coram Deo compareamus, et iusti pronunciemur ... In eandem sententiam sive potius errorem indicit Albertus Pighius in Contr. II et auctores Antididagmatis Coloniensis.[19]

In his influential study on the background to Regensburg, Stupperich appears to follow Bellarmine's analysis of the relation of Bucer, Pighius and Gropper,[20] and concluded that Gropper explicitly taught a doctrine of double justification. This conclusion requires modification. The concept of a 'double righteousness' – but *not* of a double formal cause of justification – is to be found in the earlier medieval discussion of justification, where a clear distinction is drawn (particularly within the early Dominican, and subsequently the Thomist, school) between *iustitia infusa* and *iustitia acquisita* (see §§5, 6). Justification takes place upon the basis of *iustitia infusa*, with the subsequent establishment of *iustitia acquisita*. This is most emphatically *not* a doctrine of double justification! A careful distinction is merely drawn between the righteousness which functions as the formal cause of justification (*iustitia infusa* or *iustitia inhaerens*) and the righteousness which subsequently develops within the believer through his cooperation with grace: in other words, although justification involves *duplex iustitia*, these *iustitiae* are understood to be implicated in totally different manners within the overall scheme of justification. A doctrine of 'double justification', in the strict sense of the term (as it is encountered during the Tridentine proceedings on justification: see §26), is essentially a doctrine of a *double formal cause of justification*: in other words, justification takes place on account of *duplex iustitia*. Stupperich has tended to confuse *iustitia inhaerens* with *iustitia acquisita* in his exposition of the relationship of Gropper's concepts of *iustitia imputata* and *iustitia inhaerens*, with a concomitant misunderstanding both of Gropper's doctrine of justification and its relationship to Melanchthon and Catholicism.[21] The assertion of the inseparability of forgiveness and renewal is most emphatically *not* equivalent to a doctrine of 'double justification', and this confusion over the definition of terms has enormously impeded the proper evaluation of the significance of Gropper. In the *Enchiridion*, it is clear that Gropper merely develops an earlier medieval insight in such a manner as to correct the perceived shortcomings of the Melanchthonian doctrine of justification, while at the same time indicating the common ground between the Lutheran and Catholic doctrines.

The chapter of the *Enchiridion* entitled *de iustificatione hominis* opens with the following definition of justification: iustificatio duo proprie complectitur, nempe remissionem peccatorum et interioris mentis renovationem seu repurgationem.[22] Gropper criticises Melanchthon's concept of forensic justification, which he illustrates with specific reference to the latter's analogy of the people of Rome declaring Scipio to be free: iustificari *plus* apud Paulum significat, quam iustum pronuntiari.[23] Justification is inextricably linked with the internal renewal of the individual: nemo iustificatur, nisi per innovationem voluntatis.[24] Where Gropper so evidently differs from the traditional Catholic account of justification is in his use of the concept of imputed righteousness. It appears, however, that Gropper interprets this concept in a non-Melanchthonian sense, tending to regard it as equivalent to divine acceptation.[25] Justification is not regarded as identical with the forensic pronouncement that the individual is righteous, and Gropper's divergence from Melanchthon at this point is unequivocal. It appears that Gropper regards the divine acceptation of the believer through his renewal (expressed in terms of *remissio peccatorum et renovatio interior voluntatis*) as equivalent to the imputation of righteousness, and thus merely restates the standard later medieval concept of *acceptatio divina* in language which he feels to be more acceptable to his Lutheran opponents. Far from developing a doctrine of 'double justification', Gropper merely states the inseparability of *remissio peccatorum* and *renovatio* in a thoroughly Augustinian sense. Melanchthon's definition of *iustificatio* as *acceptatio*[26] in a passage alluded to by Gropper obviously suggest such an approach.

Those who hold that Gropper develops a doctrine of 'double justification' are obliged to assert that the *Enchiridion* explicitly teaches a *double formal cause of justification*.[27] This is simply not the case. Gropper clearly asserts a single formal cause of justification (*proprie causa formalis iustificationis*), and defines it as *misericordia et gratia Dei nos innovans*.[28] Gropper rigorously excludes the possibility, necessarily associated with a doctrine of 'double justification', that the believer is justified on account of (*propter*) his renewal: iustificationem non assequimur *propter* nostram novitatem, sed *novitas*, quam Deus operatur in nobis, haec *est iustificatio nostra*.[29] It is evident that Gropper is merely restating the traditional medieval teaching that justification *includes*, but does not *take place on account of*, the interior renewal of the believer. Although Gropper's discussion of habitual grace is difficult to follow, it is evident that *gratia Dei nos innovans* – which he defines to be the single formal cause of justification – is functionally identical with the Thomist concept of *iustitia infusa seu inhaerens*, thus establishing the continuity between Gropper and the medieval tradition upon this point. Although Gropper clearly identifies important areas of continuity between the Catholic and Protestant understandings of justification, he cannot be regarded as a pre-Tridentine exponent of 'double justification' in the proper sense of the term.

Views similar to those expressed in Gropper's *Enchiridion* may be found in Contarini's *Epistola de iustificatione*, written from Regensburg on 25 May 1541. For Contarini, justification involves both becoming righteous (*iustum fieri*) and being counted as righteous (*iustum haberi*).[30] Contarini thus develops a theology which, like that of Gropper, has tended to be interpreted as a pre-Tridentine statement of the doctrine of 'double justification', explicitly recognising two types of righteousness implicated in the process of justification:

Attingimus autem ad duplicem iustitiam, alteram nobis inhaerentem, qua incipimus esse iusti et efficimur 'consortes divinae naturae' et habemus charitatem diffusam in cordibus nostris, alteram vero non inhaerentem sed nobis donatam cum Christo, iustitiam inquam Christi et omne eius meritum. Simul tempore utraque nobis donatur et utramque attingimus per fidem.[31]

Which of these *iustitiae* is prior to the other is, according to Contarini, a useless scholastic disputation;[32] the important point is that man's inherent righteousness, which is initially inchoate and imperfect, is supplemented by *iustitia Christi* as a preliminary anticipation of the state which subsequently arises through the agency of *iustitia inhaerens*.[33] The evident similarity between the views of Gropper and Contarini on justification goes some considerable way towards explaining the 'agreement' reached on justification at the Diet of Regensburg (often referred to in its Latinised form 'Ratisbon') in 1541.

Gropper's *Enchiridion* appears to have formed the basis of Article 5 of the *Liber Ratisboniensis* which formed the basis of the discussion between Protestants and Catholics at Regensburg.[34] Although agreement on the matter of justification was reached between those present at the Diet, it is clear that these individuals were simply not regarded as representative by their respective institutions: whatever personal agreement might be found to exist on the matter of justification between men such as Bucer, Contarini and Gropper, this was more than outweighed between the institutional differences between Lutheranism and Catholicism. Furthermore, the agreement appears to have been reached by a process of *zusammenleimen* – 'glueing together' (to use Luther's term), a 'scissors and paste job' (Fenlon) – which merely placed opposing views side by side, without reconciling, or even addressing, the underlying questions. It is clear that Article V *de iustificatione* represented a mere juxtaposition of the Catholic and Protestant positions, with a purely superficial engagement with the serious theological issues at stake.[35] The failure of Regensburg was of considerable political consequence, as it eventually led to the general discrediting of the Italian reforming movement known as 'Evangelism', to which we may now turn.

Evangelism was an undogmatic and transitory movement, originating within Italy itself (and the importance of Contarini's experience of 1511 should not be overlooked), rather than from Protestant currents north of the Alps.[36] The strongly Augustinian and individualist theologies of justification associated with the movement in its early phase paralleled those emerging elsewhere within Catholic Europe at the time. There can, however, be no doubt that the movement rapidly came under Protestant influence through the dissemination of printed works of the Reformers.[37] One of the most intriguing questions concerning this movement relates to the anonymous work *Trattato utilissimo del beneficio di Giesu Cristo crocifisso*, the second edition of which (1543) achieved a significant circulation throughout Europe.[38] Its first four chapters expound the doctrine of justification by faith with some vigour, and it is significant that the mediating position associated with Contarini and the Regensburg delegates appears to have been abandoned in favour of an account of the mode of justification which parallels that associated with Juan de Valdés.[39] The doctrine of justification *sola fide* is constantly interpreted thus: chiunque crede in Cristo è giustificato senza opere e senza merito alcuno.[40] It is through faith that Christ and his righteousness become the believer's, and on the basis of the union of the believer with Christ that God treats the former as righteous:

Così è necessario che noi ci vestiamo de la giustizia di Cristo per la fede, e ci occultiamo sotto la preziosa purità del nostro fratello primogenito, se vogliamo essere ricevuti per giusti nel conspetto di Dio . . . Dio ci vedrà ornati della giustizia di Cristo, senza dubbio ci accetterà per giusti e santi e degni della vita eterna.[41]

The strongly personalist understanding of justification associated with both Luther and Calvin is evident throughout the work. Through faith, the believer is united with Christ, clothed with his righteousness, and thence accepted as righteous and worthy of eternal life by God. Although there are unquestionably further recognisable allusions to the writings of northern European Reformers in the work, it is clear that the dominant influence is the form of Augustinian individualism associated with Valdés – evident, for example, in the complete omission of any reference to the implication of the church as an institution in the process of justification. Furthermore, the concept of *imputatio iustitiae* is not to be found in the work in its distinctively Protestant form. Most significant, however, is the outright rejection of the mediating theology of justification by faith *and* works associated with the members of the Viterbo circle, *quelli ... defendono la giustificazione della fede e delle opere.*[42] This point is important, as it indicates the development of a more radical faction within the Italian reforming movement in the period immediately before its suppression, critical of the mediating Regensburg theology. Although the work develops a doctrine of justification *sola fide*, it is clear that the formula is understood in a sufficiently flexible manner to accommodate those such as Reginald Pole, who retained the verbal formula, while interpreting the concept of faith in an Augustinian sense, as *fides quae per dilectionem operatur*. For Pole, the faith by which man alone was justified was a faith active through love:

Nec enim illos audiendos esse ullo modo censemus, qui sic solam fidem praedicant, ut piis caritatis actionibus detrahant: qui ignavis nihil agendi, impigris ad actiones male agendi occasionem, et licentiam suo perverso loquendi modo praebant: quos non tam perverse quidem, quam impie praedicare fidem existimamus; dum vel parum curare, vel prorsus contemnere leges, et maiorem instituta docent. Nec enim, quam praedicabant Apostoli, per quam iustificantur impii, fides eiusmodi fuit, sed quae caritatem operatur.[43]

This mediating approach appears to have exercised some restraint within the Viterbo circle, restraining its more radical members (such as Flaminio, Priuli and Vittoria) from action which could have proved prejudicial to the future conciliar pronouncement (which Pole appears to have assumed would broadly parallel his own mediating formula).[44]

The period of Italian Evangelism came to a close in 1542. Rather like the 'Prague Spring' of 1968, the period 1520–42 represented a brief interval in which ideas could be freely debated before an external authority intervened to prohibit such discussion. In 1542, Paul III, alarmed by religious unrest in Lucca, Modena and Venice, published the Bull *Licet ab initio*, re-establishing the Roman Inquisition. Whilst the influence of the northern European Reformers upon Evangelism in its later phase is undeniable, there are excellent reasons for suggesting that a form of doctrine of justification *sola fide* initially originated – independent of reforming movements in northern Europe – and subsequently achieved widespread circulation in the highest ecclesiastical circles in Italy. The failure of Regensburg to mediate between Catholicism and Protestantism forced the issue of definition of Catholic dogma upon the church, with the inevitable possibility that the temporary estrangement of the evangelical faction might become permanent schism. The convening of the Council of Trent was intended to provide the definition of Catholic doctrine so urgently required. Before dealing with this crucial period in the development of the doctrine of justification, it is necessary to consider the theologies of justification associated with the main schools of thought represented at the Council, and particularly the question of whether there existed an 'Augustinian' school, represented by Girolamo Seripando.

§26 The theological schools at Trent during the debate on justification

The Council of Trent was faced with a group of formidable problems as it assembled to debate the question of justification in June 1546. The medieval period had witnessed the emergence of a number of quite distinct schools of thought on justification (see §§14–18), clearly incompatible at points, all of which could lay claim to represent the teaching of the Catholic church. The Council of Trent was not concerned with settling long-standing debates between the various Catholic schools of theology, but with attempting a definition of the Catholic consensus on justification in the face of the Protestant challenge. The suggestion of the Bishop of Vaison, that the theologians present at Trent to debate the matter of justification should initially meet as separate Orders under their respective generals,[1] was rejected, presumably because this procedure would merely heighten the differences between the schools of thought present at Trent. In the present section, we are concerned with the identification of the main schools present at Trent, as this has an important bearing upon the relation of the final decree to late medieval Catholic theology in general.

In an important study earlier in the present century, Stakemeier argued for the existence of three theological schools at Trent during the proceedings on justification: the Thomist, Scotist and

Augustinian schools.[2] This division of the theological schools present at Trent has exercised considerable influence over subsequent discussion, and does not appear to have been subjected to critical examination. It is, in fact, quite difficult to establish the precise allegiance of many of the speakers during the proceedings on account of the similarities between the schools in relation to the points under discussion.

It is beyond question that a significant Thomist school was represented at Trent. The revival of the Thomist school had taken place in the fifteenth century under Capreolus,[3] who had established the fundamental principle that Thomas Aquinas' views should be determined on the basis of the *Summa Theologiae*, rather than the earlier *Commentary on the Sentences*. As noted in §7, Thomas' views on justification altered significantly in the intervening period, with the result that Capreolus' maxim led to a more Augustinian understanding of justification being defined as 'Thomist' than would have been regarded as legitimate earlier. It is this presupposition which underlies Cajetan's use of Thomas. In addition, Capreolus appears to have drawn upon the ferociously anti-Pelagian writings of Gregory of Rimini to emphasise the Augustinian elements of Thomas' doctrine of justification,[4] with the result that a theology of justification based jointly upon Augustine and Thomas Aquinas came to be widely current within Catholic circles.[5] The authority with which Thomas was invested may be judged from the fact that he was cited more than any theologian – other than Augustine – during the course of the Tridentine debate on justification, despite the fact that only seven of the fifty-five theologians involved in the debates were Dominicans.[6] The Salamantine school in Imperial Spain, which developed under Francisco de Vitoria, represented a similar approach to Thomas.[7] It is therefore significant that Charles V chose the Thomist Domingo de Soto, who held the chair of theology at Salamanca in the period 1532–45, as the Imperial theologian at Trent.[8] The most significant position associated with the Thomist faction present at Trent is the total and unequivocal rejection of a meritorious disposition towards justification.[9]

The Franciscan theologians were particularly prominent in the Tridentine proceedings on justification. The following analysis indicates the preponderance of the Franciscan contingent:[10]

Table 7.1 Analysis of theologians involved in the Tridentine proceedings

Order	Present at opening session	Present at sixth session
Franciscans	34	29
Dominicans	9	7
Jesuits	2	2
Carmelites	15	4
Servites	19	1
Augustinians	14	4
Secular priests	11	8

As noted earlier (§§15–17), the Franciscans were not unanimous in recognising a single authoritative doctor of their Order, and it is clear that several doctors were treated as authoritative during the course of the Tridentine proceedings, representing the early Franciscan school (such as Alexander of Hales and Bonaventure), the later Franciscan school (Duns Scotus), and even the *via moderna* (such as Gabriel Biel). The obvious reluctance on the part of certain Franciscans to concede the precedence of Scotus over Bonaventure[11] serves to emphasise the importance of this point. The most important Franciscan theologian present at Trent during the proceedings on justification was the Spanish Observant Andrés de Vega, whose *Opusculum de iustificatione* was conveniently published in time for it to be in the hands of those involved in the debate.[12]

In this work, Vega defends the notion of the necessity of a human disposition towards justification which is meritorious *de congruo*. The extreme opinions on this question, according to Vega, are the Pelagian concept of justification *ex meritis*, and the Thomist denial of all merit prior to justification.[13] Vega argues for the *via media*: the denial of merit *de condigno* and recognition of merit *de congruo* prior to grace – a doctrine which he associates with Duns Scotus and Gabriel Biel, among other recent theologians.[14] It is clear that Vega is drawing upon the common teaching of the Franciscan Order, and it is worth recalling that the whole medieval Franciscan tradition taught that the disposition for justification was meritorious *de congruo*.[15] Stakemeier appears to designate the common Franciscan teaching on this question 'Scotist' on the basis of certain presuppositions which more recent scholarship has called into question – for example, Hünermann's restriction of possible theological alternatives within

Catholicism to either Thomism or Scotism.[16] More seriously, he appears to be indirectly dependent upon Carl Stange's essays of 1900 and 1902, in which he argued that the theology of the medieval period was essentially a theology of Orders:[17] the monastic vow was taken as implying obedience to the official doctor of the Order which, according to Stange, implied recognition of the authority of Thomas Aquinas in the case of the Dominicans, and that of Duns Scotus in the case of Franciscans. As both Thomas and Scotus represented the *via antiqua*, Stakemeier was able to suggest that the influence of the *via moderna* at Trent was minimal.[18] However, although Stakemeier notes Hermelink's response to Stange of 1906, he seems to overlook its totally destructive significance, in that it was demonstrated that medieval theology was better designated a theology of *universities* rather than of *Orders*.[19] Thomas Aquinas may well have been regarded as authoritative at the Dominican house in Cologne, where the *via antiqua* was dominant in the local university, but at Erfurt, where the *via moderna* was in the ascendancy in the university faculty of arts, it was to Ockham that the Dominicans looked for guidance. Although Ockham is hardly referred to at Trent by Franciscan theologians – the Avignon condemnation (1326) of his theology as 'Pelagian or worse' doubtless hardly commending him as a reliable theological source[20] – they made frequent reference to two doctors of the Franciscan Order, Bonaventure and Scotus,[21] as well as occasional reference to two others (Alexander of Hales and Gabriel Biel). Since Bonaventure and Scotus represent very different understandings of the doctrine of justification (particularly in relation to the rôle of supernatural habits in justification) it is clear that the Franciscan contingent found itself in difficulty on occasion. In view of this broad theological base upon which the Franciscan contingent based their opinions, it is both unduly restrictive and quite inappropriate to designate this contingent as 'the *Scotist* school'.[22]

The third school which Stakemeier identified at Trent was the 'Augustinian school'. His views on this school, developed in a later study,[23] may be summarised as follows. The General of the Augustinian Order, Girolamo Seripando, defended a doctrine of *duplex iustitia* during the Tridentine proceedings on justification, which represented a theology of justification characteristic of the theologians of the Augustinian Order during the later medieval period. The 'Augustinian school' at Trent could therefore be regarded as adopting a position on justification, exemplified by Seripando, representing a theological tradition within the Augustinian Order since the time of Simon Fidati of Cassia and Hugolino of Orvieto. Stakemeier's thesis has exercised considerable influence upon accounts of the Tridentine debate on justification, and it is therefore necessary to call its foundations into question.

A careful study of Stakemeier's references to the Augustinian theologians whom he adduces as earlier representatives of this theological tradition indicates that he was only familiar with their writings at second hand, his immediate source being the highly controversial study of A. V. Müller on Luther's theological sources.[24] In this study, Müller had argued that Luther was the heir of precisely such a theological tradition within the Augustinian Order – a view which Stakemeier emphatically rejects in the case of Luther, only to attach to the Augustian contingent at Trent.[25] His evidence for this suggestion is quite unconvincing. Not only was this conclusion premature;[26] it has not stood up to subsequent critical examination.[27] The theologians of the Augustinian Order involved in the Tridentine debates on justification[28] appear to have followed the person, rather than the theology, of their General in their voting, making it impossible to suggest that there was a coherent 'school' of thought, characteristic of the Augustinian Order as a whole, represented during the Tridentine proceedings on justification. Thus in the debate of 8 October 1546 Seripando cites the Augustinian Giles of Viterbo as an earlier proponent of the doctrine of 'double justice',[29] also indicating that Jacobus Perez of Valencia is to be associated with the doctrine. However, it is significant that nowhere does he justify this assertion: the only theologian who he cites *verbatim* is Gropper, and Contarini is cited inaccurately.[30] Seripando appears merely to present a version of Gropper's theology, which is not of Augustinian provenance. It is not merely impossible to defend the view that the doctrine of *duplex iustitia* was of Augustinian provenance; it is impossible to provide convincing evidence for an 'Augustinian *school*' at Trent. We therefore see no reason for continuing the discredited practice of reporting the presence of an 'Augustinian school' during the Tridentine proceedings on justification. This is not to deny that the Augustinian contingent at Trent espoused certain specific theological attitudes: it is to call into question the implication that these attitudes were representative of the Augustinian Order as a whole, or that they corresponded to a tradition or school of thought peculiar to that Order.[31]

The Tridentine proceedings on justification suggest that the neo-Thomist school, the early Franciscan school and the later Franciscan school were all represented at Trent, along with a variety of other positions which defy rigid classification. While Trent appears to have taken some care to avoid censuring, or judging between, the traditional teachings associated with the major Orders (a policy particularly evident during the proceedings on original sin), these teachings appear to have exercised considerably less influence upon the proceedings on justification than might be expected. One possible explanation of this observation is that the whole matrix of traditional disputed questions concerning justification was recognised as occasionally having little bearing on the crucial new questions thrown up by the rise of the evangelical faction within Germany. The new questions thus raised demanded new answers, with the result that the appeal to the traditional positions of the theological schools associated with the Orders had to give way to speculation concerning the most appropriate responses to these questions. A further consideration, however, is the rise of an increasingly independent intellectual environment, particularly in Italy, which enabled theologians to break free from the thought patterns of the medieval theological schools.[32]

In the following section, we shall consider the Tridentine debates on certain crucial aspects of the doctrine of justification, with a view to casting further light upon the proper interpretation of the final *decretum de iustificatione* itself.

§27 The Tridentine proceedings on justification

The Council of Trent was the final outcome of a prolonged attempt by the papacy to convene a reforming council. The continuation of the war in Europe between the Emperor and the King of France had led to the postponement of the projected council at Mantua (1537) and the abortive convocation at Trent (1542–3). Only when the Habsburg–Valois conflict was settled by the Peace of Crépy in 1544 was there any real possibility of convening an ecumenical council. Two months after the conclusion of peace, when it became clear that there was a real possibility of a permanent cessation of hostilities, Paul III issued the Bull *Laetare Ierusalem*, announcing his intention to convene a general council for the removal of religious discord, the reform of the church, and the liberation of the faithful from the Turk.[1] Although it had been hoped that the council might open in March, the unsettled relations between the Emperor and the Pope delayed this until 13 December 1545.[2] These difficulties arose partly from the Emperor's wish that the council should discuss the reform of the church, whereas the Pope desired doctrinal clarification. A judicious compromise led to both these questions being considered in parallel.

The initial doctrinal debates concerned the relation of scripture and tradition, and original sin.[3] It was, however, recognised that the doctrine of justification was of peculiar importance. A number of crucial questions required clarification in the light of the Protestant challenge.[4] First, is justification merely *remissio peccatorum*, or does it necessarily include intrinsic sanctification through the action of grace within man? Second, what is the precise relation between faith and good works? This question required a careful response in opposition to the Protestant doctrine of justification *sola fide*. Third, what is the precise nature of the active rôle of the human will in justification, given the general Protestant tendency to assert the passivity of the will? Fourth, what is the relationship between justification and the *sacramenta mortuorum* of baptism and penance? Fifth, can the believer know with any degree of certitude whether he is, in fact, justified? Finally, is it necessary for man to dispose himself towards justification, and if so, is this disposition to be considered meritorious in any sense?

The Council initially set itself the task of dealing with six questions. On 22 June 1546, a commission of theologians laid down the following questions for discussion:[5]

1. What is justification *quoad nomen et quoad rem*; and what is to be understood when it is said that 'man is justified' (*iustificari hominem*)?
2. What are the causes of justification? What part is played by God? And what is required of man?
3. What is to be understood when it is said that 'man is justified by faith' (*iustificari hominem per fidem*)?
4. What rôle do human works and the sacraments play in justification, whether before, during or after it?
5. What precedes, accompanies and follows justification?
6. By what proofs is the Catholic doctrine supported?

Although this approach would eventually prove to be inadequate, in that it omitted important questions such as the certitude of grace, it served as a useful point of departure for the initial discussion leading up to the first draft of the decree on justification.

In the six congregations held in the period 22–28 June 1546, some thirty-four theologians addressed themselves to the questions set for discussion. Although it is far from clear upon what basis the speakers were called, it is clear that their initial concern appears to have been with the question of the *nature* of justification. Most of the speakers addressed themselves to this point, with a variety of concepts of justification being employed. The Conventual Sigismondo Fedrio da Diruta defined the term *iustificatio* as *motus quidam spiritualis de impietate ad pietatem*, and *iustificari* as *ex nocente fieri innocens*.[6] Richard of Le Mans defined *iustificatio* as *adhaesio Dei*, and *iustificari* as *redire in gratiam Dei*.[7] Gregory of Padua defined *iustificatio* in Augustinian terms, as *de impio pium facere vel iniusto iustum*, and *iustificari* as *fieri Deo gratus*.[8] Despite this remarkable variety of definitions,[9] it is clear that there existed a consensus concerning the factitive and transformational character of justification.[10] Two possible exceptions to this consensus may be noted, in the cases of the Dominican Marcus Laureus and the Franciscan Observant Andrés de Vega.

Marcus Laureus defined justification as *remissio peccatorum per gratiam*,[11] omitting any reference to the concomitant transformation of the believer. This might be taken as indicating that Laureus approached the Protestant position at this point. In fact, this conclusion cannot be drawn without further corroborating evidence, which we do not possess. As we indicated in an earlier discussion (§5), Thomas Aquinas had demonstrated, on Aristotelian grounds, that a process could be defined in terms of its *terminus*, with the result that the *processus iustificationis* could be defined simply as *remissio peccatorum*, the final element in this process. Thomas' occasional statements to the effect that *iustificatio* may be defined as *remissio peccatorum* have occasionally been misinterpreted as implying that he did not include *infusio iustitiae* as an element of justification, which is evidently incorrect. Laureus must therefore, in the absence of any evidence to the contrary, be regarded as restating the position of the chief doctor of his Order in the congregation of 23 June 1546.

Andrés de Vega defined justification in a noticably extrinsicist manner, in terms of three elements: hominem iustificari est absolutum esse a peccatis et gratiam Dei habere. Et acceptum ad vitam aeternam.[12] It is evident that Vega's conception of justification parallels that of the later Franciscan school (see §§5, 16), and is reflected in the statements of other Franciscan theologians in these congregations.[13] The weakening of the ontological link between *remissio peccatorum* and *infusio gratiae*, characteristic of both this school and the *via moderna*, places them closest to the extrinsicism of the Reformers at this point. Nevertheless, it is important to appreciate the heterogeneity of the Franciscan contingent at Trent over this point: other Franciscans defined justification in strongly intrinsicist and transformational terms, such as *regeneratio hominis interioris*,[14] or *mutatio quaedam spiritualis in peccatorem a Deo facta per infusionem iustitiae habitualis*,[15] paralleling those of the earlier Franciscan school (see §§5, 15). Although this understanding of justification does not exclude the infusion of grace and the transformation of man, the priority of the extrinsic denomination of the divine acceptation over such intrinsic qualities was rigorously upheld. This observation is of importance in relation to the question of whether there existed a *Scotist* school at Trent: as we suggested earlier (§26), the evidence strongly suggests that the theological tension already present within the Franciscan Order (particularly between the early and later Franciscan schools) is evident during the Tridentine debates on justification.

The general agreement over the nature of justification was summarised by Marcus Laureus as follows:

Omnes igitur theologi in re conveniunt, quamvis in verbis discrepent. Et in sententia dicunt, quod quoad nomen iustificatio idem est quod *iustifactio*, iustificari idem quod *iustum fieri coram Deo*. Quoad rem autem iustifactio est remissio peccatorum a Deo per gratiam. Iustificari idem est quod remitti peccata a Deo per gratiam.[16]

The discussion of the question of the nature of justification was greatly facilitated by the distinction of three stages (*status*) of justification, which permitted three different senses of the term *iustificatio* to be distinguished, thus avoiding some of the confusion evident in the initial discussions. The first *status* concerns the justification of adults, in which the unbeliever is transformed from his state of unbelief and sin to one of faith and grace; the second concerns the increase in righteousness of the justified believer, and his perseverance in the Christian life; the third concerns the justification of lapsed believers.[17]

This general consensus on the nature of justification is reflected in the first draft of the decree on justification, dating from 24 July 1546. Although it was once thought that this draft version was the work of Andrés de Vega, this is now generally regarded as doubtful.[18] The first draft consists of a brief introduction, three chapters, and a series of eighteen canons.[19] No formal definition of justification is given, although it is possible to deduce such a definition from the material appended to the first two canons. The first three canons make the distinction between the Catholic and Protestant understanding of the nature of justification clear in the following manner.

First, the opinion that a sinner may be justified solely as a matter of reputation or imputation, while remaining a sinner in fact, is rejected.

Si quis ergo dixit, impium, qui a Deo per Christum Iesum iustificatur, iniustum quidem esse et manere, sed tantum iustum reputari, non est iustum fieri, ut ipsa iustificatio sit sola imputatio iustitiae: anathema sit.[20]

Justification is thus defined in terms of a man becoming, and not merely being reputed as, righteous (*sic vere non modo reputatur, sed efficitur iustus*). Although this clearly excludes the concept of a 'legal fiction' in justification, it is not clear that it affects mainstream Protestant teaching on the question, in view of the purely notional distinction envisaged between justification and regeneration. It is, however, clear that there was a consensus that the Protestants did, in fact, restrict the meaning of the term *iustificatio* to *iustum reputatio*. This is particularly clear from the comments of the Spanish Jesuit Alfonso Salmeron, who contrasted the Catholic definition of *iustificari* as *recipere donum iustitiae seu habitum, quo ex iniusto evadimus iusti*, with Melanchthon's definition of the same term as *iustum reputari*.[21] Salmeron clearly fails to understand the significance of Melanchthon's distinction between *iustificatio* and *regeneratio*. The fact that Melanchthon understood by 'justification' *and* 'regeneration' what Catholics understood by 'justification' alone does not appear to have been appreciated. As the Catholics understood *iustificatio* to refer to Christian existence in its totality, the Protestant exclusion of *regeneratio* from *iustificatio* appeared to amount to the exclusion of any transformational dimension from Christian existence altogether. A similar difficulty is encountered with the Protestant concept of justification *per solam fidem*, which the Catholics understood to exclude works from Christian existence (whereas the Protestants, working with a quite distinct concept of justification, understood it merely to refer to the exclusion of works from the *initiation* of the Christian life). We shall return to this point below: it is, however, essential to appreciate that the full significance of the new understanding of the nature of justification associated with Melanchthon was not fully grasped by his Catholic opponents, with important consequences for the interpretation of the relevance of the Tridentine pronouncements for Protestant theologies of justification.

Second, the opinion that justification consists solely in the remission of sins, and not in the *donatio iustitiae*, is condemned.[22] Third, the opinion that the righteousness bestowed upon the believer in his justification is the righteousness of Christ won on the cross is condemned.[23] This point is of particular interest, and appears to be directed against the Lutheran doctrine of *imputatio iustitiae alienae Christi*. The righteousness, on the basis of which man is justified, is defined as *habitus divinae gratiae*, which is bestowed *by God through Christ* – in other words, God effects what Christ merited:

Promeruit quidem solus Christus Iesus sua illa magna iustitia, ut homo per eum iustus efficiatur, sed iustitia, quae in illo ipso sit, non in Christo; actus iustitiae illius Christi in eo est, non in nobis. Iustitia, qua iusti sumus, habitus est divinae gratiae, quae in nobis est, quamquam non per nos, sed per eum at a Deo; a Deo ut qui efficit, per eum ut qui meruit. Quomodo et non aliter intelligendum est apud sanctos, iustitiam Dei et Christi fieri nostram iustitiam.[24]

This statement clarifies the relationship between *iustitia Christi* and *iustitia Dei*, indicating that the former is to be understood as the meritorious cause of justification, and the latter the formal cause.

The general consensus concerning the necessity of works subsequent to the first justification evident in the earlier discussions led to the condemnation of solafideism. With the recognition, however, that the phrase *iustificari hominem per fidem* had a legitimate place in the Catholic exposition of the first justification, the condemnation of solafideism was phrased in a slightly unusual manner which made the Catholic objection to the perceived meaning of the concept unambiguous:

Si quis dixerit, quod sola fides omino, sine aliis operibus, iustificat impium, hoc est impetrat illius iustificationem, in quo sensu ab haereticis hac aetate profertur, quasi nihil aliud ad hoc ex parte hominis requiratur quam credere: anathema sit.[25]

It may also be noted that there was a general consensus that Protestants employed the terms *fides* and *credere* in a highly unorthodox sense. Alfonso Salmeron pointed out the manner in which Melanchthon interpreted the term *fides* as *fiducia divinae misericordiae*,[26] thus excluding the Catholic notion of *fides quae per dilectionem operatur*.[27] It is clear that the initial Catholic hostility to the doctrine of justification *per solam fidem* at Trent is thus based upon a quite specific understanding of both the concepts of *fides* and *iustificatio*.

Although the July debate on this draft proved inconclusive,[28] the debate of 17 August made clear the general dissatisfaction concerning it.[29] A document which was to form the basis of a revised draft was presented to the legates by Seripando on 11 August 1546.[30] This document remedied a major deficiency of the first draft – its omission of a formal definition of the term *iustificatio hominis*. Declarat praeterea, hanc de qua loquimur hominis iustificationem nihil aliud esse quam eius translationem per novam quandam et spiritualem nativitatem, ab eo statu, in quo secundum carnem natus est, filius primi Adae, sub ira et inimicitia Dei, in statum adoptionis filiorum Dei per secundum Adam Iesum Christum servatorem nostrum.[31] Of particular interest, in view of subsequent developments, is the draft's unequivocal rejection of the doctrine that the only basis upon which justification may take place is *imputatio iustitiae Christi*.[32] A significantly different approach to this question, however, is found in the draft submitted by Seripando to the legates on 29 August 1546.[33]

The new version of the decree took a radically different form from its predecessors. In its customary form, such a decree consisted of a long series of canons, with a short introduction or introductory chapters. The new draft consisted of fifteen chapters, and a mere eight canons. The significance of the document, however, lies less in its form than in the views on the formal cause of justification expressed in its eighth chapter, entitled *de duplici iustitia*,[34] as well as comparable views implied by the title of the fourth canon.[35] The fourth canon repeats the substance of the second canon of the draft of 11 August, in that it censures the opinion that we are justified *solius Christi iustitiae imputatione cum exclusione omnis iustitiae in cordibus nostris diffusae*.[36] Although the obvious interpretation of this statement is that man is justified on the basis of *donatio seu infusio iustitiae*, it is clear, from the title of this canon, that Seripando intended this merely as the rejection of the opinion that man is justified *solely* on the basis of *imputatio Christi iustitiae*. It is instructive to compare the wording of the condemned opinions in the July drafts with Seripando's versions:[37]

official July draft: ipsa iustificatio sit *sola* imputatio iustitiae
Seripando (11 August): *solius* iustitiae Christi imputatione
Seripando (29 August): *solius* Christi iustitiae imputatione

The substitution of *solius* for *sola* enables Seripando to open the way to a doctrine of justification on the basis of *iustitia duplex* – both *iustitia imputata* and *iustitia inhaerens*. Although the phrase *duplex iustitia* does not occur in the text of Seripando's draft of 29 August, the implications of those drafts were evident.[38]

The September draft of the decree omits any reference to *duplex iustitia*, and develops the teaching of Canon 3 of the July draft in such a manner as to exclude the opinion that the Christian possesses one *iustitia* deriving from God, and another deriving from Christ. Ita non sunt duae iustitiae, quae nobis dantur, Dei et Christi, sed una iustitia Dei per Iesum Christum, hoc est caritas ipsa vel gratia, qua iustificati non modo reputamur, sed vere iusti nominamur et sumus.[39] The careful phrasing of the new chapter appears to exclude the concept of *duplex iustitia* altogether. However, Canon 7 of the September draft follows the wording of Seripando's original version closely, and is clearly intended to permit the doctrine of *duplex iustitia*:

Si quis dixerit, impium iustificari *solius iustitiae Christi imputatione* aut sola peccatorum remissione, cum exclusione omnis iustitiae seu gratiae in cordibus nostris per Spiritum Sanctum diffusae et nobis inhaerentis . . . anathema sit.[40]

The excluded opinion is that the imputed righteousness of Christ *alone* is the basis of man's justification, if this is understood to exclude an inherent righteousness through the action of the Holy Spirit. The opinion that man is justified on the basis of *duplex iustitia* – that is, *iustitia imputata* and *iustitia inhaerens* – is not condemned. It is evident, from the records of the proceedings in the period 27 September–8 October 1546, that many of the delegates found themselves unable to make sense of the phrasing of the seventh chapter.[41] The case for replacing the ambiguous 'non sunt duae iustitiae' with the more explicit 'una est iustitia' was pressed with some force,[42] forcing Seripando and his supporters to make their views on the matter explicit.

In addition to Seripando, the defenders of the doctrine of *duplex iustitia* were the Augustinians Aurelius of Rocca Contrata, Marianus Feltrinus and Stephen of Sestino, the Servite Lorenzo Mazocchi, and the Spanish secular priest Antonio Solis. It is possible that another Spanish secular priest, Pedro Sarra, should be considered a supporter of the doctrine. In his defence of the doctrine, Aurelius merely recapitulates previous statements of his general, Seripando, without developing his arguments in any manner.[43] Stephen of Sestino emphasised the imperfection and inadequacy of human works in a manner which parallels Gropper's argument in the *Enchiridion* to such an extent that dependence upon this source is a probability.[44] The vote of the third Augustinian, Feltrinus, exists only in the outline of Massarelli,[45] and appears to parallel the views of Sestino. It is thus significant, in view of the hypothesis that an authentically Augustinian theology of justification is implicit in these statements, to note the clear priority of the arguments of Gropper over Augustinian theologians such as Jacobus Perez of Valencia.

The remaining supporters of the doctrine appear to have based their views upon considerations so disparate that generalisations are impossible. The vote of Solis survives only in a form which is too brief to permit analysis;[46] that of Sarra, although longer, defies interpretation.[47] Mazocchi's vote is something of an enigma:[48] although Mazocchi appears to have given his fellow-delegates the impression that he supported Seripando, the substance of the vote itself actually renders no support to the doctrine of *duplex iustitia*.[49]

The majority opinion was, however, unequivocal. Although demonstrating a near-total ignorance of the historical origins of the doctrine of *duplex iustitia*,[50] there was a general conviction that the concept of *iustitia imputata* was a theological novelty, unknown to Catholic theology throughout its existence.[51] Furthermore, it was generally agreed that the concept of imputed righteousness was an irrelevance, on account of the renovation of man in justification: non quod tunc nova fiat imputatio, ut quidam falso imaginantur, quia, ut patet sufficienter ex praemissis, ista imputatio nulla ratione requiritur.[52] Although Seripando actually employed the term *imputare* rarely (and never in his votes),[53] it seems that the demand for an explicit condemnation of justification on the basis of *iustitia imputata*[54] was essentially an indirect attack upon his position. There also appears to have been a general consensus that Seripando's appeal to *iustitia Christi* undermined the foundation of human merit.

On 31 October 1546, the September draft of the decree was rewritten in the light of the preceding debate, in which the overwhelming hostility to the concept of *duplex iustitia* (or *duae iustitiae*) had been made clear. The demand for an explicit condemnation of justification on the basis of *iustitia imputata* was met by an unequivocal assertion that man was justified on the basis of an internal righteousness:

Impii autem iustificationis, quae simul in ablutione peccatorum, simul in sanctificatione et in infusione donorum consistit, causae sunt ... formalis iustitia una Dei, qua renovamur spiritu mentis nostrae et non modo reputamur, sed vere iusti nominamur et sumus.[55]

The concept of *iustitia duplex*, incorporated at some length into the September draft, now appeared to be excluded: the formal cause of justification was explicitly identified as *iustitia una Dei*. However, the sense of the statement is clearly as follows: *the formal cause of justification is the one righteousness of God*. In other words, the document is primarily concerned with the emphasis upon the unity of the *iustitia* underlying man's justification. Seripando's position could still be accommodated without difficulty if it were conceded that there was more than one formal cause of justification. It is this ambiguous understanding of the formal cause of justification which became incorporated into the draft of the decree presented on 5 November 1546.[56] However, there were still those who felt that the doctrine of *duplex iustitia*, as defended by Seripando, was not rigorously excluded. In the congregation of 23 November, Claude Le Jay proposed that the phrase 'causa formalis iustitia una Dei' should be replaced with 'causa formalis una iustitia Dei'.[57] This alteration had the effect of defining that the one formal cause of justification was the righteousness of God, in the sense described – in other words, the possibility of a double formal cause of justification (*iustitia imputata* and *iustitia inhaerens*) was excluded. The possibility that this might be interpreted as implying that one formal cause *among others* was *iustitia Dei* required that *una* be altered to *unica* – an alteration which appears to have been agreed upon subsequently. The revised version of the eighth chapter of the decree was drawn up for discussion on 11 December 1546, incorporating this amended version of Le Jay's statement concerning the formal cause of justification: Demum unica formalis causa est iustitia illa Dei, non qua ipse iustus est, sed qua nos coram ipso iustos facit, qua videlicet ab eo donati renovamur spiritu mentis nostrae et non modo reputamur, sed vere iusti nomina-mur et sumus.[58] This unequivocal statement to the effect that the *single* formal cause of justification was the righteousness of God, in the sense defined, was approved in general congregation the same day,[59] and eventually incorporated into the final version of the decree on justification.[60] It is only at this point that the rejection of Seripando's concept of *duplex iustitia* may be considered to be complete and unequivocal.

The centrality of the concept of assurance of salvation for the Reformers, and particularly for Luther,[61] and the medieval consensus (§8) concerning the impossibility of such assurance, made it impossible for the Council to ignore the matter, despite its absence from the initial agenda. Initially, little interest was shown in the question: the records of the congregations of 22–28 June 1546 demonstrate that only two speakers deemed the matter worthy of consideration. The very different approaches adopted by Andrés de Vega[62] and Antonius Frexius[63] were indicative of the divisions which would subsequently be exposed on this question, and it is significant that these contributions are not included in the *summarium* of Marcus Laureus.[64] Although the Lutheran doctrine of assurance is included among the list of proscribed errors concerning the second *status iustificationis* tabled for discussion on 30 June,[65] little attention was paid to it.[66]

The emergence of the question of assurance as a serious issue dates from the July draft of the decree, which included as its fifteenth canon an explicit condemnation of the Lutheran doctrine of assurance as an assertion contrary to proper Christian humility.[67] It was clear, however, that this canon provoked considerable disquiet. The *notationes theologorum* revealed serious disagreement on the matter among the theologians, as well as a general desire to discuss the matter further.[68] As a result, Costacciaro invited the Conventual Antonio Delfini to prepare an expert opinion *de quaestione illa vehementer dubia, numquid Christianus certitudinem habeat, quod in gratia Dei sit, et quid hac in re opinatus fuerit subtilissimus Ioannes Scotus.*[69] In this document, Delfini interprets Scotus with the aid of Gabriel Biel,[70] indicating that Scotus cannot be regarded as an exponent of the Lutheran doctrine of assurance. Costacciaro himself clearly considered that Scotus upheld the possibility of the certitude of grace on account of the *ex opere operato* character of the sacrament of penance.[71] Zannetino, however, disagreed, and cited John Fisher as an accurate and reliable interpreter of Scotus on this point.[72] By 17 August, it was clear that there was a serious division of opinion on the matter within the council, with the Dominicans implacably opposed to any suggestion that *certitudo gratiae* was possible, and others strongly affirming such a possibility.[73] In view of this difficulty, a general congregation of 28 August 1546 determined to proceed directly merely to the condemnation of the Lutheran position, while leaving unresolved the question of the Catholic position on the matter.[74] This principle was observed in the drawing up of the September draft of the decree.

The September draft refers to the question of the certitude of grace at two points. The seventh chapter rejects the following opinion, which it attributes to 'heretics and schismatics': non omni tamen eam fiduciam et certitudinem acceptae remissionis peccatorum suorum iactanti et in ea sola quiescenti peccata dimitti dicendum est.[75] No clarification on the Catholic teaching is provided. Similarly, Canon 8 explicitly rejects any suggestion that the believer may know with certainty that he is among the predestined, or that he will persevere to the end, apart from special divine revelation.[76] The compromise of 28 August was soon recognised as unsatisfactory, and the debate on the question was resumed on 12 October 1546.[77] On 15 October, the following article was proposed for discussion: Utrum aliquis possit esse certus de sua adepta gratia secundum praesentem iustitiam, et quo genere certitudinis.[78] The discussion of this article over the period 15–26 October 1546 further emphasised the divisions within the council at this point: of the thirty-seven theologians who expressed their opinions, twenty were in favour of the possibility of certitude of grace, fifteen against, and two undecided.[79] Without exception, the Dominican theologians were opposed to the possibility of *certitudo fidei, se esse in gratia* – despite the recent arrival at the Council of the Dominican bishop Ambrogio Catharino, an outspoken supporter of the possibility.[80] The Franciscan contingent, by contrast, was deeply divided, the seven Conventuals supporting the possibility, and the Observants more or less equally divided.

The third draft of the decree was submitted for consideration on 5 November 1546, with a revised statement on the question incorporated into the decree in the form of its ninth chapter.[81] Its substance parallels that of the equivalent statement in the second draft, with an intensification of its opening reference:[82]

September draft: *non omni* tamen eam fiduciam et certitudinem
November draft: *nemini* tamen eam fiduciam et certitudinem

Although this went some way towards meeting the demands of some delegates, that the condemnation of *certitudo fidei, se esse in gratia* be strengthened and made more explicit, the new chapter failed to win their approval through its final statement, which is without parallel in the September draft: Nescit enim homo *communiter*, num divino amore dignus sit.[83] The controversy surrounded the interpretation of the enigmatic term *communiter*, which was also included in the fourteenth canon.[84] Several delegates wished the ambiguity surrounding the term to be removed by the substitution of *communi lege*;[85] others simply wished the term to be dropped altogether,[86] with a clarification of the chapter in question. By 17 December, the issue, although forcefully contested on both sides, was still unresolved. In view of the serious delays this difficulty was occasioning, del Monte proposed that the council should merely condemn the Lutheran position, and leave further discussion of the Catholic position until a future date.[87] Despite opposition from some who did not wish to see the results of months of discussion come to nothing,[88] the procedure was approved.

On 9 January 1547, four days before the final decree was published, a *convocatio praelatorum theologorum* of restricted membership met to attempt to establish a last-minute consensus on the ninth chapter *super certitudine gratiae*.[89] After three hours' debate, a compromise formula was finally agreed: nemo possit esse certus certitudine fidei, cui non potest subesse falsum, se esse in gratia Dei.[90] The formula was immediately incorporated into the fifth draft of the decree, submitted for consideration on the same day,[91] and finally approved.

With the resolution of the questions of the cause of justification and the certitude of grace, the Council of Trent was able to proceed with its extensive pronouncements concerning the Catholic teaching on justification, contained in the chapters of the final decree, as well as its specific condemnation in the canons of the errors of Protestantism. Although, strictly speaking, the decree could not be considered binding upon Catholics until the papal ratification of the Council after its closure in 1563, the decisions were widely regarded as immediately valid – despite Reginald Pole's refusal to seal the document.[92] By 1547, therefore, the teaching of the Catholic church on justification may be regarded as fixed, in the sense that the approved formulae (which permitted a certain degree of latitude of interpretation at crucial points) had been established. In the following section, we shall outline the main features of the decree, before considering the interpretation of the decree in the immediate post-Tridentine period.

§28 The Tridentine decree on justification

The Tridentine decree on justification marks a significant development in conciliar history. Up to that point, conciliar decisions had tended to be framed largely in terms of explicit condemnation, in the form of canons, of specific opinions, without substantial exposition of the Catholic teaching on the matter in question. Perhaps on account of the peculiar importance with which the doctrine of justification was recognised to be invested, the *decretum de iustificatione* devotes sixteen initial chapters to a point-by-point exposition of the Catholic teaching before proceeding to condemn thirty-three specific opinions.[1] As will become clear from the following section, there was considerable disagreement in the immediate post-Tridentine period concerning the precise interpretation of the *decretum de iustificatione*. In the present section, we propose to indicate the broad range of opinions on justification which the Council of Trent recognised as authentically Catholic. In establishing these, the following principles have been employed.

1. In that the Council was primarily concerned with distinguishing Catholic teaching from that of the Reformers, and not to settle disputed matters within the Catholic schools of theology, it follows that the previously professed theological positions of these schools may continue to be held, unless they are explicitly excluded.

2. The final decree is to be interpreted in the light of the debates which led to its formulation, in order to establish what the Tridentine fathers intended particular terms and phrases to mean.[2] Although the attempt to interpret any historical document *e mente auctorum* is notoriously difficult, we possess sufficient documentary evidence to clarify the intended meaning of at least certain otherwise obscure statements.

With these points in mind, we may turn to the analysis of the decree and its canons.

The final arrangement of the decree reflects the three *status iustificationis* which emerged during the proceedings on justification. The first nine chapters discuss the 'first justification', in which man's initial transition from a state of sin to righteousness is described.[3] This is followed by four chapters dealing with the 'second justification' – how man, once justified, may increase in righteousness.[4] The final three chapters deal with the *status tertius*, indicating how a man may forfeit his justification, and subsequently regain it through penance, and clarifying the manner in which this differs from the *status primus*.[5]

The decree opens with an analysis of man's fallen condition, inevitably incorporating certain matters touched upon in the fifth session *de peccato originali*. On account of original sin, which is a condition affecting the entire human race, man is incapable of redeeming himself. Free will is not destroyed, but is weakened and debilitated by the Fall: in eis liberum arbitrium minime exstinctum esset, viribus licet attenuatum et inclinatum.[6] The Council thus reaffirmed the position of Augustine and Orange II on this crucial point, and implicitly rejected Luther's statement: liberum arbitrium post peccatum est res de solo titulo.[7] The particularism implicit in Luther's teaching on election is excluded by the unequivocal assertion that Christ died for all men, granting grace through the merits of his passion in order that man might be born again, and hence justified. (In anticipation of the censure of a purely extrinsic conception of justification in the canons, it is affirmed that no man can be justified unless he has first been born again.)[8] Justification is defined in transformational terms, including reference to necessary alterations in man's status and nature:

Quibus verbis iustificationis impii descriptio insinuatur, ut sit translatio ab eo statu, in quo homo nascitur filius primi Adae, in statum gratiae et adoptionis filiorum Dei, per secundum Adam Iesum Christum Salvatorem nostrum; quae quidem translatio post Evangelium promulgatum sine lavacro regenerationis aut eius voto fieri non potest.[9]

The fifth and sixth chapters deal with the necessity and the mode of preparation towards justification. Man is called through prevenient grace, without reference to his merits, to dispose himself towards justification. As a consequence of man's assenting to and cooperating with this call, God touches man's heart through the illumination of his Holy Spirit.[10] The traditional medieval terminology usually employed in the discussion of the necessity for a disposition towards justification (see §7) is studiously avoided, exemplifying the general tendency to avoid scholastic language wherever possible. Indeed, the *decretum de iustificatione* is notable for its marked preference to appeal directly to scripture, passing over the vocabulary of the medieval period altogether. The preparation for justification is subsequently defined in terms of man's believing the truth of divine revelation and the divine promises (particularly the promise that God will justify the ungodly through his grace), and thence being moved to detest his sins and repent of them. This culminates in the sacrament of baptism, in which the individual declares his intention to lead a new life and observe the divine commandments.[11] Once more, the nature of the disposition towards justification is discussed in terms drawn directly from scripture, rather than from the medieval theological schools.

The seventh chapter presents a careful analysis of the causes of justification.[12] It reaffirms the transformational character of justification (non est sola peccatorum remissio, sed et sanctificatio et renovatio interioris hominis), and the causes of justification are enumerated as follows:

final cause:	the glory of God and eternal life
efficient cause:	the mercy of God
meritorious cause:	the passion of Christ
instrumental cause:	the sacrament of baptism
formal cause:	the righteousness of God.

Although this might appear to be a reversion to scholasticism, the decree is merely clarifying the various contributing factors to man's justification in the most convenient manner possible. The most significant statement concerns the formal cause of justification. The assertion that the *single* formal cause of justification (*unica formalis causa*) is 'iustitia Dei, non qua ipse iustus est, sed qua nos iustos facit'[13] represents a deliberate and conscious attempt to exclude the possibility that there exists more than one formal cause – the opinion particularly associated with Seripando during the proceedings on justification (§27). In effect, the possibility that *iustitia imputata* is a contributing cause to man's justification is intended to be excluded by this statement, despite the absence of any explicit reference to the concept. Perhaps more significantly, the entire medieval debate over whether the formal cause of justification was an intrinsic created habit of grace or the extrinsic denomination of the divine acceptation (see §§13–18) was circumvented by a reversion to the Augustinian concept of *iustitia Dei*. This does not resolve the medieval debate on this matter one way or the other, and represents an attempt to establish the common basis of both medieval understandings of the matter without using the terminology of the period. The linking of the 'first justification' with the sacrament of baptism continues the common medieval tradition of excluding the possibility of extra-sacramental justification, and parallels the subsequent linking of the recovery of justification with the sacrament of penance.

The eighth chapter deals with the concepts of 'to be justified by faith' (*iustificari per fidem*) and 'to be justified freely' (*gratis iustificari*).[14] Both these terms are to be interpreted according to the Catholic tradition: faith is to be seen as the beginning of human salvation, the foundation and root of all justification, without which it is impossible to please God. This gift is given *gratis* in the sense that none of the things which precede justification (including faith, as well as works) can be said to merit justification: gratis autem iustificari ideo dicamur, quia nihil eorum, quae iustificationem praecedunt, sive fides, sive opera, ipsam iustificationis gratiam promeretur. Although this statement clearly excludes the possibility that man may merit justification *de condigno*, it does not – and was not intended to – exclude the possibility that he may merit it *de congruo*. (As the proceedings on justification make clear, this conclusion pertains irrespective of the verb employed, whether *promereri* or *mereri*.)[15] In other words, although the traditional teaching of the Franciscan Order (that man's disposition towards justification is meritorious *de congruo*) is not explicitly permitted, there was a clear intention that it should not be excluded.

The ninth chapter deals with the question of the certitude of faith.[16] This question having been the subject of intense debate at Trent, the chapter is worded with some care. *Fiducia* on the part of the believer concerning the mercy of God, the merit of Christ and the efficacy of the sacraments is certainly appropriate; what is inappropriate is *inana haereticorum fiducia* concerning the individual's justification.

Nemini tamen fiduciam et certitudinem remissionis peccatorum suorum iactanti et in ea sola quiescenti peccata dimitti vel dismissa esse dicendum est ... immo nostra tempestate sit et magna contra Ecclesiam catholicam contentione praedicetur vana haec et ab omni pietate remota fiducia.

The tenth chapter opens the section of the *decretum* dealing with the second justification, in which man increases in righteousness. This second justification is seen as a positive duty placed upon man by virtue of the first justification. There are clear connections between the Tridentine concept of the second justification and the Reformed concept of sanctification. Whereas in the first justification, grace operates upon man, in the second, man cooperates with grace. It is thus both possible and necessary to keep the law of God.[17] The opinion that such good works as are involved in the second justification are sinful is rejected.[18] The Augustinian doctrine of final perseverance is reaffirmed: in this mortal life, no one may know whether he is among the number of the predestined, except through special revelation.[19] Although the sacrament of baptism is linked with the first justification, and that of penance with the restoration of justification, it is significant that there is no specific mention of any of the remaining sacraments in connection with the second justification.

The final three chapters deal with those who have fallen from the grace of justification through mortal sin. Those who are moved by grace may regain the grace of justification through the sacrament of penance, on account of the merit of Christ.[20] It is important to appreciate that it is only grace, and not faith, which is lost by mortal sin: the lapsed individual remains a believer. The final chapter deals with the question of merit, and goes some considerable way towards meeting Protestant criticism of the concept.[21] While insisting upon the biblical principle that good works are rewarded by God, Trent emphasises that merit is a divine gift to man, excluding human boasting. Merit remains, however, the result of man's free efforts.

Although the grace of Christ precedes and accompanies man's efforts, those efforts are real nonetheless. The believer, by his cooperation with grace, is entitled to merit and increase in justification. The man who perseveres until the end may be said to receive eternal life as a reward, the crowning gift promised by God to those who persevere. The question of the ultimate foundation of merit (*ratio meriti*), a subject of some controversy in the medieval schools (see §10), is answered in non-scholastic terms (such as the union of the believer with Christ) which permit the traditional views to be retained.

The thirty-three canons appended to the decree condemn specific heretical opinions, by no means restricted to Protestantism.[22] However, it appears that it is certain caricatures of Protestantism which are actually condemned, rather than Protestantism itself. There appears to have been considerable confusion as a consequence of the different understandings of the *nature* of justification associated with Protestants and Catholics. Canon 11 may be singled out as being of particular importance in this respect:

Si quis dixerit, homnes iustificari vel sola imputatione iustitiae Christi, vel sola peccatorum remissione, exclusa gratia et caritate, quae in cordibus eorum per Spiritum Sanctum diffundatur atque illis inhaereat, aut etiam gratiam, qua iustificamur, esse tantum favorem Dei: anathema sit.[23]

It is clear that this condemnation is aimed against a purely extrinsic conception of justification (in the Catholic sense of the term) – in other words, the view that the Christian life may begin and continue without any transformation or inner renewal of the sinner. In fact, the canon does not censure any magisterial Protestant account of *iustificatio hominis*, in that man's initial (extrinsic) justification is either understood (as with Melanchthon) to be inextricably linked with his subsequent (intrinsic) sanctification, so that the concepts are notionally distinct, but nothing more; or else both man's extrinsic justification and intrinsic sanctification are understood (as with Calvin) to be contiguous dimensions of the union of the believer with Christ. Underlying this canon appears to be the view that Protestants denied that transformation and renewal was of the *esse* of Christian existence, an error primarily due to terminological confusion, but compounded by Luther's frequently intemperate (and occasionally obscure) statements on the matter.

The degree of latitude of interpretation incorporated into the Tridentine decree on justification at points of importance makes it impossible to speak of 'the Tridentine doctrine of justification', as if there were *one such doctrine*. In fact, Trent legitimated a range of theologies as catholic, and any one of them may lay claim to be a 'Tridentine doctrine of justification'. Trent may be regarded as endorsing the medieval Catholic heritage on justification, while eliminating much of its technical vocabulary, substituting biblical or Augustinian phrases in its place. Trent thus marks a point of transition in our study, in that it marks the deliberate and systematic rejection of much of the *terminology* of the medieval schools, while retaining the *theology* which it expressed. It is possible to argue that Trent marks the end of the medieval discussion of justification, in the sense that it established a new framework within which subsequent discussion of the matter was increasingly obliged to proceed.

It will, however, be clear that the degree of latitude of interpretation implicitly endorsed by Trent did more than permit the traditional teaching of the medieval schools to be considered Catholic: it also caused uncertainty concerning the precise interpretation of the decree. The result of this uncertainty may be seen in the immediate post-Tridentine period, in which it transpired that the debate on justification within Catholicism was renewed, rather than settled. It is to this period that we now turn.

§29 The post-Tridentine debates on justification

There can be no doubt that the Tridentine decree on justification was the most significant statement on the matter ever to have been made by the Christian church. The question of its correct interpretation is therefore of the utmost importance. In his still influential account of the Tridentine debate on justification, Rückert argued that the final decree, particularly in relation to its statements concerning the meritorious nature of the disposition towards justification, represented a victory for Thomism.[1] This judgement was not universally accepted in the immediate aftermath of Trent, nor is it accepted today. In the following section, we propose to consider the interpretation of the Tridentine statement on the meritorious nature of the disposition towards justification to illustrate the difficulties associated with interpreting the decree, before proceeding to a discussion of Baianism, Molinism and Jansenism.

The eighth chapter of the Tridentine decree on justification makes the following statement:

gratis autem iustificari ideo dicamur, quia nihil eorum, quae iustificationem praecedunt, sive fides, sive opera, ipsam iustificationis gratiam promeretur.[2]

As noted earlier (§§14–18), there was a substantial body of opinion within the Franciscan Order which held that man could merit justification *de congruo*. Is this opinion excluded by this statement?

An emphatically negative answer to this question was given in the present century by Heiko A. Oberman, who drew attention to the use of the verb *promereri* in the place of the more usual *mereri* in the above statement.[3] Oberman suggests that a contrast between *mereri* and *promereri* had become well established within Catholicism by the time of the Council of Trent, the latter meaning 'merit in the full sense of the term'.[4] He thus asserts that, during the Tridentine proceedings on justification, the verb *mereri* was associated with *meritum de congruo*, and *promereri* with *meritum de condigno*.[5] The statement cited above should therefore be interpreted as follows: none of the acts which precede justification, whether faith or works, merit the grace of justification *de condigno*. The possibility of a disposition towards justification which is meritorious *de congruo* is thus not excluded by the decree.

This distinction between *promereri* and *mereri* has been rejected by subsequent commentators. Rückert drew attention to the fact that the Council of Trent was anxious to break away from the vocabulary of medieval theology, including such terms as *meritum de congruo* and *meritum de condigno*.[6] Phrases such as *mereri ex debito* or *proprie et vere mereri* were used extensively in lieu of *mereri de condigno*. Thus the following form was used in the September draft of Canon 3:

Si quis impium quibuscumque suis operibus praecedentibus dixerit posse proprie et vere iustificationem mereri coram Deo, ita ut illis debeatur gratia ipsa iustificationis: anathema sit.[7]

It is clear that this was intended as an unequivocal rejection of the Pelagian doctrine of justification *ex meritis* – in other words, the doctrine that an individual may merit his justification in the strict sense of the term (*de condigno*). Oberman suggests that *promereri* was understood by the Tridentine fathers to mean *proprie et vere mereri*, and that its use in place of the usual term *mereri* was intended to emphasise this hardening in meaning. This suggestion rests upon inadequate documentary evidence. There are no grounds for supporting that such a distinction was current in the later medieval period, or that it was recognised or employed by those present at Trent. Indeed, the supplementation of *promereri* with *vere* at points during the Tridentine proceedings suggests that the verbs *mereri* and *promereri* were regarded as synonymous.[8] Elsewhere, ample evidence is to be had that the terms were not distinguished in the manner Oberman suggests.[9] Oberman himself notes that Domingo de Soto does not distinguish the two terms,[10] and his suggestion that such a distinction is made by Andrés de Vega has been shown to be untenable.[11] In fact, this debate is quite irrelevant to the point of interpretation in question, as will become clear from the following discussion.

In what follows, we shall consider several interpretations of the Tridentine decree on justification dating from the period, including two from the pens of Tridentine *periti*. In his 1547 *de natura et gratia*, the Dominican theologian Domingo de Soto argued that Trent denied that man's disposition towards justification was meritorious *de congruo*. Conceding the necessity of a disposition towards justification,[12] Soto argues that man cannot dispose himself towards grace without the *auxilium speciale Dei*.[13] Although a purely natural disposition towards justification is conceivable, Soto insists that this is merely *dispositio impropria seu remota*.[14] Merit prior to justification is rigorously excluded, even in the weak sense of merit *de congruo*.[15] Soto thus understands Trent to have rejected explicitly the doctrine of a congruously meritorious disposition towards justification. In this, he was followed by the English Catholic émigré Thomas Stapleton, who rejected the concept of congruous merit as long since discredited.[16] The Tridentine decree is unequivocal on this matter: merit can only exist in the case of the regenerate.[17]

A very different interpretation of the Tridentine decree is associated with the Franciscan Andrés de Vega. Although Vega emphatically denied that man could merit prevenient grace,[18] it is clear that he understands this to refer to merit *de condigno*.[19] He thus expounds the eighth chapter of the Tridentine decree as follows:

Et ita hic Patres asseverant neque fidem neque *aliqua opera bona praecedentia iustificationem promereri ipsam iustificationis gratiam*. Nullus enim peccator iustificatur ex debito, nullus ex rigore iustitiae, nullus ex condignitate suorum operum, sed omnes qui iustificantur gratis a Deo iustificantur et ex gratia et misericordia et absque meritis et condignitate suorum operum.[20]

It is clear that Vega understands Trent to have excluded the opinion that man can make a claim on God *ex debito* or *ex rigore iustitiae* – but not that he may rely upon the divine benevolence and generosity. Manifesta igitur luce constat nihil repugnare opinionem asserentium meritum ex congruo verbis nostri Concilii.[21] Vega understands the terms *meritum* and *mereri* to refer solely to merit in the strictest sense of the term, but does not extend the use of the term to *congruous* merit. In other words, the Tridentine rejection of merit prior to justification is merely a rejection of the Pelagian doctrine of justification *ex meritis* – that is, justification on the basis of condign merit. The Franciscan doctrine of a congruously meritorious disposition towards justification is thus unaffected by the Tridentine statements, whether these employ the verb *promereri* or *mereri* – Vega understands *both* to mean 'merit in the strict and proper sense of the term'.

In fact, there are excellent reasons for suggesting that the Tridentine fathers intended this latitude of interpretation. The Council was concerned to exclude the possibility that man could merit – in the strict sense of the term – his own justification: it was not concerned with resolving the long-standing debate within the Catholic schools of theology on whether the immediate disposition towards justification could be deemed meritorious in a weaker sense of the term. The presence of so large a contingent of Franciscan theologians at Trent, and particularly the prominent position which they assumed during the proceedings on justification, made it improbable that the traditional teaching of their own order would be censured. In effect, both the Thomist and the Franciscan (whether inclined to accept Bonaventure or Scotus as mentor) could claim that Trent condoned their characteristic views on this matter.

The success enjoyed by early Protestant catechisms, such as Luther's *Kleiner Catchismus* of 1529, made a Catholic catechetical response imperative. Two such unofficial responses appeared soon after the Tridentine decree on justification. Peter Canisius produced his *Catechismus Major* in 1555,[22] while his work in Germany was paralleled by that of Edmund Augerius in France.[23] Work on an official catechetical response to the Reformers began in 1547, but does not appear to have been taken seriously until 1563[24] – the year which saw both the closure of the Council of Trent, and the publication of the great Reformed *Heidelberger Katechismus*. The definitive catechism of the Catholic church, the *Catechismus Romanus*, appeared in October 1566, with a subtitle (*Catechismus ex decreto Tridentini*) clearly implying that it provided an exposition of the Tridentine decrees. In fact, however, the work is an exposition of the creed, the sacraments, the decalogue and the Lord's Prayer, rather than of the Council of Trent. It is, however, possible to determine the work's teaching on justification by correlating its various elements as they are found at various points in its course.[25]

Grace always precedes, accompanies and follows man's works, and merit is impossible apart from grace.[26] The Catechism makes no distinction between condign and congruous merit, however, and its statements on merit are thus open to precisely the same latitude of interpretation as the Tridentine decree itself: once more, this appears to be deliberate.

The Council of Trent did not produce a definitive and exhaustive account of the Catholic doctrine of justification, and must be regarded as a response to past errors, rather than an anticipation of those of the future. In particular, the Council was content to affirm the reality of the human free will and the universal necessity of grace, without specifying the precise manner in which these notions might be reconciled. As with the Council's teaching on congruous merit, it seems that a certain degree of latitude of interpretations was envisaged by the Tridentine fathers in regard to their statements on these matters. A general feature of the post-Tridentine period was its patristic positivism, particularly the renewed interest in the writings of Augustine of Hippo. That the reality of the human *liberum arbitrium* and the necessity of divine grace had been reconciled by Augustine was generally accepted – but the African bishop had many post-Tridentine interpreters, eventually forcing the church to determine which represented the closest approximation to his thought.

The first major post-Tridentine controversy to arise concerning the doctrine of justification was Baianism, characterised by its rejection of *supernaturale quoad essentiam*, and the cognate distinction between 'natural' and 'supernatural'.[27] The main features of Baius' theology may be deduced from his basic assertion that man was created *rectus* by God, and that this defines his natural state.[28] Abandoning the concept of *natura pura* (whose characteristics, particularly concerning the grace with which it had been endowed, had been the subject of a long-standing debate between the Dominican and Franciscan schools: §§14–17), Baius lays down three principles upon the basis of which the characteristics and qualities of man's natural state may be established.[29] First, the quality involved must not compromise the exigencies of human nature. Second, any quality which is necessarily implicated in the specific elements of human nature must be considered as 'natural' to man. Third, a quality must be considered 'natural' to man when his nature requires it as its necessary complement, so that without it his nature suffers privative evil. Thus Adam's innocence was not a supernatural gift, but the essential complement of his human nature. These principles may be illustrated with reference to Baius' assertion that Adam was given the Holy Spirit at his creation.

As it is part of man's nature that he should be alive, Baius argues that he is necessarily endowed with whatever is necessary to life – and includes the Holy Spirit among such endowments on basic theological presuppositions. The absence of the Holy Spirit would have resulted in a privation, and hence in evil. Furthermore, those powers and faculties which lead to the completion of nature must, according to Baius, be considered as part of nature itself. The subjection of man's lower nature to his higher spiritual nature, and of the *totus homo* to God, is immediately dependent upon the inhabitation of the Holy Spirit in man *ex natura rei*. As it is unthinkable that God would deny to Adam anything essential to the completion of his being, it may be concluded that he was endowed with the Holy Spirit at creation.

This approach to the 'natural' state of man has a number of important consequences. Adam's perseverance would have resulted in his receiving beatitude as a reward: there is no need to involve divine grace in this matter, because man has certain rights over God *ex natura rei*. Thus 'natural' man receives eternal life as a reward, not as a gift. 'Natural' man has certain rights before God: the divine assistance which man requires must be considered to arise from an obligation on God's part, rather than from his generosity, in that this assistance must be regarded as an integral aspect of his 'natural' state. It is instructive to compare Augustine and Baius on this point. Both agree that man is created in such a manner as to require divine assistance, and reject the possibility that he may attain his destiny unaided, by virtue of his own powers and abilities. Augustine, however, affirms that this divine assistance is bestowed gratuitously, in order that he may obtain his *supernatural* destiny (although Augustine does not use this precise term), where Baius insists that God is under an obligation to bestow such assistance, in order that man may attain his *natural* state. The comparison with Pelagius is also instructive. Where Pelagius asserted the total autonomy of human nature, Baius simultaneously asserted its *impotence apart from grace* and the *divine obligation to bestow grace as and when required*. Where Pelagius affirms man's independence of God, Baius affirms his total dependence upon God, and thus – in the manner of a litigant rather than a beggar – demands his due assistance from God.

Baius' definition of Adam's original state carries with it the implication that Adam possessed nothing other than that which was essential to his nature, so that the deprivation of any quality of this state could only result in its vitiation. As a consequence of the Fall, man now exists in an 'unnatural' state, in that his innocence is destroyed through the privation of essential natural qualities, to be replaced with 'viciousness'.[30] Original sin is defined in terms of a *habitus concupiscentiae*, which prevents man from breaking free from sin unaided.[31] Indeed, Baius' radical dichotomy between *concupiscentia* and *caritas* leads to his asserting that all works prior to justification are sinful – far exceeding the more cautious statements of Augustine on this point, and tending to approach the more radical views of the Reformers. The problem of justification, as stated by Baius, thus comes to concern the means by which the transition from a state of concupiscence to a state of charity may be effected. However, it must be emphasised that justification is conceived in purely natural terms: it is essentially a restoration of the state of innocence and natural faculties, by which man is enabled to lead a moral existence. It is this principle which underlies the proposition, subsequently condemned by Pius V, that the *ratio meriti* is not the Holy Spirit, but obedience to the law.[32]

It is clear that Baius' theology of justification is radically different from that of Augustine, despite his attempt to recover the latter's views from the adumbrations of the medieval period. This departure from Augustine appears to arise from the rejection of the concept of *supernaturale quoad essentiam*, from which most of Baius' views ultimately derive. Although Augustine does not employ the *term* 'supernatural', this cannot be taken as an indication that the *concept* is not implicitly present in his theology of justification. The medieval development of Augustine's theology of grace (see §9) may be regarded as making this concept explicit within, rather than imposing it as an alien concept upon, this theology. By rejecting the concept of the supernatural altogether, Baius inevitably reduced Augustine's theology to pure naturalism.

Seventy-nine propositions culled from Baius' works were condemned by Pius V in the Bull *Ex omnis afflictionibus* (1 October 1567).[33] This Bull, however, was itself to prove the source of considerable controversy, which has passed into history as the affair of the *Comma Pianum*. The Bull concludes as follows:

Quas quidem sententias stricto coram nobis examine ponderatas, quamquam nonnullae aliquo pacto sustineri possent in rigore et proprio verborum sensu ab assertoribus intento *haereticas, erroneas, suspectas, temerarias, scandalosas* et *in pias aures offensionem immittentes* respective ... damnamus.[34]

The Bull was not punctuated in its original form. The affair of the *Comma Pianum* arose from the fact that the sense of the Bull was totally determined by the placing of a single comma. The Louvain theologians, and after them the Jansenists, placed the comma after 'intento', whilst their Jesuit opponents placed it after 'sustineri possent'. The former punctuation yields the following interpretation: the preceding list contains some heretical propositions, but others which are orthodox, in the sense intended by the authors. The latter punctuation yields a rather different interpretation: the list of propositions includes some which are open to an orthodox interpretation, but which are heretical as interpreted by the authors. The *magisterium* subsequently made it clear that the placing of the comma after 'intento' was unacceptable.[35]

Further controversy developed between the Dominican and Jesuit Orders in Spain, such as the acrimonious Valladolid confrontation of 1582 between Prudentius Montemayor and Domingo Báñez. This controversy entered a new phase with the publication of Luis de Molina's *Concordia* in 1588.[36] This work takes the form of a commentary upon certain sections of Thomas Aquinas' *Summa Theologiae*, and reconciles human freedom and grace by denying the efficacy of *gratia ab intrinseco*, and substituting the efficacy of grace in the divine foreknowledge *de scientia media* of human cooperation with the gift of grace.

Rejecting Thomas Aquinas' teaching on the causal relation of grace and free will,[37] Molina develops a theory of the relation between primary and secondary causes which has important consequences for his discussion of the concord between grace and the human free will in justification. This theory may be illustrated from an example Molina provides.[38] Consider the reproduction of a horse or a man. The freedom of the horse, or man, to reproduce is not in any way affected by the fact that the universal and general influence of the sun is required for that production. The sun provides a general and universal *influxus*, which forms one cause with the *influxus* of the secondary cause itself, and which derives its specific determination (that is, horse or man) from that secondary cause. As the effect proceeds from the total cause, both primary and secondary cause are necessary for the production of that effect, although they are involved in quite distinct manners. These two *influxus* do not intract directly: the interaction takes place through the *influxus* of the primary cause into the *effectus* of the secondary cause. As the secondary cause receives its *influxus* passively, its freedom is not in any sense restricted or compromised. Furthermore, the primary cause cannot be regarded as being prior to the secondary. Applying this metaphysics of causality to the question of the relation of grace and the free will, Molina draws the following conclusions: first, that the free will is responsible for its own actions; and second, that God cannot be said to be responsible for the actions of the free will.

The relationship between divine foreknowledge and human free will is resolved through an analysis of the concepts of contingency and eternity. God foreknows all that comes to pass, freely and contingently, through secondary causes.[39] This foreknowledge compromises neither the contingency of the present order of things, nor the autonomy of the human free will. Molina defines the knowledge of the behaviour of every autonomous secondary cause in all circumstances as *scientia media*.[40] This *scientia media* relates to the hypothetical and the contingent – which includes the decisions of an individual free will under a given set of circumstances.

God thus knows infallibly how each individual will respond to the grace which is offered to him, without compromising the autonomy of that individual. Molina uses this concept of the *scientia media* to reconcile the two propositions:

1. God decreed from all eternity that Paul should go to Macedonia.
2. Paul went to Macedonia of his own free will.

God knew infallibly, by his *scientia media*, that if Paul went to Troas, and thence received a call to go to Macedonia, he would obey this call. Therefore, Molina argues, God created the world with such circumstances that Paul would find himself in Troas at an opportune moment, and thence proceed to Macedonia – thus maintaining both the divine sovereignty and human freedom. The efficacy of grace is thus maintained, but is understood to arise on account of something extrinsic to grace (the consent of the human will) rather than the intrinsic nature of grace itself.[41]

This view was sharply attacked by Spanish Thomists, particularly Báñez, who upheld the notion of intrinsically efficacious grace. In contrast to sufficient grace, which confers upon man a capacity to act, efficacious grace moves man's will to action. Báñez and his supporters were particularly critical of Molina's assertion that God foreknew something because it would happen contingently through free will, and his rejection of the opinion that something happened on account of the divine foreknowledge.[42] The doctrine of *scientia media* was thus rejected in favour of the Báñezian *praemotio physica*. It is interesting to note that the term 'semi-Pelagian' was introduced during the course of this dispute by the followers of Báñez to describe the teachings of their Molinist opponents. The controversy between Jesuits and Dominicans at Valladolid in 1594 eventually became so heated that the papal nuncio at Madrid was obliged to impose silence upon the disputing parties, and referred the matter to Rome for resolution. A commission was appointed in November 1597 to consider the matter.

The celebrated *Congregatio de auxiliis* began at Rome in 1598, and continued over two pontificates until 1607.[43] Although the commission was initially in favour of censuring Molinism, pressure from representatives of both the King of Spain and the Society of Jesus led to a widening of the commission's membership and terms of reference, and the eventual declaration on 5 September 1607 that the Báñezian teaching was not Calvinist, nor the Molinist Pelagian. The Jesuit and Dominican Orders were permitted to defend their own teachings on the matter, but were forbidden to criticise each other, pending a final settlement of the question.[44] No such settlement has been made, to this day.

This deficiency was, however, overshadowed by the rise of Jansenism and the political threat which this posed to the papal influence in France.[45] Jansen's *Augustinus*, published posthumously in 1640, shows strong affinities with Baianism, particularly in its rejection of the concept of 'pure nature', and the corresponding distinction between 'nature' and 'supernature'. Jansen defines the grace conferred upon Adam at his creation as *adiutorium sine quo non*, which he distinguishes from *adiutorium quo*.[46] The former, bestowed upon Adam at his creation, is the divine grace without which he could do nothing, *tanquam lumen sanis oculis*, despite the fact that he is *sanus*. Just as a healthy man still requires light before he can see, despite his perfect vision, so man requires *adiutorium sine quo non* if he is to function properly. Just as human eyes require illumination if they are to function correctly, so man's *liberum arbitrium* requires *adiutorium sine quo non* before it too can function correctly. This *adiutorium* is thus an essential part of man's original nature.[47]

The Fall robbed man of *adiutorium sine quo non*, with a resulting radical vitiation of his nature. However, on account of the radical effects of the Fall of his faculties, which are now reduced from the natural to the subnatural level, man now requires more than light to restore his vision: he requires a cure for his blindness. By his sin,

Adam passed from a state of health to a state of decay. The grace required to free man from this *necessitas peccandi* is thus *adiutorium quo* – an *adiutorium* which is not merely necessary for good action, but which is itself intrinsically efficacious in producing such action.

Jansen thus rejects the Molinist concept of *gratia sufficiens* as an absurdity: on account of man's radically vitiated nature arising through the Fall, such grace would only be sufficient if it actually and effectually cured man's will, thereby restoring his health and permitting him to do good. Such grace was adequate in the case of Adam's natural state – but in the case of fallen man, medicinal grace (*gratia sanans*) was required in the form of *adiutorium quo*.[48] Jansen then proceeds to demonstrate that *gratia sanans* is necessary, efficacious and non-universal.[49] The second and third points are of particular importance. Jansen argues that Augustine never uses the term 'grace' unless he intends it to mean 'efficacious grace': if grace is given, the performance of the work for which it was given necessarily follows; if no such grace is given, no corresponding work results. Jansen's rejection of the universality of grace leads to his criticism of certain accounts of the effects of Christ's death, particularly those which suggested that Christ died for all men. According to Jansen, Augustine never concedes that Christ died for all men without exception, but only for those who benefited by his death.[50] When Christ is said to have died for all men in certain scriptural passages, this should be understood to mean that he died for all *types* of men (such as kings and subjects, nobles and peasants; or men of all nations or languages).[51] Augustine does not speak of Christ as being a redemption for all men, unless this is interpreted as meaning all *the faithful*. In all the writings of Augustine, Jansen stated that he found no reference to Christ dying for the sins of those unbelievers who remain in unbelief.[52] Although Christ's work is sufficient for all men, it is efficacious only for some. Jansen thus rejects the opinion that God must confer his grace upon the man who does *quod in se est*, claiming the support of Augustine in doing so.[53]

It was clear, in the light of the rise of Jansenism, that the Tridentine decree on justification required supplementation. On 31 May 1653, Innocent X condemned five Jansenist propositions in the Bull *Cum occasione*,[54] to be followed by more extensive condemnation of Jansenist positions (as stated by Pasquier Quesnel) in the 1713 papal constitution *Unigenitus filius Dei*.[55] The strongly political overtones to the condemnation of Jansenism, particularly evident in the association of the movement with Gallicanism,[56] lend weight to the suggestion that *Unigenitus* should be seen as a political, rather than a theological, document.

The post-Tridentine debates on justification ended with the magisterial toleration of the various forms of Thomism and Molinism, and the rejection of Jansenism and Baianism. Although individual Catholic theologians have subsequently written extensively on the question of justification,[57] the broad outlines of the Catholic teaching on the matter may be regarded as having been finally fixed by 1713.

Two points may be noted in closing this chapter. First, it may be emphasised that, despite the considerable degree of convergence evident at points between Jansenism and Protestantism, the entire post-Tridentine Catholic tradition (including those otherwise considered heterodox, such as Baianists and Jansenists) continued to regard justification as a process in which man was made righteous, involving the actualisation rather than the imputation of righteousness. The Protestant conception of justification was not adopted even by those who came closest to Protestant understandings of the mode in which justification came about. The continuity within the western tradition concerning the nature of justification was upheld by its post-Tridentine representatives. Second, the very term 'justification' itself appears to have been gradually eliminated from the homiletical and catechetical literature of Catholicism. Although the term is employed extensively in the polemical works of the sixteenth century, and may still be encountered in sermons of the seventeenth,[58] it seems that the associations of the term led to an increased reluctance to employ it from the late seventeenth century onwards – despite the extensive use of the concept by the Council of Trent. The dating of this elimination suggests that it may have been a reaction to Jansenism, rather than Protestantism. The general reintroduction of the term into the vocabulary of Catholicism appears to date from the Second Vatican Council.

8. The legacy of the English Reformation

§30 The English Reformation: Tyndale to Hooker

The Reformation in England drew its inspiration primarily from its continental counterpart, although the Lollard movement had done much to instil the anti-clerical and anti-sacramental attitudes upon which the English Reformers would base their appeal to the doctrine of justification *sola fide*.[1] The strongly political cast of the English Reformation tended to result in theological issues having a secondary and derivative importance, which goes some way towards accounting for the theological mediocrity of the movement. Furthermore, the English Reformers appear to have busied themselves chiefly with eucharistic controversies – unnecessarily drawing attention to their differences in doing so[2] – rather than with the doctrine of justification. It is, however, clear that the doctrines of justification circulating in English reforming circles in the 1520s and early 1530s were quite distinct from those of the mainstream continental Reformation, thus raising the question of the sources of these doctrines. Although the Cambridge 'White Horse circle' met to discuss the works of Luther in the 1520s, it is clear that few of the Reformer's distinctive ideas became generally accepted in England.[3]

There are excellent reasons for supposing that essentially Augustinian doctrines of justification were in circulation in England independent of the influence of Luther, and that the doctrines of justification which developed as an indirect consequence of such influence appear to have omitted the idea of the *reputatio iustitiae Christi alienae* – a central feature of Luther's conception of justification – altogether. Thomas Bilney, for example, a leading figure of the 'White Horse circle', developed a concept of justification framed solely in terms of the non-imputation of sin, omitting any reference to the concept of the 'imputation of righteousness'.[4] Similarly, William Tyndale, although making extensive use of Luther in his early polemical works,[5] tends to interpret justification as 'making righteous'.[6] Tyndale's emphasis upon the renewing and transforming work of the Holy Spirit within man is quite distinct from Luther's emphasis upon faith, and clearly parallels Augustine's transformational concept of justification. John Frith reproduces a sanative concept of justification, clearly Augustinian in its structure.[7] Frith's most characteristic definition of justification is that it consists of the non-imputation of sin,[8] omitting any references to the imputation of righteousness. The first clear and unambiguous statement of the concept of the imputation of righteousness to be found in the writings of an English Reformer may be found in the 1534 edition of Robert Barnes' *Supplication unto King Henry VIII*. The vague statements of the 1531 edition on this matter[9] are expanded to yield an unequivocal statement of the concept of imputed righteousness.[10] Barnes, however, was exceptional in his understanding of, and affinity with, Lutheranism: the early English Reformation as a whole appears to have been characterised by theologies of justification which demonstrate many points of contact with their continental counterparts, except in their understanding of the *nature* of justification. In 1531, George Joye defined justification thus:

To be justified, or to be made righteous before God by this faith, is nothing else but to be absolved from sin of God, to be forgiven, or to have no sin imputed of him by God.[11]

The assertion that justification is the forgiveness or non-imputation of sin *without* the simultaneous assertion that righteousness is imputed to the believer, or *with* the assertion that justification is to be understood as *making* righteous, appears to be characteristic of the English Reformation until the late 1530s.

The years between Henry VIII's break with Rome and his death saw the publication of a series of formularies of faith, which attempted to define the theological position of the new national church: the Ten Articles (July 1536); the Bishops' Book (August 1537); the Six Articles (statute enacted June 1539); and the King's Book (published May 1543). While these formularies of faith give insights perhaps more into the political, rather than the theological, concerns of the period, their statements on justification are particularly interesting to the extent that they refer to the *nature* of that concept.

The Ten Articles of July 1536 deal with justification and the three sacraments, amongst other matters. Although the influence of Lutheranism upon these Articles, mediated through the Wittenberg Articles of the same year,[12] is well established, this influence appears to have been minimal in relation to their statements on justification. Justification is defined in an Augustinian manner:

Justification signifieth remission of our sins, and our acceptance or reconciliation into the grace and favour of God, that is to say, our perfect renovation in Christ.[13]

Although grace is clearly conceived extrinsically as the *favor Dei*, justification continues to be defined non-forensically. This definition of justification is, in fact, based upon that of Philip Melanchthon's 1535 *Loci communes*:[14]

Iustificatio significat remissionem peccatorum et reconciliationem seu acceptationem personae ad vitam aeternam. Nam Hebraeis iustificare est forense verbum; ut si dicam, populus Romanus iustificavit Scipionem accusatum a tribunis, id est, absolvit seu iustum pronuntiavit.[15]

It is clearly significant that the entire second sentence, which contains an unequivocal assertion of the *forensic* character of justification, has been omitted, and a final phrase ('perfect renovation in Christ') substituted which completely eliminates any possibility of a distinction between *iustificatio* and *regeneratio*. This Article was incorporated *verbatim* into the Bishops' Book of the following year.[16] Elsewhere, the Bishops' Book emphasised the *communication* – and not the *imputation* – of the righteousness of Christ to the believer:

He hath planted and grafted me into his own body, and made me a member of the same, and he hath communicated and made me participant of his justice, his power, his life, his felicity, and all of his goods.[17]

Although this Book contains extracts from William Marshall's 1535 *Primer*, which is held to be based upon Luther's 1523 *Betbuchlein*,[18] the influence of Lutheranism upon the work is not marked.

The King's Book of 1543 contained an entirely new article on justification, abandoning the previous definition, based partly on Melanchthon, in favour of a definition which could be taken directly from the works of Augustine himself:

Justification . . . signifieth the making of us rightous afore God, where before we were unrighteous.[19]

The phrase 'afore God' here appears to reflect the Augustinian and medieval *apud Deum*, rather than the Lutheran *coram Deo*. Elsewhere in the Book, the teachings of baptism as the first justification, and of 'restoration to justification' through penance, may be found – clearly indicative of a concept of justification continuous with the medieval Catholic tradition.

A work of particular importance in establishing the position of the early English national church on the nature of justification is the *Homily of Salvation*, usually regarded as the work of Thomas Cranmer himself.[20] In many respects, the *Homily* is Melanchthonian. For example, the obvious similarity between the explanations of Cranmer and Melanchthon concerning the correct interpretation of the phrase *sola fide* have often been noted.[21] The *Homily* is, in fact, a fine exposition of the Melanchthonian doctrine of justification *per solan fidem*. The verbal similarity between Melanchthon and Cranmer on the rôle of the law is also striking,[22] as is their similarity in relation to the fiduciary character of faith and the Anselmian approach to the death of Christ. However, Melanchthon's influence is conspicuously absent in Cranmer's discussion of the nature of justification. Cranmer interprets justification to mean 'making righteous',[23] which clearly reflects the strongly factitive Augustinian concept of justification evident in the collection of patristic texts assembled by Cranmer in support of the position he develops in the *Homily*.[24] Although Cranmer rejects Augustine's doctrine of justification on the basis of *fides quae per dilectionem operatur*, excluding charity from his account of man's justification, he does not extend this criticism to Augustine's understanding of the *nature* of justification.

This raises an important point. The English Reformers appear to have understood that their continental colleagues developed a doctrine of justification *by fayth onely*, and that its leading feature was the total exclusion of human works from man's justification. Several of them also appear to have understood that this faith was 'reputed' as righteousness, possibly drawing on the use of this term in the *Apology* for the Augsburg Confession. They do not, however, appear to have realised precisely what was meant by the very different concept of the imputation of righteousness, or its potential theological significance. In general, the English Reformers appear to have worked with a doctrine of justification in which man was understood to be *made* righteous *by fayth onely*, with good works being the natural consequence of justifying faith – a possible interpretation of the Lutheran teaching, as stated in the important confessional documents of 1530, but not the most reliable such interpretation.

The year 1547 marked the beginning of the reign of Edward VII, and the dawning of new possibilities for the English Reformers to consolidate the Protestantism of the national church. 'Since these churches of ours are in great want of learned men',[25] Cranmer wrote to various continental Reformers, inviting them to England to supervise the religious developments which he envisaged – including the clarification of points of doctrine. Of these points, the most important was the following: does justification make a man really righteous, or does it merely make him acceptable to God as though he were really righteous?[26] By 1549, Bucer and Fagius felt able to write to their colleagues in Strasbourg to the effect that 'the doctrine of justification is purely and soundly taught' in England.[27] It is not clear what moved them to this judgement: even as late as 1571, the teaching of the English church on this matter was unclear. The 1552 Article *de hominis iustificatione* affirms that 'justification *ex sola fide Iesu Christi*, in the sense in which it is explained in the *Homelia de iustificatione*', is the most important and healthy doctrine of Christians.[28] The fact that this Article refers interested readers to the *Homily of Justification* (almost certainly Cranmer's *Homily of Salvation*) for further details, when this Homily simultaneously develops an Augustinian concept of justification and a Melanchthonian doctrine of justification *per solam fidem*, further indicates that, at least in this respect, the English Reformation had yet to assimilate the teaching of its continental counterpart. It is, of course, possible that the English Reformers were misled through the occasional references in the *Apology* of the Augsburg Confession which do indeed refer to justification as 'making righteous', and which use the term 'repute', rather than 'impute'.[29] Although the *Homily* clearly states the doctrine of justification *per solam fidem* in an orthodox Melanchthonian sense (apparently with extracts from the *Loci* being worked into the text), it is significant that the crucial concept of imputed righteousness is absent. The 1563 Articles, however, contain an important addition. The reader is referred to the *Homily* merely for details of *the manner in which faith justifies*;[30] justification itself is defined as follows:

Tantum propter meritum Domini ac Servatoris nostri Iesu Christi, per fidem, non propter opera et merita nostra, iusti coram Deo reputamur.[31]

This is clearly a much more precise statement of the Melanchthonian doctrine of justification *per solam fidem*; indeed, this entire sentence could be constructed from Melanchthon's statements in the 1530 *Apologia*. Four phrases or terms may be singled out for particular comment. The use of the Melanchthonian term *per fidem* – rather than *propter fidem* or simply *fide* – makes it clear that faith is the *instrument* of justification, as explained by Melanchthon in the *Apologia* and in the *Loci*. 'Propter opera et merita nostra', with the possessive pronoun present where it is absent in the earlier reference to faith, makes it clear that man is not justified on account of any quality which he may possess, and implies that *fides* is not to be understood as such a quality. Once more, the technical expressions of the *Confessio Augustana* and its associated *Apologia* found their way into this Article – a point confirmed by the use of the crucial phrase *coram Deo*, characteristic of the forensic language of the Melanchthonian sources upon which it is so closely dependent. Finally, the use of the term *reputamur* is significant, in that it is the term used most frequently by Melanchthon in the 1530 *Apology* to describe the forensic aspect of justification: 'reputentur esse iusti coram Deo;[32] fide propter Christum coram Deum [sic] iusti reputemur'.[33] Although the term *reputatio* was displaced at a relatively early stage by *imputatio*, the fact remains that it was the former which was employed by Melanchthon in the documents which appear to have exercised so significant an influence over the English Reformers at this point. It is therefore evident that the 1563 Article on justification is intended to clarify the somewhat vague statement of 1552 along Lutheran lines. It will, nevertheless, be clear that the Article does not distinguish between the idea of *the imputation of faith for righteousness* and the quite distinct idea of the *the imputation of the righteousness of Christ*. The former expresses the notion that God accepts, reckons or 'reputes' the faith of the believer to be 'righteousness'; the latter, which corresponds to the teaching characteristic of the continental Reformation by this stage, expresses the notion that faith is the means by which the extrinsic righteousness of Christ is appropriated by the individual believer. The importance of the distinction may be seen from the later seventeenth-century controversy among Independent and Presbyterian divines, in which Thomas Gataker, John Graile, John Owen and Joshua Watson held the latter, and Richard Baxter, Christopher Cartwright, John Goodwin and Benjamin Woodbridge the former, to be the formal cause of justification (see §32). Although there are reasons for supposing that the early English Reformers actually inclined towards the former position, the latter became established as normative within the English national church by the end of the sixteenth century.

Despite this clear alignment with the Lutheran Reformation, rather than the Swiss Reformations of Zurich or Geneva, the Elizabethan period witnessed a general decline in the fortunes of Lutheranism in England. The returning Marian exiles, many of whom were promptly elevated to the episcopacy in the aftermath of the deprivations of 1559, had generally spent their time of exile in cities (such as Zurich, Strasbourg and Geneva) strongly influenced by the Reformed, rather than Lutheran, theology.[34] Although Elizabeth herself had read Melanchthon's *Loci* as a girl (the 1538 edition was dedicated to her father), and in 1559 expressed the wish that the 'Augustanean Confession' be maintained in the realm, it is clear that the Reformed theology made considerable headway in England during the final decades of the sixteenth century. The tension between Episcopalians and Presbyterians (both of whom were obliged to consider themselves members of the same church as a result of the Act of Uniformity) led to a number of important apologetic works appearing justifying the existence and teachings of the Episcopal national church. The most important of these for our purposes are Richard Hooker's sermons on the book of Habakkuk, preached in 1586, although not published until 1612.[35] In these sermons, Hooker addresses himself to issues such as the 'grand question which hangeth yet in controversy between us and the Church of Rome, about the matter of justifying righteousness'.[36] In his response, it is clear that Hooker attempts to construct a mediating doctrine of justification between Catholicism and Protestantism, which avoids the discredited eirenicon of double justification. Hooker considers that the chief error of his Catholic opponents is their teaching that a habit of grace is infused into man at his first justification to produce an inherent and real righteousness within man, which may subsequently be increased, by merit acquired through good works, in the second justification.[37] For Hooker, God bestows upon man justifying and sanctifying righteousness in his justification at one and the same time: the distinction between the two lies in the fact that the former is external to man, and imputed to him, while the latter is worked within him by the Holy Spirit.[38] Hooker distinguishes habitual and *actual* sanctifying righteousness, the former being the righteousness with which the soul is endowed through the indwelling of the Holy Spirit, and the latter the right-eousness which results from the action of that Spirit.[39] At the instant of his justification, man is simultaneously accepted as righteous in Christ and given the Holy Spirit, which is the formal cause of his subsequent actual sanctifying righteousness. Hooker interprets the phrase 'justification by faith alone' as follows:

We teach that faith alone justifieth: whereas we by this speech never meant to exclude either hope and charity from being always joined as inseparable mates with faith in the man that is justified; or works from being added as necessary duties, required at the hands of every justified man: but to shew that faith is the only hand that putteth on Christ unto justification; and Christ the only garment, which being so put on, covereth the shame of our defiled natures, hideth the imperfections of our works, preserveth us blameless in the sight of God, before whom otherwise the very weakness of our faith were cause sufficient to make us culpable.[40]

As Hooker concedes, however, faith is itself a work of the Holy Spirit within man,[41] so that faith is both the prerequisite and consequence of justification.[42]

It will thus be clear that Hooker's understanding of the nature of justification is similar to that of Calvin. Man is justified *per fidem propter Christum*.[43] Justification is to be conceived Christologically, in terms of the appropriation of the personal presence of Christ within the believer through the Holy Spirit, on account of which he is declared righteous and the process of sanctification initiated. A clear distinction is thus drawn between justification through imputed righteousness, and sanctification through inherent righteousness. The importance of this distinction will become clear in the section which follows.

§31 Anglicanism: the Caroline Divines

Just as the seventeenth century witnessed the consolidation of the two main theological streams of the Continental Reformation in the shape of Lutheran and Reformed Orthodoxy, so the theological developments initiated by the English Reformation may be regarded as having been consolidated in the century which followed. The 'golden age of Anglican divinity' took place in a century which witnessed considerable change in England, including the turmoil and the uncertainty occasioned by the Civil War and Interregnum, and the theological and ecclesiological changes introduced by the Westminster Assembly. Despite the political revolution of 1688, and the no less significant, and practically simultaneous, revolution in the world of ideas accompanying the publication of Newton's *Principia mathematica* and Locke's *Essay concerning Human Understanding*, the Church of England appeared to remain relatively unaltered, retaining both her episcopal system of church government, and the reigning monarch as her head. Nevertheless, significant alterations had taken place within Anglican theology: for example, the origins of Deism may be detected in the writings of certain post-Reformation divines.

In the present section, we propose to illustrate an important discontinuity in Anglican thinking on justification over the period 1600–1700, and assess its significance.[1]

The seventeenth-century churchmen collectively known as the Caroline Divines may, in general, be regarded as exponents of an Arminianism which immediately distinguishes them from their Puritan opponents. In May 1595, William Barrett, a fellow of Caius College, Cambridge, preached a sermon which touched off the predestinarian controversy ultimately leading to the nine Lambeth Articles of 1595.[2] These strongly predestinarian Articles never had any force, other than as the private judgement of those who drafted them. The seventeenth century saw their failing to achieve any authority within the Church of England, particularly when John Reynolds failed to persuade the Hampton Court Conference of 1604 to append them to the Thirty-Nine Articles of Religion. This left Article XVII – easily harmonised with an Arminian doctrine of election – as the sole authoritative pronouncement of the Church of England on the matter.

Although there can be little doubt that the Reformed doctrine of election continued to be widely held, particularly within Puritan circles, increasing opposition to the doctrine, largely from academic sources, was evident in the early seventeenth century. Thus Richard Hooker at Oxford, and Launcelot Andrewes at Cambridge, developed an 'Arminianism before Arminius', which received considerable impetus through the influence of William Laud, subsequently translated to Canterbury. Like Vincent of Lérins, Andrewes declined to support the latest continental speculation on predestination precisely because he felt it to be an evident innovation. The Arminianism of the leading divines of the period – and the intense hostility towards them from Puritans[3] – is perhaps best illustrated from the controversy surrounding the publication of Henry Hammond's *Practical Catechism* in 1644.[4] This work may be regarded as a classic statement of the soteriological convictions of the Laudian party, asserting unequivocally that Christ died for all men.[5] This view was variously described by his opponents: Cheynell accused him of subscribing to the doctrine of universal salvation; others charged him with Arminianism. The response of Clement Barksdale to this latter charge is particularly significant:

You are mistaken when you think the Doctrine of Universall Redemption Arminianisme. It was the Doctrine of the Church of England before Arminius was borne. We learne it out of the old Church-Catechisme. I believe in Iesus Christ, Who hath redeemed mee and all mankind. And the Church hath learned it out of the plaine Scripture, where Christ is the Lamb of God that taketh away the sinnes of the world.[6]

In this, Barksdale must be regarded as substantially correct. The Bezan doctrine of limited atonement was somewhat late in arriving in England, by which time the older Melanchthonian view had become incorporated into the confessional material of the English national church – such as the catechism of 1549. This evidently poses a nice problem in relation to terminology: should one style men such as Peter Baro (d. 1599) as an 'Arminian *avant la lettre*',[7] or accept that their teaching was typical of the period before the Arminian controversy brought the matter to a head and a new theological term into existence? Most Anglican divines in the late sixteenth and early seventeenth centuries appear to have based their soteriology on the dialectic between universal redemption and universal salvation, declining to accept the Bezan solution of their Puritan opponents.[8] More significantly, the early Caroline Divines appear to have been unanimous in their rejection of the doctrine of justification by inherent righteousness.

In 1701, two letters of Thomas Barlow (1607–71), sometime Bishop of Lincoln, were published.[9] Addressed to a priest in his diocese, the letters condemn the tendency to harmonise Paul and James to yield a doctrine of justification by faith *and* works, particularly on account of its associated denial of the imputation of the righteousness of Christ in justification. As we shall indicate later in the present section, this doctrine is characteristic of the post-Reformation Caroline Divines. The real significance of the letters, however, lies in their historical insight. Barlow states that Anglican divines

who have writ of our justification *coram Deo* before the late unhappy rebellion, such as Bishop Jewel, Hooker, Reynolds, Whittaker, Field, Downham, John White, etc., do constantly prove and vindicate the imputation of our blessed Saviour's Righteousness against the contrary doctrine of Racovia and Rome, Papists and Socinians. So that in truth it is only you, and some Neotericks who (since the year 1640) deny such imputation.[10]

In this respect, Barlow must be judged correct. In the case of every divine which he mentions, the doctrine of justification by imputed righteousness is defended, reflecting the general theological consensus upon this point in the Caroline church up to 1640. Had he so desired, Barlow could have added Ussher, Hall, Jackson, Davenant,

Cosin, and Andrewes to his list.[11] Thus George Downham defined justification as 'a most gracious and righteous action of God whereby he, imputing the righteousness of Christ to a believing sinner, absolveth him from his sinnes and accepteth him as righteous in Christ.'[12] In common with his contemporaries, Downham distinguished between the *imputation* of the righteousness of Christ, as the formal cause of man's justification, and the *infusion* of righteousness in his subsequent sanctification. The Tridentine doctrine of justification by inherent righteousness (or, more strictly, the doctrine that the formal cause of justification was inherent righteousness) was criticised on six counts,[13] closely paralleling similar criticisms made of the Tridentine teaching – particularly as presented in the writings of Bellarmine – by Lutheran and Reformed apologists. Indeed, in the period 1590–1640, the Caroline Divines may be regarded as developing an understanding of justification which parallels that of Lutheran Orthodoxy, and criticising both Rome (on the formal cause of justification) and Geneva (on the nature of predestination) on grounds similar to those by then well established within Lutheranism.

Isolated traces of an emerging discontinuity may be detected in the final years of the troubled reign of Charles I. Henry Hammond reverted to the more Augustinian definition of justification associated with the earlier period of the English Reformation, including the non-imputation of sin, but *not* the imputation of righteousness, among its elements. In his *Practical Catechism*, Hammond defines justification as:

God's accepting our persons, and not imputing our sins, His covering or pardoning our iniquities, His being so reconciled unto us sinners, that He determines not to punish us eternally.[14]

A similar understanding of justification may be found in the works of William Forbes, particularly his posthumously published *Considerationes*. In this work, Forbes reverts to the Augustinian understanding of justification as 'an entity, one by aggregation, and compounded of two, which by necessary conjunction and co-ordination are one only' – in other words, justification subsumes both the forgiveness of sins and the regeneration of man through inherent righteousness.[15] The 'whole sanctification or renewal of man ought to be comprehended in the expression "forgiveness of sins"'.[16]

The idea of justification *sola fide* is also criticised by the same authors. Hammond agrees that regeneration must be regarded as a precondition of justification,[17] while Forbes, conceding that faith justifies 'in a singular manner', denies that it is faith, *and faith alone* which justifies. Works cannot be excluded from justification, precisely because faith is itself a work.[18] This understanding of the implication of both faith and works in justification is, of course, a necessary consequence of the reversion to the Augustinian concept of justification, which subsumes the new life of the believer under the aegis of justification, rather than sanctification.

The leading features of the doctrines of justification characteristic of the leading Anglican divines in the period of the Restoration may thus be shown to have been anticipated in the earlier part of the century. These leading features are:[19]

1. Justification is treated as both an event and a process, subsuming regeneration or sanctification.
2. The formal cause of justification is held to be *either* inherent righteousness, *or* inherent and imputed righteousness – but *not* inherent righteousness alone.
3. The teachings of Paul and James are harmonised in such a manner that both faith and works are held to be involved in man's justification, frequently on the basis of the explicitly stated presupposition that faith is itself a work.

The most significant expositions of this understanding of justification are Jeremy Taylor's Dublin sermons of 1662,[20] and George Bull's *Harmonia Apostolica* (1669–70) – the 'apostles' in question being, of course, Paul and James.[21] Of particular interest is Bull's apparent awareness that his views on justification are at variance with those of an earlier generation of Anglican divines: he acknowledges significant points of disagreement with Hooker on the question of justifying righteousness.[22] Nevertheless, whatever its relationship with the earlier Caroline divinity may have been, it is clear that the 'theology of holy living' came to exercise a profound influence over later Caroline theology in general, and particularly its moral theology. This is not to say that there were no critics of this new theology of justification among the later Caroline Divines: Barlow, Barrow and Beveridge, for example, argued that Paul was referring to justification *coram Deo* and James to justification *coram hominibus*,[23] thus challenging the *harmonia apostolica* of the 'holy living' school. Similarly, many of the earlier Caroline Divines – such as Bramhall and Sanderson – survived until the period of the post-Restoration Caroline church, maintaining the older view of the nature of the formal causes of justification.[24]

In his *Learned Discourse of Justification*, delivered towards the end of the sixteenth century, Richard Hooker spoke of 'that grand question, which hangeth yet in controversy between us and the Church of Rome, about the matter of justifying righteousness'.[25] The following century saw disagreement concerning precisely this 'grand question' arise within the Church of England itself. Whereas the Anglican tradition had been virtually unanimous upon this, and related, questions until about 1640 (the earlier Caroline divines following Hooker himself in insisting that justifying righteousness was imputed to man; that faith was not a work of man; that justification and sanctification were to be distinguished), the later period of Caroline divinity came to be dominated by the theology of 'holy living', with a quite distinct – indeed, one might go so far as to say totally different – understanding of justification (justifying right-eousness is inherent to man; faith is a work of man; justification subsumes sanctification). Although the intervention of the Common-wealth between these two periods of Caroline divinity suggests that the new directions within the Anglican theology of justification may have arisen as a conscious reaction against that of the Westminster divines, the origins of these new directions may be found in the earlier Caroline period. Even in the later period, however, significant support for the older view persisted.

These observations are clearly of significance in relation to John Henry Newman's attempt to construct a *via media* doctrine of justification on the basis of the teachings of the later Caroline Divines, such as Bull and Taylor (see §33). Newman's own doctrine of justification, as expounded in the 1837 *Lectures on Justification*, is essentially coterminous with that of the later Caroline Divines just mentioned. However, Newman appears to appreciate that his own teaching on justification is at variance with some of the pre-Common-wealth divines. Thus Newman appeals to 'the three who have sometimes been considered the special lights of our later church, Hooker, Taylor and Barrow':[26] while he feels able to claim the support of the latter two for his own teaching, he is obliged to report that Hooker 'decides the contrary way, declaring not only for one special view of justification ... but that the opposite opinion is a virtual denial of gospel truth'.[27] This 'opposite opinion' bears a remarkable resemblance to the position carefully established by Newman himself. Furthermore, it is questionable, to say the least, whether Barrow may be cited as an antecedent of Newman's position, on account of his strong affinities with the earlier Caroline theology of justification: Newman merely cites Barrow to demonstrate the latter's awareness of the confusion and uncertainty concerning the terminology of justification, and his cautionary comments arising as a consequence;[28] this does not, however, inhibit Barrow from unequivocally affirming the earlier Anglican teaching of justification by imputed, rather than inherent, righteousness, and by faith, rather than by works.[29] Newman's claim to present an 'Anglican' theology of justification appears to involve the unwarranted restriction of 'Anglican' sources to the 'holy living' divines, with the total exclusion of several earlier generations of Anglican divines – men such as Andrewes, Beveridge, Davenant, Downham, Hooker, Jewel, Reynolds, Ussher and Whittaker. The case for the 'Anglican' provenance of Newman's *via media* doctrine of justification thus rests upon the teachings of a small, and unrepresentative, group of theologians operating over a period of a mere thirty or so years, which immediately followed the greatest discontinuity within English history – the period of the Commonwealth. It is therefore nothing less than absurd to regard certain divines of the Restoration period as in any way representing a classic statement of the essence of 'Anglican' thinking on justification, in that it represents an arbitrary historical positivism. Anglicanism cannot be defined with reference to the teachings of such a small group of theologians, operating over so short a period of time, contradicting a previously well-established tradition, and subject to considerable contemporary criticism. If any such group *could* be singled out in this manner, it is the group of *earlier* Anglican theologians, operating in the period immediately following the Elizabethan Settlement – for whom Hooker is generally regarded as spokesman.

We shall return to consider Newman's teaching later (§33). Our attention is now claimed by what is probably the most significant contribution of the English Reformation to Christendom: Puritanism.

§32 Puritanism: from the Old World to the New

The term 'Puritan' is notoriously difficult to define,[1] this difficulty unquestionably reflecting the fact that it was a term of stigmatisation used uncritically in a wide variety of social contexts over a long period of time. As early as 1565, Catholic exiles from Elizabethan England were complaining of the 'hot puritans of the new clergy',[2] and it is possible that Shakespeare's Malvolio (1600) exemplifies the stereotyped puritan of the new 'character' literature, particularly in the aftermath of the Marprelate Tracts. For the purposes of the present study, the term 'Puritanism' may be regarded as the English manifestation, especially during the period 1564–1640, of Reformed theology which laid particular emphasis upon both the experimental basis of faith and the divine sovereignty in election.[3] In this period, Puritans may be regarded as those members of the English national church who, although critical of its theology, church polity and liturgy, chose to remain within it; terms such as 'Brownist', 'Separatist' or 'Barrowist' were used to refer to those who, though criticising the same church for substantially the same reasons, did so from without its bounds.[4] Although some historians have suggested that Puritanism is the 'earlier and English form of that mutation from the Protestantism of the Reformation which on the Continent is called Pietism',[5] it must be emphasised that the Arminianism which is so characteristic a feature of Pietism is rejected by Puritan theologians in favour of the *decretum absolutum*. Indeed, the term is recorded as being used in 1622 to refer specifically to anti-Arminian elements.[6] More recently, the particular form of predestinarianism associated with Puritanism has been characterised as 'experimental predestinarianism',[7] thus capturing the twin elements of the characteristic Puritan understanding of justification. It is perfectly legitimate to suggest that perhaps the most important feature of Puritan spirituality – the quest for assurance – results from the tension inherent between the emphasis simultaneously placed upon an emotional searching for communion with God (unquestionably paralleling later Pietism in this respect) and upon the divine sovereignty in election.

The tension between Anglicanism and Puritanism led to the great exodus of pilgrim fathers from the old England to the new. The early American Puritans were refugees from an intolerant England. An old theology thus came to be planted in the New World, where it developed unhindered. The legacy of Puritanism is to be sought chiefly in American, where its influence upon the piety and culture of a new nation, with no indigenous theology or culture to oppose it, was incalculable. Just as no student of European history can neglect the Reformation, as no student of American history can neglect the Puritans, who shaped a nation in the image of their God.

One of the most important features of Puritan theologies of justification is the federal foundation upon which they are based. The concept of a covenant between God and man underlies the soteriology of the *via moderna* (§17), the young Luther (§§11, 20) and Reformed Orthodoxy (§24). It is the version of this federal theology initially associated with the Reformed theologian Heinrich Bullinger and subsequently with the Heidelberg theologians Zacharias Ursinus, Kaspar Olevianus and Girolamo Zanchius which appears to underlie that of Puritanism. The concept of a covenant between God and man, on the basis of which the justification of the latter may proceed, appears to have been introduced to the English Reformation by William Tyndale. Tyndale's covenant theology is only evident in his writings subsequent to 1530, and is probably best seen in the 1534 Genesis prologue:

> Seek, therefore, in the scripture, as thou readest it, chiefly and above all, the covenants made between God and us; that is to say, the law and commandments which God commandeth us to do; and then the mercy promised unto all them that submit themselves unto the law. For all the promises throughout the whole scripture do include a covenant: that is, God binding himself to fulfil that mercy unto thee only if thou wilt endeavour thyself to keep his laws.[8]

It must be pointed out, however, that the covenant theology which established itself within English Puritanism was significantly different from that of Tyndale: for example, Tyndale recognises but *one* covenant between God and man, whereas Reformed Orthodoxy and Puritanism recognised *two*. Tyndale's influence upon the theology of the English church appears to have been ephemeral: while martyrs had their uses, the later sixteenth century saw the recognition of an even greater need – a systematic exposition of the theological foundations of the English Reformation.

The introduction of the covenant concept into the English church appears to have been largely due to the influence of Bullinger, whose *Decades* were published in English translation in 1577, and subsequently commended by Archbishop Whitgift. In the same year, John Knewstub delivered a series of lectures in London, in which he expounded the soteriological benefits of the 'league' between God and man.[9] The first clear statement of the concept of the *double* covenant may be found in Dudley Fenner's highly influential *Theologia sacra* (1585), but passed into general circulation through William Perkins' *Armilla aurea* (1590). Although Perkins' theology is essentially Bezan, his piety is overwhelmingly Puritan, demonstrating the intense concern with casuistry and personal election so characteristic of Cambridge Puritanism at the time. The *Armilla*, based largely upon Beza's *Summa totius theologiae*, did much to promote the Bezan doctrines of election and limited atonement in the period before the Synod of Dort, and its perhaps most famous feature – the 'chart of salvation', resembling an early map of the London Underground[10] –

permitted those who found theologising difficult to follow the course of their election along well-established Bezan paths with the minimum of effort. Perkins declared that the outward means of election is the covenant, which is God's

contract with men concerning the obtaining life eternall upon a certain condition. This covenant consisteth of two parts: God's promise to man, man's promise to God. God's promise to man is that whereby he bindeth himself to man to be his God, if he perform the condition. Man's promise to God is that whereby he voweth his allegiance unto his Lord and to perform the condition betweene them.[11]

Following the Heidelberg theologians, he distinguishes between a covenant of works and a covenant of grace, this latter being 'that whereby God, freely promising Christ and his benefits, exacteth againe of man that he would by faith receive Christ and repent of his sinnes'.[12]

We shall return to consider the federal foundations of the Puritan soteriology later. A second aspect of this theology which claims our attention is the concept of 'temporary faith', intimately linked with the Puritan quest for assurance of election. Perkins' discussion of the question: how may I know that I am among the elect? exemplifies both the Puritan preoccupation with, and response to, this issue.[13] The earlier Reformed appeal to the present existence of faith as the basis of assurance was negated by the rise of the Bezan doctrine of limited atonement. The reprobate may seem to have a faith at every point identical with that of the elect, but it is merely a 'temporarie faith', which fails to apply the promises of God to the believer. The individual believer is therefore prevented from knowing whether his is a true or a temporary faith, and thus from knowing whether he is among the elect or reprobate. Perkins produces the following syllogism for troubled consciences:[14]

Everyone that beleeves is the childe of God.
But I doe beleeve.
Therefore I am the childe of God.

Unfortunately, as Perkins himself appears to have appreciated (in that he died in the conflict of a troubled conscience, uncertain as to whether he was among the elect), the similarity between the faith of the elect and reprobate excluded such an appeal as the basis of assurance. Similarly, Miles Mosse argued that the fact that the reprobate were able to recognise the divine mercy, and thus trust in the gospel promises, was to no avail, in that they were unable to be 'ingrafted into Christ'.[15] It is precisely this difficulty which led to the later shift in emphasis away from faith to *personal sanctification* as the basis of assurance. As Samuel Clarke put it: 'Kings may pardon traytours, but they cannot change their hearts; but Christ pardons none, but he makes them new creatures.'[16] Thus man has grounds for assurance in the stirrings of the new creature within him:

> As a woman that hath felt her childe stirre, concludes that she hath conceived, though she does not always feel it stirre; so if upon good grounds we have found God's grace and favour, by the powerful work of God upon our souls, we may be assured of spiritual life, although we find it not so sensibly at work in us at all times.[17]

This particular approach to the question may also be shown to have been common among Perkins' contemporaries. Thus William Bradshaw appealed to personal holiness as the proper ground of assurance; Richard Rogers argued that man could clinch his election by purity of heart: George Webb followed the earlier medieval tradition in suggesting that an earnest desire for godliness constituted reasonable grounds for assurance; John Dod even developed an existentialist approach paralleling Luther's concept of *Anfechtung* – only the elect *are* troubled in conscience concerning their election, the reprobate being exempt from any such anxiety.[18]

It is of interest to note that the Westminster Confession (1647), while explicitly following Beza in teaching limited atonement,[19] is somewhat vague concerning the pastoral consequence of such a teaching. Perkins' doctrine of temporary faith, by which the reprobate believe but are not saved, is passed over in discrete silence.[20] The Confession concedes that believers may have their assurance shaken,[21] but stipulates that it is the 'duty of every man to give all diligences to make his calling and election sure'.[22] *Si non es praedestinatus, fac ut praedestineris?*

In general, the English Puritans may be regarded as following Reformed Orthodoxy in their teaching on justification, particularly in relation to the doctrines of election and the imputation of the righteousness of Christ. The strongly anti-Arminian character of English Puritanism is best illustrated from the writings of John Owen, evident in his first work, *A Display of Arminianism*.[23] In this work, Owen reduced the Arminian teaching to two points: first, the precise object of Christ's death; second, the efficacy and end of his death.[24] The controversy was thus defined in terms of the identity of those on whose behalf Christ died, and what he merited or otherwise obtained on their behalf. Both these points were developed at greater length in *Salus electorum, sanguis Jesu* (1647). Although Owen displays the usual Puritan veneration for scripture, it is significant that this work is essentially a logical analysis of the Arminian doctrine of universal redemption. Owen argues that the Arminian proposition 'Christ died for all men' contains within itself the further proposition 'Christ died for nobody', in that no men are actually and effectively saved by his death. For Owen, it is beyond dispute that all men are not saved: therefore, if Christ died to save all men, he has failed in his mission – which is unthinkable.[25] For Owen, the Arminians subscribe to a doctrine of conditional redemption, so that God may be said to have given Christ to obtain peace, reconciliation and forgiveness of sins for all men, 'provided that they do believe'.[26] Thus the Arminians treat the 'blood of Christ'

as a medicine in a box, laid up for all that shall come to have any of it, and so applied now to one, then to the other, without any respect or difference, as though it should be intended no more for one than for another; so that although he hath obtained all the good that he hath purchased for us, yet it is left indifferent and uncertain whether it shall ever be ours or no.[27]

For Owen, 'salvation indeed is bestowed conditionally, but faith, which is the condition is absolutely procured'.[28]

Although Owen himself taught that the formal cause of justification was the imputation of the righteousness of Christ, the controversy surrounding Baxter's *Aphorisms of Justification* (1649) served to demonstrate the remarkable variety of opinions within Puritanism on this question. For Baxter himself, the formal cause of justification was the faith of the believing individual, imputed or reputed as righteousness on account of the righteousness of Christ.[29] Underlying this doctrine is a federal scheme characteristic of Puritanism, in which a distinction is drawn between the old and new covenants. According to Baxter, Christ has fulfilled the old covenant, and therefore made it possible for man to be justified on the basis of the somewhat more lenient terms of the new.[30] The righteousness of Christ in fulfilling the old covenant is thus the meritorious cause of justification, in that it is on account of this fulfilment that the faith of the believer may be the formal cause of justification under the new covenant. A similar teaching may be found in John Goodwin's *Imputatio fidei* and George Walker's *Defence*, although these two writers differed on the grounds on which man's faith could be treated as righteousness: for Walker, man's faith is reckoned as righteousness only because it apprehends Christ as its object,[31] whereas Goodwin argued that the remission of sin implied that the sinner was 'compleately and perfectly righteous',[32] and thus did not require the imputation of the righteousness of Christ. In many respects, the disagreements over the formal cause of justification within seventeenth-century Puritanism parallel those within contemporary Anglicanism (see §31). Nevertheless, it is clear that the most favoured view was unquestionably that adopted by John Owen and others – that the formal cause of justification was none other than the imputed righteousness of Christ,[33] thus aligning the English movement with continental Reformed Orthodoxy.

In the year 1633, the *Griffin* set sail from Holland for the New World, carrying with her two refugees from Laudian England: Thomas Hooker and John Cotton. Both were to prove of considerable significance in the establishment of Puritanism in New England. It was not, however, merely English Puritanism, but also the tensions within English Puritanism, which sailed with the *Griffin* to America, there to flare up once more with renewed vigour. Of particular significance was the issue of 'preparationism', to which we now turn.

We have already noted the importance of assurance as both a theological and a practical aspect of Puritan spirituality, and the tendency to treat the experimental aspects of the Christian life (such as faith or regeneration) as grounds of assurance. During his period as a preacher in the Surrey parish of Esher, Hooker was called to counsel one Mrs Joan Drake, who was convinced that she was beyond salvation. Although we have no record of Hooker's advice to her – which succeeded where that of others had failed – it is probable that it is incorporated into the 1629 sermon *Poor Doubting Christian drawne unto Christ.*[34] In this sermon, Hooker rejected the experimental basis of assurance:

A man's faith may be somewhat strong, when his feeling is nothing at all. David was justified and sanctified, and yet wanted this joy; and so Job rested upon God, when he had but little feeling ... Therefore away with your feeling, and go to the promise.[35]

Having rejected experience as the foundation and criterion of assurance, Hooker substituted the process of preparation in its place. It is within man's natural powers to be sufficiently contrite to permit God to justify him: 'when the heart is fitted and prepared, the Lord Jesus comes immediately into it'.[36] The absence of Christian experience is therefore of secondary importance in relation to the matter of assurance: developing an argument which parallels the federal theology of the *via moderna* (see §§7, 11, 17), Hooker argues that, once man has satisfied the minimum precondition for justification, he may rely upon God's faithfulness to his promises of mercy to ensure his subsequent justification and assurance of the same. Man's preparation for justification (the 'fitting of the sinner for his being in Christ'), in which the heart is 'fitted and prepared for Christ', thus constitutes the grounds of assurance.

A similar understanding of the relation of man's preparation for grace and his assurance of the same may be found in the early writings of John Cotton. In an early discussion of Revelation 3.20, he argued that conversion consists of an act of God, knocking at the door of man's heart, followed by an act of man, opening the door in order that God may enter.[37] Once man has performed this necessary act, he may rest assured that God will do the rest – which he, and only he, may do. In an intriguing exposition of Isaiah 40.3–4, he declares: 'if we smooth the way for him, then he will come into our hearts'.[38] Before his departure from England, however, Cotton's theology appears to have undergone a significant alteration. Prior to this point, Cotton and Hooker had assumed that man was naturally capable of preparing himself for justification (once more, it is necessary to point out the similarity with the soteriology of the *via moderna* on this point). But what if man's depravity was such that he could not prepare himself? In a development which parallels that of Luther over the period 1513–16, Cotton appears to have arrived at the insight that there is no saving preparation for grace prior to union with Christ: Christ is offered in a promise of free grace without any previous gracious qualification stipulated.[39] In other words, man cannot turn to God of his own volition: he requires God to take hold of him. Christ is given to the sinner upon the basis of an absolute, rather than a conditional, promise.[40] As a result, Cotton makes faith itself the basis of man's assurance, rather than preparation or sanctification. Cotton's rejection of sanctification as the basis of assurance was based upon his conviction that this was to revert to the covenant of works from the covenant of grace. Unfortunately for him, his views appear to have been misunderstood by some of his more intimate circle, most notably by Mrs Anne Hutchinson. Prior to her demise at the hands of the Indians in late 1643, Mrs Hutchinson suggested that every minister in Massachusetts Bay – with the exception of Cotton – was preaching nothing more and nothing less than a covenant of works.[41] The resulting controversy did not seriously damage his reputation. More significant, however, was his evasion of the crucial question which Hooker had addressed so directly: although Cotton implies that the believer knows that he has faith, he has nothing to say concerning how that faith may be obtained in the first place.

The controversy over 'the heart prepared' is of importance in a number of respects, particularly as it indicates the manner in which Puritan thinking on justification and assurance were related. Although Hooker and Cotton adopt very different theologies of justification (the former asserting the activity, the latter the passivity, of man prior to his justification), they share a common desire to establish the grounds of assurance within the context of that theology. It is therefore of importance to note that the grounds of assurance are the consequence of a prior understanding of the mode in which man is justified.

The later seventeenth and early eighteenth century saw New England Puritanism in decline.[42] The emphasis upon human impotence in the face of the divine omnipotence, a cornerstone of mainstream Puritan thought, tended to induce religious paralysis rather than renewal. As a consequence, subsequent generations of New Englanders were largely unconverted, obliging the churches to introduce the 'Half-Way Covenant', by which baptised persons of moral character would be treated as church members, save in certain respects.[43] The emphasis on the 'means of grace' – apparently peculiar to New England – permitted pastors to admit the unregenerate to church services on the basis of the principle that the public reading of the Bible, the preaching of the Word (and, in the Stoddardean system, the attending of the Lord's Supper) were means by which divine grace could be bestowed upon man.

This situation was radically altered through the 'Great Awakening', particularly associated with Jonathan Edwards.[44] In 1734, Edwards preached a series of sermons on the theme of 'justification by faith'.[45] Although these sermons contained nothing which could be described as radical innovations, the earnestness with which they were preached appears to have proved decisive in achieving their astonishing and celebrated effects. The intense emphasis placed by Edwards and others upon the need for spiritual rebirth was such that it became the criterion of church membership, thus ensuring the demise of the Half-Way Covenant.

The Great Awakening was based upon a covenant theology similar to that which had long been accepted in New England. God is understood to have entered into an agreement with man, by which he promised to pardon those who have faith in him, upon condition that man promises to work towards his sanctification. Edwards' discussion of the covenant of grace parallels that of Reformed Orthodoxy: God has made a covenant of redemption with Christ from all eternity, by which man would be redeemed, and the covenant of grace is the temporal manifestation of this eternal covenant.[46] Just as the imputation of the sin of Adam to his posterity is the consequence of his being the federal representative of all mankind in the covenant of works,[47] so the imputation of the righteousness of Christ to the elect is the consequence of his being their federal representative in the covenant of redemption, actualised in the covenant of grace.[48]

Edwards' somewhat traditional presentation of the federal basis of justification was developed and modified by his followers. Joseph Bellamy modified the Bezan foundations of the 'New England Theology'[49] by following Grotius in insisting that Christ's sufferings were a penal example stipulated by God as the moral governor of the universe, rather than a satisfaction rendered to God as the offended party. Samuel Hopkins explicitly rejected the 'Old Calvinist' emphasis upon the 'means of grace' – the principle upon which the Half-Way Covenant was based – although his chief contribution to the development of the movement was his understanding of the positive rôle of sin within the economy of salvation.[50]

Of particular significance was the rise of federal Arminianism within New England Puritanism. Recognising that the federal condition required of man for justification was faith (which the 'Old Calvinists' regarded as a divine gift to man), the Arminians regarded faith as a condition, equivalent to obedience, capable of being met by all men. In many respects, the Arminian party within the Puritan movement may be regarded as the direct equivalent of European Pietism, the one significant difference between Puritanism and Pietism (the doctrine of election) having been abandoned. Indeed, there are excellent grounds for suggesting a direct link between the two movements through the correspondence between Cotton Mather and the Halle Pietists.[51] The Arminians thus followed the 'Old Calvinists' in relation to the principle of the 'means of grace': grace was understood to be available to all men, particularly through 'means' such as reading the Bible, attending public worship and hearing the proclamation of the Word. As Jonathan Mayhew stated this principle: 'Tho' God is omnipotent, yet he seldom or never works wholly without means.'[52] The Arminians thus sided with the 'Old Calvinists' over the question of unregenerate church membership, proclaiming the universality of grace:

The Gospel takes no Notice of different Kinds or Sorts of Grace – Sorts of Grace specifically different, – one of which may be call'd *special* and the other not so; – one of which, from the peculiar and distinguishing Nature of it, shall prove converting and saving, and the other not.[53]

The emphasis upon the necessity of both faith and works in justification was usually justified with reference to the need to harmonise the opinions of Paul and James,[54] with both faith and works being understood 'as the *gracious Terms* and *Conditions*, appointed by the Redeemer, without which we shall not be *pardon'd* and *accepted*'.[55]

Although the effects of the Great Awakening in New England were to extend far beyond the purely religious sphere, the revival in preaching and intense interest in personal conversion and religious experience thus resulted in a number of differences on the question of justification becoming evident within New England Puritanism, in many respects paralleling similar developments within continental Protestant theology.

It is now necessary to return to England in order to consider one of the most significant discussions of the doctrine of justification to emerge within the Anglican church: John Henry Newman's *Lectures on Justification*.

§33 John Henry Newman's *Lectures on Justification*

As noted in §31, the Restoration of Charles II in 1660 appears to have been the occasion for the introduction of a new Anglican theology of justification, which asserted the positive rôle of inherent righteousness in justification, with faith being understood as a human work. If these later Anglican divines believed in justification *sola fide*, it was in the sense that faith justifies *in its own particular manner*. These features of the later Caroline understanding of justification were emphasised by the 'High Churchmen'[1] of the later eighteenth century in their polemic against the possibility that their Evangelical counterparts might cause the faithful to become complacent or negligent of good works through their preaching of the doctrine of justification *sola fide*. The nineteenth century saw the theological differences between High Churchmen and Evangelicals on this matter fairly well established, and not the subject of major controversy. Indeed, both parties to the debate emphasised the need for personal holiness as a result of justification, showing a remarkable uniformity in their respective teachings on piety. It is a fact which is often overlooked, that many Evangelicals – such as C. R. Sumner –

followed the early stages of the Oxford Movement with great sympathy.

This relative calm was shattered through the publication (1834–7) of the *Remains* of Alexander Knox, a lay theologian of some considerable talent. The *Remains* included his 1810 essay *On Justification*,[2] in which Knox argued that the Church of England, far from teaching a doctrine of *forensic* justification in her Homilies and Articles, was actually committed to a doctrine of *moral* justification. 'In the judgement of the Church of England justification by faith contains in it the vitalisation which *vera et viva fides* (true and lively faith) produces in the subject; as well as the reputation of righteousness, which follows *coram Deo* (before God).'[3] Noting Cranmer's frequent references to patristic writers in the *Homily of Salvation*, and the failure of the church historian Joseph Milner to demonstrate that such writers taught a forensic doctrine of justification, Knox suggested that the patristic consensus favoured a doctrine of moral justification.[4] The editor of Knox's *Remains*, John Henry Newman, subsequently (1837) delivered a course of lectures at Oxford in which he defended and enlarged upon Knox's essay of 1810. It is with these *Lectures on Justification*, easily the most significant theological writing to emerge from the Oxford Movement, that we are concerned in the present section. In these lectures, Newman defined what he took to be a *via media* understanding of justification, which allowed an authentically *Anglican* concept of justification to be defended in the face of the distortions of both Protestantism and Roman Catholicism.[5] Newman thus declared his intention to 'build up a system of theology out of the Anglican divines', and indicated that the lectures were a 'tentative inquiry' towards that end.[6]

Newman's theology of justification rests primarily upon an historical analysis of the doctrines of justification associated with Luther (and to a much lesser extent, with Melanchthon), with Roman Catholic theologians such as Bellarmine and Vásquez, and with the Caroline Divines. It is therefore of the utmost importance to appreciate that in every case, and supremely in the case of Luther himself, Newman's historico-theological analysis appears to be seriously and irredeemably inaccurate. In other words, Newman's construction of a *via media* doctrine of justification appears to rest upon a fallacious interpretation of both the extremes to which he was opposed, as well as of the Caroline divinity of the seventeenth century, which he regarded as a prototype of his own position. We shall develop these criticisms at the appropriate point in the present section.

The essential feature of Newman's understanding of the nature of justification is his insistence upon the real presence of the Trinity within the soul of the justified believer, conceived in broadly realist terms which undoubtedly reflect his interest in and positive evaluation of the Greek fathers, such as Athanasius.[7] It is this understanding of the nature of justification which underlies the most difficult stanza of his most famous hymn:

> And that a higher gift than grace,
> Should flesh and blood refine;
> God's presence and his very self,
> And essence all-divine.[8]

It is God himself, the 'essence all-divine', who dwells within and thus 'refines' sinful man, in the process of justification. '*This* is to be justified, to receive the Divine Presence within us, and be made a Temple of the Holy Ghost.'[9] Justification thus refers to a present reality, the 'indwelling in us of God the Father and the Word Incarnate through the Holy Ghost'.[10] Although this divine presence is to be understood in Trinitarian terms, Newman makes it clear that it is most appropriately understood as the presence of Christ himself. 'If to justify be to impart a certain inward token of our personal redemption, and if the presence of God within us is such a token, our justification must consist in God's coming to us and dwelling in us.'[11] This real presence of the Trinity within the soul of the believer has certain associated and necessary consequences, which Newman identifies as being *counted righteous* and being *made righteous*. Both justification and sanctification are bestowed simultaneously with the gift of the divine presence within the souls of the justified. In other words, Newman understands the primary and fundamental sense of the term 'justification' to be the indwelling of the Trinity within the souls of the believer, which has as its necessary consequence those aspects of his conversion which are traditionally (although Newman feels *inappropriately*) termed 'justification' (that is, being counted as righteous) and 'sanctification' (that is, being made righteous).[12] This is made clear in what is probably the most important passage in the *Lectures*:

We now may see what the connection really is between justification and renewal. They are both included in that one great gift of God, the indwelling of Christ in the Christian soul. That dwelling is *ipso facto* our sanctification and justification, as its necessary results. It is the divine presence which justifies us, not faith, as say the Protestant schools, not renewal, as say the Roman. The word of justification is the substantive and living Word of God, entering the soul, illuminating and cleansing it, as fire brightens and purifies material substances. He who justifies also sanctifies, because it is He. The first blessing runs into the second as its necessary limit; and the second being rejected, carries away with it the first. And the one cannot be separated from the other except in idea, unless the sun's rays can be separated from the sun, or the power of purifying from fire or water.[13]

Justification is therefore *notionally distinct* from sanctification, although inseparable from it, in that they are both aspects of one and the same thing – the indwelling of the Holy Trinity within the soul of the believer. This distinction between justification and renewal allows Newman to maintain a proleptic relation between them: 'Justification is at first what renewal could but be at last; and therefore is by no means a mere result or consequence of renewal, but a real, though not a separate act of God's mercy.'[14] The distinction between justification and sanctification is thus 'purely mental',[15] relating to the single act of divine mercy, and does not necessitate the division of that act itself.

In his tenth lecture, Newman turns his attention to the vexed question of the precise rôle of faith in justification. Newman rejects a purely fiduciary interpretation of faith as excluding other Christian virtues, such as love or obedience. Whilst Newman would not go so far as to state 'that there is no such thing as a trusting in Christ's mercy for salvation, and a comfort resulting from it',[16] he insists that this is inadequate to characterise true Christian faith. The evil and good alike can trust in God's mercy, whereas the good and the evil are distinguished on account of the former's charity, love and obedience. The Protestant understanding of faith, as Newman perceives it, is thus not so much wrong, as incomplete.[17] Following Bull and Taylor (see §31), Newman argues that faith and works must both be said to justify, although in different manners.[18] Thus the fact that all acknowledge that it is Christ who justifies does not prevent the simultaneous assertion that faith justifies, nor does the fact that faith justifies exclude works from justifying:

It seems then, that whereas faith on our part fitly corresponds, or is the correlative, as it is called, to grace on God's part, sacraments are but the manifestation of grace, and good works are but the manifestation of faith; so that, whether we say we are justified by faith, or by works or by sacraments, all these but mean this one doctrine, that we are justified by grace, which is given through sacraments, impetrated by faith, manifested in works.[19]

The importance of Newman's *Lectures* lies in their representing an attempt to construct an authentically *Anglican* doctrine of justification representing the *via media* between Protestantism and Roman Catholicism, on the basis of the following understanding of the spectrum of theologies of justification:[20]

Luther	Gerhard	Melanchthon	*Via Media*	Pighius	Bellarmine	Vasquez

←――――――――――――――――――――― ――――――――――――――――――――→

Protestant   Roman Catholic

This evaluation is essentially correct. It may, however, be noted that Newman tends to direct his invective chiefly against the Protestant, rather than the Roman Catholic region, of this spectrum, and that the Protestant divines whom he singles out for discussion are Lutheran, rather than Reformed. In view of the fact that Newman was addressing himself to the contemporary situation within the Church of England in the context of the predominantly Protestant theological climate of England, it is understandable that he should wish to direct particular attention to his Protestant opponents. His failure to deal at any length with Reformed theologians is, however, unjustified: Lutheranism exerted a minimal influence over English theology since 1600,[21] although a Melanchthonian influence upon the Homilies and Articles may be conceded. From 1600 onwards, the main Protestant influence upon English theology was *Reformed*, rather than *Lutheran* – in other words, due to Calvin and Beza (in an equally great variety of manners and refractions), rather than Luther. Newman, presumably on account of the intimate association between Luther and the doctrines of justification, appears to assume unconsciously that contemporary Protestant opinions on this matter were essentially those of Luther himself – which is clearly not the case.

The construction of the *via media* upon dialectical principles inevitably means that its validity is dependent upon the accuracy with which the extremes are represented and analysed. Furthermore, as Newman appears to regard the Caroline Divines as precursors or representatives of the *via media*, it will be clear that the accuracy of his understanding of their position is crucial in ascertaining the 'Anglican' character of the resulting doctrine. In what follows, we propose to examine the accuracy of Newman's presentation of two of the three elements upon whose basis the *via media* is constructed: Luther and the Caroline Divines.

1. Luther[22]

Newman's critique of Luther in the *Lectures* appears to rest upon the quite fallacious assumption that the Reformer regards faith as a human work. His criticism of Luther for his insistence upon the fiduciary aspects of faith, while neglecting hope, love and obedience, reflects his basic conviction that Luther singled out the *human activity of trust in God* as the defining characteristic of justifying faith. This criticism is inept.[23] For Luther, man is passive towards his justification; he takes no part in his own justification, which is totally the work of God. Faith itself, however it may be defined, is a work of God within man. God operates upon man in justification, and man contributes nothing to the process apart from being the inert material upon which God operates – a view which, as noted earlier (§30), coincides with that of Richard Hooker.[24] The misunderstanding of Luther which Newman reproduces coincides with that of George Bull (see §31), and it appears that Newman merely projected the Caroline caricature of Luther on to what little of the Reformer he troubled to read. Newman understood Luther to teach that man is *active* in justification, and that the nature of this human activity is defined in terms of fiduciary apprehension of the benefits of Christ, without reference to such *desiderata* as hope, love and obedience. In fact, of course, Luther rarely uses the phrase *sola fide*, and where he does use it, it is clear that the reference is to *fides Christi* – a *Christological* concept, with the emphasis placed upon the real and redeeming presence of Christ in the believer, rather than the faith which procured this in the first place. The 1521 treatise *Rationis Latomianae confutatio* makes it clear that *Christ and faith* are *given simultaneously* to the sinner in his justification. The distinguishing mark of faith is not its 'fiduciary' character – and how influential Newman's caricature has become in English-speaking circles! – but the real and redeeming presence of Christ in the soul of the believer. For Luther, *fides Christi*, upon the basis of which alone justification takes place, is the real presence of Christ in the believer, brought about by the gracious working of the Holy Spirit – in fact, something remarkably close to Newman's own position. Luther does not understand 'justification by faith' to mean that man puts his trust in God, and is justified on that account: indeed, such an understanding of the phrase was rigorously excluded by the confessional material of both the Lutheran and Reformed churches – rather, it means that God bestows upon that man faith and grace, without his cooperation, effecting within him the real and redeeming presence of Christ as the 'righteousness of God' within him, and justifying him on *this* account. In effect, the phrase *sola fide* is merely a convenient statement of the justification of man upon Christological grounds without his cooperation. Luther does not understand the 'righteousness of God' to be some impersonal attribute of God fictitiously ascribed to man – it is none other than Christ himself. 'The Christ who is grasped by faith and lives in the heart of the true Christian righteousness, on account of which God counts us righteous, and grants us eternal life.'[25] Similar statements are made frequently in the course of the work from which this citation is taken. Newman's own statement concerning this point should be compared with this: 'This indwelling [of the divine presence] accurately answers . . . to what the righteousness which justifies has already been shown to consist in.'[26] These statements clearly presuppose precisely the same understanding of the basis and nature of justification. Luther's statement noted immediately above is, however, taken from the 1535 Galatians commentary, from which most of Newman's citations from Luther are drawn. Why did Newman not notice it, or the many others in the same work which express substantially the same idea? It seems to us that Newman did not read Luther at first hand. If this conclusion can be shown to be false, then, reluctantly, we are forced to draw the more serious conclusion that Newman deliberately misrepresents Luther. We shall indicate the grounds for this suggestion in what follows.

In his discussion of the relation between faith and works, Newman takes the remarkable step of citing Luther in support of his own opinion that justification is to be ascribed to 'believing deeds' (that is, both faith and works, as taught by Bull and Taylor). Newman prefaces his citation of Luther on this point with the caustic remark that this opinion might appear unusual, coming from Luther, but that the Reformer was obliged to concede this point 'in consequence of the stress of texts urged against him'.[27] He then quotes, in English translation, Luther's comments on Galatians 3.10 as they appear in the 1535 Galatians commentary:

'It is usual with us', he says, 'to view faith, sometimes apart from its work, sometimes with it. For as an artist speaks variously of his materials, and a gardener of a tree, as in bearing or not, so also the Holy Ghost speaks variously in Scripture concerning faith; at one time of what may be called abstract faith, faith as such: at another of concrete faith, faith in composition, or embodied. Faith as such, or abstract, is meant when Scripture speaks of justification, as such, or of the justified (Vid. Rom. and Gal.) But when it speaks of rewards and works, then it speaks of faith in composition, concrete or embodied. For instance: 'Faith which worketh by love'; 'This do and thou shalt live'; 'If thou wilt enter into life, keep the commandments'; 'Whoso doeth these things, shall live in them'; 'Cease to do evil, learn to do well.' In these and similar texts, which occur without number, in which mention is made of doing, believing doings are always meant; as, when it says, 'This do, and thou shalt live', it means, 'First see that thou art believing, that thy reason is right and thy will good, that thou hast faith in Christ; that being secured, work.' Then he proceeds:– 'How is it wonderful, that to that embodied faith, that is, faith working, as was Abel's, in other words, to believing works, are annexed merits and rewards? Why should not Scripture speak thus variously of faith, considering it so speaks even of Christ, God and man; sometimes of His entire person, sometimes of one or other of His two natures, the Divine or human? When it speaks of one or other of these, it speaks of Christ in the abstract; when of the Divine made one with the human in the one person, of Christ as if in composition and incarnate. There is a well-known rule in the schools concerning the 'communicatio idiomatum', when the attributes of His divinity are ascribed to His humanity, as is frequent in Scripture; for instance, in Luke ii. the Angel calls the infant born of the Virgin Mary, 'the Saviour' of men, and 'the Lord' both of Angels and men, and in the preceding chapter, 'the Son of God'. Hence I may say with literal truth, That Infant who is lying in a manger and in the Virgin's bosom, created heaven and earth, and is the Lord of Angels. . . . As it is truly said, Jesus the Son of Mary created all things, so is justification ascribed to faith incarnate or to believing deeds.'[28]

As it stands, this citation is quite astonishing, in that the final sentence appears to state unequivocally the principle of justification by 'believing deeds' – an excellent description of the teaching both of Newman and certain later Caroline Divines. The argument of the passage is clear, if not entirely persuasive: just as it is possible to employ the standard principle of the communication of attributes to Christ, so that attributes of his divinity may be applied to his humanity, so justification may be ascribed to believing deeds. The essential point which Newman wishes us to grasp is that even Luther is obliged to concede a positive rôle for works in justification.

Astonishment, however, gives way to intense irritation when the sections of this passage which have been omitted are considered. Thus the final dramatic sentence of this citation is preceded by four periods, suggesting that a sentence or portion of a sentence irrelevant for Newman's purposes, but not significant in determining the meaning of the passage, has been omitted. In view of the great length of the citation up to this point, this might appear quite unnecessary: omission of portions of previous sentences would have done little detrimental to the sense of the passage. Why this verbal economy at this stage? In fact, Newman has omitted not a portion of a sentence, or still a single, or even a couple of sentences. An *entire section* has been omitted, which so qualifies the final sentence as to exclude Newman's interpretation of it. The omitted section is so long that we ourselves have been forced to omit the list of scriptural citations given by Luther, indicated by three periods. The section which Newman chose to omit is here reproduced, with the parts Newman did include printed in italics:

That Infant who is lying in a manger and the Virgin's bosom, created heaven and earth, and is the Lord of Angels. I am indeed speaking about a man here. But 'man' in this proposition is obviously a new term, and, as the sophists say, stands for the divinity; that is, this God who became man created all things. Here creation is attributed to the divinity alone, since the humanity does not create. Nevertheless, it is correct to say that 'the man created', because the divinity, which alone creates, is incarnate with the humanity, and therefore the humanity participates in the attributes of both predicates ... Therefore the meaning of the passage: 'This do, and thou shalt live', is, 'You will live on account of this faithful doing; this doing will give you life solely on account of faith.' Thus justification belongs to faith alone, just as creation belongs to the divinity. *As it is truly said, Jesus the Son of Mary created all things, so is justification ascribed to faith incarnate or to believing deeds.*[29]

The significance of the omitted section lies in the fact that it unequivocally qualifies the final sentence as a statement of the principle that justification is by faith alone, and indicates that scriptural passages which indicate the necessary implication of works in salvation are to be understood primarily and fundamentally as an assertion of the necessity of *faith*. The statement 'Jesus the Son of Mary created all things' is a statement that God alone is creator, just as the statement 'Justification is ascribed to ... believing deeds' remains a statement that faith alone justifies.

We are thus confronted with two possibilities. Either Newman encountered this passage at second hand, already in its mutilated form; or else he deliberately chose to omit a section on account of its evident significance. We incline towards the former, not merely out of respect for Newman, but on account of a further consideration: where Newman cites Luther elsewhere in Latin, it frequently appears as a garbled version of the original. For example, he cites Luther's 'paradox of justification' as follows: sola fides, non fides formata charitate, iustificat: fides justificat sine et ante charitem.[30] The closest approximation to this we have been able to find is: sola fide, non fide formata charitate iustificat ... haec fides sine et ante charitatem iustificat.[31] As Newman normally cites his sources with some care, it is probable that his references derive from an inaccurate secondary source, accurately cited.

It will be clear that Newman has failed to grasp the essence of Luther's understanding of justification, and to appreciate the similarities between his own position and that of the Reformer. A similar critique could be made of his totally inadequate references to Calvin. Had Newman studied Calvin seriously, he could hardly have failed to notice the remarkable similarities between them on the nature of justification. Thus Calvin regards both justification and sanctification as notionally distinct yet inseparable aspects of the believer's incorporation into Christ through the Holy Spirit in a mystical union. 'Christ, when he enlightens us with faith by the power of the Spirit, simultaneously grafts us into his body, that we may become partakers of all his benefits.'[32] This corresponds exactly to Newman's view, that justification and renewal 'are both included in that one great gift of God, the indwelling of Christ in the Christian soul'.[33] The similarity between Newman and Calvin may arise through their common respect for, and use of, the works of Athanasius. Newman's purely superficial engagement with the thought of the Reformation prevents him from even observing, let alone evaluating, their evident similarity on the Christological conception of justification.

2 The Caroline Divines

As we noted in §31, a distinction may be drawn between the pre-Commonwealth divines up to 1640, and certain of the divines writing in the post-Restoration period. The latter were essentially unanimous in asserting that the formal cause of justification was imputed, rather than inherent, righteousness, and excluded the idea of justification by 'believing deeds'. Newman, however, develops a theology of justification which corresponds, in many respects, to that of certain of the post-Restoration divines, such as Bull and Taylor. As we indicated in §31, this view by no means represented the unanimous, and probably not even the *majority*, opinion within contemporary Anglicanism. Yet Newman appears to suggest that this understanding of the formal cause of justification is characteristic of Anglicanism, and may be taken to define the *via media* between Protestant and Roman Catholic. Put crudely, but nonetheless accurately, Newman appears to believe that Protestants taught that man was justified on account of faith (which, as we have seen, is an Arminian, rather than an Orthodox view) and that Roman Catholics taught that man was justified on account of his works or renewal – and therefore that the *via media* consisted in the affirmation that man is justified on account of both faith and works. This view corresponds with that of the 'holy living' school within later Caroline divinity, which appears to establish the 'Anglican' character of this mediating doctrine. However, as we have seen, the discontinuity within Anglicanism over the period 1550–1700 on precisely this point is sufficient to negate any attempt to characterise such a position as 'Anglican'.

It is interesting to consider, in concluding, Newman's understanding of the Roman Catholic position on justification. Newman nowhere attempts a detailed analysis of the teaching of Bellarmine and Vásquez, forcing us to base our tentative conclusions upon the few passing statements made in the *Lectures* concerning Roman Catholicism in general. Newman clearly believes the Roman Catholic teaching to be that man is justified on account of his renewal.[34] Like many contemporary Evangelicals, Newman appears to have assumed that the notion of factitive justification implies that the analytic divine verdict of justification is based upon the inherent righteousness of the individual, *achieved through moral renewal* – whereas the reference is, of course, to the *infusion* of *divine* righteousness which is the *cause* of subsequent moral renewal, and is not identical with that renewal itself. The evidence contained within the body of the *Lectures* is suggestive, but not conclusive, that Newman simply did not understand the Tridentine doctrine of justification.

There is thus every reason to state that Newman's construction of a *via media* doctrine of justification unquestionably rests upon an historico-theological analysis of the dialectic between Protestantism and Roman Catholicism which is seriously inaccurate in the case of Luther, and may well be, although conclusive evidence may never be forthcoming, equally inaccurate in the case of Roman Catholicism. The demonstration of a serious misrepresentation of one extreme is, however, adequate, given Newman's dialectical construction of the *via media*, to invalidate its results. Furthermore, there are excellent reasons for calling into question the 'Anglican' character and provenance of the *via media* which Newman thus constructs. This is not necessarily to say that a *via media* cannot be constructed, although its possibility is remote, to say the least; rather, it is to say that, if such a possibility is conceded, Newman failed in his attempt to construct one.

The publication of *Tract 90* on 27 February 1841 effectively ended Newman's usefulness to the Oxford Movement. The purpose of the *Tract* was to demonstrate that the Thirty-Nine Articles, 'the offspring of an uncatholic age, are, through God's good providence, to say the least, not uncatholic, and may be subscribed to by those who aim at being Catholic in heart and doctrine'.[35] For many of its readers, however, the *Tract* merely confirmed what they had long suspected – that Newman was closer to Rome than to Canterbury on most issues of substance. In fact, the *Tract* merely restates, rather than develops, the views on justification expressed in the *Lectures*, and the greatest offence appears to have been caused by the passages relating to purgatory (Article 22) and the sacrifice of the mass (Article 31). The publication of the *Tract*, however, marked the beginning of the decline of the Oxford Movement's interest in justification as other, more pressing, theological considerations came to the fore. As with the Reformation, the ecclesiological was never far behind the soteriological question. The Tractarian interest in justification as a theological issue appears to have been entirely due to Newman's personal influence, and it declined accordingly during the remainder of the nineteenth century, never to be revived.[36]

In the present section, we have been concerned with Newman's conception of the *via media* on justification, which it has proved necessary to reject as untenable. The *dialectical* approach to the *via media* adopted by Newman is immediately invalidated if the thesis and antithesis are misunderstood or misrepresented. Furthermore, it will be clear that, in the case of Newman's *Lectures on Justification*, the *via media* thus established is identified with reference to the later Caroline Divines, which Newman regarded as encapsulating the essence of Anglicanism, at least in this respect. This presupposition must be considered to represent an arbitrary historical positivism, for the following reasons. First, Anglicanism cannot be defined with reference to what such a small group of theologians, operating over so short a period of time, taught. Second, if any such group *can* be singled out, the first generation of Anglican theologians (including Cranmer, Jewel and Hooker) have a far greater claim to merit the distinction, rather than the later Caroline Divines. Third, as our analysis of the development of Anglican theology on justification in the seventeenth century indicated (see §31), the later divines of the period were associated with a doctrine of justification which marked a reversal of the accepted teaching of the earlier Caroline Divines, as well as that of the divines of the Elizabethan Settlement, concerning a crucial element of Newman's doctrine of justification (namely, the nature of justifying righteousness). Newman's appeal to the post-Restoration Caroline Divines as the embodiment of an 'Anglican' theology of justification must therefore be regarded as inept.

The fact that Newman's attempt to construct a *via media* doctrine of justification is irredeemably discredited does not, however, invalidate the general principle of such a mediating doctrine of justification. Clearly, if it were possible to establish, in the light of the best possible scholarship available, the leading characteristics of Protestant and Catholic theologies of justification, it should, in principle, be possible to construct a *via media* doctrine on the basis of a dialectical approach such as that employed by Newman. In the remainder of this section, we propose to demonstrate that this is an impossibility, on account of the *naïveté* of its historical and theological presuppositions.

To illustrate this point, let us consider how the essence of Protestant doctrines of justification might be determined. The simplest solution is to select a leading theologian of Protestant inclination, and establish with the utmost impartiality precisely what his teaching on justification is.[37] Simple solutions, however, are notoriously seductive. How, it may reasonably be asked, may such a theologian be selected in the first place? For example, should that theologian be Lutheran or Reformed? And should he be selected from the early sixteenth, or the later seventeenth, century? In effect, the very process of selection itself dictates the resulting profile of a 'typically Protestant' theology of justification. This conclusion is given added weight through the observation that Protestant doctrines of justification have been subject to a process of continual modification from the time of the Reformation onwards, with the result that what may have been 'typical' of Lutheranism in 1525 was not so in 1725. Furthermore, there is a serious theological problem associated with establishing whether movements such as Pietism or the *Aufklärung* can be regarded as Protestant in their teachings on justification. The direct appeal to the confessional material of Protestantism (such as the Formula of Concord) is also of questionable value, as it is not clear what force such material has today. In general, it may be pointed out that the spirit of free inquiry and emphasis upon scripture, rather than tradition, which is so characteristic of Protestantism militates against the historical approach to the *via media*.

In the case of Catholicism, it might be thought that the emphasis upon tradition, coupled with the authority of the *magisterium* in matters of doctrine, facilitates the establishment of the essence of its theology of justification. This is clearly not, however, the case. We have already drawn attention to the fact that Trent legitimated a *range* of theologies of justification, rather than a single, well-defined, doctrine of justification (see §28). Furthermore, the post-Tridentine debates on justification, culminating in the disputes *de auxiliis* (see

§29), indicate the variety of opinions subsequently associated with Catholic theologians.[38] The fact that neo-Thomist and Molinist alike may claim to represent Catholic thinking on justification indicates the difficulty in identifying a *single, well-defined* doctrine of justification which is characteristic of Catholicism – yet the dialectical approach necessitates precisely such an identification.

Finally, it may be pointed out that the dialectical approach to the *via media* has a disquieting tendency to lead to a theology of justification which is already discredited – the 'Regensburg theology' of 1541 (see §25), rejected by Protestant and Catholic alike.[39]

An attempt to construct a *via media* theology of justification is thus not merely artificial, but rests upon unacceptable historical and theological presuppositions. If Protestant and Catholic held theologies of justification which were rigidly defined and mutually exclusive at points of importance, there would clearly be considerable value in attempting to mediate between the two. This is, however, evidently not the case. The fact that the Council of Trent legitimates a *range* of theologies of justification, and that this range is contiguous with certain Protestant theologies of justification at crucial points, suggests that the pursuit of the *via media* is one of the less significant of theological activities. The common heritage of Protestant and Catholic alike may be explored without reference to the obsolete concept of the *via media*.

9. The modern period

Introduction

Practically every period in human history since the time of the Italian Renaissance of the *Quattrocento* may lay at least some claim to having initiated the 'modern' period. For instance, Renaissance Italy may be regarded as having laid the foundations of modern political theory,[1] and may thus be regarded as marking the transition to the 'modern' understanding of this particular matter. Similarly, the theologians of the *via moderna* designated themselves as 'modern' in their rejection of the reality of universals.[2] In the case of the development of Christology, it is clear that the Enlightenment marks the opening of the 'modern' period.[3] The question thus arises: when may the transition to the 'modern' understanding of the theology of justification be deemed to have taken place?

The answer traditionally given to this question is that the modern discussion of the question dates from the period of the Reformation.[4] While it is certainly true that the Reformation marked an irreversible change in many aspects of man's self-understanding,[5] it is clear, not merely that the Reformers discussed the question of man's justification *coram Deo* within the same general framework as their medieval counterparts,[6] but also that there existed a substantial number of uncontroverted presuppositions relating to the doctrine – such as the presupposition of the necessity of the reconciliation of man to God, traditionally expressed in the dogma of original sin. The growing recognition of the medieval character of the Reformation in general[7] must be extended to include its theologies of justification. The theocentricity underlying Luther's so-called 'Copernican Revolution' was a well-established feature of certain schools of thought in the late medieval period,[8] and cannot be considered to represent a permanent universal alteration in theological outlook which parallels that attending the recognition of the heliocentricity of the solar system. The rise of anthropocentric theologies of justification within both the Lutheran and Reformed traditions in the late seventeenth century, apparently to attain a dominant position in the eighteenth and nineteenth centuries, effectively calls into question the suggestion that Luther's theocentricity can be deemed quintessentially 'modern'.

If there is a 'modern' period in the development of the doctrine of justification, that period must be regarded as having been initiated by the Enlightenment in England, France and Germany in the eighteenth century. It was this movement which called into question the presuppositions (such as the dogma of original sin) upon which theologies of justification, whether Protestant or Catholic, had until then been based, and which dictated the means by which such presuppositions might be defended. We therefore begin our discussion of the 'modern period' with an analysis of the significance of the Enlightenment for the development of the doctrine.

§34 The Enlightenment critique of Orthodox doctrines of justification

The origins of the Enlightenment critique of Orthodox doctrines of justification may be located in the new emphasis upon the autonomy of man as a moral agent so characteristic of the movement. The new optimism concerning the capacity of the natural human faculties to understand and master the world led to those moral and religious systems which called into question the autonomy of man being held in suspicion. The particular hostility demonstrated by the theologians and philosophers of the Enlightenment towards the Orthodox dogma of original sin was ultimately a rejection of the implied heteronomous conditioning and moral inadequacy of the individual. In that the Orthodox theology of justification – whether Lutheran, Reformed or Catholic – presupposed the essential natural alienation of the individual from God (in other words, that an individual enters the world already alienated from God, rather than that he becomes alienated from God through his subsequent actions), it will be evident that a serious challenge was posed to such theologies by the rise of the moral optimism and rationalism of the Enlightenment. In the present section, we are particularly concerned with the critique of Orthodox Protestant theologies of justification associated initially with English Deism, and subsequently with the German *Aufklärung*.[1]

The founder of English Deism is usually, although incorrectly, considered to be Edward Herbert, Lord Cherbury.[2] Deeply influenced by Bodinus' *Colloquium* of 1588, he subsequently published his highly influential treatise *De veritate religionis* (1624). This work was essentially an attack on empiricism, arguing for the existence of *notitiae communes* or *ideae innatae* within every man upon which a system of eudaemonistic ethics might be constructed.[3] The strongly religious orientation of Cherbury's thought is indicated by the central position occupied by the *quinque notitiae communes circa religionem*, given to all men by nature in such a manner that they could function as the basis of human moral action (and thence as the means by which eternal life might ultimately be gained), without the necessity of a special revelation. These *notitiae* were originally stated in the following form:

1. Esse Supremum aliquod Numen.
2. Istud Numen debere coli.
3. Probam facultatum conformationem praecipuam partem cultus divini semper habitam fuisse.
4. Vitia et scelera quaecumque expiari debere ex poenitentia.
5. Esse praemium vel poenam post hanc vitam.[4]

The third *notitia* immediately identifies the moral emphasis which distinguished Herbert even from Christian humanists, in that the real aim of religion is identified to be the promotion of morality. The fourth sets him apart from Orthodoxy in relation to the question of forgiveness (note how the term *scelera* is adopted in preference to *peccata*). Where Orthodoxy held that man is justified *per fidem propter Christum*, Herbert asserted that forgiveness takes place *propter poenitentiam*. In this, he is not merely adopting the characteristically Arminian doctrine of justification *propter fidem* (that is, that forgiveness is contingent upon a human, rather than a divine, act);[5] any reference to the implication of Christ in divine forgiveness is omitted.

The Stoicism evident in Herbert's concept of *notitia communes* is also evident in his concept of the self-determination of the will (αὐτεξουσία) which stands in diametrical opposition to even the most modest Augustinian view of the corruption or compromise of the human will through original sin (see §4). Such views were developed and modified in the later seventeenth century. Thus John Toland's *Christianity not Mysterious* rejects the view that human reason is corrupted through original sin to such an extent that it is unable to recognise the truths of the gospel.[6] Similarly, John Locke (upon whom Toland is clearly dependent) earlier rejected the idea of original sin as unworthy of God.[7] The man who is totally obedient to

God is the man who attains eternal life. Locke, however, concedes the weakness of human nature, and permits any deficiencies in human obedience to the law of God to be supplemented:

The rule therefore, of right, is the same that ever it was; the obligation to observe it is also the same: the difference between the law of works, and the law of faith, is only this: that the law of works makes no allowance for failing on any occasion ... But by the law of faith, faith is allowed to supply the defect of full obedience: and so the believers are admitted to life and immortality, as if they were righteous.[8]

Although Locke defines the *theological* element of faith to be belief that 'Jesus is the Messiah',[9] it must be emphasised that Locke insists upon the necessity of a *moral* element in faith. The theological element of faith is itself inadequate to justify, and must be supplemented with the moral element.[10] 'These two, faith and repentance, i.e., believing Jesus to be the Messiah, and a good life, are the indispensable conditions of the new covenant, to be performed by all those who would obtain eternal life.'[11] It is clear that Locke reduces the dogmatic content of Christianity to a single statement, in order to permit the believer to lead a moral life untroubled by intricate matters of doctrine.[12] Thus the work of Christ may be defined in terms of the 'great encouragement he brought to a virtuous and pious life'.[13]

The moralist understanding of the divine nature so characteristic of Latitudinarianism and the later Deism may be regarded as being substantiated by the theological method which Locke developed in his *Essay concerning Human Understanding* (1690).[14] The emphasis this essay laid upon the necessity of the universalisation of method had profound consequences for Anglican theological method in the eighteenth century, in that it lent weight to two significant developments. First, the Lockean insistence upon the necessity of demonstration in the establishment of positive knowledge paralleled the rise in interest in natural theology on the part of Anglican theologians at the time, with a concomitant decline in interest in the concept of supernatural revelation.[15] Second, the moralism so characteristic of seventeenth-century Anglicanism[16] became transformed into the rationalism of the eighteenth, assisted by the Lockean 'construction' of the concept of God by the projection of human moral values *ad infinitum*.

The basic features of Locke's epistemology may be summarised as follows: all knowledge, whether sensitive, intuitive or demonstrative, derives from experience.[17] Demonstrative knowledge, characterised by generality and certainty, must begin from and be based upon experience, as the abstract ideas which are linked in the mind are the result of the 'resolution' or 'abstraction' of the 'materials' given to the mind in experience.[18] The abstract ideas, upon which knowledge is based, are obtained through the analysis (Locke prefers the term 'decomposition') of the complexity of sentient states. On the basis of this assumption, Locke denies the existence of innate ideas, and innate speculative or moral principles. The theological significance of this empiricist presupposition lies in the fact that the existence of an innate idea of God is denied: 'though the knowledge of a God, be the most natural discovery of humane reason, yet the *idea of him*, is *not innate*'.[19]

The essential question which thus arises is the following: given that 'God' is not an innate idea, but one which can only be derived from experience, how can God's character be determined *empirically*?[20] Having established that there indeed exists 'an eternal, most powerful, and most knowing Being; which whether anyone will please to call God, it matters not',[21] Locke turns to the question of the character of this being. Having demonstrated that complex ideas are 'composed' by the association of simple ideas, Locke argues that the complex idea of 'God' is 'composed' by the association of certain simple ideas with the idea of *infinity*:

If we examine the *Idea* we have of the incomprehensible supreme Being, we shall find, that we come by it the same way; and that the complex *Ideas* we have both of God, and separate Spirits, are made up of the simple *Ideas* we receive from *Reflection*; *v.g.* having from what we experiment in our selves, got the *Ideas* of Existence and Duration; of Knowledge and Power; of Pleasure and Happiness; and of several other Qualities and Powers, which it is better to have than to be without; when we would frame an *Idea* the most suitable we can to the supreme Being, we enlarge every one of these with our *Idea* of Infinity; and so putting them together, make our complex *Idea of God*.[22]

For Locke, 'there is no *Idea* we attribute to God, bating Infinity, which is not also a part of our complex *Idea* of other Spirits'.[23] The concept of 'God' is therefore constructed through the mind's infinite enlargement of its ideas, received from sensation and reflection, of 'Qualities and Powers, which it is better to have than to be without'.

The egocentricity of Locke's account of experience thus inevitably leads to the moral character of God being constructed in terms of the moral value-judgements of the individual. If moral ideas were capable of being established demonstratively, on the basis of the analysis of experience, this difficulty could be avoided: however, Locke's statements on the grounds of morality are inconsistent.[24] The basic theological method employed by him in the *Essay* leads to the establishment of the moral character of God by the projection of human ideas of good, justice, and so forth, *ad infinitum* – and thus inevitably leads to the endorsement, rather than the critique, of human concepts of morality. In an age increasingly dominated by rationalism, it was inevitable that God should be deemed to act according to precisely such concepts, and be modelled upon the institution which was increasingly being recognised as the ultimate arbiter of justice – the state.

According to Thomas Hobbes, the state imposes certain restrictions upon man in order that he may benefit as a consequence. The ultimate reality to be reckoned with is the claim of the individual to self-preservation and happiness. As all men have a natural claim to all things, the only restraining factor which can be brought into operation to prevent universal war is the rational acceptance of certain self-imposed restrictions. The subjective right of the individual is therefore transposed into an objective right by a *translatio iuris*, by which each individual transfers to the state a portion of his individual rights.[25] In effect, the state may be regarded as representing the general will of the individuals which compose it, offering them protection and promising to each his due. 'For Justice, that is to say, Performance of Covenant, and giving to every man his due, is a Dictate of the Law of Nature.'[26] The state is thus conceived as *persona civilis*, whose function is to promote the happiness and well-being of man.[27] The application of such insights leads to an empirically derived concept of God modelled on the state as the philanthropic preserver of mankind, and the rejection of theological notions (such as that of eternal punishment)[28] which cannot be justified on the basis of this criterion of preservation.

Precisely such a eudaemonistic concept of God is to be found in the Deist writings, such as Tindal's *Christianity as Old as the Creation*. God's commands are given purely in order to benefit mankind:

Nothing can be a Part of the Divine Law, but what tends to promote the common Interest, and mutual Happiness of his rational Creatures . . . As God can require nothing of us, but what makes for our Happiness; so he . . . can forbid us those Things only, which tend to our Hurt.[29]

The later phase of Deism involved not merely the rejection of the concept of original sin and an emphasis upon the moral character of Christianity, but a sustained attack upon central dogmas of the

Christian faith which were held to be at variance with reason. Significantly, most of these dogmas related to the Christological dimension of the doctrine of justification. In *The True Gospel of Jesus Christ* (1738), Thomas Chubb asserted the identity of the *lex Christi* with the law of reason, which has always been in existence.[30] Chubb thus summarised the 'Gospel of Jesus Christ, or the Christian revelation', in three propositions:[31]

1. Man must ground his life and actions on the eternal and unchangeable rule of action which is grounded in the reason of things.
2. God requires repentance and reformation of the man who departs from this rule of life if he is to be forgiven.
3. God will judge man on the basis of whether he has lived in accordance with this rule.

Christ has a place in this soteriological scheme only in so far as he established the laws with reference to which man must live – laws which may be established equally well on the basis of unaided reason. 'Christ preached his own life, if I may so speak, and lived his own doctrine.'[32] Thus Chubb argues that the essential moral simplicity of Christianity has been compromised by certain unjustifiable theological beliefs – such as the doctrine of imputed righteousness, and the vicarious significance of the death of Christ. The only manner in which Christ could effect the salvation of man was by summoning him to repentance and conversion.[33] Thus Paul's statement that the 'blood of Christ takes away sin' is to be understood in the sense that the moral example of the death of Christ moves the sinner to repentance, and hence leads to his forgiveness on this account.[34] Christ saves men 'by his working a personal change in them', in that this alteration leads to their becoming worthy of divine forgiveness and salvation. The basis upon which God favours one man rather than another lies in man himself.[35]

The strongly naturalist and rationalist cast of Chubb's analysis parallels the general outlook of later Deism. Thus Thomas Morgan argued that Christianity represented the 'best rendering' of the law of nature,[36] and that Christ was a superior moral legislator to Moses, Zarathustra, Confucius or Mahomet.[37] For Morgan, it is axiomatic that God acts and legislates only in such a manner as is 'necessary to the Wellbeing and Happiness of Mankind throughout the whole period of their existence'.[38] The essential feature of the Deist soteriology was the rejection of the concept of the *mediatorship* of Christ in favour of the 'republication' by Christ of the eudaemonistic laws of nature. Although the notion of the mediation of Christ between God and man was defended with some vigour, particularly in Joseph Butler's influential *Analogy of Religion* (1736),[39] the Deist critique of this and related ideas was received with some sympathy, initially in England, and subsequently in France[40] and Germany. The traditional structure of the Christian doctrine of justification was discarded, occasionally on the basis of criticism paralleling those made earlier by Socinus, in favour of a purely moral conception of the matter. Man is justified *propter fidem*, in the Arminian sense – in other words, he is justified on the basis of his unaided act of repentance, inspired by the moral example and teaching of Christ, and motivated by the knowledge of the good which this repentance will bring him. The strongly eudaemonistic cast of Deist ethics lent weight to the assertion that morality was the foundation and criterion of religion, thus inverting the traditional understanding of the relation of the two.

The period 1690–1750 may be characterised as the period in which rationalism dominated English theology. The great Evangelical Awakening of England under the influence of the particular form of Pietism known as Methodism followed this period, and may be regarded as bringing its popular appeal to an end.[41] In Germany, by contrast, rationalism followed the rise of Pietism, and was deeply influenced by this movement[42] – despite the evident and considerable influence of English Deism upon its German counterpart at points. Many of the *Aufklärer* were of Pietist origins. The Pietist critique of the theologies of justification of Protestant (especially Lutheran) Orthodoxy was based upon the conviction that they did not encourage moral regeneration (see §24). For the Pietist, the object of justification was the potentially or actually morally regenerate man, whose moral regeneration both caused and demonstrated his justification. This emphasis upon the moral dimension of justification, and the rejection of the view that justification entailed a synthetic, rather than an analytic, judgement, is also characteristic of the early *Aufklärung*. Thus Johann Franz Budde makes no reference to the concept of *iustificatio impii* where it might be expected, and insists that it is the regenerate alone who may be justified: certum enim est, in homine, qui iustificatur, mutationem quamdam contingere.[43] It is necessary that the object of the divine justification possesses an inherent quality, or undergoes a transformation (*mutatio*) in order that such a quality may come about, which legitimates this pronouncement: 'illa [mutatio] tamen, quae per regenerationem exsistit, in iustificatione supponitur, cum nemo iustificetur nisi regenitus'.[44] Although justification is understood as a forensic divine declaration, it is presupposed that this declaration is based upon an inherent quality within man. Thus Christoph Matthaeus Pfaff defines justification as 'actus ille iudicalis, quo Deus ex mera gratia, intuitu redemptionis a Christo facta, quae vera fide iam a nobis apprehenditur, a reatu et poena peccati nos absolvit nosque perfectae sic iustos pronunciat atque declarat,'[45] while developing a moralist understanding of the *ratio iustificationis*. In his *Elementa theologiae dogmaticae* (1758), Lorenz von Mosheim explicitly stated the transformational concept of justification underlying his moralist soteriology: generatim iustificatio est actio Dei, per quam iniustus ita mutatur, ut iustus fiat.[46] Although clearly developing a theology of *iustificatio regenerati*, Mosheim still feels able to retain the forensic structure of the *actus iustificationis* inherited from Lutheran Orthodoxy:

Actus ... Dei, qui iustificatio nominatur, tametsi simplex et unus est, in tres tamen actus secari et dividi potest:
I.   in imputationem iustitiae Christi
II. in absolutionem a culpa et poena et
III. in attributionem iuris ad gratiam et gloriam.[47]

These three aspects of the believer's justification are, however, contingent upon his already having been converted, possessing faith, and being regenerate.[48] The divine judgement implicit in the process of justification is necessarily *iudicium secundum veritatem*, and is thus grounded in the qualities which such a judgement presupposes already being present in the object of justification.

In many respects, the early *Aufklärung* paralleled later Pietism in its theology of justification, retaining the concept of justification as *actus forensis Dei*, whilst substituting an analytical concept of the divine judgement in place of Orthodoxy's synthetic equivalent. While Pietism and Orthodoxy shared a common understanding of the work of Christ, on the other hand, it was, however, clear that a major assault upon precisely such an understanding by the theologians of the *Aufklärung* was not far removed. In the earlier part of this section, the theological significance of emerging theories of the nature and function of the state (such as that of Hobbes) was noted. Such theories represented the state as the means towards the end of the welfare of the individual, and this understanding of the *persona civilis* had been extended to include God as the moral governor of the universe, working towards the end of its welfare. Hobbes had extended this teleological understanding of the state to include a rationale for the state punishment of individuals: given that the state exists as a means towards the end of the welfare of the individual, the function of punishment is essentially to deter the individual from committing acts which are detrimental to his own welfare, or reforming him, should such deterrence fail.[49] The *Aufklärung* is particularly significant, in that this understanding of the basis of punishment came to be applied to God, with important consequences for the Christian doctrine of justification.[50] The explicit transfer of Hobbes' understanding of the basis of punishment from the theory of the state to the theology of justification is particularly associated with Johann Konrad Dippel, and we propose to consider it in some detail.[51]

Dippel transferred to God the function of the state – that is, the well-being of the individual, along with the understanding of the rationale of punishment within this context. On this basis, Dippel argued that God could not conceivably wish to destroy a sinner, since this is at variance with his understanding of the divine purpose, but merely to eradicate his sin and reform him. For Dippel, the consequences of sin relate solely to man, in that his well-being is affected by its existence. In marked contrast to Anselm of Canterbury and Protestant Orthodoxy, Dippel argued that sin has no effect upon God whatsoever, except indirectly, in that his love for mankind is grieved by the disadvantages which sin is perceived to bring to them. There is no need for God to punish sin, in that sin brings its own natural punishment with it, on account of its dysteleological character. If God does threaten man with punishment – as Dippel reluctantly concedes to be the case – it is solely with the object of deterring man from sin. God's threats against man do not arise from sin being committed *against* God, but on account of the potential frustration of the divine purposes in creating man in the first place. God, in his love for man, works actively towards his well-being – and is therefore obliged, as is the state, to discourage inherently self-destructive actions, which pose a threat to man's well-being. Thus Dippel prefers not to speak of 'retributive' or 'vindictive justice',[52] and is reluctant to speak of the divine 'wrath', lest this be misunderstood as divine wrath against *sinners*, rather than *sin*.

The consequences of this understanding of the nature of God for Dippel's understanding of the doctrine of reconciliation are considerable. First, Dippel departs from the Orthodox understanding of the scheme of reconciliation, in that he declines to allow a divine wrath directed against sinners, which the death of Christ can be said to appease or satisfy. Second, as sin is accompanied by its own natural punishments, it is clear that there is no sense in which Dippel may speak of Christ having removed man's punishment for sin. Dippel understands Christ's passion and death as a model for human conquest of sin, which has no soteriological significance until it is successfully imitated. Christ's death cannot be said to remit the divine punishment of man's sins, in that sin has its own natural punishment, which God cannot remove, save by abrogating the natural order.[53]

Although Dippel's criticisms of the Orthodox doctrine of reconciliation made relatively little impact at the time of their publication, similar criticisms made later were to have considerable effect. An excellent example of the latter is to be found in Johann Gottlieb Töllner's celebrated criticism of the satisfactory value of the active obedience of Christ. In his celebrated monograph *Der thätige Gehorsam Christi untersucht* (1768), Töllner rejected the thesis of the independent satisfactory value of the active obedience of Christ (see §24) with a rigour never before encountered. Earlier, Piscator had argued that Christ's active obedience (that is, his obedience to the law) was essentially a presupposition of his passive obedience (that is, his suffering and death upon the cross). Töllner's thesis is far more radical, and is based upon the analysis of the concepts of the person and office of Christ, and the nature of vicarious satisfaction itself.

Töllner argues that Christ, as man, was under the common human obligation to obey the law.[54] As such, he was only able to fulfil the law for himself, and not for others. This thesis thus calls into question the Lutheran doctrine of *exlex*, according to which Christ was under no such obligation whatsoever (see §24). The possibility of the *obedientia Christi activa* possessing any independent vicarious satisfactory value can thus only be maintained if it can be shown that one of two conditions has been satisfied. Either Christ must be the authorised federal representative of mankind, so that the actions which he performs on behalf of mankind may be duly accredited to them; or else Christ's obedience must be accepted by God as if it were performed on behalf of those whom he represents. Although Töllner gives no indication that he is familiar with the Reformed teaching on this question, it will be clear that the specified conditions correspond to the Reformed understanding of Christ as *caput et sponsor electorum* (see §24), by which the union between Christ and the believer in justification permits a *commercium admirabile* between them, as a result of which Christ's righteousness and merit become the believer's, and the latter's sin and guilt Christ's. Töllner, however, rejects the first condition as unproven, and the second as unprovable, and accordingly feels able to deny the notion of Christ's active obedience being of benefit to man.

On the basis of this conclusion, Töllner argues that the concept of vicarious satisfaction for sin may be rejected: 'nun ist es augenscheinlich, wie ohne den ganzen thätigen Gehorsam Christi die vertretende Genugthuung desselben unmöglich gewesen wäre'.[55] Töllner then argues, in the manner noted above, that it is the renewal (*Heiligung*) of the individual which leads to the bestowal of grace (*Begnadigung*), rather than the satisfaction of Christ. The obedience of Christ is an essentially moral quality, which inspires a corresponding moral quality within man – upon the basis of which man is forgiven and justified. Thus Töllner explicitly appeals to the Socinian critique of the satisfaction-doctrine of Orthodoxy, arguing that Socinus 'übersah richtig, daß das Wesentliche in der Religion auf die Tugend ankomme'.[56] The man who is justified is the morally regenerate man, whose justification does not depend upon the allegedly 'objective' value of the death of Christ, but upon the subjective moral influence which it exerts upon him. Töllner draws the conclusion that all explanations of the significance of the death of Christ (*alle Erklärungsarten vom versöhnenden Tode Christi*) actually reduce to one essential point: that Christ's death is the grounds of our assurance of God's graciousness towards us, and confirms the reliability of previous divine promises concerning the bestowal of divine grace.[57] This single point, it may be emphasised, pertains to man's perception of God, rather than the divine relationship with or attitude towards man. Christ represents God to man, and not man to God.

These insights were developed by Gotthelf Samuel Steinbart in his strongly moralist *Glückseligkeitslehre* (1778). For Steinbart, the divine dispensation towards mankind was totally concerned with the promotion of 'a supremely excellent and complete morality',[58] which finds its personification in Jesus Christ. God demands nothing of man which is not directly and totally beneficial to man himself. Steinbart thus insists that God asks nothing of his children other than that which leads immediately to their increased happiness and perfection.[59] Steinbart's tendency to employ the term *Besserung* where *Heiligung* had traditionally been used serves to emphasise the moral cast of his theology.[60] The essential simplicity of this moral gospel has, however, become obscured, according to Steinbart, by the intrusion of 'arbitrary hypotheses', of which the most significant are the following:[61]

1. The Augustinian doctrine of original sin.
2. The Augustinian doctrine of predestination.
3. The Anselmian doctrine of the satisfaction of Christ.
4. The Protestant doctrine of the imputation of the righteousness of Christ.

It will be evident that all these 'arbitrary hypotheses' are of direct relevance to our study. On the basis of extensive historical arguments,[62] Steinbart concludes that the origins of these concepts are such as to call their continued use into question. Thus Augustine's doctrines of original sin and predestination represent vestiges of his Manichaeism, which should be eliminated in order that the teaching of the Greek fathers and Pelagius might be recognised as the older and authentic Christian teaching on the matter. Similarly, Anselm's concept of vicarious satisfaction represents a further distortion, based upon Augustinian presuppositions, of the original moral interpretation of Christ's death. The concept arises through the union of the Manichaean good and evil principles in one God, so that they constitute a permanent and internally irreconcilable tension which must be resolved from outside the Godhead.[63] No such tension may be found in the teaching of Jesus.[64] Furthermore, Steinbart appeals to Töllner's critique of the *obedientia Christi activa* as a devastating theological critique of a concept already virtually discredited on the grounds of its questionable historical origins.[65]

What, then, does Steinbart understand to be the objective grounds of man's justification? According to Steinbart, Christ redeemed man from false understandings of God – such as the idea of God as wrathful, as a tyrant, or as one who imposed arbitrary penalties or conditions upon man.[66] Following the view – ultimately due to Hobbes – which we noted above, Steinbart insists that the only penalties due to man are those which are the immediate natural consequences of his sins, or which are necessary to reform man, in order that he may avoid such natural penalties in future. Steinbart dismisses questions such as the necessity and significance of Christ's passion and death as beyond meaningful discussion,[67] and irrelevant to human happiness and moral perfection. The concept of vicarious satisfaction is both impossible theologically, and unnecessary practically.[68]

It will be clear that the general position of the *Aufklärung* in relation to the objective grounds of justification leads to the total disintegration of the Orthodox doctrine of reconciliation. The emphasis upon the intellectual and moral autonomy of man, particularly evident in the writings of Töllner,[69] calls into question the crucial Orthodox assertion that man was *naturally* alienated from God. For the *Aufklärer*, man is not naturally alienated from God, although he may impose such an alienation upon himself by his acts of sin. These acts of sin, however, are conceived dysteleologically – in other words, they work against man's own interests, defined in terms of his happiness and moral perfection. Sin is defined with reference to the injury it causes to man: God is only affected by sin indirectly, in so far as he is concerned with man's destiny. Sin is most emphatically *not* understood as an offence against God, for which an appropriate satisfaction is required. If Christ's death has any significance for man, this significance is to be located in the effect which it has on man himself. This important conclusion finds its expression in the 'moral' or 'exemplarist' interpretation of the death of Christ,[70] characteristic of the theologians of the later *Aufklärung*. Christ's death is understood to serve as a supreme example or inspiration to man, motivating and encouraging him to emulate the outstanding moral character of Christ, in order that he may become *der wirkliche gute Mensch*.[71] The strong moralism and naturalism of the *Aufklärung* is evident in this moralist reduction of the Christian understanding of the nature of salvation, and the manner in which it is related to the death of Christ.[72] If Christ may be said to redeem man, it is in the restricted sense of 'redeeming man from false concepts of God'. Thus Steinbart declares that Christ has redeemed man from the *idea* of God as a tyrant, and from the *idea* of Satan, illustrating with some clarity the notion of 'redemption' as 'intellectual liberation' so characteristic of the rationalism of the movement.

By the year 1780, therefore, the foundations of the Christian doctrine of justification had been subjected to such destructive criticism by the Enlightenment in England, France and Germany that it appeared impossible that they could ever be restored. In fact, however, the period which lay ahead saw the Enlightenment criticism of Orthodoxy itself subjected to destructive criticism, with significant results for the development of the doctrine. We thus turn to consider the distinctive contributions of Kant and Schleiermacher to the re-establishment of the doctrine of reconciliation.

§35 The critique of the *Aufklärung* soteriology: Kant and Schleiermacher

The soteriologies of the later *Aufklärung* can be characterised in terms of their rationalism, moralism and naturalism (see §34). Religion, and most religious categories (particularly those relating to soteriology), were regarded as essentially ethical in character, expressing general universal moral truths in a particular (though not necessarily the most appropriate) manner. Whatever conditions might be conceded to be attached to man's justification were regarded as essentially moral in character. Furthermore, fundamental to the *Aufklärung* soteriologies was the axiom of the soteriological autonomy of the individual: each individual must be regarded as possessing whatever soteriological resources were necessary for his justification. In the present section, we are concerned with two critiques of the soteriologies of the *Aufklärung* which emerged in the period 1790–1830. Both concerned the relation between religion and morality, Kant demonstrating that the traditional Enlightenment account of this relationship was inadequate, and Schleiermacher developing a purely religious account of the Christian faith, thus severing this relationship altogether. In addition, Schleiermacher's critique of the adequacy of the soteriological resources of the individual posed a significant challenge to the fundamental axiom upon which the soteriologies of the *Aufklärung* were based.

The modern era in European thought, particularly epistemology, is frequently regarded as having been initiated by Kant.[1] Kant has rightly been compared with Copernicus in relation to the ideological revolution which he occasioned, particularly in relation to his concept of the synthetic *a priori* judgement. Although the Kantian proclamation of the inalienable subjectivity of judgements has important consequences for Christian theology, it must be emphasised that Kant's significance in relation to the development of the doctrine of justification lies in his insistence upon the autonomy and absoluteness of the moral consciousness, which has profound implications for the doctrine of reconciliation. Indeed, Kant's significance to the development of the doctrine lies in his analysis of the presuppositions of the concept of reconciliation which lies in the consciousness of moral freedom and moral guilt,[2] which led him to criticise the moral and exemplarist soteriologies of the *Aufklärung*.[3]

Although Kant's exposition of the relationship between morality and religion is to be found in his *Kritik*, his most lucid and sustained discussion of the matter may be found in the important essay of 1793, *Religion innerhalb der Grenzen der bloßen Vernunft*.[4] This work appeared some eleven years after the appearance of the *Kritik der reinen Vernunft*, and has as its presuppositions certain of the fundamental doctrines of this earlier work – for example, the unconditional authority of the moral law, the autonomy of the rational human subject, the critical evaluation of the transcendent metaphysical impulse, and the assertion of the primacy of practical reason. It is the first of these presuppositions which is of particular importance, especially when Kant is viewed in relation to his context within the later *Aufklärung*.

The cornerstone of Kant's theology in general is the priority of the apprehension of moral obligation over anything else. For Kant, it is a fundamental axiom of theology, that all which man believes himself to be capable of doing to please God, apart from a moral way of life, is mere 'religious delusion' (*Religionswahn*) and 'pseudo-worship' (*Afterdienst*) of God:

Ich nehme erstlich folgenden Satz als einen keines Beweises benötigten Grundsatz an: alles, was außer dem guten Lebenswandel der Mensch noch thun zu können vermeint, um Gott wohlgefällig zu werden, ist bloßer Religionswahn und Afterdienst Gottes.[5]

Kant's emphasis upon the moral basis of the Christian religion, with the concomitant rejection of 'arbitrary demands' made by God of man, clearly parallels that of the *Aufklärung*. However, Kant diverges from the movement at two significant points. First, the essentially utilitarian or eudaemonistic approach to morality is replaced with an emphasis upon the concept of moral obligation as an end in itself (rather than as a means towards the end of man's perfection or happiness), expressed in terms of the concept of the 'highest good'.[6] Second, Kant argues that to base morality upon the known commands of God would be to concede the heteronomous character of ethics: rather, morality must be held to be based upon the self-imposed 'categorical (or unconditional) imperative' (*unbedingte Forderung*) of the autonomous human will. Man's sense of moral obligation (*das Sollen*) is prior to the correlation of virtue and happiness. Furthermore, Kant insists that the apprehension of the categorical imperative is quite independent of the idea of 'another Being above man' (in other words, God): however, Kant allows that the *idea* of such a Being may subsequently arise, through an act of faith which correlates the apprehension of *das Sollen* with the existence of God as a 'moral legislator apart from man'. The religiously disposed individual will interpret *das Sollen* as an expression of divine obligations laid upon him, an interpretation which Kant's critical philosophy places beyond the scope of pure reason, even if it does not involve conceding that religion is essentially a postulate of practical reason.

Kant notes that the presupposition of man's duty to pursue the highest good has as its necessary presupposition the possibility of moral perfection. For Kant, the denial of the possibility of moral perfection has as its corollary the denial of the possibility of the highest good, in that the former is the unconditioned component of the latter. Therefore the rejection of the possibility of the highest good entails the rejection of the moral law, which Kant dismisses as an *absurdum practicum*. For Kant, the apprehension of *das Sollen* has as its fundamental and necessary presupposition the possibility of moral perfection. It is of the utmost importance to appreciate that this presupposition forces him to break with the *Aufklärung* on several crucial points. The reasons for this will become clear when his concept of 'radical evil' is considered.[7]

It is to Kant's credit that he recognised that man is a free creature, with an ability to misuse precisely that freedom. His account of moral obligation is able to take account of the possibility that man will ignore his apprehension of *das Sollen*. (It may be noted that he excludes the suggestion that a man may deliberately choose to do evil, knowing it to be evil). The moral qualities of the will, both good and evil, are the consequences of human freedom. Man himself must determine whether he is morally good or evil; if he does not, or is unable to, he cannot be held responsible for his moral condition, and thus cannot be considered to be good or evil *morally*.[8] The consciousness of moral obligation leads Kant to conclude that man must be free to exercise or decline to exercise that obligation – otherwise the concept of 'obligation' becomes evacuated of its moral content. For Kant, as for the *Aufklärung* as a whole, the notion of original sin is to be rejected – and hence the origin of human evil is to be sought within the human will. But why should the human will choose evil? If there is no evil within man until he himself causes it, how does the will come to be corrupted in such a manner?

Kant answers this crucial question by developing the concept of the dispositional aspect of the human will (*Willkur*) to account for this fundamental ambivalence within human volition. While he defines evil in terms of a lesser good, so that the evil man is the man who subordinates the demands of *das Sollen* to the demands of his sensible nature, it is clear that even this approach to the existence of evil calls into question the possibility of moral perfection. The thesis of 'radical evil' excludes the essential presupposition upon which Kant's ethics are based, in that it indicates that the most which can realistically be expected is progress towards, rather than attainment of, the end of moral perfection. Kant thus (re)defines moral perfection in terms of a 'disposition' (*Gesinnung*) towards this (unattainable) objective, which is now recognised as an *Urbild*, which man recognises as good, and towards which he actively works.

Having defined a 'good disposition' as the intention to work towards the *Urbild* of moral perfection, Kant takes the remarkable step of asserting that God treats the man who possesses an *intention* to work towards moral perfection *as if he were already in full possession of that perfection*. Although he concedes that man has no right to expect God to treat him in this remarkable manner, he insists that God gratuitously (*aus Gnaden*) reckons the *Gesinnung* as the *Urbild*:

Hier ist nun derjenige Überschuß über das Verdienst der Werke, der oben vermißt wurde, und ein Verdienst, das uns aus Gnaden zugerechnet wird. Denn damit das, was bei uns in Erdenleben (vielleicht auch in allen künftigen Zeiten und allen Welten) immer nur im bloßen Werden ist (nämlich ein Gott wohlgefälliger Mensch zu sein), uns, gleich *als ob* wir schon hier in vollen Besitz desselben wären, zugerechnet werde, dazu haben wir doch wohl keinen Rechtsanspruch (nach der empirischen Selbsterkenntnis), so weit wir uns selbst kennen (unsere Gesinnung nicht unmittelbar, sondern nur nach unseren Thaten ermessen).[9]

The reappearance of an *als-ob-Theologie*, or 'legal fiction', so vigorously rejected by Pietism and the *Aufklärung*, in the works of Kant is of considerable importance. As we noted earlier, the later *Aufklärer* had stressed that *Begnadigung* was contingent upon *Verbesserung*: for Kant, it is clear that grace is implicated at the earliest phase of justification. The 'man who is pleasing to God' (*der wohlgefällige Mensch*) is only 'pleasing' on the basis of a gratuitous act by which God overlooks his deficiencies. As he puts this elsewhere, the man who attempts to be pleasing to God 'in so far as it lies within his ability' (*so viel in seinem Vermögen ist*)[10] may rely upon God to 'supplement' (*ergänzen*) his deficiencies:

Man muß mit allen Kräften der heiligen Gesinnung eines Gott wohlgefälligen Lebenswandels nachstreben, um glauben zu können, daß die (uns schon durch die Vernunft versicherte) Liebe desselben zur Menschheit, sofern sie seinem Willen nach allem ihrem Vermögen nachstrebt, in Rücksicht auf die redliche Gesinnung den Mangel der That, auf welche Art es auch sei, ergänzen werde.[11]

The obvious parallels between Kant and the *via moderna* at this point will be evident (see §17), particularly in their mutual presupposition that the man who does his best (*quod in se est – so viel in seinem*

Vermögen ist) will become pleasing to, or accepted by, God *as an act of grace, rather than strict justice*.

The divergence between Kant and the *Aufklärung* becomes increasingly evident from Kant's discus..'on of how God may justify an individual leading an immoral life who subsequently decides to repent. Kant insists that this is a *real* possibility – as, indeed, it must be, if the practical possibility of the unconditioned component of the highest good is to be maintained, even in the weakest of senses. However, Kant notes three difficulties raised by this possibility, of which the third is of particular significance.[12] The individual who alters his evil disposition to the good is nevertheless the same individual who formerly committed evil acts, and as a result is burdened with the guilt associated with that evil.[13] How can God justify such an individual? Kant actually merely demonstrates that it is acceptable for God to permit guilt to go unpunished, and defers his solution of how such an individual may be justified (in the strict sense) until a later section of the work. This solution is, however, of enormous significance.

Kant's solution to this difficulty is, in fact, apparently irreconcilable with the general principles upon which his moral philosophy is based, particularly the axiom that an individual is responsible for *his own* moral actions. No individual can be good on behalf of another, nor can the goodness of a morally outstanding individual be permitted to remove the guilt of another. The basis of Kant's rejection of the concept of vicarious satisfaction (*stellvertretende Genugthuung*) is the principle that guilt, like merit, is strictly non-transferable. It is therefore remarkable that Kant's solution to the difficulty noted above is based upon the assertion that the individual who turns away from his evil disposition to adopt a good disposition may be regarded as having become a different person: the old disposition *ist moralisch ein anderer* from the new.[14] The discontinuity between the old and the new disposition is such that Kant denies that they may be predicated of the same moral individual. This conclusion appears to rest upon the assumption that the disposition itself is the only acceptable basis of establishing the identity of the moral agent. Having established this point, Kant takes the remarkable step of asserting that the new disposition 'takes the place' (*vertritt*) of the old in respect of the guilt which is rightly attached to the latter disposition.[15] It is on account of the new disposition that man's former guilt is cancelled, and that he is justified before God. On the basis of these assumptions, Kant asserts that the man who attempts to be pleasing to God may rest assured of the truth expressed by the doctrine of reconciliation, which represents his former sins as abolished (*abgetan*):

Dieser Muth, auf eigenen Fußen zu stehen, wird nun selbst durch die darauf folgende Versöhnungslehre gestärkt, indem sie, was nicht zu ändern ist, als abgethan vorstellt und nun den Pfad zu einem neuen Lebenswandel für uns eröffnet.[16]

In effect, Kant interprets the doctrine of reconciliation to mean that the man who determines to keep the moral law, whatever his previous history may have been, has the right to hope that his moral past may be abolished, and present moral deficiencies supplemented, through divine grace. The relation between *Begnadigung* and *Verbesserung* is thus demonstrated to be considerably more complex than the *Aufklärer* recognised.

The significance of Kant's *Religion* lies in the deduction of the necessity of divine grace *as a postulate of practical reason*. The deep pessimism of his doctrine of 'radical evil' is counteracted by his optimism concerning the rôle of divine grace in the supplementation of a good disposition, and the abolition of the moral guilt of a prior evil disposition (by a process of vicarious satisfaction). Although Kant cannot be said to have advanced the Orthodox doctrine of reconciliation (or, indeed, to have intended to), it is clear that the doctrines of justification and reconciliation were shown to have their proper and necessary place within moral philosophy, even if stated in forms quite distinct from their Orthodox equivalents. The naïve moralism of the *Aufklärung* was thus called into question through the Kantian analysis of the moral dimension of reconciliation.[17]

The remarkable rise of German Romanticism in the closing years of the eighteenth century is generally regarded as a reaction of 'spirit' against 'reason', in that the latter was regarded as quite inadequate to analyse the depths of human feeling (*Gefühl*).[18] Although Schleiermacher was not himself a *Romantiker*, it is clear that the new significance attached to human *Gefühl* permitted him to develop an account of Christian faith which dissociated it from the hitherto prevailing rationalist reductions of the concept. The fundamental fact (*Grundtatsache*) of Christian dogmatics is the existence of the individual's faith or 'piety' (*Frömmigkeit*), and it is the task of Christian dogmatics to give an account of the content of this *datum*, rather than to establish it in the first place.[19] Thus Schleiermacher distinguishes between Christian dogmatics (which begins from an inward perception), historical sciences (which begin from an outward perception), and deductive sciences (which begin from a fundamental principle (*Grundsatz*)).[20] The essence of 'piety', which Schleiermacher holds to be the irreducible element in every religion, is not some rational or moral principle, but 'feeling' (*Gefühl*), the immediate self-consciousness.[21] Thus Christian doctrines are, in essence, individually accounts of Christian religious feelings.[22] Schleiermacher constructs his dogmatics upon the basis of the fact of redemption in Christ, and thence upon the antithesis of sin and grace.[23] In Part I of *Der christliche Glaube*, Schleiermacher discussed the human religious consciousness (*Bewußtsein*) in isolation from this antithesis. Although this consciousness is presupposed by Christian piety, the specifically Christian consciousness is to be distinguished from it, in that it is the 'feeling of absolute dependence (*das Gefühl schlechthinniger Abhängigkeit*)', which faith interprets as a consciousness of God.[24]

Having established Christian piety, and particularly the 'feeling of absolute dependence', as the starting point for Christian theology, Schleiermacher argues that the origins of this piety are to be explained soteriologically in terms of the perceived effects of Christ upon the collective consciousness of the Christian community. It must be emphasised that this represents a purely *religious* approach to the matter, which sharply distinguishes it from the moralism of the *Aufklärung*. Schleiermacher attributes to Christ an 'absolutely powerful God-consciousness (*schlechthin kräftiges Gottesbewußtsein*)', charged with such assimilative power that it is able to effect the redemption of mankind.[25] The essence of redemption is that the God-consciousness already present in human nature, although feeble and repressed, becomes stimulated and elevated through the 'entrance of the living influence of Christ'.[26] As the redeemer (*Erlöser*), Christ is distinguished from all other men both in degree and kind by the uninterrupted power of his God-consciousness. The redemptive activity of Christ consists in his assuming individuals into the power of his God-consciousness. On the basis of this presupposition, Schleiermacher criticises the soteriologies of both the *Aufklärung* and Orthodoxy.[27]

For Schleiermacher, the *Aufklärer* treated Christ solely as a prophet, regarding him primarily as the teacher of an *idea* of God, or the exemplar of a religious or moral principle. This view – which Schleiermacher designates the 'empirical' understanding of the work of Christ – 'attributes a redemptive activity on the part of Christ, but one which is held to consist only in bringing about an increasing perfection in us, and which cannot take place other than by teaching and example'.[28] If this account of the significance of Christ is correct, Schleiermacher argues that belief in redemption *im eigentlichen Sinne* becomes an impossibility. The Orthodox understanding of the work of Christ – which Schleiermacher designates as 'magical' – attributes to Christ a purely objective transaction which is 'not mediated by anything natural'. This approach, which Schleiermacher considers to approximate to Docetism, is incapable of doing justice to the historical figure of Jesus of Nazareth: if Christ were able to exert his influence in this supernaturalist manner, it would have been possible for him to work in precisely the same way at any time, so that his personal appearance in history would have been superfluous.[29] Underlying this observation is Schleiermacher's conviction that the supranaturalist approach involves a non-natural concept of divine causality. For Schleiermacher, divine causality operates through natural means – and at this point, his affinity with the *Aufklärung* is evident. The assimilative power of Christ's dominant God-consciousness is mediated to man through natural channels.

Having discussed how the individual believer enters into fellowship with Christ, Schleiermacher moves on to consider how this expresses itself in the life of the believer.[30] It is clear that Schleiermacher is obliged to follow the arguments of the *Aufklärung*, and hold that justification is contingent upon a real change in man:

Rechtfertigung sezt etwas voraus in Beziehung worauf jemand gerechtfertigt wird; und da in dem höchsten Wesen kein Irrthum möglich ist, so wird angenommen, zwischen dem vorher und jezt sei dem Menschen etwas begegnet, wodurch das frühere göttliche Mißfallen aufgehoben wird, und ohne welches er nicht habe können ein Gegenstand des göttlichen Wohlgefallens werden.[31]

The same emphasis is to be found here as in the writings of Töllner, Steinbart and Teller: justification is contingent upon a prior alteration within man. Where Schleiermacher diverges so radically from the *Aufklärung* in this respect is the nature of the alteration. For the *Aufklärer*, the alteration was to be conceived morally (note the tendency to refer to the condition as *Besserung*, rather than *Heiligung*: see §34). For Schleiermacher, the alteration was to be conceived *religiously* as 'laying hold of Christ in a believing manner (*Christum gläubig ergreifen*)'.[32] Although conceding that this might appear to suggest that man is capable of justifying himself, Schleiermacher states that justification actually derives from the assumption of man into fellowship with Christ,[33] and adopts an understanding of man's rôle in justification which is sharply distinguished from that of the *Aufklärung*.

Schleiermacher, developing the Kantian concept of radical evil, argues that man is unable to attain a dominant God-consciousness unaided. There is an inherent disposition within man towards sin, understood as a 'total incapacity for the good',[34] which leads man to recognise his need for external assistance (*Hülfe*).[35] This point is also developed in Schleiermacher's important discussion of the four 'natural heresies' of Christianity – the Docetic and Ebionite interpretations of the person of Christ, and the Pelagian and Manichaean interpretations of man's soteriological resources.[36] As Schleiermacher observes, the understanding of man's soteriological resources must be such that it can account for the necessity of redemption from outside humanity itself – in other words, that it can explain why all men cannot be redeemers. The understanding of the object of redemption – man – must be such that it can accommodate the two presuppositions fundamental to Schleiermacher's soteriology: that man requires redemption from outside humanity; and that he is capable of receiving or accepting that redemption, once it is offered to him: 'wenn die Menschen sollen erlöst werden, so müssen sie eben sowohl der Erlösung bedürftig sein, als auch fähig sie anzunehmen'.[37] If man's need for redemption is conceded, and yet his impotence to provide such redemption is denied, the conclusion must be drawn, that man himself could be the agent of his own redemption. Redemption could then be effected, either by the soteriologically sufficient individual, or by one individual for another: and if not by all men, then at least by some, to varying degrees. If man's impotence to redeem himself is conceded, and yet his ability to appropriate that redemption, once offered, is denied, it will be clear that redemption is an impossibility. Broadly speaking, these two positions correspond to the Pelagian and Manichaean heresies, although the specific historical forms taken by these heresies differ somewhat from Schleiermacher's characterisations of them.

The importance of this discussion relates to Schleiermacher's definition of the distinctive feature of Christianity being the principle that 'all religious emotions are related to redemption in Christ'.[38] The *Aufklärung* axiom of the soteriological autonomy of man eliminated this distinctive element, in that the principle of redemption from outside humanity was regarded as violating human autonomy. Schleiermacher's careful statement of the heteronomous character of human soteriological resources leads to the position of the *Aufklärung* on this question being recognised as Pelagian (by Schleiermacher's definition).

A further point at which Schleiermacher criticises the soteriologies of the *Aufklärung* relates to the concept of sin. Schleiermacher, as is well known, subordinates sin to the divine purpose of redemption, regarding the human recognition of sin as the necessary prelude to his redemption. The first consciousness of the actuality of sin is effectively the first presentiment of the possibility of redemption.[39] Schleiermacher rejects the *Aufklärung* axiom of the reformatory character of punishment,[40] as well as the distinction between natural and arbitrary punishments (see §34).[41] For him, a positive correlation is established by the divine righteousness between sin and penalty for sin *as a means of generating the consciousness of redemption*.[42] The view – which assumes the status of an axiom in the soteriologies of the *Aufklärung* – that the divine righteousness recognises a positive correlation between human good (such as moral action) and divine reward (such as justification) is rejected. Defining the 'righteousness of God' as 'the divine causality by which a connection is established between evil and actual sin in the state of universal sinfulness', Schleiermacher concedes that this represents a considerable restriction upon the term, in that no correlation between good and reward is recognised.[43] However, he defends this restriction by observing that the Christian consciousness recognises no such positive correlation between human good and divine reward, save in the specific and unique case of Christ.[44] Consciousness of the divine righteousness is thus consciousness of the divine punitive justice (*strafende Gerechtigkeit*) alone,[45] thus leading to the realisation of the possibility of redemption. It is therefore evident that Schleiermacher has replaced the moral understandings of divine punishment and the divine righteousness, characteristic of the *Aufklärung*, with *religious* understandings of the concepts, and that these are subordinated to a *religious* concept of salvation.

It is thus clear that the essential presuppositions of the soteriologies of the *Aufklärung* were called into question by developments during the period 1790–1830. The following are of particular importance:

1. The Kantian analysis of the concept of moral autonomy in the light of the principle of radical evil, which demonstrated the superficiality of the moralism of the Enlightenment.

2. Schleiermacher's rejection of the equation of religion and morality, and the associated moral interpretation of soteriological concepts (such as the preconditions of justification, the righteousness of God, or the work of Christ).

3. Schleiermacher's demonstration of the heteronomous character of man's soteriological resources.

Although the rationalist spirit of the *Aufklärung* remained influential for some considerable time thereafter, it exercised a steadily diminishing influence over the articulation of the doctrine of justification in the remainder of the period 1830–1914. While the rise of rationalism in England had been checked through the great Evangelical revival of the late eighteenth century, thus largely obviating the necessity for such critiques of rationalist soteriologies, the situation in Germany demanded that rationalism be refuted on different grounds. The very different character of the English and German discussions of justification in the period 1780–1914 ultimately reflects the different relationship of Pietism and rationalism in the two countries. In England, the rise of Pietism subsequent to rationalism led to the critical questions raised by the Deists being largely ignored, so that the discussion of justification within the English church over the period 1780–1914 is essentially a continuation, and occasionally an extension, of the debate between Anglican and Puritan (see §§ 30–3), rather than a new development in its own right. The German situation, in contrast, demanded the development of new theological methods and insights, in order that rationalism might be defeated – and thus the period 1780–1914 witnessed significant and genuine *developments* in the theology of justification, as rationalism was initially checked, to be followed by a sustained period of consolidation. It is to the developments which are associated with this period of consolidation that we now turn.

§36 The consolidation of the doctrine 1820–1914: Ritschl

Although Schleiermacher's soteriology was subjected to considerable criticism in the period 1820–70,[1] it is clear that it made a permanent impact upon the German theological consciousness. The purely rationalist or moralist account of the justification of man before God was subjected to a significant reversal. If this reversal was to become permanent, however, it was necessary that the anti-rationalist offensive should be consolidated, particularly through the reintroduction of an objective dimension to the doctrine of justification. Initially, it was not clear whether this was a real possibility, let alone how this might be attained. In his influential study of the development of the doctrine of reconciliation, published in 1838, Ferdinand Christian Baur asserted, on the basis of his Hegelian understanding of the nature of historical development,[2] that an element of this doctrine, once eliminated, could no longer be restored. Baur's Hegelianism led him to suggest that objective soteriological concepts had been permanently eliminated from the doctrine of reconciliation. The use of Hegelian speculative categories was widespread within theological circles, and is particularly evident in the first work of one of Baur's most promising pupils: Albrecht Ritschl's *Die Entstehung des altkatholischen Kirche* (1850). As most of Baur's contemporaries were sympathetic to his Hegelian presuppositions, and thus to his views on the development of the doctrine of reconciliation, it was thus far from clear how this consolidation might take place, in that the objective elements of the doctrine rejected by the *Aufklärung* were generally regarded as irretrievably lost.

The sudden collapse of Hegelianism in the fifth decade of the nineteenth century led to a general rejection of the Hegelian understanding of the nature of historical development. The consequences of this development are immediately evident from the second edition of Ritschl's *Entstehung* (1857), in which a break with both Baur and Hegelianism is evident. More significant, from the standpoint of the present study, was Ritschl's decision to reinvestigate the development of the Christian doctrine of justification without the restrictions of the Hegelian interpretative framework imposed upon it by Baur. After a series of preparatory articles in *Jahrbuch für deutsche Theologie*, the first volume of his *Christliche Lehre von der Rechtfertigung und Versöhnung* was published in 1870. The full importance of this historical analysis in consolidating the doctrine of justification has not been fully appreciated. In this work, Ritschl was able to demonstrate that, contrary to Baur's axiom, elements eliminated from the doctrine of reconciliation by one generation had subsequently been reappropriated by another. The closing sentences of this important study merit consideration:

I may now appeal to the delineation of the history of the doctrines of reconciliation and justification, which here closes, to test whether or not [Baur's] belief in the progress of knowledge in a direct line is one to which we are of necessity driven by the facts. At all events, the last link recognised by my predecessor in the history unfolded by him . . . has been so surpassed that an older position has again been taken up.[3]

Having thus demonstrated that Baur's *a priori* imposition of the speculative and unempirical categories of Hegel's philosophy of history was incapable of accounting for the objectively given historical data pertaining to the development of the doctrine of reconciliation, Ritschl was able to move towards the positive restatement of the doctrine through the reappropriation of *objective* soteriological concepts (such as sin) without being impeded by the constraints imposed upon such a restatement by Baur's understanding of the nature of historical development. It is this positive restatement which forms the subject of the third volume of his *Christliche Lehre von der Rechtfertigung und Versöhnung*.[4]

For Ritschl, all religion is exclusively soteriological in character, seeking a resolution of the contradiction in which man finds himself, in that he is at one and the same time a part of the world of nature, dependent upon and confined to the natural order, and yet also a spiritual entity motivated by his determination to maintain his independence of nature.[5] Religion is therefore essentially an interpretation of man's relation to God and the world, based upon the belief that God may effect the redemption of man.[6] Ritschl's theology in its entirety is based upon the centrality of God's redemptive action in history, with its associated (and subsequent) human response and obligations. In the second edition of *Die Entstehung der altkatholischen Kirche*, Ritschl drew an important, and highly influential, distinction between early authentic Christianity, and its later inauthentic form, which resulted from the intrusion of elements essentially alien to the gospel itself. According to Ritschl, Christianity was essentially soteriologically orientated, but became corrupted through the intrusion of Hellenistic metaphysics into a Christologically orientated religion. Ritschl's intense suspicion of the rôle of metaphysics in theology reflects his fundamental conviction that man has no true knowledge of God outside the sphere of his redemptive activity, and that even then, this knowledge takes the form of value-judgements (*Werthurtheile*), which cannot be allowed to be equivalent to disinterested and impartial knowledge.

In his polemic against the claims of idealistic rationalism, Ritschl argues that the specifically Christian knowledge of God takes the form of *Werthurtheile* evoked by divine revelation.[7] For him, we know the nature of God and Christ only in terms of their perceived significance for us. Thus he makes frequent approving reference to Melanchthon's celebrated dictum: Hoc est Christum cognoscere, beneficia eius cognoscere.[8] Ritschl's theological method is based upon the assumption that faith is grounded in the saving revelation of God in Christ, so that the actual justification of man is defined as the point of departure for all Christian statements concerning God. All the believer's statements concerning God and Christ reflect the importance which he personally attaches to them, and cannot be divorced from his faith. Thus for Ritschl, the question: who is Christ? must reduce to the more pertinent and radical question: who is Christ *for me*? this latter constituting a *Werthurtheil* upon which theology is based. Exploiting the Kantian insistence upon the inalienable subjectivity of value-judgements, Ritschl insists that the *Bild* cannot be separated from the *Ding-an-sich*. Thus man cannot consider the person of Christ (the *Ding-an-sich*) in isolation from the work of Christ (the *Bild*). This point is made with particular clarity in the first edition of Ritschl's *Hauptwerk*, where the Christological consequences of the phenomenalist thesis that *Dinge-an-sich* escape our perception altogether (except in the form in which they are perceived and evaluated) are analysed.[9] Ritschl thus argues that our knowledge of the person of Christ, in so far as this represents a genuine possibility, derives from our knowledge of the work of Christ – in other words, that soteriology is prior to Christology in the theological *ordo cognoscendi*. Ritschl's celebrated reluctance to avert his gaze from the phenomenal aspects of reality to their ontological foundation inevitably leads to a certain lack of interest in the *Christusbild* which underlies his soteriological concentration.

This point is brought out with particular importance by Ritschl in his introduction to his historical study of the development of the doctrines of justification and reconciliation:

The Christian doctrine of justification and reconciliation . . . constitutes the real centre of the theological system. In it is developed the determinate and direct result of the historical revelation of God's purpose of grace through Christ.[10]

Of course, it may be emphasised that the affirmation of the subjectivity of religious value-judgements does not entail the denial of their objective foundation: faith, in making its value-judgements, bases them upon the objective reality of the saving revelation of God in Jesus Christ. It is clear that Ritschl regards man's justification as the fundamental datum from which all theological discussion must proceed, and upon which it is ultimately grounded.[11] This conviction expresses itself in the manner in which Ritschl's systematic exposition of Christian theology proceeds. An initial examination of the concept of justification (§§5–26) is followed by an analysis of the presuppositions of man's justification, such as the doctrines of sin and the work and person of Christ (§§27–50). After a discussion of the difficulties which might be thought to arise from the doctrine (§§51–61), the work ends with an analysis of the consequences of man's justification (§§62–8).

Ritschl's initial definition of justification is of immediate significance, in that it represents the reintroduction of objective concepts into the systematic discussion of the doctrine. 'Justification, or the forgiveness of sins (as the religious operation of God upon men, fundamental within Christianity), is the acceptance of sinners into that fellowship with God within which their salvation will be effected and developed into eternal life.'[12] Ritschl's explicit identification of justification and the remission of sins indicates his concern to emphasise the objective dimension of justification, and represents a reappropriation of certain aspects of the concept associated with the Reformation in general, and Luther in particular.[13] Thus Ritschl identifies Luther's statement in the 1518 sermon on the sacrament of penance, 'alßo sihestu, das die gantz Kirch voll ist vogebung der sund',[14] as the key to the reformer's theology of justification,[15] and hence incorporated it into his own positive exposition of the doctrine. For Ritschl, sin separates man from God, effecting the withdrawal of God's presence from the sinner; justification is therefore the divine operation through which the sinner is restored to fellowship with God. The objective dimension of justification is therefore prior to, although inseparable from, the subjective consciousness of this forgiveness.[16] Ritschl thus criticises an earlier generation of Lutheran theologians for their excessive objectivism, which led to justification becoming divorced from personal experience and practice.[17] Of considerably greater importance, however, is Ritschl's critique of the axiom of the *Aufklärung*, that God enters into no real relationship with man, unless the man in question is morally regenerate. This principle amounts to the destruction of the central and fundamental presupposition of Christianity which, according to Ritschl, is that God justifies *sinners*. Ritschl stresses that justification necessarily finds its expression in the lifestyle of the individual:[18] justification (*Rechtfertigung*), which is concerned with the restoration of man's fellowship with God, necessarily finds its concrete expression in reconciliation (*Versöhnung*), the lifestyle of the reconciled community. In so far as the moral implications of justification and reconciliation derive from and are grounded in man's new relationship to God, established in justification, it may be said that reconciliation is the ethical complement of justification – in other words, that the *moral* aspects of this fellowship with God are secondary to its specifically *religious* character.

It will be evident that Ritschl has reinterpreted the concept of 'reconciliation' (*Versöhnung*). For Orthodoxy, 'reconciliation' referred to the objective basis of justification, especially the historical work of Christ. Ritschl inverted the traditional frame of reference, so that God is now understood as the *subject*, rather than the *object*, of reconciliation.[19] Indeed, Ritschl appears to regard the terms *Rechtfertigung* and *Versöhnung* as being essentially synonymous, their difference lying in the aspects of the God–man relationship to which they referred. *Rechtfertigung* refers to the divine judgement, understood as an unconditional act of will, independent of whether an individual or a community appropriates it. *Versöhnung* refers to the same basic concept of a synthetic divine judgement, as it is appropriated by an individual or community. In other words, *Versöhnung* expresses as an actual result the effect which is intended in *Rechtfertigung* – that the individual or community who is justified actually enters into the intended relationship.

For Ritschl, God's gracious gift of justification is inextricably and irrevocably linked with the ethical consequences of this divine act: 'Christianity, so to speak, resembles not a circle described from a single centre, but an ellipse which is determined by two *foci*.'[20] The first *focus* is 'redemption through Christ', and the second 'the ethical interpretation of Christianity through the idea of the Kingdom of God'. His conviction that Lutheran Orthodoxy had tended to concentrate upon redemption without correlating it with Christian existence led to his insistence upon the necessity of correlating the divine and human elements in justification and reconciliation. However, it is evident that Ritschl had some difficulty in establishing the relative weighting to be given to the two *foci* of his theology: in the first edition of the work (1870), it seems that the ethical *focus* is regarded as the more significant, whereas the second (1883) and third (1888) editions gave the *focus* of redemption greater weight.[21]

Ritschl's statement that justification involves a *synthetic* judgement on the part of God represents a decisive break with the soteriologies of the *Aufklärung* and their precursors within Pietism, which even Schleiermacher had not felt able to make. In making this assertion, Ritschl clearly considers himself to be reappropriating a vital element of the Reformation and Orthodox soteriologies rejected by the 'Age of Reason'. If justification involves an *analytic* judgement on the part of God, God is understood to 'analyse' the righteousness which is already present in the *objectum iustificationis*, and on the basis of this analysis, to pronounce the sentence of justification. This pronouncement is thus based upon a quality already present within man, prior to his justification, which God recognises and proclaims in the

subsequent verdict of justification. 'Righteousness' is already predicated of man – the function of the pronouncement of justification is to
endorse man's present status *coram Deo*. It will be evident that this
corresponds to the moralist soteriology of the *Aufklärung*. If, on the
other hand, justification involves a *synthetic* judgement, God is
understood to act in a creative manner, adding something to man
which was not his previously. God 'synthesises' the righteousness
upon the basis of which the divine verdict of justification proceeds: in
justification, a predicate is added to man which is not already
included in the notion of 'sinner' ('ein Prädicat gesetzt wird, welches
nicht schon in dem Begriffe des Sünders eingeschlossen ist').[22]
Ritschl declares his intention to break free from the moralism of
Catholicism[23] and the *Aufklärung* (the latter he considers to be
Socinian in character) by affirming that justification is a creative act of
the divine will which, in declaring the sinner to be righteous, *effects*
rather than *endorses* the righteousness of man. It will be evident that
Ritschl's insistence upon the synthetic character of the divine judgement of justification eliminates any claim by the morally renewed
man to be justified on that account.[24] Ritschl thus argues that Pietism
(and, by inference, the *Aufklärung*) represent an 'inversion of the
Reformation point of view'.

Although Ritschl is severely critical of the soteriologies of the
Aufklärung, it is also clear that he regards the theologies of justification associated with Orthodoxy as open to criticism, singling out
the judicial approach to justification and the concept of original sin
for particular comment.

Fundamental to Ritschl's critique of an analytic understanding of
the divine judgement of justification is the question of the positive
laws or principles by which such a judgement may be undertaken.
'Every judicial judgement is an analytic judgement of knowledge.
The subsequent decree of punishment or acquittal is also an analytic
judgement, in that it is a conclusion based upon the prohibitive or
permissive law [*Schluß aus dem verbietenden oder erlaubenden Gesetz*]
and the knowledge of the guilt or innocence of the person involved.'[25]
If God's justifying verdict is based upon *law*, the question of God's
status in regard to that law must be positively established. This
question is, of course, particularly associated with the Arminian
theologian Hugo Grotius,[26] and Ritschl may be regarded as extending
the critique of the Orthodox doctrine of justification associated with
this Arminian divine to exclude totally a judicial interpretation of
justification.

'The attribute of God on the basis of which the older theology attempts to understand justification is that of lawgiver [*Gesetzgeber*] and judge [*Richter*].'[27] By these terms, Ritschl intends to convey the quite distinct concepts of God as *rector* and *iudex* (underlying Grotius' critique of Orthodox theologies of justification). Ritschl points out how the divine pardon of the sinner in justification was generally treated by Orthodoxy as analogous to the bestowal of pardon upon a guilty individual by a head of state. On the basis of this analogy, it was argued that justification could be interpreted as a judicial act of God, by which the individual was found guilty of sin, and yet pardoned through precisely the same legal process. Any apparent contradiction between the divine justice and the divine grace could be resolved by developing a theory of penal substitution, so that any hint of injustice in relation to the pardoning of the guilty individual could be remedied.

Ritschl, however, argued that the exercise of the head of state's right to pardon is not comparable to the divine justification of the sinner. The head of state is obliged to act in accord with the best interests of the individual members of the state, and the established law is merely a means towards that end. As such, the law is subordinate to the greater good of the state:

The right of granting pardon [*Begnadigung*] . . . follows from the fact that the legal order is merely a means to the moral ends of the people, and that consequences of legal action are conceivable, which are incongruous with the respect which is due to public morality, as well as to the moral position of guilty persons.[28]

The ability of the head of state to take certain moral liberties with the established law is a direct consequence of the fact that the moral good of the people is to be considered as being of greater importance than the strict observance of the law, which is merely a means to that end. As such, the question of whether a guilty individual should be pardoned is not one of *law*, but one of *public moral interests*. The state may thus relax a law with this end in view, without its action being deemed to be improper.[29] The reason why the state is able to take such liberties with the established law is that it maintains two potentially conflicting principles at one and the same time – the need to obey the law, and the need to act towards the greatest good of the people. Although these principles are usually reconcilable, situations inevitably must arise when they cannot be maintained simultaneously – and Ritschl argues that, on such occasions, it is the latter which must be upheld. It is therefore, according to Ritschl, impossible to model God upon the institution of the state and assert that his action in justification is *judicial*, in that it is clearly *extra-judicial*. Ritschl thus notes with approval Tieftrunk's emphasis upon the subordination of God's rôle as lawgiver to that of public benefactor.[30] It is clear that Ritschl regards this extra-judicial approach to justification as avoiding the impasse of the Orthodox doctrine of God as the righteous God who justifies men, despite their being sinners, in order to develop an understanding of justification based upon a teleological principle of paralleling that of the state as public benefactor.

Ritschl locates this teleological element of Christianity in the concept of the 'Kingdom of God' (*Reich Gottes*). In adopting this position, Ritschl was following a general trend among the theologians of his time.[31] Ritschl's innovation lay in the significance he attached to the concept in connection with his doctrines of justification and reconciliation. His biblical investigations had led him to the conclusion that the concept of the Kingdom of God was both the key to the preaching of Jesus, and the unifying principle of the Old and New Testaments.[32] Ritschl thus rejects the 'Scotist' principle of God as *dominium absolutum* and the juristic concept of God, modelled upon the state, in favour of the concept of God as the originator and ground of the teleological principle of the Kingdom of God.[33] All else in Christian theology is to be regarded as subordinated to this goal. This general principle is of particular importance in connection with Ritschl's discussion of the divine attributes. Thus God's eternity may be taken to refer to the fact that God 'remains the same, and maintains the same purpose and plan by which he creates and directs the world'.[34] Similarly, the divine attribute of 'righteousness' (*Gerechtigkeit*) is defined teleologically, in terms of the Kingdom of God:

Omnipotence receives the particular character of *righteousness* in the particular revelation of the old and new covenants. By 'righteousness', the Old Testament signifies the consistency of the divine direction towards salvation [*die Folgerichtigkeit der göttlichen Leitung zum Heil*] ... In so far as the righteousness of God achieves his dominion in accordance with its dominant purpose of salvation ... it is *faithfulness*. Thus in the New Testament the righteousness of God is also recognised as the criterion of the special actions by which the community of Christ is brought into existence and led on to perfection. Such righteousness therefore cannot be distinguished from the grace of God.[35]

Ritschl regards this deobjectified teleological understanding of the 'righteousness of God' as having circumvented the difficulties of the Orthodox concept, and to amount to a recovery of the teaching of the

Old and New Testaments,[36] as well as of Luther.[37] The concept
clearly marks a break with the concept of *iustitia distributiva* (whether
in the form associated with Orthodoxy, Pietism or the *Aufklärung*),
and permits Ritschl to avoid discussion of the question of how God
can justify sinful man (in that his understanding of the divine
righteousness relates solely to the manner in which God *does* justify
sinners).

On the basis of this teleological understanding of the economy of
salvation, Ritschl mounts a sustained critique of the soteriology of
Lutheran Orthodoxy. He characterises the Orthodox approach to the
locus iustificationis as follows:[38]

1. A doctrine of original sin is developed on the basis of texts such as
    Romans 5.12, by which original sin is deduced from the actual sin
    of Adam and Eve.
2. The fact of this universally inherited sin of the human race is then
    used as the basis of the demonstration of the necessity of redemp-
    tion. The mode of this redemption is determined by comparing sin
    with the divine attribute of retributive righteousness, following the
    general method of Anselm of Canterbury.
3. From this, the doctrine of the person and work of Christ is
    deduced, as is its application to the individual and community of
    believers.

Ritschl argues that this approach is based upon purely rational ideas
of God, sin and redemption, and is quite unsuited either to the
positive exposition of the doctrine, or to its defence against its
rationalist critics. In particular, Ritschl objects to the Augustinian
doctrine of original sin as implying a false hypostasisation of mankind
over and against the individuals who are its members, and as failing to
account for the fact that all men are sinful to different degrees. Ritschl
is at his closest to the soteriologies of the *Aufklärung* at this point.

It will, however, be clear that Ritschl's exposition of the doctrine of
justification represents a significant consolidation of the doctrine in
the face of earlier rationalist criticism. Three points may be singled
out as being of particular importance:

1. The demonstration, on the basis of an historical analysis of the
development of the doctrine of justification, that elements of the
doctrine rejected in one cultural situation might subsequently be
reappropriated in another. Thus the Enlightenment critique of the
Orthodox doctrine, and particularly its elimination of any objective
dimension to justification, was not of permanent significance. It is
difficult for the modern reader to appreciate the full force of this

point, in that he is unlikely to share the Hegelian framework within which theologians such as F. C. Baur constructed their thesis of the irreversibility of theological development.

2. The reappropriation of objective elements in the discussion of justification. Schleiermacher, although providing a strongly anti-rationalist foundation for his soteriology, had not taken this crucial step in re-establishing the traditional framework of the doctrine of justification.

3. The explicit statement that justification involves a *synthetic*, rather than an *analytic* judgement, which eliminated the theological foundation of the moral soteriologies of the *Aufklärung*.

It is also clear that Ritschl's analysis of the distinction between *rector* and *iudex* has considerable implications for certain Enlightenment soteriologies: indeed, it is significant that the *Aufklärer* (Tieftrunk) singled out by Ritschl for approval in his exposition of this matter was one of the few who had responded to the Kantian critique of the moralism of the Enlightenment (see §35).

Nevertheless, a strong degree of affinity may still be detected between the *Aufklärung*, Schleiermacher and Ritschl in relation to their discussion of the work of Christ. The subjectivism of the earlier period is still evident in Ritschl's exposition of the work of Christ. Christ is the revealer of certain significant (and not necessarily rational) insights concerning an unchangeable situation between God and man, rather than the founder of a new relationship between God and man.[39] For Martin Kähler, there remained an essential continuity between Ritschl and the *Aufklärung* at precisely this point.[40] According to Kähler, such a subjective approach to the meaning of the death of Christ represented a radical devaluation of its significance (*eine Entwertung des Werkes Christi*), in that Christ tends to be reduced to a mere symbol of the grace of God, without having any essential connection with that grace. It is this point which underlies his criticism of Ritschl's interpretation of the concepts of *Rechtfertigung* and *Versöhnung*: for Kähler, the latter corresponds to the objectively altered situation between God and man, arising through the historic work of Christ, while *Rechtfertigung* refers to a specific aspect of this situation – the individual's appropriation of this reconciliation through faith. The objective reality of reconciliation is necessarily prior to the subjective consciousness of this reconciliation.

Despite Kähler's strictures, the period 1880–1914 was characterised by the emergence of a significant degree of broad consensus relating to the question of justification. Drawing heavily upon the theme of the 'religious personality' of the historical Jesus, it was generally assumed that man's justification came about through the influence of this supremely powerful religious personality as it impinged upon his existence. The anti-rationalist character of this view may be judged by the general concession of an objective dimension to justification, and the non-rational character of the 'religious personality'. Although the development of critical biblical studies was gradually undermining this theology,[41] it would remain dominant until the year 1914, when the outbreak of the First World War posed a radical, and ultimately irresistible, challenge to its foundations. It is to that challenge which we now turn.

§37 The dialectical theology of justification: Barth

The outbreak of the First World War ushered in a new period in European theology, as the bourgeois optimism of the dawn of the century gave way to the sombre realism of the immediate post-war period. The impact of the war upon German theology, and particularly preaching, was momentous.[1] The link between Christianity and culture, one of the most significant achievements of Ritschl's theological synthesis, was widely regarded as discredited through the Kaiser's war policies.[2] The growing sense of the 'otherness' of God is reflected in many developments of the period, particularly Karl Holl's famous lecture of 31 October 1917, delivered before the University of Berlin, which inaugurated the Luther renaissance by demonstrating how radically Luther's concept of God differed from the somewhat emasculated deity of liberal Protestantism.[3] Such radical developments in the world of religious ideas could not fail to have an impact upon the doctrine of justification. To illustrate this impact, we turn to consider Karl Barth's lecture of 16 January 1916 in the Aarau Stadtkirche, on the theme of 'the righteousness of God'.[4]

Even today, the rhetorical power of this lecture may still be felt, and the passage of time has done nothing to diminish the force of Barth's sustained critique of man's self-assertion in the face of God, which he links with the question of the true meaning of the 'righteousness of God'. For Barth, the 'deepest, inmost and most certain fact of life, is that "God is righteous"'.[5] This fact is brought home to man by his conscience, which affirms the existence of a righteous God in the midst of human unrighteousness, which Barth recognised in the forces of capitalism as much as in the war which was raging over the face of Europe as he spoke.[6] Deep within man's inmost being lies the desire for the righteousness of God – and yet paradoxically, just when this divine righteousness appears to be on the verge of altering man's nature and conduct, man asserts his own self-righteousness. He is unable to contemplate the concept of a 'righteousness' which lies beyond his own control. Man welcomes the intervention of divine righteousness if it puts an end to wars or general strikes – but feels threatened by it when he realises that behind the *results* of human unrighteousness lies the unfathomable reality of *human righteousness* itself. The abolition of the consequences of human unrighteousness necessarily entails the abolition of human unrighteousness itself, and hence an entirely new existence.[7] Unable to accept this, man deforms the 'righteousness of God' into various forms of human righteousness, of which Barth singles out three types for particular criticism.

1. Moral righteousness (*die Gerechtigkeit unserer Moral*).[8] Barth rejects those spheres of human existence within which *Kulturprotestantismus* had located the locus of human morality (such as the family, or the state), on the grounds that, by restricting moral action to these spheres, man is simply ignoring the obvious fact that his action is immoral in others. For Barth, the existence of the capitalist system and the war demonstrated the invalidity of this thesis, as *both* were perpetrated in the name of morality.

2. Legal righteousness (*die Gerechtigkeit des Staates und der Juristen*).[9] Barth emphasises (prophetically, as the Third Reich was to demonstrate)[10] that human law is essentially orientated towards the ends specified by the state itself. At best, law could be regarded as an attempt to restrict the effect of human unrighteousness; at worst, it resulted in the establishment and perpetuation of human unrighteousness by the agencies of the state itself. Once more, Barth cites the war as exemplifying the defection of human ideas of 'righteousness' from those which conscience dictated should be recognised as divine.

3. Religious righteousness (*die religiöse Gerechtigkeit*).[11] Foreshadowing his mature critique of religion, Barth argues that man's religion, like his morality, is a tower of Babel, erected by man in the face of, and in defiance of, what his conscience tells him to be right.

In these three ways, Barth argues that man is failing to take the 'righteousness of God' seriously, lest it overwhelm and transform him: 'wir haben es nicht weiter gebracht als bis zu einem schlaftrunkenen Spiel mit den Schattenbildern der göttlichen Gerechtigkeit'.[12]

For Barth, the First World War both questions and demonstrates the righteousness of God. It *questions* that righteousness, in that man is unable to understand how a 'righteous' God could permit such an outrage; it *demonstrates* that same righteousness, in that it shows up human caricatures of divine righteousness for what they really are. Man has made his own concepts of righteousness into a God, so that God is simply the 'great personal or impersonal, mystical, philosophical or naïve Profundity and patron saint of our human righteousness, morality, state, civilisation, or religion'.[13] For Barth, the war has destroyed this image of God for ever, exposing it as an idol. By asserting his own concept of righteousness in the face of God, man constructed a 'righteous' God who was the first and least mourned casualty of the war.[14] The 'death' of this God has forced man to recognise that the 'righteousness of God' is qualitatively different from, and stands over and against, human concepts of righteousness.

This lecture is of considerable significance in a number of respects. Of particular importance is the dialectic between human and divine righteousness, which marks an unequivocal break with the 'liberal' understanding of the nature of history, progress and civilisation. 'God's will is not a superior projection of our own will: it stands in opposition to our will as one that is totally distinct [*als ein gänzlich anderer*].'[15] It is this infinite qualitative distinction between human and divine righteousness which forms the basis of Barth's repeated assertion that God is, and must be recognised as, God.

The radical emphasis upon the 'otherness' of God so evident in Barth's programmatic critique of concepts of the 'righteousness of God' clearly parallels the theological concerns of the young Luther.[16] It might therefore be thought that Barth's early dialectical theology, or mature 'theology of the Word of God', might represent a recovery of the Reformer's insights into the significance of the *articulus iustificationis*. In fact, this is not the case, and Barth actually remains within the framework established by the *Aufklärer*, Schleiermacher and Ritschl for the discussion of the justification of man before God.

Barth's mature theology may be regarded as extended reflection upon the fact that God has spoken to man – *Deus dixit* – abrogating the epistemological chasm separating them in doing so. God has spoken, in the fullness of time, and it is this event – or these events – which stand at the heart of Barth's theological concerns. It is the task of any authentic and responsible *Christian* theology to attempt to unfold the nature and identity of the God who had spoken to sinners in the man-ward movement envisaged in the *Deus dixit*. The structures and the inner nexus of relationships presupposed by the fact –

not the *idea* – of the *Deus dixit* determines what Christian theology has to say concerning the God who thus speaks. Barth thus abandons his earlier attempt, in the *Christliche Dogmatik*, to construct a 'grammatical' doctrine of the Trinity, based upon the idea or notion of revelation, in terms of the logical analysis of the event of the *Deus dixit* in terms of its implied subject, object and predicate: it is now the *fact*, rather than the *idea*, of revelation which claims Barth's attention. In effect, Barth develops an *Offenbarungspositivismus* in which the concrete structure of revelation as it has happened, and as it still happens, is interpreted theologically. To interpret the idea of revelation would, in effect, be to reduce theology to anthropology, in that a prior human model with its attending epistemological presuppositions is required for an analysis of the idea in question. Although revelation is a unitary act, it nevertheless possesses a divinely grounded unity in that diversity, which Barth formulates as 'Das Wort Gottes in seiner dreifachen Gestalt'. God speaks in history, but is not bound by its categories: the divine event of revelation can be actualised in every human circumstance, and is not confined to any given historical form under which he may speak (although Barth concedes that revelation demands historical predicates). The *function* of Barth's concept of the three-fold form of the Word of God is therefore to provide a secure theological foundation for Barth's insistence that God, who has spoken his final and supreme Word in Jesus Christ, still speaks to man today – and in every conceivable historical human circumstance. The single assumption, which alone can be recognised as a leading principle in Christian theology, is that God has spoken: *Dominus dixit*.

It is clear that Barth's theological system is, in essence, the unfolding of the inner structures and relationships which characterise the *fact* that God has spoken. The theological enterprise could thus be characterised as an exercise in *Nach-Denken*, following out the order of revelation in the man-ward movement of God in history. God has spoken to man across the epistemological chasm which separates them, and by so speaking to him, discloses both the reality of that separation and also the possibility of its abrogation. Barth confronts us with the paradox that man's inability to hear the Word of God is disclosed to him by that very Word. It is the reality of this divine abrogation of this epistemological chasm between God and man, and hence of the axiom *homo peccator non capax verbi Dei*, which stands at the heart of Barth's theological system.

But is the fact that God has spoken to man really what the gospel is all about? For Luther, the gospel was primarily concerned with the forgiveness of sins, whereas for Barth it is primarily concerned with the possibility of the right knowledge of God. Barth has placed the *divine revelation to sinful man* at the point where Luther placed the *divine justification of sinful man*. Although there are clearly points of contact between Luther and Barth, it is equally clear that Barth cannot share Luther's high estimation for the *articulus iustificationis*. In what follows, we propose to indicate why this is the case.

In the course of his exposition of the doctrine of justification,[17] Barth finds himself obliged to disagree with Ernst Wolf's analysis of the significance of the *articulus iustificationis* for the Reformers in general, and Luther in particular.[18] Wolf locates the significance of the *articulus iustificationis* in terms of its function, which he conveniently finds expressed in the celebrated dictum of Luther: 'articulus iustificationis est magister et princeps, dominus, rector et iudex super omnia genera doctrinarum, qui conservat et gubernat omnem doctrinam ecclesiasticam et erigit conscientiam nostram coram Deo'.[19] Wolf summarises Luther's understanding of the function of the *articulus iustificationis* in terms of its defining the 'centre and limits of Reformation theology' (*Mitte und Grenze reformatorischer Theologie*), which he elaborates as follows:

Mitte – das heißt: alles in reformatorischer Theologie ist auf sie bezogen; in ihr wird ja das *subiectum theologiae* zentral erfaßt.
Grenze – das heißt: alles, was außerhalb des durch diese Mitte Bestimmten und Zusammengefaßten liegt, ist '*error et venenum*' in theologia.[20]

Wolf illustrates this interpretation of the function of the *articulus iustificationis* with reference to Luther's anthropology and ecclesiology, with convincing results, and thus establishes two important principles concerning this function. First, the *articulus iustificationis* is established as the leading principle of Luther's theology, as is the priority of soteriological considerations within the same context. Second, the *subjectum theologiae* is defined as God's salvific activity towards sinful man. The modesty of Barth's soteriological interests is emphasised when compared with Luther's insistence upon their dominating rôle in positive theological speculation. Furthermore, the secondary and derivative rôle of revelation within the context of Luther's theology will be evident,[21] although Barth does not seem to appreciate this point.

Barth is thus clearly obliged to dispute Wolf's analysis,[22] which he does in an important discussion of the *temporary* significance of the *articulus iustificationis.* He acknowledges the peculiar importance which Luther attached to the doctrine, and further concedes that Luther did not regard the *articulus iustificationis* as the *primus et principalis articulus* merely in the polemic against Rome, but against all form of sectarianism. However, he notes that no evangelical theologian – with the possible exception of Martin Kähler – ever dared to construct a dogmatics with the *articulus* at its centre. This observation leads Barth to his critique of such a procedure. Conceding that the *articulus iustificationis* has been regarded as being *the* Word of the gospel on several occasions in the history of the church, he points out that these occasions represented instances where the gospel, understood as the free grace of God, was under threat – such as the Pelagian controversy. Barth then argues that it is necessary to free the theological enterprise from the contingencies of such controversies.[23] Barth then asserts that the *articulus iustificationis* is not central to the Christian proclamation:

Sie war nun einmal auch in der Kirche Jesu Christi nicht immer und nicht überall das Wort des Evangeliums, und es würde einen Akt allzu krampfhafter und ungerechter Ausschließlichkeit bedeuten, wenn man sie als solches ausgeben und behandeln würde.[24]

In one sense, this is clearly correct: it is true that the *articulus iustificationis* has not always been regarded as the centre of theological speculation. However, in that the *lex orandi* continually proclaims the centrality of the soteriological dimension of Christianity to Christian prayer, adoration and worship, in that the community of faith is understood to be based upon a soteriological foundation, it is possible that Barth has not represented the situation accurately. Furthermore, the fundamentally soteriological orientation of the patristic Trinitarian and Christological debates[25] leads to the conclusion that the Trinitarian and Christological dogmas are ultimately an expression of the soteriological convictions of the early church, whatever reinterpretation Barth may choose to place upon them. If the *articulus iustificationis* is taken to represent an assertion of the priority of soteriological considerations within the sphere of the church, Barth's statement must be regarded as seriously misleading.

It is, however clear that Barth's chief reason for relegating the *articulus iustificationis* to a secondary position is that it poses a serious and comprehensive threat to his own theological method. It is for this reason that he singles out Wolf's study of the function of the *articulus iustificationis* within the theology of the early Reformers for particular criticism. He therefore argues that the *articulus stantis et cadentis ecclesiae*, properly understood, is not the doctrine of justification as such, but its 'basis and culmination' in the 'confession of Jesus Christ'. This point is, however, hardly disputed, and is made by Wolf himself. The *articulus iustificationis* is merely a convenient statement of the salvific activity of God towards man, concentrated in Jesus Christ. While Barth is prepared to retain the traditional designation of the *articulus iustificationis* as the *articulus stantis et cadentis ecclesiae*, it is only on account of the community of faith's need to know of the objective basis of its existence: 'ohne die Wahrheit der Rechtfertigungslehre gäbe und gibt es gewiß keine wahre christliche Kirche'.[26] Nevertheless, so long as the essential truth of this article is not denied, Barth argues that it may withdraw into the background:

Gerade des Menschen Rechtfertigung und gerade das Vertrauen auf die objecktive Wahrheit der Rechtfertigungslehre verbietet uns das Postulat, daß ihr theologischer Vollzug in der wahren Kirche *semper, ubique et ab omnibus* als das *unum necessarium*, als die ganze Mitte oder als die einzige Spitze der christliche Botschaft und Lehre angesehen und behandelt werden müsse.[27]

In fact, it is clear that Barth's criticism of those who see in the *articulus iustificationis* the centre of the Christian faith is merely a consequence of his theological method. Soteriology is necessarily secondary to the fact of revelation, *Deus dixit*. As we noted earlier, Barth's own theology may be regarded as a reaction against the anthropocentricity of the liberal school – a reaction particularly evident in his inversion of the liberal understanding of God and man as epistemic object and subject respectively.[28] It will therefore be clear that Barth's theology is subject to precisely the same charge as that levelled by him against those who made the *articulus iustificationis* the centre of their theology. Barth has merely inverted the liberal theology, without fundamentally altering its frame of reference.[29] As such, he may be regarded as perpetuating the theological interests and concerns of the liberal school – particularly the question of how God may be known. The theologians of the liberal school were simply not concerned with the question of 'guilt' or of 'righteousness *coram Deo*', in that they possessed no sense of human bondage or slavery to sin. Thus Albrecht Ritschl regarded Luther's *de servo arbitrio* (1525), which develops the notion of man's bondage to sin in some depth (see §21), as 'an unfortunate botch' (*unglückliches Machwerk*) – although it was precisely this work which Rudolf Otto singled out as the 'psychological key' to understanding Luther. Similarly, Karl Holl's celebrated 1917 lecture on Luther was primarily concerned with the correct *knowledge* of God, rather than the soteriological dimension of his thought.[30] It is significant that the Luther renaissance initially served to emphasise the Reformer's emphasis upon the deity and 'otherness' of God, rather than the importance of the *articulus iustificationis* within the context of his theology. Dialectical theology was initially passionately concerned with the question of the right knowledge of God, inspired by a conviction of man's ignorance of God and the impossibility of any theologically significant natural knowledge of God. There is no means by which the yawning chasm (which Barth designates a 'crevasse') between God and man may be bridged from man's side – hence the news that God has bridged this chasm from his side must be taken with the utmost seriousness.

Early dialectical theology thus took up one aspect of Luther's theology (the 'otherness' of God) and abandoned the other (man's bondage to sin). Hence for the young Barth, as we have seen, the significance of the 'righteousness of God' lay in the fact that it was diametrically opposed to human concepts of righteousness. The lack of interest in man's bondage to sin, so characteristic of the liberal school and nineteenth-century theology in general, thus passed into the dialectical theology of the early twentieth century. The theological drama which constitutes the Christian faith is thus held to concern man and his knowledge of God, rather than the salvation of sinful man, caught up in the cosmic conflict between God and sin, the world and the devil.[31] Such a conflict is an impossibility within the context of Barth's theology, in that Barth shares with Hegel the difficulty of accommodating sin within an essentially monistic system. Barth has simply no concept of a divine engagement with the forces of sin or evil (unless these are understood in the epistemically reduced sense of 'ignorance' or 'misunderstanding'): instead, we find only talk about God making himself *known* to man. Barth even reduces the cross – traditionally the *locus* of precisely such a conflict – into a monologue between God the Father and God the Son.[32] The impartation of knowledge is no substitute for a direct confrontation with sin, death and evil.

The most significant aspect of Barth's criticism of the rôle allocated by Wolf to the *articulus iustificationis* lies in the different theological methods which they presuppose. For the later Barth, the concept of 'Christomonism' (Althaus) or 'Christological concentration' (von Balthasar) becomes of increasing importance. This Christological concentration finds its expression not in the history of Jesus of

Nazareth in general, or even in the crucifixion or resurrection in particular, but in the pre-existence of Christ, before all eternity.[33] The reason for this lies in Barth's understanding of the divine freedom to reveal, or not to reveal, himself, and is particularly well expressed in his critique of Hegel.[34] The antecedence of the doctrine of the eternal generation of the Son preserves the divine freedom in revelation. As a result, Barth now finds himself obliged to assert that Christ is equally present at every stage of the history of salvation. That redemption presupposes sin is a difficulty which cannot really be accommodated within Barth's essentially supralapsarian understanding of the Fall. It is simply impossible to accommodate the existence of sin and evil in a convincing manner within the context of a theology which presupposes that the historical process is absolutely determined by what is already perfected at the beginning of time. For Paul, sin 'entered into the world'; Barth cannot convincingly speak of sin 'entering into' such a Christologically determined historical process.[35]

Setting aside for a moment Barth's general lack of interest in soteriology, it will be clear that his emphasis upon what has been Christologically determined from all eternity leads to a certain lack of interest in what pertains here and now. The *articulus iustificationis* deals with man's predicament here and now, as he is enslaved by sin and unable to redeem himself. Barth's interests clearly lie elsewhere than with sinful man, even if it is possible to argue that his theology ultimately represents the outcome of anthropological and epistemological considerations.

A further point of importance relates to theological method in general. If the starting point for theological speculation is defined to be the *articulus iustificationis*, it is clear that an analytic and inductive method must be followed, arguing from the particular event of the divine justification of the sinner to the context in which it is set (such as the decrees of election). It can be shown that this methodology characterised the first period of Reformed theology, and is also characteristic of Arminius.[36] However, the onset of Reformed Orthodoxy (see §24) saw the starting point for theological speculation shifted from the concrete event of the justification of the sinner in Christ to the divine decrees of election and reprobation. Instead of an analytic and inductive method, a synthetic and deductive method was employed, involving the appeal from general principles (such as the divine decree to elect) to particular events (such as the justification of the elect in Christ). As a result, justification is accorded a place of low priority in the *ordo salutis*, in that it is merely the concrete actualisation of the prior divine decision of election. It will be clear that Barth approximates more closely to the theological method of Reformed Orthodoxy than to that of Calvin. The synthetic and deductive approach necessitated by his insistence upon the antecedence of the doctrine of the eternal generation of the Son leads to the incarnation, death and resurrection of Christ being placed low in the order of priorities within the context of his theological method. In that it is the application of a synthetic and deductive theological method by the theologians of Reformed Orthodoxy (such as Beza) which leads to the abstract *decretum absolutum*, so heavily criticised by Barth, it is somewhat ironical that his own theological method approximates so closely to this method.

Barth's modest soteriological concerns also express themselves in his doctrine of the work of Christ, in which a remarkable degree of continuity is evident with the *Aufklärung*, Schleiermacher and Ritschl,[37] demonstrating once more Barth's close affinity with the theological framework of the liberal school, despite substantial differences in substance. At first glance, Barth's theology of the work of Christ appears to be irreconcilably opposed to that of the *Aufklärung*. In his study of Protestant theology in the eighteenth and nineteenth centuries, Barth frequently displays his contempt for the theology of the *Aufklärung*.[38] Yet, as an analysis of the relation of his doctrine of the work of Christ, the passive nature of justifying faith and the related doctrine of the *servum arbitrium*, and the doctrine of election makes clear, Barth reproduces the main features of the *Aufklärung* soteriology. To make this point, we must begin with an analysis of Barth's Christological concentration of man's knowledge of God.

For Barth, theology is essentially an exposition of the identity and significance of Jesus Christ.[39] In effect, Barth turns the whole of theology into Christology, in that the doctrines of creation, election and redemption are considered in so far as they are determined by Christological considerations. Thus in the exposition of his doctrine of election, Barth insists that the concept must not be regarded as a theological abstraction which bears witness to the divine omnipotence. He consciously distances himself from the pronouncements of the Synod of Dort (see §24) by reinterpreting Calvin's concept of the *speculum electionis* to mean that Jesus Christ is at one and the same time the electing God and the elected man. If Christ were not the former, it would be necessary to look for the basis of election outside of Christ, and thus be driven to the doctrine of the *decretum absolutum* – which Barth considers unthinkable. Furthermore, in Jesus Christ the divine decision to become man is expressed tangibly. As there is a duality in this election, Barth feels himself able to retain the term *praedestinatio gemina*, while totally altering its traditional meaning.[40] Whereas Reformed Orthodoxy had interpreted the term to mean that God irresistibly wills some to eternal life and others to eternal death (§24), Barth argues that it refers to the divine decision to will *man* to election, salvation and life, and *God himself* to reprobation, perdition and death.[41] It is God himself who is condemned and rejected by his own judgement, and not those whom he elected in Christ. God thus chose as his own portion the negative element of the divine predestination, so that the positive element alone might be man's: in so far as predestination involves a negative verdict, that verdict is not pronounced against man.[42] In other words, although Barth concedes that predestination includes a negative element, this has no bearing upon man whatsoever.[43]

It is clear that God has elected man unilaterally (*einseitig*) and autocratically (*selbstherrlich*),[44] without any cooperation upon man's part.[45] Christ took man's place as his federal representative and substitute, so that whatever needed to be done for our salvation has been done, without man's consent or cooperation. Indeed, Barth insists upon the total inability of man to justify himself, or to cooperate with God in a significant manner with God in bringing about his salvation. For Barth, it is necessary to take a positive stand against the delusion (*Wahn*) of man's *liberum arbitrium* and cooperation with God, and to recognise that the Word of God includes a 'knowledge of the *servum arbitrium*, and the inability of man to give God his due and thus justify himself'.[46] If man is to have any say in his own justification – as the Catholic tradition within western Christianity has insisted to be the case – he must have the freedom to respond to divine grace. Barth follows the 1525 Luther (§21) and Calvin in asserting that man possesses no such freedom.[47] The freedom of man's will is totally and irreparably compromised by sin.[48] Barth's insistence upon the bondage of the human will, and his evident agreement with Calvin that faith is *res mere passiva*,[49] serve to emphasise further that man is absolutely and totally unable to make any response whatsoever to the divine initiative in justification. When this doctrine of the soteriological impotence of man is related with Barth's theology of election, an astonishing situation results.

For Barth, it is impossible for God to select man to reprobation, as we have noted above. God has already elected this element of *praedestinatio gemina* for himself. In so far as predestination includes a 'No!', this 'No!' is not spoken against man.[50] Man is totally unable to reject whatever God may have elected for him. This point is made by Barth repeatedly, as he emphasises the ultimate impotence of unbelief in the face of divine grace. Unbelief does not cancel God's decision to elect man. God's judgement has been executed against Christ, and will never be executed against man himself, in whose place Christ stood. Man may believe, or he may not believe – but whether he believes or not is quite irrelevant to his election. It may seem impossible for man to be elected, on account of his sin and unbelief – but in fact, precisely the opposite is the case. It is impossible for man not to be elected. As is well known, this aspect of Barth's theology has been criticised for its apocatastasian tendencies.[51] His doctrine of election, when linked with his understanding of the capacities of fallen man, necessarily leads to a doctrine of universal restoration: all men are saved, whether they know it or not, and whether they care for it or not.

With this point in mind, it will be clear that the crucial question now concerns man's knowledge of this election. Barth frequently emphasises that Christ is the *locus* of man's self-knowledge as a theological entity. Thus man only knows himself to be a sinner, and what this implies for his theological existence and status, in the light of Jesus Christ.[52] Similarly, Barth insists that man's election is disclosed to him through the *speculum electionis*, Jesus Christ. In his discussion of both the positive and negative dimensions of the death and resurrection of Christ, Barth reveals an overriding concern for the *knowledge* which results:

Im Spiegel des für uns dahingegebenen und als dieser Dahingegebene gehorsamen Jesus Christus *wird offenbar*, wer wir sind: wir als die, für die er dahingegebenen wurde, sich selbst gehorsam dahingegeben hat. Im Licht der Demut, in deren Bewährung er als wahrer Gott für uns gehandelt, d.h. gelitten hat und gestorben ist, sind wir *durchschaut, erkannt und haben wir uns selbst zu erkennen* als die Hochmütigen, die sich selbst Gott, Herr, Richter, Helfer sein wollen, die als solche von Gott abgewichen und also Sünder sind ... Und so ist und bleibt die *Erkenntnis* der Gnade Gottes und des aus ihr fließenden Trostes in diesem Urteil und also die *Erkenntnis* seines positiven Sinnes gebunden daran, daß wir nicht aufhören, uns auch als in Ihm Verurteilten *zu erkennen*.[53]

It is on the basis of the Christologically disclosed knowledge of the reconciliation of the world to God that the community of faith stands or falls:

Und gäbe es keine Erkenntnis der hier waltenden Gerechtigkeit Gottes oder Erkenntnis nur in Form von Verkennung, getrübt und entstellt durch teilweise oder gänzliche Mißverständnisse, wie könnte dann die Gemeinde dem Irrtum und Zerfall und der Glaube dem Zweifel, der Auflösung in allerlei Unglauben und Aberglauben entrinnen?[54]

The astonishingly frequent references to *Erkenntnis* and its cognates, where one might expect to find reference to *Heil* or *Versöhnung*, is one of the more remarkable aspects of Barth's discussion of man's justification *coram Deo*, suggesting that Barth regards man's knowledge and insight, rather than God's activity, as forming the centre of theological reflection. Barth's entire discussion of the justification of man appears to refer to man's epistemic situation – in other words, to his *Christologically disclosed knowledge of the Christologically determined situation*.

Barth's frequently observed emphasis upon salvation as *Erkenntnis* is easily understood: given that all men are saved eventually – which is the inevitable conclusion which must be drawn from his doctrines of election and *servum arbitrium* – the *present knowledge* of this situation is clearly of enormous importance. As all men will be saved eventually, it becomes of some importance that this salvation be actualised in the present – for such is the basic presupposition of Christian dogmatics and ethics alike. Both these disciplines are totally and absolutely dependent upon the presupposition that *man knows that he is saved*. Furthermore, in that dogmatics is a discipline which is carried out within the community of faith, it must reflect the basic presupposition upon which that community is grounded – in other words, the knowledge of its present salvation. Barth's repeated emphasis upon the cognitive character of salvation is perfectly consistent with this theology of election, in that, whatever salvation may be ultimately, it is certainly a deliverance from false thinking at present. Man may feel that all is lost, that there is no hope of salvation in a world permeated by sin and unbelief – and yet precisely the opposite is, in fact, the case. As Brunner has pointed out,[55] Barth's doctrine of election may be compared to a group of men who think that they are about to drown in a stormy sea, whereas the water is actually so shallow that there is no possibility whatsoever of drowning – this knowledge has, however, been withheld from them. What is necessary is that they be informed of the *true* situation which underlies the *apparent* situation. Thus Barth's doctrine of faith permits the believer to see beyond the sinful world of unbelief to the triumph of divine grace which lies behind it, and is disclosed in

Christ, the *speculum electionis*. As all men will be saved eventually, apparently quite independently of their inclinations or interest, it is quite natural that Barth's attention should be concentrated upon the resolution of the epistemological confusion with which the believer is faced. Christ is thus the mirror, or *locus*, in which the Christologically determined situation is disclosed to man.

With this point in mind, let us return to Martin Kähler's criticism of the soteriologies of the *Aufklärung*, Schleiermacher and the liberal school (see §35). For Kähler, a theology of the work of Christ could be classified under one of two types: the first, which corresponds to that of the *Aufklärung*, understands Christ to have communicated certain significant insights concerning an unchangeable situation; the second, which corresponds to his own view, understands Christ to be the founder of an altered situation.[56] Kähler's distinction allows two quite different approaches to the death of Christ to be identified:

1. Those which regard man's predicament as being *ignorance of the true situation*. Man *is* saved, but does not realise it: upon being informed of the true situation, he is enabled to act upon the basis of this knowledge, and adjust and reorientate his existence to what he now realises to be the true state of affairs. In so far as any alteration takes place in the situation, it is in man's subjective awareness; indeed, one could argue that the true situation is irrelevant, unless man recognises it as such – thus emphasising the necessity of being informed of it.

2. Those which regard man's predicament as being *bondage to sin or evil*. Man is enslaved, and may not realise it: upon being informed of the true situation, he still requires liberation. The knowledge of man's bondage may well lead to a recognition of the possibility of liberation, and hence the search for the means of that liberation – but such liberation is not identical with, or given simultaneously with, or even a necessary consequence of, the knowledge of man's true situation. A victory of good over evil, of grace over sin, is required, which man may appropriate and make his own, if he is to break free from the hegemony of sin – and precisely such a victory is to be had in the death of Christ upon the cross.

It is clear that Barth's understanding of the work of Christ falls into the first of these categories. For Barth and the *Aufklärer* (see §34), Christ is supremely the revealer of the knowledge of man's true situation, by which man is liberated from false understandings of his situation. For Barth, the death of Christ does not in any sense change the soteriological situation, in that this has been determined from all eternity – rather, he discloses the Christologically determined situation to man. Man's dilemma concerns his knowledge of God, rather than his bondage to sin or evil (unless these are understood in the epistemically reduced sense of 'ignorance' or 'confusion').[57]

It will therefore be clear that Barth's new emphasis upon the theocentricity of theology, and particularly his recognition of the divinity of God, is not associated with a revival in interest in the *articulus iustificationis*. Indeed, Barth operates within the same theological framework as the *Aufklärer*, Schleiermacher and the liberal school at this point, despite their evident differences at others.

§38 Justification as a hermeneutical principle

Barth is the last major theologian to be discussed in the present study. This is not to say that justification has ceased to be of theological significance in the last decades, but reflects the fact that sufficient time has not elapsed to establish a proper historical perspective, with reference to which the significance of more recent developments may be judged. In this concluding section, we propose merely to indicate the general features of more recent developments, which are particularly associated with the recognition of the doctrine of justification as a hermeneutical principle. Another generation will have to pass judgement upon their significance, in the light of subsequent developments.

The development of the doctrine of justification within the Christian tradition may be regarded as a systematic engagement with four major questions concerning the church's proclamation of the justification of sinful man.

1. How is the concept of the 'justification of the ungodly' to be understood?
2. How is the 'justification of the ungodly' possible?
3. In what sense is the proclamation of the 'justification of the ungodly' relevant?
4. How may the proclamation of the 'justification of the ungodly' be established as a legitimate and necessary interpretation of the history of Jesus of Nazareth?

The development of the doctrine in the pre-modern period (that is, to about 1700) may be regarded as a systematic engagement with the first two such questions.[1] As the present chapter has indicated, the modern period was not totally unconcerned with these questions (see §34), but nevertheless found itself increasingly forced to consider the two latter such questions. The rise of increasingly sophisticated methods of biblical criticism led to the suggestion, increasingly voiced during the later nineteenth century, that there existed a radical disjuncture between the preaching of Jesus and Paul, so that the doctrine of justification represented a gross distortion of the essentially simple message of Jesus.[2] In the late nineteenth century, liberal theologians such as Schweitzer, Wernle and Wrede argued that the Pauline doctrine of justification by faith was of purely historical interest, being an aspect of Paul's anti-Jewish polemic rather than the positive proclamation of a universal theology of redemption. The rise of European secularism in the aftermath of the First World War led to increased scepticism concerning the relevance of God to 'modern emancipated man',[3] with a consequent decline in the perceived significance of Luther's celebrated question concerning the quest for a gracious God.[4] Whereas earlier generations of theologians were primarily concerned with the exposition and analysis of the church's proclamation of the divine justification of sinful man, Western theologians of the present century have found themselves increasingly obliged to defend its relevance and legitimacy in the face of fundamental challenges to both.

In response to the first challenge, the present century has witnessed a growing tendency to relate the doctrine of justification to the question of the meaning of human existence, rather than the more restricted sphere of man's justification *coram Deo*.[5] It is this trend which underlies the existentialist reinterpretation of the doctrine, associated with Bultmann, Tillich and Ebeling, to which we now turn.

In his highly influential *Sein und Zeit* (1927), Martin Heidegger employed the phenomenological method of Husserl to develop an existential understanding of the structures of human existence.[6] Arguing that the basic meaning of *Existenz* derives from *ex-sistere*, 'to stand outside', Heidegger characterised man's existence in terms of his ability to stand outside the world of things. What is it that distinguishes the existence of man from that of inanimate objects? Heidegger argues that there are three fundamental senses in which man's peculiar way of being (*Dasein*) may be distinguished from that of things (*Vorhandenheit*).[7]

1. Man transcends the subject–object relationship, in that he is at one and the same time both subject and object to himself. He has the unique ability to reflect upon his nature, to understand himself, and to be open to himself in his being. He may properly be said to be at

one with himself, or at war with himself, in that his relation to *Dasein* is open and alterable.

2. Human existence must be regarded as open-ended, in that man is never fixed or complete in his being. In other words, it is to be understood in terms of possibility, rather than actuality.

3. Human existence must be regarded as individual. Heidegger lays emphasis upon the 'individuality' (*Jemeinigkeit*) of existence, which cannot be separated from the individual in question.

Like Kierkegaard, Heidegger is concerned with man in his subjectivity.[8] Whereas the traditional approach to questions of existence involved an ontic inquiry concerning entities (*das Seiende*), Heidegger argues that the question should be approached from an ontological perspective, inquiring concerning 'Being' (*Sein*) itself.

Although it is clear that Heidegger's analysis of human existence in general is of considerable potential theological significance,[9] the aspect of his analysis which is of particular relevance to our study is his distinction between authentic (*eigentlich*) and inauthentic (*ineigentlich*) existence.[10] Man exists in the world, which defines the arena within which he is confronted with the various possibilities open to him. Man is in the world, and is bound up with its existence, even though he is quite distinct from its way of being. The possibility that man will be overwhelmed by the way of being which the world represents, and thus 'fall' from an authentic to an inauthentic mode of existence, is an essential element of Heidegger's analysis of existence. Man may fall away (*abfallen*) from himself, obliterating his awareness of the essential distinction from the world by becoming absorbed in it, and thus becoming 'uprooted' (*entwurzelt*) from his proper way of being.[11] Man thus becomes alienated from his true existence through his fall into the world.[12] Although it is tempting to equate *Verfallenheit* directly with the theological concept of original sin, it is clear that Heidegger maintains that fallenness and alienation are merely existential *possibilities open to man*, rather than a normative definition of human existence.

The relevance of this existential analysis of human existence to the Christian theology of justification was indicated by Heidegger himself, who pointed out that Luther's doctrine of justification, especially when considered in relation to the question of the assurance of salvation, could be interpreted in existentialist categories.[13] Although critics have subsequently pointed out that Luther is primarily concerned with the justification of man *coram Deo*, rather than the self-justification of man in his particular existential situation,[14] it is this understanding of the significance of the doctrine of justification which achieved considerable influence through the works of Bultmann and Tillich.

For Bultmann, the New Testament is concerned with the fundamental question of the nature of human existence. The Christian kerygma, expressed in mythical form in the New Testament, is a divine word addressed directly to man, revealing that his present state of existence is inauthentic, and making known the possibility of authentic existence through the Christ-event, upon condition of the decision (*Entscheidung*) of faith.[15] Man is a 'potentiality to be' (*ein Sein-Können*), whose innate potentiality for authentic existence is exposed and developed by the kerygma. The Pauline concept of justification by faith thus concerns a fundamental aspect of human existence. In man's decision of faith, in response to the kerygma, he attains his authentic self (*sein eigentliches Sein*).[16] Although Bultmann was criticised for his use of Heidegger's analysis of human existence, in that it appeared to reduce the gospel to an analysis of the condition of natural man,[17] Bultmann argued that the specifically Christian answer to the question of how authentic existence might be attained served to distinguish the gospel from secular understandings of human existence.[18]

A similar existential interpretation of the doctrine of justification is associated with Paul Tillich. In an important essay of 1924, Tillich noted that the doctrine of justification applied not merely to the religious aspects of moral life, but also to the intellectual life of religion, in that it is not merely the *sinner*, but also the *doubter*, who is justified by faith.[19] Tillich thus extends the scope of the doctrine to the universal human situation of despair and doubt concerning the meaning of existence. Tillich thus argues that the doctrine of justification, when rightly understood, lies at the heart of the Christian faith.[20] While nineteenth-century man was characterised by his idealism, his twentieth-century counterpart is characterised by existential despair and anxiety – and it is to this latter man that the Christian message must be made relevant. Tillich attempts this task by the 'method of correlation', by which the Christian proclamation is 'correlated' with the existential questions arising from human existence.[21] For Tillich, the doctrine of justification addresses a genuine human need: man must learn to accept that he is accepted, despite being unacceptable.[22]

Similarly, Gerhard Ebeling argues that the concept of 'justification' is as strange to modern man 'as an Egyptian sphinx', and argues that the concept must be demythologised and interpreted in order that it may be shown to have an essential connection with human existence and its problems.[23] For Ebeling, in the event of justification, a fundamental change in man's situation takes place, by which he is transferred from the state of non-existence (*Nichtsein*) to that of authentic existence (*Sein*).[24] Although Ebeling's approach to the doctrine may appear to parallel that of Bultmann or Tillich, Ebeling has gone far beyond them in drawing attention to the hermeneutical insights which lay at the basis of Luther's doctrine of justification *sola fide*, thus clarifying the nature of the doctrine as a critical principle in judging thought and practice. According to Ebeling, the central point of the Christian faith is that the proclamation of the grace of God in word and sacrament is itself the saving event, in that it proclaims the death and resurrection of Christ, and thence effects what it proclaims.

On the basis of this analysis, it will be clear that there has been a growing tendency to treat the doctrine of justification as an hermeneutical principle for interpreting, and subsequently transforming, human existence. As a result, there has been a corresponding increased emphasis upon both the subjective or anthropological dimension of the doctrine, as well as upon the proclamation which brings about this existential transformation of the human situation.[25] This increased emphasis upon the rôle of the kerygma, or the Word of God, evidently raises the question of the legitimation of the kerygma – in other words, whether the soteriological or existential interpretation placed upon the history of Jesus of Nazareth by the Christian church, and expressed in the doctrine of justification, is justifiable. Lying behind the kerygma of the justification of the ungodly is the problem of the justification of the kerygma itself.

This problem is particularly linked with the question of the relation between the preaching of Jesus and the proclamation of Paul – in other words, the question of how a legitimate and theologically coherent account may be given of the transition from the preaching of Jesus to the proclamation about Jesus. The *Aufklärer* suggested that the Pauline interpretation of Jesus (expressed in the doctrine of justification) was an improper and unnecessary dogmatic transformation of what was originally an essentially ethical proclamation. The rise of the 'New Quest of the Historical Jesus' since 1953 has, however, been based upon the explicitly acknowledged presupposition that there is an essential continuity between the history of Jesus of Nazareth and the proclamation of Christ.[26] In the Christian proclamation, the proclaimer himself becomes the proclaimed, as the one who calls to faith becomes the one who is believed. It may therefore be argued that the proclamation of the justification of the ungodly is an historically and theologically legitimate interpretation of the significance of the history of Jesus of Nazareth.[27] A further refinement of this development is the argument that it is axiomatic that there is an essential continuity between the 'Jesus of history' and the 'Christ of faith', so that the *articulus iustificationis* is treated as the axiomatic foundation of the Christian faith.[28]

It will thus be evident that the twentieth century has not witnessed a general abandonment of the doctrine of justification, but rather the discussion of aspects of the doctrine which were taken for granted by earlier generations. The difficulties which contemporary western theologians have been obliged to consider were not envisaged in the pre-modern period. Although the church continues to proclaim the justification of man through the free grace of God, and although this message continues to find a response in those to whom it is addressed, there has been growing recognition of the need to establish and defend the relevance and legitimacy of this proclamation in the first place.

At this point, our study of the development of the doctrine must end. It is too soon to pass judgement upon the significance of developments within recent decades. The increase in ecumenical conversations has led to the establishment of a broad – and apparently genuine – consensus between Catholic and Protestant on the matter of justification.[29] Increasingly precise historical investigation of the origins of the Reformation and the nature of the sixteenth-century debates on justification has led to the recognition that many of the disputed questions on justification involved conceptual differences, or differences in emphasis, rather than substantial disagreement on the basic question of salvation. The confessionally biased historical caricatures of the past have now been generally abandoned, so that issues which were once thought to necessitate divisions within Christendom are no longer viewed in this manner. It remains to be seen what the consequences of such agreement will finally be.

It will be evident that the present study, although clearly incomplete and inadequate, permits certain significant general conclusions to be drawn. First, it will be clear that the development of the doctrine of justification indicates the general consensus of the church down the ages to the effect that the human situation has been transformed through the action of God in Jesus Christ. The precise nature of this action, and the manner in which it impinges upon man, were and are the subject of continuing debate. The only significant challenge to this consensus dates from the time of Enlightenment, and its impact has diminished with the recognition of the questionable character of its presuppositions.

Second, the action of God in transforming man's situation is regarded as based upon the grace of God alone. Although man is generally understood to be involved in his justification in some manner, and to have certain definite obligations laid upon him as a consequence of his justification, the Christian tradition has invariably emphasised the priority of the gracious divine action. Even the theologians of the *via moderna* expressed this in the theologoumenon of the *pactum* between God and man, understood as a concrete expression of the divine grace and liberality. Once more, it is necessary to note the challenge posed to this consensus during the period of the Enlightenment, when it was occasionally suggested that man's actions were prior to – and, indeed, the occasion, or even the *cause*, of – the divine grace: the Kantian critique of this opinion proved decisive.

Third, it will be clear that the development of the doctrine is neither linear nor continuous, in that developments often took place in an essentially sporadic or episodic manner, with one generation often reappropriating elements of the doctrine discarded by an earlier period. It is therefore both improper and impossible to argue for a consistent general pattern of doctrinal development, either as the basis upon which the future development[30] of the doctrine may be predicted, or as a major element in establishing the propriety or legitimacy of present thinking on the doctrine.

One final point must be made before bringing this work to a close. The relevance and urgency of the doctrine of justification relates to the identity and existence of the Christian church, and hence to Christian theology, in so far as this is seen as a consequence of the existence of the church. The full significance of the doctrine relates to its proclamation from the pulpit, rather than its discussion in the university seminar room. The Reformation represents a rare instance of a situation in which these two aspects of the doctrine temporarily converge. In this respect, our analysis of the development of the doctrine, particularly since the time of the Enlightenment, is potentially misleading, in that we have been obliged to concentrate upon the academic analysis of the doctrine, rather than the form it has taken, and still takes, in the popular preaching and literature of the church. Were this deficiency in both historical and theological perspective corrected, it would be clear that the doctrine may still lay claim to be the *articulus stantis et cadentis ecclesiae*.[31]

In the present study, we have been concerned with the documentation and analysis of the manner in which previous generations of Christians have understood and articulated the remarkable insight that God justifies sinners. It is this heritage which the Christian tradition has bequeathed to us, in order that we might make it, and the task of articulating and defending it, our own.

> Was du erebt von deinen Vätern hast,
> Erwirb es, um es zu besitzen.[32]

Abbreviations

ARG	*Archiv für Reformationsgeschichte*
BSLK	*Bekenntnisschriften der evangelisch-lutherischen Kirche*
BSRK	*Bekenntnisschriften der reformierten Kirche*
ChH	*Church History*
CR	Corpus Reformatorum
CT	Concilium Tridentinum: diariorum, actorum, epistolarum, tractatuum nova collectio
D.	Enchiridion Symbolorum
EE	*Estudios eclesiásticos*
EThL	*Ephemerides Theologicae Lovanienses*
FcS	*Franciscan Studies*
FS	*Franziskanische Studien*
HThR	*Harvard Theological Review*
JEH	*Journal of Ecclesiastical History*
KuD	*Kerygma und Dogma*
OS	*Calvini Opera Selecta*
REAug	*Revue des études augustiniennes*
RET	*Revista española de teología*
RSPhTh	*Revue des sciences philosophiques et théologiques*
SJTh	*Scottish Journal of Theology*
StA	*Melanchthons Werke in Auswahl: Studienausgabe*
StTh	*Studia Theologica*
WA	D. Martin Luthers Werke: Kritische Gesamtausgabe
ZKG	*Zeitschrift für Kirchengeschichte*
ZKTh	*Zeitschrift Für Katholische Theologie*
ZSTh	*Zeitschrift für systematische Theologie*
ZThK	*Zeitschrift für Theologie und Kirche*

Notes

Introduction to chapter 6

1 See Wolf, 'Die Rechtfertigungslehre als Mitte und Grenze reformatorischer Theologie'. For a useful (if purely descriptive) general survey of the thought of the Reformers on this matter, see Henry Strohl, *La pensée de la Réforme* (Neuchâtel, 1951), 29–45 (on 'faith'); 85–120 (on 'justification by faith').

2 e.g., see WA 25.332.12–13; 39 I.205.2–5; 40 I.72.20–1; *BSLK* 416.22–3.

3 On the basis of his analysis of Valentin Löscher's *Timotheus Verinus* (Wittenberg, 1714), Loofs argued that this celebrated phrase actually dates from the eighteenth century, and is characteristic of Lutheran theologians alone: 'Der articulus stantis et cadentis ecclesiae', 345. In fact, it appears to have been in use at least a century earlier. Thus the Reformed theologian J. H. Alsted begins his discussion (1618) of the justification of man before God with the following assertion: 'articulus iustificationis dicitur articulus stantis et cadentis ecclesiae' (*Theologia scholastica didactica*, 711). Precursors of the phrase may, of course, be found in the writings of Luther himself: e.g., WA 40 III.352.3, 'quia isto articulo stante stat Ecclesia, ruente ruit Ecclesia'.

4 See Heiko A. Oberman, 'Headwaters of the Reformation: *Initia Lutheri – Initia Reformationis*', in *Luther and the Dawn of the Modern Era*, ed. H. A. Oberman (Leiden, 1974), 40–88.

5 e.g., see Benjamin B. Warfield, *Calvin and Augustine* (Philadelphia, 1956), 322: 'The Reformation, inwardly considered, was just the triumph of Augustine's doctrine of grace over Augustine's doctrine of the church.'

6 On the late medieval Augustinian renaissance, see H. A. Oberman, *Werden und Wertung der Reformation* (Tübingen, 1977), 82–140; on the Amorbach edition of Augustine, see J. de Ghellinck, 'La première édition imprimée des "opera omnia S. Augustini"', in *Miscellanea J. Gessler* I (Antwerp, 1948), 530–47. For useful insights into the Reformers' use of patristic sources, see Peter Fraenkel, *Testimonia Patrum: The Function of the Patristic Argument in the Theology of Philip Melanchthon* (Genève, 1961); Alfred Schindler, *Zwingli und die Kirchenväter* (Zürich, 1984).

7 See §19 and McGrath, 'Forerunners of the Reformation? A Critical

Examination of the Evidence for Precursors of the Reformation Doctrines of Justification', *HThR* 75 (1982), 219–42 for further discussion.

8 See A. J. Beachy, *The Concept of Grace in the Radical Reformers* (Nieuwkoop, 1977), for a discussion of the tendency of the radical Reformers to supplement or replace the notion of *imputatio iustitiae* with that of an essential ontological change within man (often conceived realistically, as 'deification').

§20

1 WA 9.42.35–43.6; 44.1–4. Cf. McGrath, *Luther's Theology of the Cross*, 82–5.

2 WA 3.289.1–5; 4.261.32–9; 262.2–7. Cf. O. Bayer, *Promissio: Geschichte der reformatorischen Wende in Luthers Theologie* (Göttingen, 1971), 119–23; 128–43; 313–17; McGrath, *Luther's Theology of the Cross*, 85–92.

3 Note especially WA 4.262.2–7. Cf. §7 of the present study.

4 WA 54.185.12–186.21. English translations in Rupp, *The Righteousness of God*, 121–2; McGrath, *Luther's Theology of the Cross*, 95–8. For the debate in the literature, see Gerhard Pfeiffer, 'Das Ringen des jungen Luthers um die Gerechtigkeit Gottes', *Luther-Jahrbuch* 26 (1959), 25–55; Regin Prenter, *Der barmherzige Richter: Iustitia Dei passiva in Luthers Dictata super Psalterium 1513–1515* (København, 1961); Albrecht Peters, 'Luthers Turmerlebnis', *ZSTh* 3 (1961), 203–36; Bornkamm, 'Zur Frage der Iustitia Dei beim jungen Luther'; Kurt Aland, *Der Weg zur Reformation: Zeitpunkt und Charakter des reformatorischen Erlebnisses Martin Luthers* (München, 1965); Oberman, '"Iustitia Christi" and "Iustitia Dei"'; McGrath, *Luther's Theology of the Cross*.

5 WA 54.185.12–20.

6 Heinrich Denifle, *Luther and Luthertum in der ersten Entwickelung, quellenmäßig dargestellt* (2 vols: Mainz, 1904), especially 392–5; 404–15.

7 *Die abendländischen Schriftausleger bis Luther über Iustitia Dei (Röm. 1.17) und Iustificatio* (Mainz, 1905).

8 Biel, *In II Sent.* dist. xxvii q. unica a. 3 dub. 5; ed. Werbeck/Hoffmann, 2.525.11–526.17: 'Homo non potest evidenter scire se facere quod in se est ...'

9 For a detailed analysis of the nature, date and theological significance of this 'discovery', see McGrath, *Luther's Theology of the Cross*, 95–147; 153–61.

10 These *lectures* (now published in WA 57.5–108) should not be confused with the Galatians *commentary* of 1519 (WA 2.436–618). Although the commentary is clearly based upon the lectures, there are significant differences.

11 For this important phrase, see WA 3.588.8; 4.127.10; 231.7; 56.282.9–13. Bizer asserts that *fides* and *humilitas* are synonymous over the period 1513–18, with excellent reasons for doing so: *Fides ex auditu*, 19–21.

12 WA 3.124.12–14; 4.91.4–5; 111.33–7; 262.2–7. Cf. Bayer, *Promissio:*

Geschichte der reformatorische Werde in Luthers Theologie, 128; McGrath, *Luther's Theology of the Cross*, 89–92.

13 For the argument, see McGrath, *Luther's Theology of the Cross*, 113–19.
14 Most notably by Vogelsang, *Die Anfänge von Luthers Christologie*.
15 For the argument, see McGrath, *Luther's Theology of the Cross*, 119–28.
16 WA 56.379.1–15.
17 It is possible that Luther has come to this conclusion toward the end of the *Dictata*: WA 4.309.6–11 is highly suggestive.
18 WA 56.385.15–22. Note the occurrence of the term *servum arbitrium*.
19 WA 56.382.26–7; 502.32–503.5.
20 Luther's marginal comments on Biel are of importance here: unfortunately, their date remains uncertain: H. Volz, 'Luthers Randbemerkungen zu zwei Schriften Gabriel Biels: Kritische Anmerkungen zu Hermann Degerings Publikation', *ZKG* 81 (1970), 207–19.
21 McGrath, *Luther's Theology of the Cross*, 100–13. See also §6.
22 McGrath, 'Mira et nova diffinitio iustitiae'.
23 McGrath, *Luther's Theology of the Cross*, 153–61.
24 Scholion to Galatians 2.16; WA 57.69.14–16; cf. WA 2.503.34–6. Note also the 1516 statement: 'Iustitia autem ista non est ea, de qua Aristoteles 5. Ethicorum vel iurisperiti agunt, sed fides seu gratia Christ iustificans' (WA 31 1.456.36). (We have taken the liberty of correcting the clearly incorrect '3. Ethicorum'.) It is Luther's critique of the concept of *iustitia* underlying the soteriology of the *via moderna* which lies at the heart of his later critique of Aristotle: see McGrath, *Luther's Theology of the Cross*, 136–41.
25 For the reasons, see McGrath, *Luther's Theology of the Cross*, 141–2.
26 e.g., see Rich, *Anfänge*, 73–95. Cf. CR (Zwingli) 1.224.11–2: 'Hat der Luter da getruncken, da wir getruncken habend, so hatt er mit uns gemein die euangelisch leer.' Recently, however, Neuser has suggested that, in his reminiscences, Zwingli tends defensively to minimise his debts to both Luther and Erasmus: Wilhelm H. Neuser, *Die reformatorische Wende bei Zwingli* (Neukirchen, 1977). However, Zwingli's dependence upon Luther is still to be dated from the 1520s.

§21

1 WA 56.502.32–503.5 is particularly significant here.
2 WA 40 1.357.18–22.
3 The historical background to this question is complex: see McGrath, *Luther's Theology of the Cross*, 27–71.
4 For this suggestion, see McGrath, 'John Calvin and Late Medieval Thought'.
5 Holl, 'Die Rechtfertigungslehre in Luthers Vorlesung über den Römerbrief mit besonderer Rücksicht auf die Frage der Heilsgewißheit', in *Gesammelte Aufsätze*, 1.111–54.
6 Holl, 'Rechtfertigungslehre', 117.
7 Holl, 'Rechtfertigungslehre', 123.

8 Holl, 'Rechtfertigungslehre', 128.

9 e.g., Regin Prenter, *Spiritus Creator: Studien zu Luthers Theologie* (München, 1954).

10 See E. Schott, *Fleisch und Geist nach Luthers Lehre* (Leipzig, 1930); W. Joest, *Ontologie der Person bei Luther* (Göttingen, 1967); Gerhard Ebeling, *Lutherstudien* II: *Disputatio de homine 1. Teil. Text und Traditionshintergrund* (Tübingen, 1977); H.-M. Barth, 'Martin Luther disputiert über den Menschen: Ein Beitrag zu Luthers Anthropologie', *KuD* 27 (1981), 154–66.

11 WA 56.347.2–11.

12 WA 56.343.16–19.

13 WA 56.270.9–11; 343.16–23; 351.23–352.7. Cf. Hermann, *Luthers These 'Gerecht und Sünder zugleich'*.

14 WA 56.268.27–269.2. Cf. 269.25–30.

15 WA 56.442.17, 20–3.

16 e.g., see P. S. Schubert, *Augustins Lex-Aeterna-Lehre nach Inhalt und Quellen* (Münster, 1924). See §4 for further discussion.

17 WA 56.3.6; 157.2.

18 WA 40 I.229.28; cf. 229.4.

19 WA 5.608.16.

20 e.g., *WA* 56.259.14.

21 Walter von Loewenich, 'Zur Gnadenlehre bei Augustin und Luther', in *idem, Von Augustine zu Luther* (Witten, 1959), 75–87; 83.

22 WA 56.442.3.

23 WA 40 II.24.2–3.

24 WA 56.347.11–13.

25 WA 57.232.26. Cf. Schwarz, *Fides, spes und caritas beim jungen Luther*, 50, where Luther is shown to have employed the traditional understanding of *fides* in 1509–10.

26 WA 57.215.16–20. On the existential dimension of Luther's concept of faith, see L. Pinomaa, *Der existenzielle Charakter der Theologie Luthers* (Helsinki, 1940).

27 On this important concept, see P. T. Bühler, *Die Anfechtung bei Luther* (Zürich, 1942); H. Beintker, *Die Überwindung der Anfechtung bei Luther* (Berlin, 1954).

28 WA 57.233.16–19.

29 WA 8.106.10–13.

30 e.g., *WA* 8.106.18–22; 107.21.

31 e.g., *WA* 56.279.22: 'Ideo recte dixi, quod extrinsecum nobis est omne bonum nostrum, quod est Christus.'

32 WA 56.287.23–4.

33 The best study of this aspect of Luther's theology is Harry J. McSorley, *Luther – Right or Wrong?*, 217–73; 297–366.

34 WA 1.224 Thesis 4. On Luther's attack on the *via moderna*, personified by Gabriel Biel, see Grane, *Contra Gabrielem*, 369–85.

35 WA 1.354 Thesis 13. Cf. D. 776. See further H. Roos, 'Die Quellen der Bulle "Exsurge Domine"', in *Geschichte und Gegenwart: Festschrift für*

Michael Schmaus, ed. J. Auer and H. Volk (3 vols: München, 1957), 3.909–26.

36 See D. 781, and compare with the *in globo* condemnation of D. 484–90 and 690. See McSorley, *Luther: Right or Wrong?*, 251–3. Luther was, of course, condemned at the end of the Diet of Worms (25 May 1525) for teaching a pagan determinism which denied free will: see *Deutsche Reichstagakten unter Karl V* (2 vols: Göttingen, 1962), 2.647.1–3. More generally, see *Lutherprozess und Lutherbann*, ed. Remigius Bäumer (Münster, 1972).

37 WA 7.146.6–12; 18.615.12–17.

38 WA 7.144.34–145.4; 18.709.28–36.

39 WA 18.709.28–36 should be read carefully here.

40 WA 18.615.13–16 leaves no room whatsoever for contingency on the part of any created being, including man, whether he is a sinner or not.

41 e.g., G. L. Plitt, 'Luthers Streit mit Erasmus über den freien Willen in den Jahren 1525–25', *Studien der evangelisch-protestantischen Geistlichen des Grossherzogthums Baden* 2 (1876), 205–14.

42 See B. Lohse, *Ratio und Fides: Eine Untersuchung über die Ratio in der Theologie Luthers* (Göttingen, 1958), 82–6; B. A. Gerrish, *Grace and Reason: A Study in the Theology of Martin Luther* (Oxford, 1962), 84–99; McGrath, *Luther's Theology of the Cross*, 136–41.

43 WA 40 I.347.27.

44 WA 40 I.204.11–14.

45 See T. M. McDonough, *The Law and the Gospel in Luther: A Study of Martin Luther's Confessional Writings* (Oxford, 1963); Modalsi, *Das Gericht nach den Werken: Ein Beitrag zu Luthers Lehre vom Gesetz*; Peters, *Glaube und Werk: Luthers Rechtfertigungslehre im Lichte der Heiligen Schrift*.

46 WA 39 I.96.6–8.

47 WA 39 I.254.27–30.

48 WA 39 I.208.9–10.

49 WA 39 I.96.9–14.

50 It is clear that Luther owed little to mysticism: H. A. Oberman, 'Simul gemitus et raptus: Luther und die Mystik', in *Kirche, Mystik, Heiligung und das Natürliche bei Luther*, ed. I. Asheim (Göttingen, 1967), 20–59; K.-H. zur Mühlen, *Nos extra nos: Luthers Theologie zwischen Mystik und Scholastik* (Tübingen, 1972); S. E. Ozment, *Homo Spiritualis: A Comparative Study of the Anthropology of Johannes Tauler, Jean Gerson and Martin Luther (1509–15) in the Context of their Theological Thought* (Leiden, 1969). It is also probable that Luther owed little to the *schola Augustiniana moderna*, although further discussion of this point is required: McGrath, *Luther's Theology of the Cross*, 27–40; 63–71. See further below.

51 See McGrath, *Luther's Theology of the Cross*, 95–147, especially 113–19.

52 F. de Lagarde, *Naissance de l'esprit laïque au déclin du Moyen Age* (6 vols: Paris, 1948), 6.86–8.

53 C. Feckes, *Die Rechtfertigungslehre des Gabriel Biels und seine Stellung innerhalb der nominalistischen Schule* (Münster, 1925), 12.

54 H. A. Oberman, *The Harvest of Medieval Theology: Gabriel Biel and Late Medieval Nominalism* (Cambridge, Mass., 1963).

55 Vignaux, 'Sur Luther et Ockham'.

56 See McGrath, *Luther's Theology of the Cross*, 27–40; 63–71. It is significant that Staupitz cites older Augustinian theologians (i.e., members of the *schola Aegidiana*, rather than the *schola Augustiniana moderna*) as theological sources: Ernst Wolf, *Staupitz und Luther: Ein Beitrag zur Theologie des Johannes von Staupitz und deren Bedeutung für Luthers theologischen Werdegang* (Leipzig, 1929), 23–5.

57 As established by Leif Grane, 'Gregor von Rimini und Luthers Leipziger Disputation', *StTh* 22 (1968), 29–49. The crucial text is *Resolutiones Lutherianae super propositionibus suis Lipsiae disputatis*: *WA* 2.394.31–395.6: 'Certum est enim, Modernos (quos vocant) cum Schotistis et Thomistis in hac re (id est libero arbitrio et gratia) consentire, excepto uno Gregorio Ariminense, quem omnes damnant, qui et ipse eos Pelagianis deteriores esse et recte et efficaciter convincit. Is enim solus inter scholasticos contra omnes scholasticos recentiores cum Carolostadio, id est Augustino et Apostolo Paulo, consentit. Nam Pelagiani, etsi sine gratia opus bonum fieri posse asseruerint, non tamen sine gratia coelum obtineri dixerunt. Idem certe dicunt Scholastici, dum sine gratia opus bonum, sed non meritorium fieri docent. Deinde super Pelagianos addunt, hominem habere dictamen naturale rectae rationis, cui se possit naturaliter conformare voluntas, ubi Pelagiani hominem adiuvari per legem dei dixerunt.'

58 See Oberman, *Werden und Wertung der Reformation*, 110–12.

59 e.g., A. V. Müller, *Luther und Tauler auf ihren theologischen Zusammenhang neu untersucht* (Bern, 1918), 25.

60 The best study remains Ozment's *Homo Spiritualis*.

61 Ozment, *Homo Spiritualis*, 215.

62 e.g., see S. E. Ozment, 'Homo Viator: Luther and Late Medieval Theology', *HThR* 62 (1969), 275–87.

§22

1 See Gordon Rupp, *Patterns of Reformation* (London, 1969), 55–63; McGrath, *Luther's Theology of the Cross*, 44–6. For Karlstadt's own account, see Karlstadt, *De spiritu et litera*, ed. Kähler, 4.13–28.

2 *De spiritu et litera*, 5.4–10.3.

3 For the text of these theses, see *De spiritu et litera*, 11*–37*. He also published 405 theses partly directed against Eck: *Vollständige Reformations-Acta und Documenta*, ed. V. E. Löscher (3 vols: Leipzig, 1720–3), 2.79–104.

4 e.g., *De spiritu et litera*, 28*, Theses 103–5. Karlstadt actually uses the term 'gospel' infrequently over the period 1516–21, and it is somewhat misleading for Kriechbaum to devote an important section of her work to the antithesis of 'law and gospel': Kriechbaum, *Grundzüge der Theologie Karlstadts*, 39–76.

5 *De spiritu et litera*, 71.14–15: 'Sola igitur gratia Dei per Iesum Christum dominum nostrum nos adiuvat'; 91.17–20; 16* Theses 21–2. On the basis of Theses 106 and 109, Kähler suggests that Karlstadt appears to have modified Augustine's concept of *litera occidens* slightly: *De spiritu et litera*, 29*.

6 *De spiritu et litera*, 69.27–31. Cf. 55.32–56.2.

7 Cf. Oberman, *Werden und Wertung der Reformation* (Tübingen, 1977), 110–12.

8 *De spiritu et litera*, 43*. Cf. Kriechbaum, *Grundzüge der Theologie Karlstadts*, 42–5.

9 In his study of Karlstadt, Sider appears to misunderstand the term 'forensic justification', apparently regarding it as synonymous with 'the merciful pardoning of sins': Sider, *Andreas Bodenstein von Karlstadt*, 67–8; 122–5; 258–9. Although Sider frequently refers to the concept of 'imputed righteousness' the texts which he adduces do not support his interpretation of the concept. Furthermore, he recognises that Karlstadt continues to emphasise the interior regeneration implicit in justification: e.g., see 126–9; 258. Karlstadt's doctrine of justification is no more forensic than that of Augustine, which he reproduces remarkably faithfully. The term 'forensic' derives from the Latin *forum* – the place in which judicial and other business was transacted – and in relation to the doctrine of justification, refers to a purely legal declaration that the sinner is righteous, *without or prior to* the concomitant actualisation of righteousness in the sinner.

10 *De spiritu et litera*, 32* Thesis 138.

11 Augustine, *Enn. in Psalm.* 140.15. See further Nygren, 'Simul iustus et peccator bei Augustin und Luther'.

12 Holfelder, *Ausbildung von Bugenhagens Rechtfertigungslehre*, 24–42. For the concept of the non-imputation of sin in his commentary on the Psalter, see Holfelder, *Tentatio et consolatio*, 173–98.

13 As pointed out, with documentation, by Holfelder, *Ausbildung von Bugenhagens Rechtfertigungslehre*, 23 n. 25.

14 cf. *ibid.*, 59n. 6.

15 *ibid.*, 41n. 74.

16 Bugenhagen, *Annotationes im epistolas Pauli* (1525); cited in Holfelder, *Ausbildung von Bugenhagens Rechtfertigungslehre*, 24.

17 Cf. Melanchthon, *Locus de gratia* (1521); *StA* 2.85.16–88.4.

18 H. Bornkamm, 'Humanismus und Reform im Menschenbild Melanchthons' in *idem*, *Das Jahrhundert der Reformation* (Göttingen, 1961), 69–87.

19 *StA* 1.24 Thesis 9, 'Ergo Christi beneficium est iustitia'; Thesis 10, 'Omnis iustitia nostra est gratuita dei imputatio.'

20 *Annotationes in Evangelium Matthaei*; *StA* 4.173.5–6. But see Bizer, *Theologie der Verheißung*, 123–8.

21 *StA* 2.86.23–5; cf. 2.86.26–8; 106.20–2. See W. Maurer, *Der junge Melanchthon zwischen Humanismus und Reformation 2. Der Theologe* (Göttingen, 1969), 361–8.

22 See Bizer, *Theologie der Verheißung*, 82–5.

23 e.g., see CR (Melanchthon) 14.1068; 1080. Cf. Bornkamm, 'Menschen-bild Melanchthons'.

24 The analogy first appears in the 1533 edition of the *Loci*: CR (Mel-anchthon) 21.421. For the 1555 edition, see *StA* 2.359.10–18. On the case of Scipio, see *Realencyclopädie der classischen Alterthumswissenschaft*, ed. August Pauly, IV/I (Leipzig, 1900), 1475–83. For the differences between Luther and Melanchthon at this point, see H. Lindroth, *Försoningen: En dogmhistorisk och systematisk undetsökning* (Uppsala, 1935), 242–3; Josef-son, *Ödmjukhet och tro: En studie i den unge Luthers teologi* (Stockholm, 1939), 127; 179; Robert Stupperich, 'Die Rechtfertigungslehre bei Luther und Melanchthon 1530–1536', in *Luther und Melanchthon: Refer-ate und Berichte des Zweitens Internationalen Kongresses für Lutherforschung* (Göttingen, 1961), 73–88; L. Haikola, 'Melanchthons und Luthers Lehre von der Rechtfertigung', in *Luther und Melanchthon*, 89–103; Greschat, *Melanchthon neben Luther*.

25 *BSLK* 56.1–10.

26 *Apologia* art. 21 para. 19; *BSLK* 320.40–6: 'Ut si quis amicus pro amico solvis aes alienum, debitor alieno merito tamquam proprio liberatur. Ita Christi merita nobis donantur, ut iusti reputemur fiducia meritorum Christi, cum in eum credimus, tamquam propria merita haberemus.'

27 *Apologia*, art. 4 para. 305; *BSLK* 219.43–5.

28 *Apologia*, art. 4 para. 252; *BSLK* 209.32–4.

29 *Apologia*, art. 4 para. 214; *BSLK* 201.23.

30 *Apologia*, art. 4 para. 72; *BSLK* 174.37–40. Note also the continuation of this citation (41–4): 'Ideo primum volumus hoc ostendere, quod sola fides ex iniusto iustum efficiat, hoc est, accipiat remissionem peccatorum.' See also art. 4 para 78; *BSLK* 175.37–9: 'Igitur sola fide iustificamur, intelligendo iustificationem, ex iniusto iustum effici seu regenerari'; art. 4 para. 117; *BSLK* 184.9–11: '... quod sola fide iustificemur, hoc est, ex iniustis iusti efficiamur seu regeneremur'.

31 e.g., see Loofs, *Leitfaden*, 825–6 n. 16. For a careful study and an attempt to resolve the ambiguity, see Pfnür, *Einig in der Rechtfertigungslehre?*, 155–81, especially 157–68; 178–81.

32 See F. C. Baur, *Brevis disquisitio in Andreae Osiandi de iustificatione doctrinam* (Berlin, 1831). Niesel, 'Calvin wider Osianders Rechtfertigung-slehre', while dealing primarily with Calvin's critique of Osiander, gives a useful exposition of the latter's views. Cf. Osiander, *Von dem einigen Mittler* G iiij: 'a solche irren all sehr grewlich, Erstlich das sie das wortlein Rechtfertigen verstehen und auslegen allein fur gerecht halten und sprechen, und nicht der that und in der wahrheit gerecht machen'.

33 These are chiefly to be found in the Fourth Gospel: note the texts cited in *Von dem einigen Mittler*, E iib and following.

34 Perhaps the best account of the views and influence of Stancari may be found in C. A. Selig, *Vollständige Historie des Augsburger Confession* (3 vols: Halle, 1730), 2.714–947.

35 WA 1.96.6–8: 'Opera sunt necessaria ad salutem, sed non causant

salutem, quia fides sola dat vitam.' Cf. WA 30 II.663.3–5; 39 I.254.27–30.
For an excellent study, see Modalsi, *Gericht nach den Werken*, 83–9.

36 WA 39 I.46.20.

37 WA 6.204.25–6; 206.36.

38 *StA* 4.153–4.

39 *StA* 2.148.22–4; 149.19–21.

40 Amsdorf, *Das die propositio (Gute werck sind sur Seligkeit schedlich) eine rechte ware christliche propositio sey* (Magdeburg, 1559). In his preface to Luther's sermons on John 18–20, published in 1557, Amsdorf represented Luther as teaching that good works were unnecessary and harmful: *WA* 28.765–7. See further Kolb, *Nikolaus von Amsdorf*, 123–80, especially 158–62.

41 Cf. W. Joest, *Gesetz und Freiheit: Das Problem des tertius usus legis bei Luther und neutestamentliche Parainese*, 3rd edn (Göttingen, 1961); J. Seehawer, *Zur Lehre vom Gebrauch des Gesetzes und zur Geschichte des späteren Antinomianismus* (Rostok, 1887).

42 Melanchthon cites Chrysostom's gloss on John 6.44 in this connection: see N. P. Williams, *The Grace of God* (London, 1930), 81.

43 A. Evard, *Etude sur les variations du dogme de la prédestination et du libre arbitrie dans la théologie de Melanchthon* (Laval, 1901).

44 See the letter to Brenz of 30 September 1531 (No. 1010): CR (Melanchthon) 2.547.

45 Strigel, *Loci theologici*, ed. Petzel (4 vols: Neustadt, 1581–4). These volumes are very heavily dependent upon Melanchthon. The best study remains that of H. Merz, *Historia vitae et controversiae V. Strigelii* (Tübingen, 1732).

46 Both Amsdorf and Flacius were strident defenders of the 'Gnesio-Lutheran' principle of absolute predestination, which they held to be compromised by Pfeffinger: Kolb, *Nikolaus von Amsdorf*, 188–201. Curiously, Amsdorf accused Pfeffinger of Scotism (Kolb, *Nikolaus von Amsdorf*, 196–7), although Amsdorf's predestinarianism is often thought to reflect his own Scotist background.

47 Chemnitz, *Examen*, 129.a 7–16.

48 *ibid.*, 130.b 15–18.

49 Chemnitz, *Loci Theologici*, Pars II, 626. *Examen*, 130.b 24–48; 131.b 18–23; 132.b 1–3.

50 *Loci*, Pars II, 642 '[Augustinus] involvit et obscurat mentem Pauli.'

51 *Examen*, 131.a 39–41.

52 *BSLK*, 913–36.

53 *BSLK* III.9; 917.15–33. Note, however, III.54 (932.45–933.17), where the indwelling of the essential righteousness of God in the believer is conceded, but distinguished from *iustitia fidei*, the righteousness on the basis of which man is justified.

54 *BSLK* III.17; 919.24–9.

55 *BSLK* III.60; 935.14–19.

56 *BSLK* III.4; 914.19–916.3; III.12; 918.10–12; III.56; 933.36–934.11.

57 *BSLK* Epitome IV.6; 787.19–22; IV.18; 789.30–2.

58 *BSLK* Epitome IV.16; 789.15–20. The exact phrases condemned are due to Georg Major.

59 *BSLK* Epitome II.11; 779.1–17. Note also the assertion 'homo nihil agit aut operatur, sed tantum patitur': II.89; 910.16–18.

60 *BSLK* Epitome I.15; 773.28 'cum magnes allii succo illinitur'.

61 *BSLK* Epitome II.6; 778.4–14.

62 *BSLK* XI.5; 1065.23–7.

63 *BSLK* XI.4; 1065.2–6.

64 *BSLK* XI.81; 1086.26–41: 'enim Deus non est causa peccati'. Cf. XI.41 (1076.4–16), where the possibility that the reprobate's contempt for the Word of God is a consequence of divine predestination is also rejected.

65 *BSLK* Epitome II.18; 780.30–781.3. Cf. II.83; 906.5–24.

66 *BSLK* II.44; 889.11–41. On this, see McSorley, *Luther – Right or Wrong?*, 360–2.

67 See Werner Elert, 'Deutschrechtliche Züge in Luthers Rechtfertigungslehre', *ZSTh* 12 (1935), 22–35.

68 Erasmus, *Novum Instrumentum omne* (Basileae, 1516), 429: 'Accepto fert: λογίζηται, id est, imputat sive acceptum fert. Est autem acceptum fere, debere, sive pro accepto habere, quod non acceperis, *quae apud iure consultos vocatur acceptilatio*'.

§23

1 See Bernd Moeller, 'Die deutschen Humanisten und die Anfänge der Reformation', *ZKG* 70 (1959), 46–61; *idem*, 'Die Ursprünge der reformierten Kirche', *Theologische Literaturzeitung* 100 (1975), 642–53.

2 See E.-W. Kohls, *Die Theologie des Erasmus* (2 vols: Basel, 1966), 1.143–58.

3 Cf. Kohls, 'Die Bedeutung literarischer Überlieferung bei Erasmus', *Archiv für Kulturgeschichte* 48 (1966), 291–33, especially 226–7.

4 For a useful discussion of Erasmus' moralist exegesis of scripture, see Henning Graf Reventloh, *The Authority of the Bible and the Rise of the Modern World* (London, 1984), 39–48.

5 e.g., see Richard Stauffer, 'Einfluß und Kritik des Humanismus in Zwinglis "Commentarius de vera et falsa religione"', *Zwingliana* 16 (1983), 97–110 (which should be compared with the older study of J. F. Gerhard Goeters, 'Zwinglis Werdegang als Erasmianer', in *Reformation und Humanismus: Robert Stupperich zum 65. Geburtstag*, ed. M. Greschat and J. F. G. Goeters (Witten, 1969), 225–71); Christine Christ, 'Das Schriftverständnis von Zwingli und Erasmus im Jahre 1522', *Zwingliana* 16 (1983), 111–25; F. Krüger, *Bucer and Erasmus: Eine Untersuchung zum Einfluß des Erasmus auf die Theologie Martin Bucers* (Wiesbaden, 1970). The strong emphasis upon personal responsibility for sin which causes Zwingli to abandon the traditional Augustinian understanding of original sin (and which underlies his moralist theology of justification) may be due to Erasmian influence: see Rudolf Pfister, *Das Problem der Erbsünde bei Zwingli* (Leipzig, 1939). Zwingli's discussion of the relation of original sin

and baptism suggests that he regards the former to be insignificant theologically until it is actualised as a conscious and deliberate act of sin, in knowledge of the demands of the law: CR (Zwingli) 3.760.

6 CR (Zwingli) 1.67.17–20. For a useful analysis of this *Pestlied*, see Rich, *Anfänge*, 112–19.

7 e.g., Beatus Rhenanus: see CR 7.115.10–4.

8 e.g., see CR 7.328.17–20. See Rich, *Anfänge*, 56–70.

9 CR 2.649.19–21. Note the emphasis upon doing God's will at CR 3.29.25–7. For further discussion, see Heinrich Schmid, *Zwinglis Lehre von der göttlichen und menschlichen Gerechtigkeit* (Zürich, 1959).

10 CR 2.6434.2.5. See further McGrath, 'Humanist Elements in the Early Reformed Doctrine of Justification'.

11 CR 2.76.18–21.

12 CR 1.178.1; 2.496.22.

13 Cited in Zwingli, *Opera*, ed. M. Schuler and J. Schulthess (8 vols: Zürich, 1929–42), 4.185. Zwingli's tendency to identify *lex* and *evangelium* leads to a similar conclusion: Rich, *Anfänge*, 64–7.

14 Henri Strohl, *La pensée de la Réforme* (Neuchâtel, 1951), 107. Cf. E. Staehelin, *Das theologische Lebenswerk Johannes Oecolampadius* (Leipzig, 1939); E. G. Rupp, *Patterns of Salvation* (London, 1969), 3–48; 17: 'His was always the faith of a moralist.'

15 Strohl, *La pensée de la Réforme*, 108.

16 Bullinger, *Sermonum decades quinque*, 157b. Note also the emphasis upon the consonance of Paul and James, also evident in *De gratia dei iustificante*, 65–7.

17 This is clearly seen from his early preoccupation with the works of Erasmus: Martin Greschat, 'Martin Bucers Bücherverzeichnis', *Archiv für Kulturgeschichte* 57 (1975), 162–85.

18 This is well brought out by Karl Koch, *Studium Pietatis: Martin Bucer als Ethiker* (Neukirchen, 1962), 10–15, on the basis of his correspondence with Beatus Rhenanus.

19 *Enarrationes in sacra quattuor evangelia* (1530), 48 B-C; 49 C. Cf. Koch, *Studium Pietatis*, 67.

20 *Metaphrasis et enarratio in epist. D. Pauli ad Romanos*, 231 A-B; 232 D-E. Elsewhere in the same work, he notes a three-fold scheme, which includes the final glorification of the sinner as its third element: 119 A-B. See Johannes Müller, *Martin Bucers Hermeneutik* (Heidelberg, 1965), 122 n. 184.

21 Robert Stupperich, 'Der Ursprung des Regensburger Buches von 1541 und seine Rechtfertigungslehre', *ARG* 36 (1939), 88–116.

22 *Metaphrasis et enarratio in epist. D. Pauli ad Romanos*, 11–14. Cf. W. P. Stephens, *The Holy Spirit in the Theology of Martin Bucer* (Cambridge, 1970), 48–100, especially 55–61.

23 August Lang, *Der Evangelienkommentar Martin Butzers und die Grundzüge seiner Theologie* (Leipzig, 1900), 8; 137; 377–8; idem, *Puritanismus und Pietismus: Studien zu ihrer Entwicklung vom M. Butzer bis zum Methodismus* (Gütersloh, 1941), 13–71. Unfortunately, Lang's assertion that Bucer

was devoid of humanist influence has not stood up to critical evaluation. For further comment see Eduard Ellwein, *Vom neuen Leben: de novitate vitae* (München, 1932), *passim*. However, Bucer's ideological flexibility may go some way towards explaining difficulties in interpretation at such points: see Martin Greschat, 'Der Ansatz der Theologie Martin Bucers', *Theologische Literaturzeitung* 103 (1978), 81–96.

24 e.g., *Metaphrasis et enarratio in epist. D. Pauli ad Romanos*, 405 c. It is not clear whether this should be understood as a logical or a chronological sequence: Stephens, *Martin Bucer*, 30, suggests it is logical, although the more careful analysis of Müller, *Martin Bucers Hermeneutik*, 24 n. 38 suggests it is chronological.

25 Stephens, *Martin Bucer*, 99, states that 'there is an unbreakable link holding together predestination, vocation, justification, *sanctification* and glorification' (our italics): the reference given makes no mention of sanctification (99 n. 2). Similarly, Stephens' entire section on 'sanctification' (71–98) represents the imposition of an alien structure upon Bucer's thought, and cannot be supported on the basis of the texts cited. Bucer must be allowed to speak for himself rather than having a later structure imposed upon him.

26 See Emmanuel Graf von Korff, *Die Anfänge der Föderaltheologie und ihre erste Ausgestaltung in Zürich und Holland* (Bonn, 1908).

27 Schrenk, *Gottesreich und Bund*, 36–7, argues that Zwingli derived the concept from the Radical Reformers. Zwingli's covenantal theology is undoubtedly closely linked with his theology of baptism: see David C. Steinmetz, 'The Baptism of John and the Baptism of Jesus in Huldrych Zwingli, Balthasar Hubmeier and Late Medieval Theology', in *Continuity and Discontinuity in Church History*, ed. F. F. Church and Timothy George (Leiden, 1979), 169–81; Timothy George, 'The Presuppositions of Zwingli's Baptismal Theology', in *Prophet, Pastor, Protestant: The Work of Huldrych Zwingli after Five Hundred Years*, ed. E. J. Furcha and H. Wayne Pipkin (Allinson Park, Pennsylvania, 1984), 71–87. On Bullinger, see Peter Walser, *Die Prädestination bei Heinrich Bullinger im Zusammenhang mit seiner Gotteslehre* (Zürich, 1957), 234–49. On the differences between Bullinger and Zwingli, see J. Wayne Baker, *Heinrich Bullinger and the Covenant: The Other Reformed Tradition* (Athens, Ohio, 1980), 1–25.

28 e.g., see Hans H. Wolff, *Die Einheit des Bundes: Das Verhältnis von Altem und Neuem Bund bei Calvin* (Neukirchen, 1958).

29 On the distinction between 'testament' and 'covenant', and its importance for the development of the later Reformed federal soteriologies, see Kenneth L. Hagen, 'From Testament to Covenant in the Early Sixteenth Century', *Sixteenth Century Journal* 3 (1972), 1–24.

30 Although the main features of Calvin's theology of justification may be found in his exegetical works (e.g., see H. P. Santmire, 'Justification in Calvin's 1540 Romans Commentary', *ChH* 33 (1963), 294–313), we propose to develop our analysis upon the basis of the 1559 *Institutio*. It is only in this later work that the distinction between Calvin and

Osiander on the nature of the believer's relation to Christ is fully clarified. Furthermore, the propagation of Reformed theology in the later sixteenth century was largely due to the 1559 *Institutio*, either in translation or in a condensed edition, rather than his biblical commentaries.

31 *Christianae religionis institutio* (Basileae, 1536), III; *OS* 1.73. For the differences between the 1536 and 1539 editions, see A. Autin, *L'Institution chrétienne de Calvin* (Paris, 1929), 47–83; *OS* 3.vi–xv. The 1539 edition contains a chapter (*VI. de iustificatione fidei et meritis operum*) which represents a massive expansion of the brief comments of the first edition.

32 *Institutio* (1559), III.xi.2; *OS* 4.183.7–10.

33 *Institutio*, III.xi.11; *OS* 4.193.2–5; 193.17–194.21.

34 See McGrath, 'John Calvin and Late Medieval Thought', for an analysis. Calvin's doctrine of the *meritum Christi* – of importance in this respect – is discussed in relation to the late medieval doctrine of merit (§10).

35 *Institutio*, III.xi.23; *OS* 4.206.29–32. Thus Calvin criticises Augustine's intrinsic concept of justifying righteousness: *Institutio*, III.xi.15; *OS* 4.199.25–200.6

36 For Calvin's attitude to the Augsburg Confession, see Willem Nijenhuis, 'Calvin en de Augsburgse Confessie', *Nederlands Theologisch Tijdschrift* 15 (1960–1), 416–33.

37 *Institutio*, III.xi.10; *OS* 4.191.31–192.4. This section should be read with some care.

38 See Niesel, 'Calvin wider Osianders Rechtfertigungslehre'. Also of relevance here is Calvin's attitude to the Regensburg article of justification (1541): see W. H. Neuser, 'Calvins Urteil über den Rechtfertigungsartikel des Regensburger Buches', in *Reformation und Humanismus: Robert Stupperich zum 65. Geburtstag*, ed. M. Greschat and J. F. G. Goeters (Witten, 1969), 176–94.

39 *Institutio*, III.xi.1, 6. For further discussion and references, see Boisset, 'Justification et sanctification chez Calvin'; Stadtland, *Rechtfertigung und Heiligung*; McGrath, 'Humanist Elements in the Early Reformed Doctrine of Justification', 14–16.

40 For the phrase, see CR (Calvin) 50.437–8.

41 *Institutio*, III.xi.7; *OS* 4.188.24–5: 'Quod obiicit, vim iustificandi non inesse fidei ex seipsa, se quatenus Christum recipit, libenter admitto.' For Calvin's definition of faith, see *Institutio*, III.ii.7.

42 *Institutio*, IV.xvii.42; III.xvii.11; III.xviii.10.

43 *Institutio*, III.xi.7.

44 CR (Calvin) 49.61; *Institutio*, III.xi.7.

45 Thus J. R. Packer, in *John Calvin*, ed. G. E. Duffield (Abingdon, 1966), 157. Cf. W. Niesel, *The Theology of Calvin* (London, 1956), 130. Göhler suggests that there is *no* central doctrine in the theology of Calvin: *Calvins Lehre von der Heiligung*, 81. It must also be noted that the circumstances of Calvin's 'conversion' were quite different from those attending Luther's theological breakthrough, in that soteriological questions do not appear to have been pre-eminent: see P. Sprenger, *Das Rätsel um die Bekehrung Calvins* (Neukirchen, 1960); A. Ganoczy, *Le jeune Calvin:*

Genèse et évolution de sa vocation réformatrice (Wiesbaden, 1966), 286–304; Harro Höpfl, *The Christian Polity of John Calvin* (Cambridge, 1985), 219–26.

46 That this is also the case with early Scottish Reformed theology (e.g., that of John Knox or the *Scots Confession* of 1560) has been brought out by T. F. Torrance, 'Justification: Its Radical Nature and Place in Reformed Doctrine and Life', *SJTh* 13 (1960), 225–46, especially 225–7.

47 See Alexander Schweizer, *Die protestantischen Centraldogmen in ihrer Entwicklung innerhalb der reformirten Kirche* (2 vols: Zürich, 1854–6). Schweizer, however, argues that Calvin treats the doctrine of predestination as central – a conclusion which modern Calvin scholarship has not endorsed.

§24

1 See Alister E. McGrath, 'Reformation to Enlightenment', in *The Science of Theology*, ed. P. D. L. Avis (London, 1986), for a discussion. The parallels between Protestant and medieval Catholic scholasticism are well brought out by Robert Scharlemann, *Aquinas and Gerhard: Theological Controversy and Construction in Medieval and Protestant Scholasticism* (New Haven, 1964). The scholasticism of Gerhard's soteriology is best seen from his Aristotelian analysis of the causes of justification: see Richard Schröder, *Johann Gerhards lutherische Christologie und die aristotelische Metaphysik* (Tübingen, 1983), 69–97.

2 See E. Bizer, *Frühorthodoxie und Rationalismus* (Zürich, 1963), 5–15.

3 See Otto Gründler, *Die Gotteslehre Giralmo Zanchis* (Neukirchen, 1965); Walter Kickel, *Vernunft und Offenbarung bei Theodor Beza* (Neukirchen, 1967); J. S. Bray, *Theodore Beza's Doctrine of Predestination* (Nieuwkoop, 1975); J. P. Donnelly, *Calvinism and Scholasticism in Vermigli's Doctrine of Man and Grace* (Leiden, 1976).

4 See Kickel, *Vernunft und Offenbarung*, 167–8, for an excellent discussion of this point. While Calvin regarded Christ as the *speculum electionis* (see CR (Calvin) 35.479), Beza regarded the decrees of election and reprobation as the *speculum* in which the glory of God was reflected (*Tractationes theologicae*, 3.403).

5 For the reasons why, see the second of the *Treze Sermons*: CR (Calvin) 58.31–44. These points are also emphasised by Basil Hall, 'Calvin against the Calvinists', in *John Calvin*, ed. G. E. Duffield (Abingdon, 1966), 19–37, especially 25–8. Unfortunately, Hall is incorrect in his assertion (27) that Beza altered Calvin's teaching on the *nature* of justification by including both remission of sin and acceptance of the sinner as righteous, where Calvin included only the former element: it is clear (see §22) that Calvin included both – e.g., *Institutio*, III.11.2; *OS* 4.183.7–10.

6 *BSRK* 843.15–861.8 On the final point, see Jürgen Moltmann, *Prädestination und Perseveranz: Geschichte und Bedeutung der reformierten Lehre 'de perseverantia sanctorum'* (Neukirchen, 1961), especially 110–62. For details of the Arminian controversy over the decisions of the Synod of

Dort, see A. W. Harrison, *The Beginnings of Arminianism to the Synod of Dort* (London, 1926). On the background to Dort, see Gustav Adolf Benrath, 'Die hessische Kirche und die Synode in Dordrecht', *Jahrbuch der Hessischen Kirchengeschichtlichen Vereinigung* 20 (1969), 56–81.

7 See *Acta et scripta synodalia Dodrecena ministrorum remonstrantium* (Harderwijk, 1622), 1.71–4.

8 Schrenk, *Gottesreich und Bund*, 63. On the theological significance of the covenant-motif in later Reformed and Puritan theology, see Perry Miller, 'The Marrow of Puritan Divinity', in *Errand into the Wilderness* (Cambridge, Mass., 1956), 48–98.

9 Especially his *Summa religionis Christianae* (Nystadt, 1584). The study of F. A. Lampe, *Einleitung zu dem Geheimnis des Gnadenbundes* (Marburg/Frankfurt, 1782), is still useful as a source.

10 *Christianae theologiae compendium* 1, 7. Man's obligations to God under the *foedus operum* may be defined as the general obligation to love God and one's neighbour, and the specific obligation to eat of the tree of the knowledge of good and evil: Lampe, *Einleitung*, 25. For a well-documented discussion of the *foedus operum* within Reformed theology, see H. Heppe, *Die Dogmatik der evangelisch-reformierten Kirche*, ed. E. Bizer (Neukirchen, 1958), 224–54. On the pre-Cocceian covenant in Scotland, see S. A. Burrell, 'The Covenant Ideas as a Revolutionary Symbol: Scotland, 1596–1637', *ChH* 27 (1958), 338–50; R. L. Greaves, 'John Knox and the Covenant Tradition', *Journal of Ecclesiastical History* 24 (1973), 23–32; J. B. Torrance, 'Covenant or Contract? A Study of the Theological Background of Worship in Seventeenth Century Scotland', *SJTh* 23 (1970), 51–76; *idem*, 'The Covenant Concept in Scottish Theology', *SJTh* 34 (1981), 225–43.

11 *Compendium* I, 21. For a general survey, see Heppe, *Dogmatik*, 295–322.

12 *Summa doctrinae de foedere et testamento Dei* IV, 6. See further Heiner Faulenbach, *Weg und Ziel der Erkenntnis Christi: Eine Untersuchung zur Theologie des Johannes Coccejus* (Neukirchen, 1973).

13 e.g., see Burmann, *Synopsis Theologiae*, II.xv.2.

14 *Opera* (Genevae, 1642), 544–52.

15 Thesis 46 is particularly important: 'in foedere subserviente Deus ius suum non alio fine exigit, quam ut homines convicti imbecilitatis suae ad Christum confugiant' (*Opera*, 548).

16 See Moltmann, 'Prädestination und Heilsgeschichte bei Moyse Amyraut'; Laplanche, *Orthodoxie et prédication*; Armstrong, *Calvinism and the Amyraut Heresy*.

17 Armstrong, *Calvinism and the Amyraut Heresy*, 222–40.

18 Thesis 2; in *Syntagma thesium theologicarum* (2 vols: Saumur, 1641), 1.212.

19 *Defense de la doctrine de Calvin sur le sujet de l'election* (Saumur, 1644), 544. The whole of this chapter (512–68) should be studied. Note also 312–13, where Amyraut makes it clear that he regards the doctrine of election to function as an *ex post facto* explanation of why some believe and others do not, rather than as a speculative principle of deductive theology. For the manner in which Amyraut reconciles the universality of the offer of

salvation and the particularity of faith, see *Brief traitté de la prédestination* (Saumur, 1634), 89–90; Laplanche, *Orthodoxie et prédication*, 87–108.

20 See Wilhelm Dantine, *Die Gerechtmachung der Gottlosen: Eine dogmatische Untersuchung* (München, 1959), 15–29; H. E. Weber, *Reformation, Orthodoxie und Rationalismus*, 2nd edn (2 vols: Gütersloh, 1940–51), I/1.126.

21 On the Lutheran side, see Hafenreffer, *Loci theologici*, 664; Koenig, *Theologia positiva acroamatica*, §562; 208; Brochmand, *Universae theologiae systema*, 1.471. On the Reformed, see Heidegger, *Medulla*, XXII, 4; 169; XXI, 6; 169; XXII, 26; 183; Wollebius, *Christianae theologiae compendium*, 1.xxx.2; 234; Bucanus, *Institutiones theologicae*, XXXI, 6; 332; Alsted, *Theologia scholastica didactica*, IV.xxv.1; 709; Musculus, *Loci communes*, 262–3. Note the explicit criticism of Augustine evident in certain of these citations (e.g., Musculus).

For an analysis of the Aristotelian foundations of Johann Gerhard's understanding of the causality of justification, see Richard Schröder, *Johann Gerhards lutherische Christologie und die aristotelische Metaphysik* (Tübingen, 1983), 69–96. For a description of Quenstedt's doctrine of justification, which illustrates Lutheran Orthodoxy at its best, see R. D. Preuss, 'The Justification of a Sinner before God as taught in Later Lutheran Orthodoxy', *SJTh* 13 (1960), 262–77. On the forensic character of justification, see 270–7. For the general character of Quenstedt's theology, see Jörg Baur, *Die Vernunft zwischen Ontologie und Evangelium: Eine Untersuchung zur Theologie Johann Andreas Quenstedt* (Gütersloh, 1962),.

22 See Bucanus, *Institutiones theologicae* XXXI, 27; 341: 'Iustitia Christi aliena est, quatenus extra nos est ... sed aliena non est, quatenus nobis destinata est ... Est etiam nostra illa iustitia, quatenus illud ipsum eius subjectum, nempe Christus, noster est adeoque spiritualiter per fidem factus est unus nobiscum.' Cf. Polanus, *Syntagma* IV, 27; 781. For an excellent introduction to the thought of Polanus, see Heiner Faulenbach, *Die Struktur der Theologie des Amandus Polanus von Polansdorf* (Zürich, 1967), which remedies the theological deficiencies of the older study of Ernst Staehelin, *Amandus Polanus von Polansdorf* (Basel, 1955).

23 It is not strictly correct to suggest that Piscator denied that Christ's active obedience was totally devoid of satisfactory value. Piscator asserted that the active obedience of Christ affected the satisfactory value of his death, in that without Christ's sinless and obedient life, his passion could not have had any satisfactory value. Thus the *obedientia activa* may be said to possess *indirect* satisfactory value.

24 *Loci theologici*, ed. Cotta, loc. xvii cap. 4; 7.260.

25 *Loci theologici* 7.261.

26 See the important discussion in Ritschl, *The Christian Doctrine of Justification and Reconciliation* (Edinburgh, 1872), 248–67, especially 256.

27 It may be noted that federal theologians, such as Burmann, discussed the *obedientia activa* in terms of Christ's *natural* submission to the law as on account of his *being* a man, and his *federal* submission to the law by virtue of his *becoming* man on behalf of the elect.

28 The best study of Socinianism remains O. Fock, *Der Socianismus nach seiner Stellung* (Kiel, 1847). A useful analysis in English is to be found in R. S. Franks, *The Work of Christ* (London, 1962), 362–77.

29 Fock, *Der Socianismus*, 552; 615–39.

30 For an excellent description of the Lutheran and Reformed teaching on the work of Christ, exemplified by Quenstedt and Heidegger respectively, see Franks, *The Work of Christ*, 410–47.

31 There appears to have been considerable confusion within Lutheranism upon the relation of Christ's merits and satisfaction. Gerhard appears to treat the concepts as identical, although a distinction between them emerges later: see Koenig, *Theologia positiva acroamatica*, §§219–20; §§150–1. See also Ritschl, *Justification and Reconciliation*, 261.

32 On the Lutheran side, see Koenig, *Theologia positiva acroamatica*, §217; 150; §232; 153; Brochmand, *Universae theologiae systema*, 1.709–11; Gerhard, *Loci theologici*; in *Opera* 7.70. On the Reformed, see Heidegger, *Medulla*, XIX, 15; 53; Wollebius, *Christianae theologiae compendium*, I.xvii.4; 117; Polanus, *Syntagma*, VI, 27; 266–82.

33 *Loci theologici* locus xvii, *de iustificatione per fidem, prooemium*; ed. Cotta, 7.1: 'Calviniani errant in articulo praedestinationis; ergo et in articulo iustificationis, quia iustificatio est praedestinationis executio.'

34 To the Tridentine assertion (*decretum de iustificatione*, cap. 6) of the universality of the passion and benefits of Christ, cited at CR (Calvin) 7.431, Calvin replies (435) 'Tertium et quartum caput non attingo.' For the background to this work, see T. W. Casteel, 'Calvin and Trent: Calvin's Reaction to the Council of Trent in the Context of His Conciliar Thought', *HThR* 63 (1970), 91–117.

35 Beza, *Tractationes theologicae*, 1.344; 363; 418. See Hall, 'Calvin against the Calvinists', 27; Bray, *Beza's Doctrine of Predestination, passim*.

36 Heidegger, *Medulla*, XIXI, 56; 77–8.

37 *Compendium theologiae*, VI.xviii.2.

38 Interestingly, Koenig does not even include *iustificatio* in his *ordo salutis: Theologia positiva acroamatica*, §426; 184 (although it is possible that he intends to subsume it under *regeneratio* – cf. §447; 188). See further Bengt Hägglund, 'Rechtfertigung – Wiedergeburt – Erneuerung in der nachreformatorischen Theologie', *KuD* 5 (1959), 318–37; Carl E. Braaten, 'The Correlation between Justification and Faith in Classical Lutheran Dogmatics', in *Symposium on Seventeenth Century Lutheranism* (St Louis, 1962), 77–90.

39 *Christianae theologiae libri II*, facing prolegomena at beginning of work. Only a small part of a complex chart is reproduced. The inclusion of glorification as a consequence of the *unio mystica* between Christ and the believer can be illustrated from many Reformed works of the period, including those otherwise deemed heterodox – e.g., Amyraut, *Brief traitté*, 86–7.

40 See A. B. Ritschl, *Geschichte des Pietismus* (3 vols: Bonn, 1880–6); M. Schian, *Orthodoxie und Pietismus in Kampf um die Predigt* (Giessen, 1912); Martin Schmidt, *Wiedergeburt und neuer Mensch: Gesammelte Studien zur*

Geschichte des Pietismus (Witten, 1969); McGrath, 'Reformation to Enlightenment'.

41 See A. J. Beachy, *The Concept of Grace in the Radical Reformers* (Nieuwkoop, 1977), especially 28–9, who demonstrates the transformational concept of justification widely employed within the movement, generally articulated in terms of the concept of 'deification'.

42 Robert Barclay, *An Apologie for the True Christian Divinity*, 13th edn (Manchester, 1869), 136.

43 *Apologie*, 131.

44 E. Hirsch, *Geschichte der neuern evangelischen Theologie* (5 vols: Gütersloh, 1949–51), 2.245–9.

45 Ritschl, *Justification and Reconciliation*, 515.

46 See Schian, *Orthodoxie und Pietismus*, 86–97; Jörg Baur, *Salus Christiana: Die Rechtfertigungslehre in der Geschichte des christlichen Heilsverständnisses* (Gütersloh, 1969), 87–110; Erhard Peschke, 'Speners Wiederburtslehre und ihr Verhältnis zu Franckes Lehre von der Bekehrung', in *Traditio – Krisis – Renovatio aus theologische Sicht* (Marburg, 1976), 206–24; Dietrich Meyer, 'Zinzendorfs Sehnsucht nach der "naturellen Heiligkeit"', in *Traditio – Krisis – Renovatio*, 284–97; Horst Weigelt, *Pietismus-Studien* I (Stuttgart, 1965), 105–18. The Methodist movement may be regarded as the English manifestation of Pietism: see E. von Eicken, *Rechtfertigung und Heiligung bei John Wesley* (Heidelburg, 1934); D. Lerch, *Heil und Heiligung bei John Wesley* (Zürich, 1941); H. Lindström, *Wesley and Sanctification: A Study in the Doctrine of Salvation* (London, 1956).

47 Schmidt, *Wiedergeburt und neuer Mensch*, 273.

48 On this controversy, see H.-M. Rotermund, *Orthodoxie und Pietismus: Valentin Ernst Löschers 'Timotheus Verinus' in der Auseinandersetzung mit der Schule August Hermann Franckes* (Berlin, 1960), 48–51.

49 E. Peschke, *Studien zur Theologie August Hermann Franckes* I (Berlin, 1964), 47.

50 The concept is first encountered in the writings of Spener: Hirsch, *Geschichte*, 2.148. In England, the doctrine is particularly associated with Wesley, who expressed it in his concept of 'entire sanctification'.

51 See the criticism of Wesley on this point by the Reformed divine James Buchanan, *The Doctrine of Justification* (1867; reprinted London, 1961), 192–4.

52 See Baur, *Salus Christiana*, 91–5; Buchanan, *Doctrine of Justification*, 193–4.

53 Rotermund, *Orthodoxie und Pietismus*, 56–7. Löscher saw in this the spectre of Osiandrism.

54 Wesley, *Works*, 10.366.

55 Wesley, *Standard Sermons*, 1.120. Baur notes the general Pietist hostility towards the *als-ob-Theologie* of Lutheran Orthodoxy: *Salus Christiana*, 94.

56 Cf. Spener, *Das Gericht der Verstockung* (Frankfurt, 1701), 24–7. Traces of the idea may be found in Dannhauer's *Hodosophia Christiana sive theologia positiva* (Strasbourg, 1649).

Introduction to chapter 7

1 See Jedin, *Geschichte des Konzils von Trientes*, 2.140-2. The earlier (and somewhat impressionistic) study of Catholic responses to the Lutheran doctrine of justification in the period 1520-45 of H. Laemmer, *Die vortridentinisch-katholische Theologie des Reformationszeitalter* (Berlin, 1858), 137-99, has now given way to the detailed study of Pfnür, *Einig in der Rechtfertigungslehre?*, 273-378.

2 H. Schmidt, *Bruckenschlag zwischen den Konfessionen* (Paderborn, 1951), 162.

3 For useful studies of the late medieval religious outlook, see J. Toussaert, *Le Sentiment religieux en Flandre à la fin du Moyen Age* (Paris, 1963); P. Heath, *The English Parish Clergy on the Eve of the Reformation* (London/ Toronto, 1969); M. Bowker, *The Secular Clergy in the Diocese of Lincoln* (Cambridge, 1968).

4 Pfnür, *Einig in der Rechtfertigungslehre?*, 369-78.

5 The full implications of the forensic dimension of the Melanchthonian concept of justification occasionally appear to have been recognised – e.g., in the case of Johannes Dietenberger, *Phimostoms Scripturariorum* (1530), and Johannes Mensing, *Antapologie* (1535): see Pfnür, *Einig in der Rechtfertigungslehre?*, 280 n. 66; 359-60.

6 See *WA* 18.786.26-8.

§25

1 The renaissance within the late medieval Spanish church is particularly associated with Francisco Ximénez de Cisneros: see J. Garcia Oro, *Cisneros y la reforma del clero español en tiempo de los reyes católicos* (Madrid, 1971). On the reforming synods of Alcalá and Talavera, see L. Fernández de Retana, *Cisneros y su siglo: Estudio histórico de la vida y actuación publica del Cardenal Ximénez de Cisneros* (2 vols: Madrid, 1929-30), 1.497-8.

2 See Nieto, *Juan de Valdés and the Origins of the Spanish and Italian Reformation* (Geneva, 1970), 13-88 for a discussion.

3 The relevant portions of the confessions of Pedro Ruiz de Alcaraz and Isabella de la Cruz should be noted: e.g., see Nieto, *Juan de Valdés*, 62 n. 49; 64 nn. 55-6. See further M. Serrano y Sanz, 'Pedro Ruiz de Alcaraz, illuminado alcarreno del siglo XVI', *Revista de archivos, bibliotecas y museos* 8 (1903), 1-16; 126-39; A. Selke de Sánchez, 'Alguno datos nuevos sobre los primeros alumbrados: El edicto de 1525 y su relación con el proceso de Alcaraz', *Bulletin Hispanique* 54 (1952), 125-52; Nieto, *Juan de Valdés*, 60-88.

4 The parallels with Quakerism have often been noted: e.g., R. M. Jones, 'A Quaker Forerunner', *Friends' Quarterly Examiner* 66 (1932), 47-57. For the question of the nature and extent of Protestant influence upon the later Spanish Reformation, see J. I. Tellechea Idígoras, *Melanchton y Carranza: Préstamos y afinados* (Salamanca, 1979), 36-201.

5 See Ortolani, *Pietro Carnesecchi*, 172. For further discussion, see Fr.

Domingo de Sta. Teresa, *Juan de Valdés 1498(?)–1541: su pensamiento religioso y las corrientes espirituales de su tiempo* (Roma, 1957), 284–316; M. J. Montsérin, 'La andadura humana de Juan de Valdés', in *Dialogo de doctrina cristiana* (Biblioteca de visionarios, heterodoxos y marginados: Madrid, 1979), 161–89.

6 *Las ciento diez divinas consideraciones*, ed. Idígoras, 85.

7 *Las ciento diez divinas consideraciones*, 85–6.

8 *Las ciento diez divinas consideraciones*, 291.

9 For a discussion of the Lutheran works which may have been available in Spain at the time, see Nieto, *Juan de Valdés*, 66 n. 1. Of course, it must be remembered that the Luther known in Spain was a vague and distant figure, quite unlike the reality: see J. I. Tellechea Idígoras, 'Lutero desde Españo', *Revista de Occidente* 29 (1983), 5–32.

10 See P. O. Kristeller, 'Augustine and the Early Renaissance', in *Studies in Renaissance Thought and Letters* (Rome, 1956), 355–72 for details of such works. On the first printed edition of Augustine, see J. de Ghellinck, 'La première édition imprimée des "Opera omnia S. Augustina"', in *Miscellanea J. Gessler* I (Antwerp, 1948), 530–47. A pronounced Augustinianism may be found in Jacques Lefèvre d'Etaples' 1512 Pauline commentaries: A. Renaudet, *Préréforme et humanisme à Paris pendant les premières guerres d'Italie 1494–1517*, 2nd ed (Paris, 1953), 622–34; R. M. Cameron, 'The Charges of Lutheranism brought against Jacques Lefèvre d'Etaples', *HThR* 63 (1970), 119–49.

11 For a careful study, see R. Cessi, 'Paolinismo preluterano', *Rendiconti dell' Academia nazionale dei Lincei*, Classe di scienze morali, storiche e filologe Ser. VIII, 12 (1957), 3–30. Note also that Valdés was regarded as *iuvenis divi Pauli studiosissimus*: J. N. Bakhuizen van den Brink, *Juan de Valdés réformateur en Espagne et en Italie* (Genève, 1969), 16.

12 On whom see J. Leclerq, *Un humaniste érémite: le bienheureux P. Giustiniani (1476–1528)* (Rome, 1951).

13 For the correspondence, discovered in 1957, see Hubert Jedin, 'Contarini und Camaldoli', *Archivio italiano per la storia della pietà* 2 (1959), 51–117. For the comparison with Luther, see *idem*, 'Ein Turmerlebnis des jungen Contarini', in *Kirche des Glaubens – Kirche des Geschichte* (2 vols: Freiburg, 1966), 1.167–80.

14 The episode of Easter Eve 1511, which he recounts to Giustiniani in a letter of 24 April 1511 (Jedin, 'Contarini und Camaldoli', 64), should be studied in full.

15 Jedin, 'Contarini und Camaldoli', 117. This letter, dated 7 February 1523, is the last surviving letter in the collection discovered by Jedin.

16 Supporting text, as cited by Peter McNair, *The Anatomy of Apostasy: Peter Martyr in Italy* (Oxford, 1967), 8 n. 1: 'Ego iampridem antequam insigne Lutheri nomen esset, abhinc triginta et eo amplius fortasse annis, cum adhuc Martinus se non aperuisset, et pro veritate scribebam, ea dicebam, ut quidam veritatis inimici famosos libellos, nominatim appellato me, templi ualuis affigerent, quod scilicet depressum hominem, Deus exaltatum uolebam.' The influence of Luther in Italy dates from the mid

1520s: see D. Cantimori, *Eretici Italiani del Cinquecento* (Firenze, 1939), 24; E. G. Gleason, 'Sixteenth Century Italian Interpretations of Luther', *ARG* 60 (1969), 160–73.

17 *Regesten und Briefe des Kardinals Gasparo Contarinis*, ed. Dittrich, No. 90; 358. A similar view appears to have been expressed at the time by Reginald Pole: see C. Corviersi, 'Compendio di Processi del Santo Uffizio', *Archivio della Società Romana di Storia Patria* 3 (1880), 261–91; 449–73; 284: 'Polus defendit et nititur probare doctrinam Lutheranam de iustificatione esse veram.' However, Pole appears to have interpreted justifying faith as *fides quae per dilectionem operatur*, a view to which Luther was radically opposed: see Pole, *De Concilio* (Romae/Venetiis, 1562), 24v–25v. (On the basis of internal evidence, this work may be deduced to have been written in April 1545: see 1r–v; 58v). See further n. 43 below.

18 e.g., see S. Ehses, 'Johannes Groppers Rechtfertigungslehre auf dem Konzil von Trient', *Römische Quartalschrift* 20 (1906), 175–88; 184; Hanns Rückert, *Die theologische Entwicklung Gasparo Contarinis* (Bonn, 1926), 97 n. 1. The suggestion that Kaspar Schatzgeyer developed a doctrine of *duplex iustitia* rests upon a misunderstanding of the significance of the Scotist analysis of the elements of justification: see Valens Heynck, 'Bemerkungen zu dem Buche von O. Müller, *Die Rechtfertigungslehre nominalistischer Reformationsgegner*', *FS* 28 (1941), 129–51, especially 145–50. There is no convincing evidence that Contarini's views on justification derive from Gropper's *Enchiridion*: see Rückert, *Die theologische Entwicklung Gasparo Contarinis*, 102–4, where it is shown that there are excellent reasons for supposing that Contarini reflects theological currents prevalent in Italy in the 1530s. The discovery of the Contarini–Giustiniani correspondence some thirty years after Rückert's investigation has enormously strengthened his conclusions.

The movement to which Rückert refers is now generally known as 'Evangelism': see E. M. Jung, 'On the Nature of Evangelism in Sixteenth Century Italy', *Journal of the History of Ideas* 14 (1953), 511–27.

19 Bellarmine, *Disputationum . . . de controversiis Christianae fidei* (Ingolstadt, 1601), 1028. Cf. 1096–7. Bellarmine may base his views upon the vote of Seripando at Trent, in which Contarini, Cajetan, Pighius, Julius Pflug and Gropper are identified with the doctrine of 'double justification': CT 5.487.33–4.

20 Robert Stupperich, *Der Humanismus und die Wiedervereinigung der Konfession* (Leipzig, 1936), 11–36. Cf. Walter Lipgens, *Kardinal Johannes Gropper (1503–1559) und die Anfänge der katholischen Reform in Deutschland* (Münster, 1951), 100–8; 192–203.

21 As pointed out by Braunisch, *Die Theologie der Rechtfertigung im 'Enchiridion' (1538) des Johannes Gropper*, especially 419–38.

22 *Enchiridion Christianae institutiones* (Coloniae, 1538), fol. 163r. Cf. fol. 163v: 'Nam quis iustificatum dixerit eum, cui tantum sunt remissa peccata, non autem voluntas etiam commutata, nempe ex mala facta bona? Quemadmodum nemo servum nequam, ob id tantum, quod ei

indulgens dominus noxam clementer remiserit iustificatum dixerit, nisi is bonam quoque voluntatem (qua posthac servus non inutilis sed frugi esse contendat) ceperit?'

23 *Enchiridion*, fol. 163r (Marg). The Melanchthonian text to which Gropper alludes is cited as n. 24 of §21 of the present study.

24 *Enchiridion*, fol. 163v (Marg).

25 e.g., *Enchiridion*, fol. 129v treats *imputatio iustitiae* and *acceptatio* as synonymous.

26 CR (Melanchthon) 21.421: 'Sumpsit igitur Paulus verbum iustificandi ex consuetudine Hebraici sermonis pro acceptatione, id est, pro reconciliatione et remissione peccatorum.' On this, see Braunisch, *Die Theologie der Rechtfertigung im 'Enchiridion'*, 367: 'Die melanchthonische "imputatio iustitiae Christi" als positives Pendant der Sündenvergebung kennt das "Enchiridion" nicht. Um der Begriffsverwirrung bezüglich der Lehre von der "doppelten Gerechtigkeit" vorzubeugen, muß klar unterscheiden werden: Wo Melanchthon "remissio" und "imputatio" einander zuordnet und in beiden Momenten primär das Rechtfertigungsereignis erblickt ... betont Gropper die Einheit von Vergebung und Erneuerung.'

27 e.g., W. van Gulik, *Johannes Gropper (1503–1559): Ein Beitrag zur Kirchengeschichte Deutschlands* (Freiburg, 1906), 54 n. 5.

28 *Enchiridion*, fol. 167v. For an excellent critical analysis, see Braunisch, *Die Theologie der Rechtfertigung im 'Enchiridion'*, 360–72; 381–98, especially 394–6.

29 *Enchiridion*, fol. 167v (Marg).

30 Contarini, *Epistola de iustificatione*; in Corpus Catholicorum VII, ed. F. Hünermann (Münster, 1923), 24.1–2. See also n. 33 below. Those at Rome who read the letter were sceptical concerning its catholicity: see *Epistolae Reginaldi Poli Cardinalis* (5 vols: Bresciae, 1744–57), 3.ccxxxi-xl.

31 *Epistola de iustificatione*, 28.12–18.

32 *Epistola de iustificatione*, 26.18–19.

33 *Epistola de iustificatione*, 29.19–38; see further Rückert, *Die theologische Entwicklung Gasparo Contarinis*, 93. Rückert's suggestion (86 n. 2) that Contarini affirms that *iustitia inhaerens* and *iustitia imputata* function as the double formal cause of justification cannot be sustained on the basis of the text cited in its support: the adverb *formaliter* is transferred from its proper clause to one subsequent, from which it does not appear to have been elided.

34 Text of the article in CR (Melanchthon) 4.198–201. The parallels between the two documents have been brought out by Stupperich, 'Der Ursprung des "Regensburger Buches" von 1541 und seine Rechtfertigungslehre'. For the background to the discussion at Regensburg, see Peter Matheson, *Cardinal Contarini at Regensburg* (Oxford, 1972) 101–7. It may be noted that three of the five major theological figures present were amenable to this doctrine of *duplex iustitia* – Bucer, Contarini and Gropper. Eck was critical of the document, and Melanchthon more favourably disposed towards it. For Luther's attitude to Regensburg on

justification, see von Loewenich, *Duplex Iustitia*, 48–55; for Calvin's, see W. H. Neuser, 'Calvins Urteil über den Rechtfertigungsartikel des Regensburger Buches', in *Reformation und Humanismus: Robert Stupperich zum 65. Geburstag*, ed. M. Greschat and J. F. G. Goeters (Witten, 1969), 176–94.

35 See Peter Matheson, *Cardinal Contarini at Regensburg* (Oxford, 1972), 181: 'The dialogue between Protestantism and Catholicism at the Diet of Regensburg in 1541 did not fail. It never took place'; von Loewenich, *Duplex Iustitia*, 34–8; Dermot Fenlon, *Heresy and Obedience in Tridentine Italy* (Cambridge, 1972), 45–68; V. Pfnür, *Die Einigung bei den Religionsgesprächen von Worms und Regensburg (1540–41)* (Gütersloh, 1980). For a more positive (although now generally discredited) assessment, see Stupperich, *Humanismus und die Wiedervereinigung der Konfession*, 120–4.

36 *Contra* McNair, *Anatomy of Apostasy*, 1–50, especially 8. See further n. 18 above.

37 See Carlo de Frede, 'La stampa nel Cinquecento e la diffusione della Riforma in Italia', *Atti della Accademia Pontiniana* (Napoli) 13 (1963–64), 87–91; *idem*, 'Per la storia della stampa nel Cinquecento in rapporto con la diffusione della Riforma in Italia', in *Gutenberger Jahrbuch 1964* (Mainz, 1964), 175–84; E. G. Gleason, 'Sixteenth Century Italian Interpretations of Luther', *ARG* 60 (1969), 160–73. The Viterbo Circle appears to have been of particular importance in this respect in the 1530s and early 1540s: see Fenlon, *Heresy and Obedience*, 69–99, for an excellent introduction.

38 See *Il Beneficio di Cristo*, ed. Caponetto, 469–96, for details of the work. Note particularly the suggestion that Giulio Contarini's *sententia* on justification at Trent may reflect the direct influence of this work: see Domingo de Sta. Teresa, *Juan de Valdés*, 297–301.

39 See Caponetto, *loc. cit.* For the suggestion that the work is Lutheran in inspiration, see A. C. Politi, *Compendio d'errori et inganni luterani contenuti in un libretto intitolato Trattato utilissimo del beneficio di Cristo crocifisso* (Roma, 1544). However, the influence of Calvin's 1539 *Institutio* is much more evident: see Tomasso Bozza, *Il Beneficio di Cristo e la Istituzione della religione cristiana di Calvino* (Roma, 1961), 4–5. An examination of the critical apparatus of Caponetto's critical edition makes evident the dependence upon Valdés in the first four chapters at points of crucial significance. Bozza's thesis that the work is essentially a summary of the 1539 *Institutio* raises a number of difficulties, of which we here note three. First, chapter 1 does not develop the anthropological pessimism characteristic of Calvin where it would be expected; second, chapter 6 develops a doctrine of the eucharist based directly upon Augustine, rather than Calvin; third, the 1539 *Institutio* is unlikely to have penetrated sufficiently far south in the time necessary to exercise so significant an influence upon the work.

For a more recent survey of the influence of Juan de Valdés in Italy, see Salvatore Caponetto, 'Richerche recenti su Juan de Valdés e il valdesianismo in Italia', *Bullettino della Società di Storia valdese* 150 (1981), 50–7.

40 Beneficio di Cristo, cap. 4; 37.261–2; cf. 37.272–4. On the phrase *sola fide* as used by Grimaldi at the time, see M. W. Anderson, *Peter Martyr: A Reformer in Exile* (Nieuwkoop, 1975), 271–2.
41 *Il Beneficio di Cristo*, cap. 4; 38.281–9.
42 *Il Beneficio di Cristo*, cap. 4; 46.514–47.515.
43 Pole, *De Concilio*, 24r–v.
44 See Fenlon, *Heresy and Obedience*, 203–4.

§26

1 CT 5.259.3–6.
2 Stakemeier, 'Die theologische Schulen'. The older study of H. Lennerz, 'Das Konzil von Trient und die theologischen Schulmeinungen', *Scholastick* 4 (1929), 38–53, should also be noted. A major deficiency of Stakemeier's study is the implicit implication that the proceedings on justification were of interest only to academic theologians, whereas it is clear that many bishops regarded the matter as of practical and spiritual importance: see Giuseppe Alberigo, *I vescovi italiani at Concilio di Trento (1545–7)* (Firenze, 1959), 337–94.
3 M. Grabmann, 'Johannes Capreolus O.P., der "princeps Thomistarum", und seine Stellung in der Geschichte der Thomistenschule', in *Mittelalterliches Geistesleben: Abhandlungen zur Geschichte der Scholastik und Mystik* III, ed. L. Ott (München, 1956), 370–410.
4 This was first pointed out by Friedrich Stegmüller, 'Gratia sanans: Zur Schicksal des Augustinismus in der Salmantizienerschule', in *Aurelius Augustinus: Festschrift der Görres-Gesellschaft zum 1500. Tod des heiligen Augustinus*, ed. M. Grabmann and J. Mausbach (Köln, 1930), 395–409; 402–3.
5 See Joseph Hefner, *Die Entstehungsgeschichte des Trienter Rechtfertigungsdekretes* (Paderborn, 1909), 68. It is important to appreciate the significance of the pre-Tridentine Dominican polemic in ensuring the ascendancy of the views of Thomas: see A. Walz, 'La polemica domenicana pre-tridentina', *Sapientia* 9 (1956), 469–87.
6 See the *Index nominum et rerum* of CT 5.1053–72. On the Thomist school at Trent, see Stakemeier, 'Die theologischen Schulen', 199–207; 322–31.
7 See Stegmüller, *Francisco de Vitoria y la doctrina de gracia en la escuela salmantina*. The most significant product of this school was the massive *Cursus theologicus Summam D. Thomae complectens*, written in the period 1631–1701: see O. Merl, *Theologia Salmanticensis: Untersuchung über Entstehung, Lehrrichtung und Quellen des theologischen Kurzus der spanischen Karmeliten* (Regensburg, 1947).
8 See Stegmüller, 'Zur Gnadenlehre des spanischen Konzilstheologen Domingo de Soto'; Becker, *Rechtfgertigungslehre*.
9 See Becker, *Rechtfertigungslehre*, 141–53. On this question, with particular reference to Francisco de Vitoria, see Xiberta, 'La causa meritoria de la justificación'.
10 Those present at the opening session were ascertained from the list

published in CT 5.1041–4. The list published at CT 5.819–20 is misleading, as it notes only those present at the closing session on 13 January 1547: the numbers given for the sixth session are based upon an analysis of those actually taking part in the debate.

11 See the comments of Bonaventura Pius de Costacciaro, dated 28 December 1546: CT 5.741.28–32. The quite distinct positions of Bonaventure and Scotus noted here made a Franciscan consensus upon the matter difficult.

12 Sagués, 'Un libro pretridentino de Andrés de Vega sobre la justificación'.

13 *Opusculum de iustificatione*, fol. 146–8. Perhaps with Capreolus in mind, Vega links Thomas Aquinas and Gregory of Rimini together as exponents of the 'no merit whatsoever prior to justification' school.

14 *Opusculum de iustificatione*, fol. 148: 'theologi recentiores, Gabriel, Maiores, Almanyus et similes; et ante illos, ne adeo nova existemetur, videtur iam tempore doctoris subtilis fuisse haec opinio communis in scholis'.

15 Heynck, 'Der Anteil des Konzilstheologen Andreas de Vega O.F.M. an dem ersten amtlichen Entwurf des Trienter Rechtfertigungsdekretes', 57. We have confirmed this conclusion for all three phases of Franciscan theology (i.e., the early and later Franciscan schools, and the *via moderna*, which is contiguous with the later school): see §§15–17.

16 e.g., Hünermann, *Wesen und Notwendigkeit der aktuellen Gnade nach dem Konzil von Trient*, 5 n. 1; cf. Stakemeier, 'Die theologischen Schulen', 341.

17 Carl Stange, 'Über Luthers Beziehungen zur Theologie seines Ordens', *Neue kirchliche Zeitschrift* 11 (1900), 574–85; *idem*, 'Luther über Gregor von Rimini', *Neue kirchliche Zeitschrift* 13 (1902), 721–7.

18 Stakemeier, 'Die theologischen Schulen', 342–3.

19 Heinrich Hermelink, *Die theologische Fakultät in Tübingen vor der Reformation* (Stuttgart, 1906). Stakemeier merely notes this study: Stakemeier, 'Die theologischen Schulen', 342 n. 3.

20 For the incompetence of the theologians who censured Ockham's doctrine of justification as 'Pelagian', see McGrath, *Luther's Theology of the Cross*, 53–8.

21 As noted by Stakemeier himself: e.g., 'Die theologischen Schulen', 344–5.

22 The controversy at Trent over Scotus' views on the certitude of grace raises further questions over the 'Scotism' of the Franciscan contingent: see Heynck, 'A Controversy at the Council of Trent'. Heynck correctly notes (257) the much greater faithfulness of the Conventuals than the Observants to the earlier Franciscan tradition.

23 See Stakemeier, *Augustinus und die Augustiner*.

24 A. V. Müller, *Luthers theologische Quellen: Seine Verteidigung gegen Denifle und Grisar* (Giessen, 1912); cf. Wilfred Werbeck, *Jacobus Perez von Valencia: Untersuchungen zu seinem Psalmenkommentar* (Tübingen, 1959), 212 n. 6. See also §18 of the present work.

25 Stakemeier, *Augustinus und die Augustiner*, 21–2.

26 As Jedin pointed out, the sources required for such a conclusion were not available in 1937: H. Jedin, in *Theologische Revue* 37 (1938), 425–30.

27 See §18; McGrath, '"Augustinianism?" A critical assessment of the so-called "Medieval Augustinian Tradition" on Justification', *Augustiniana* 31 (1981), 247–67, *passim*. The study of Anselm Forster, *Gesetz und Evangelium bei Girolamo Seripando* (Paderborn, 1963), indicates the conventional character of much of Seripando's views.

28 See D. Gutiérrez, *Los Agustinos en el Concilio de Trento* (El Escorial, 1947); A. Zumkeller, 'Die Augustiner-Eremiten und das Konzil von Trient', in *Das Weltkonzil von Trient*, 2.523–40.

29 Seripando appears to have derived his Platonism from Giles: H. Jedin, *Girolamo Seripando* (2 vols: Wurzburg, 1937), 1.68–9; 80–2.

30 CT 12.668.16–18. Cf. 12.313.26–9. Seripando also links Cajetan and Pighius with the idea elsewhere: CT 12.665.16–667.43.

31 It should not be overlooked that this also involves the rejection of the suggestion that Luther and Seripando represent equally possible outcomes of an 'Augustinian' theology. However, there were prelates present at Trent, associated with the Viterbo circle, who unquestionably approximated to Luther on several matters of importance: see Dermot Fenlon, *Heresy and Obedience in Tridentine Italy* (Cambridge, 1972), 116–60.

32 See Alberigo, *I vescovi italiani*, 388–9. Alberigo is primarily concerned with the intellectual climate in Italy, from which most of those involved in the Tridentine proceedings on justification were drawn. His conclusions, however, would appear to have a wider validity.

§27

1 See Jedin, *Geschichte des Konzils*, vol. 1, for details.

2 CT 2.409.

3 The importance and inseparability of the doctrines of original sin and justification had been stressed in the Legates' report of 15 April 1546 (CT 10.548–60). However, the two doctrines were eventually discussed in isolation.

4 For a slightly different list, see Jedin, *Geschichte des Konzils*, 2.142–4. It should be borne in mind that the council was committed to the simultaneous discussion of the questions of residence and of translation.

5 CT 5.261.26–35. For background information to such congregations, see H. Lennerz, 'De congregationibus theologorum in Concilio Tridentino', *Gregorianum* 26 (1945), 7–21. For similar information in relation to votes, see *idem*, 'Voten auf dem Konzil von Trient', *Gregorianum* 15 (1934), 577–88.

6 CT 5.262.18–19.

7 CT 5.262.20–1.

8 CT 5.262.31–5.

9 See the opinions noted by Marcus Laureus: CT 5.279.6–26.

10 See the following: CT 5.263.9–10; 22–3; 27–9; 31–2; 264.1–5; 264.43–265.2; 265.12–14; 272.40–1; 273.11–12; 45–6; 274.35–6; 275.25–6.

11 CT 5.264.31–2.

12 CT 5.275.9–11.

13 e.g., Antonio Delfini: CT 5.274.21–30. Note particularly the reference to *tectio seu non imputatio peccatorum* (274.24). See further Santoro, 'La giustificazione in Giovanni Antonio Delfini, teologo del Concilio di Trento'.

14 CT 5.278.20–1.

15 CT 5.278.1–2.

16 CT 5.279.27–31 (our italics).

17 See the list of errors noted at CT 5.281–2. The subsequent discussion follows this division, with interest particularly concerning the *primus status*: e.g., see CT 5.287–96; 298–310.

18 See the careful study of Valens Heynck, 'Der Anteil des Konzilstheologen Andreas de Vega an dem ersten amtlichen Entwurf des Trienter Rechtfertigungsdekretes', *FS* 33 (1951), 49–81.

19 CT 5.384–91. The numeration of the canons is confusing, and errors of reference are frequent in the secondary literature. The Görres edition numbers the chapters and canons consecutively, without distinguishing them, so that the paragraph numbered '4' is actually Canon 1, that numbered '18' is Canon 15, etc. It is clear from the *notationes theologorum* (CT 5.392.1–394.6) that the first three chapters were actually treated *as canons*. Thus a reference to 'Canon 18' (CT 5.393.36) refers to the section numbered '18' (CT 5.390.22–40), even though, strictly speaking, this is actually the *fifteenth* canon.

20 Canon 1: CT 5.386.12–14.

21 CT 5.266.3–28. The full text cited from Melanchthon's Romans prologue reads: 'Iustificari proprie est iustum reputari, quia iustus significat relative acceptum Deo. Et sic iustitiam in Pauli disputationibus non esse qua iusti sumus, sed relative qua iusti habemur etiam non existentes, quia accepti sumus Deo propter fidem, id est fiduciam divinae misericordiae.'

22 Canon 2: CT 5.386.18–20.

23 Canon 3: CT 5.386.25–7.

24 CT 5.386.28–33.

25 Canon 9: CT 5.387.40–2.

26 CT 5.268.43–4.

27 It was on the basis of this concept of faith that Pole had hoped a compromise might be possible between Protestants and Catholics: see §24.

28 CT 5.392–4. An exception may be noted: objections were raised to Canon 11, dealing with the certitude of grace in its present form (396.36–41).

29 CT 5.408–14. The postponement of the debate occurred on account of political considerations.

30 Seripando's draft is to be found in CT 5.821–8.

31 Cap. 4: CT 5.823.6–9.

32 Canon 3: CT 5.824.33–5. This canon also condemns the doctrine of justification *sola fide*.

33 CT 5.828–3. The first four chapters correspond to those of the draft of 11

August. The date given in the Görres edition (19 August) is incorrect, and should be amended to 29 August.

34 CT 5.829.40–9.

35 Canon 4: CT 5.832.25–6.

36 CT 5.832.27–8; cf. 5.824.33–4.

37 CT 5.386.13–14; 824.33–4; 832.27–8.

38 The phrase does, of course, occur in the titles of the respective chapter and canon, as noted above. See further P. Pas, 'La doctrine de la double justice au Concile de Trente', *EThL* 30 (1954), 5–53.

39 Cap. 7: CT 5.423.34–6.

40 Canon 7: CT 5.427.1–7 (our italics).

41 e.g., see Pas, 'La doctrine de la double justice', 20–3.

42 e.g., CT 5.492.10–11; 496.2 'Tenet quod una sit iustitia tantum, qua iustificamur, videlicet nobis inhaerens.' The objections noted at CT 5.505.26–7 should be noted. To the twenty-two votes recorded in the Görres edition of the *Acta* should be added those of Salmeron and Hervet: see J. Olazarán, 'En el IV centenario de un voto tridentino del jesuito Alfonso Salmerón sobre la doble justicia', *EE* 20 (1946), 211–40; *idem*, 'Voto tridentino de Gentian Hervet sobre la certeza de la gracia y la doble justicia', *Archivio Teologico Granadino* 9 (1946), 127–59.

43 See Aurelius' vote of 19 October 1546: CT 5.561.47–564.12. For the similarities, compare CT 5.563.4–13 with 12.665.2–12; 5.563.35–6 with 12.667.46–668.9; 5.563.37–42 with 12.635.37–42 and 5.374.10–15.

44 e.g., compare CT 5.609.22–7 with Gropper, *Enchiridion*, fol. 132v; 5.611.17–24 with *Enchiridion*, fol. 168r–v.

45 CT 5.599.4–10.

46 CT 5.576.31–5.

47 CT 5.547.8–549.43.

48 CT 5.581.17–590.19.

49 It is possible that certain statements made (e.g., 5.584.29–30: 'quo ad hunc actum nihil absurdi de nova nostra imputatione ad vitam, si novo actu resurgimus') may have aroused the suspicions of his more critical hearers.

50 Thus there is to be found no reference to Gropper or his *Enchiridion*, or to the Diet of Regensburg, throughout the entire debate. However, the personal association of Reginald Pole with similar views was known to many delegates: see Dermot Fenlon, *Heresy and Obedience in Tridentine Italy* (Cambridge, 1972), 161–95.

51 e.g., see CT 5.564.38–9; 569.8; 579.5–6; 602.37–42; 617.27–9.

52 CT 5.541.45–6. For a full study of the main lines of criticism directed against Seripando's position, see Pas, 'La doctrine de la double justice', 31–43.

53 e.g., see CT 5.489.31–2; 12.671.16, 32.

54 e.g., CT 5.643.31–2; 644.34; 644.31–2; 647.12–15; 649.10–11.

55 CT 5.512.12–20.

56 CT 5.636.30–637.11. Note especially 35–6: 'formalis iustitia una Dei'.

57 CT 5.658.24–6.

58 CT 5.700.25–8.
59 CT 5.701.14–704.14.
60 Cap. 7; D. 799. There is a slight alteration in the wording, which does not affect the sense of the statement in question.
61 e.g., see H. J. Iwand, *Nachgelassene Werke: 5. Luthers Theologie* (München, 1974), 64–104, especially 90–104. For the general problem at Trent, see Guérard des Lauriers, 'Saint Augustin et la question de la certitude de la grâce au Concile de Trente'; Heynck, 'Zur Kontroverse über die Gnadengewissheit auf dem Konzil von Trient'; Huthmacher, 'La certitude de la grâce au Concile de Trente'; Schierse, 'Das Trienterkonzil und die Frage nach der christliche Gewissheit'; Stakemeier, *Das Konzil von Trient über die Heilsgewissheit.*
62 CT 5.275.14–16, rejecting the possibility, apart from special divine revelation.
63 CT 5.277.42–3, in which the possibility is upheld.
64 CT 5.279.6–281.15.
65 CT 5.282.24–5: '9. Quod iustificatus tenetur credere, se esse in gratia et sibi non imputari peccata, et se esse praedestinatum'.
66 It is discussed, in passing, at CT 5.324.34–42. Seripando noted the point (CT 12.634.31–635.11), but did not permit his views to be included in the general discussion.
67 CT 5.390.22–40, especially 37–40. On the numeration of the canons, see n. 19 above.
68 CT 5.393.36–41. On the numeration of the canon, see n. 19.
69 CT 5.410 n. 1. The reference to Scotus is significant: as Heynck has shown, there was considerable confusion among the delegates (particularly the Franciscans) concerning Scotus' views on the certitude of grace; Heynck, 'A Controversy at the Council of Trent', *passim.* On Delfini, see Friedrich Lauchert, *Die italienischen literarischen Gegner Luthers* (Freiburg, 1912), 487–536; Santoro, 'La giustificazione in Giovanni Antonio Delfini'.
70 For the document, see CT 12.651.22–658.14. For the appeal to Biel's interpretation of Scotus, see CT 12.657.53–658.11.
71 CT 5.404.41–3. He appears to have been supported in this assertion by the General of the Carmelites (CT 5.404.50) and Martellus of Fiessole (CT 5.406.16–18).
72 CT 10.586.22–587.20.
73 Thus the Generals of both the Conventuals and Observants spoke in favour of the latter: CT 5.410.1–2; 5.410.5–6. The English bishop Richard Pate, himself suspected by many of Lutheranism, also spoke in support of this latter position on 28 August 1546: CT 5.419.18–19. His views were expressed even more forcefully on 13 November: CT 5.648.4–5: 'Homo iustificatus secundum praesentem iustitiam potest esse certus certitudine fidei, se esse in gratia Dei.'
74 CT 5.418.1–9; 419.44.
75 Cap. 7; CT 5.424.12–13.
76 Canon 8; CT 5.427.8–11. It should be recalled that the term *praedestinatio* is used in the positive sense of 'predestination to life'.

77 Note the comments of del Monte: CT 5.497.3–4; cf. 497.12–15. For some comments of the theologians on the respective chapter and canon, see CT 5.505.46–51; 5.508.40–2.

78 CT 5.523.17–19.

79 For the names of the theologians in each group, see Massarelli's lists at CT 5.632.31–633.10. We have taken the liberty of transferring the secular priest Andrés de Navarra from the list of supporters of *certitudo fidei, se esse in gratia* to that of its opponents. His vote (CT 5.559.14–561.46) clearly opposes the concept; we are unable to account for Massarelli's error.

80 See J. Olazarán, 'La controversia Soto–Caterino–Vega sobre le certeza de la gracia', *EE* 19 (1942), 145–83; Beltrán de Heredia, 'Controversia de certitudine gratiae entre Domingo de Soto y Ambrosio Catarino'; Oltra, *Die Gewissheit des Gnadenstandes bei Andres de Vega*. His vote of 22 November 1546 is of particular importance: CT 5.655.34–657.18.

81 Cap. 9; CT 5.637.12–21. The contents of Canon 8 of the September draft are to be found in Canons 12 and 13; CT 5.649.39–42. A new canon on the subject follows: Canon 14: CT 5.649.43–4.

82 September draft, cap. 7: CT 5.424.13; November draft, cap. 9: CT 5.637.14–15.

83 CT 5.637.20–1 (our italics).

84 Canon 14: CT 5.649.43–4: 'Si quis dixerit, omnes renatos et iustificatos teneri ad hoc, ut certo credant, se esse in gratia Dei, aut iustificatos *communiter* certo scire, se esse in gratia Dei: anathema sit.'

85 e.g., CT 5.643.4–5; 643.43; 644.39; 645.11–12; 647.37–8; 653.21.

86 e.g., CT 5.655.36–7; 5.662.9–11.

87 CT 5.727.1–11.

88 The objection of Pachecco should be noted (CT 5.727.12–17), as well as del Monte's reply (CT 5.727.18–27). Pachecco's final rejoinder makes his hostility to this proposal evident: CT 5.727.28–30.

89 CT 5.772.10–773.5.

90 CT 5.773.4–5. Their evident relief is recorded: 773.5.

91 CT 5.777.1–10.

92 Ehses notes the absence of Pole's seal from the volume of the Bologna edition of 1548 specially reserved to receive it: CT 5.xxv.10–xxvi.40.

§28

1 D. 729a–843. The unusual structure of the *decretum de iustificatione* is best seen by comparing it with the *decretum super peccato originali*, which immediately precedes it (D. 787–92). See further Brunner, 'Die Rechtfertigungslehre des Konzils von Trient'; Buuck, 'Zum Rechtfertigungsdekret'; Joest, 'Die tridentinische Rechtfertigungslehre'; Walz, 'La giustificazione tridentina'.

2 One of the most significant shortcomings of Hans Küng's analysis of the Tridentine decree (*Rechtfertigung: Die Lehre Karl Barths und eine katholische Besinnung*) is his failure to deal with the decree in its proper historical

perspective. We have discussed Küng's analysis of Trent critically elsewhere: 'ARCIC II and Justification', 27–42, especially 34–9.

3 D. 793–802.
4 D. 803–6.
5 D. 807–10.
6 Cap. 1; D. 793.
7 Proposition 36, as condemned in *Exsurge Domine* (15 June 1520): D. 776.
8 Cap. 3; D. 795.
9 Cap. 4; D. 796.
10 Cap. 5; D. 797.
11 Cap. 6; D. 798. The charge of 'neo-semipelagianism' levelled against the decree at this point is quite absurd: F. Loofs, *Leitfaden zum Studium der Dogmengeschichte*, 4th edn (Halle, 1906), 668–9. A similar criticism must be levelled at the study of A. Th. Jörgenssen, 'Was verstand man in der Reformationszeit unter Pelagianismus?', *ThStK* 83 (1910), 63–82, in which any theology of justification which recognises the necessity of a preparation for justification is treated as 'semi-Pelagian'.
12 Cap. 7; D. 799.
13 The reference is to Augustine, *de Trinitate*, XIV.xii.15: cf. §§3, 5.
14 Cap. 8; D. 801.
15 The dispute concerning the sense of the verb *promereri* is considered in §28.
16 Cap. 9; D. 802.
17 Cap. 11; D. 804.
18 Cap. 11; D. 804.
19 Cap. 12; D. 805. Cf. Cap. 13; D. 806.
20 Cap. 14; D. 807.
21 Cap. 16; D. 809–10.
22 The specific condemnation of Pelagianism in the opening canons is significant, as it represents a much-needed magisterial clarification in this area.
23 Canon 11; D. 821.

§29

1 Rückert, *Die Rechtfertigungslehre auf dem Tridentinischen Konzil*, 185. Cf. Gonzáles Rivas, 'Los teólogos salmantinos y el decreto de la justificación'.
2 D. 801.
3 Oberman, 'Das tridentinische Rechtfertigungsdekret'. The verb *promereri* also occurs at one additional point in the decree itself (chapter 16; D. 809: 'consequendum vere promeruisse censeantur'), and in canon 2 (D.812: 'vitam aeternam promereri possit'). The supplementation of *promereri* with *vere* in chapter 16 is itself sufficient to raise doubts concerning Oberman's thesis.
4 Oberman, 'Das tridentinische Rechtfertigungsdekret', 268–78.
5 Oberman, 'Das tridentinische Rechtfertigungsdekret', 278.
6 Rückert, 'Promereri: Eine Studie zum tridentinischen Rechtfertigungs-

dekret als Antwort an H. A. Oberman'.

7 CT 5.426.35–7.

8 See the proceedings of 2 January 1547; CT 5.753.17–20; 9 January 1547: CT 5.777.16–19.

9 CT 5.737.15–16; 20–1.

10 Oberman, 'Das tridentinische Rechtfertigungsdekret', 278–9.

11 See Heynck, 'Die Bedeutung von "mereri" und "promereri" bei dem Konzilstheologen Andreas de Vega O.F.M.'.

12 *De natura et gratia*, ii.1; fol. 96r.

13 *De natura et gratia*, ii.3; fol. 102r.

14 *De natura et gratia*, ii.3; fol. 101r–v.

15 *De natura et gratia*, ii.4; fol. 109r–111v. Soto's views on congruous merit prior to justification were defended by Suaréz (although the latter was reluctant to concede any form of disposition, however remote, towards justification): *de gratia*, VIII.vii.9; *Opera*, ed. Vivés (28 vols: Paris, 1856–61), 9.339–42.

16 *De universa iustificationis doctrina*, viii.16; in *Opera*, 2.265B. See further Seybold, *Glaube und Rechtfertigung*.

17 See the references collected by Seybold, *Glaube und Rechtfertigung*, 89 n. 189.

18 *De iustificatione doctrina universa*, vi.10; fol. 86.

19 *De iustificatione doctrina universa*, vii.8; fol. 137.

20 *De iustificatione doctrina universa*, viii.10; fol. 192. We have italicised the allusion to the text of the decree.

21 *De iustificatione doctrina universa*, viii.10; fol. 194.

22 *Summa doctrina Christianae* (Vienna, 1555); modern edition in *S. Petri Canisii ... catechismi Latini et Germanici*, ed. F. Streicher (Romae, 1933), 1.1–75; a shorter version appeared the following year: Streicher, 1.263–71. For further details, see O. Braunsberger, *Entstehung und erste Entwicklung der Katechismen des seligen Petrus Canisius* (Freiburg, 1893).

23 See F. J. Brand, *Die Katechismen des Edmundus Augerius in historischer, dogmatisch-moralischer und katechetischer Bearbeitung* (Freiburg, 1917). The demand for such works appears to have been greatest in northern Europe.

24 P. Paschini, 'Il Catechismo Romano del Concilio di Trento: sua originali e sua prima diffusione', in *Cinquecento Romano e riforma cattolico* (Roma, 1958), 67–91.

25 See G. Bellinger, *Der Catechismus Romanus und die Reformation* (Paderborn, 1958), 95–8. Bellinger's suggestion (97–8) that the Catechism teaches the necessity of a disposition for justification, based on faith and penitence, does not appear to be borne out by the evidence.

26 *Catechismus Romanus* (Leipzig, 1852), II.v.68; 247.

27 For the general background, see J. B. du Chesne, *Histoire du Baïanisme* (Douai, 1731); F. X. Linsenmann, *Michael Baius und die Grundlegung des Jansenismus* (Tübingen, 1867); F.-X. Jansens, *Baius et le Baïanisme* (Louvain, 1927); N. Abercrombie, *The Origins of Jansenism*, 87–93; 137–42. On the theological issues, see Alfaro, 'Sobrenatural y pecado

original en Bayo'; Kaiser, *Natur und Gnade im Urstand*; Henri de Lubac, *Augustinisme et théologie moderne* (Paris, 1965), 15–48.

28 *de prima hominis iustitia*, 1; *Opera*, 49.

29 *de prima hominis iustitia*, 9; *Opera*, 62–3. Cf. Kaiser, *Natur und Gnade im Urstand*, 69–157.

30 *de peccato originis*, 2–13; *Opera*, 3–13.

31 *de peccato originis*, 11; *Opera*, 12.

32 Proposition 13; *Opera*, 51; cf. D. 1013: 'Opera bona, a filiis adoptionis facta, non accipiunt rationem meriti ex eo, quod fiunt per spiritum adoptionis inhabitantem corda filiorum Dei, sed tantum ex eo, quod sunt conformia legi, quodque per ea praestatur oboedientia legi.'

33 D. 1001–80.

34 D. 1080. See further E. van Eijl, 'L'Interprétation de la Bulle de Pie V portant condamnation de Baius', *Revue d'Histoire Ecclésiastique* 1 (1955), 499–542.

35 See the footnote to D. 1080.

36 The best study remains G. Schneemann, *Die Entstehung und Entwickelung der thomistisch-molinistischen Kontroverse* (2 vols: Freiburg, 1879–80). More recently, see F. Stegmüller, *Geschichte des Molinismus* (Münster, 1935).

37 As stated in *Summa Theologiae*, Ia q. 105 a. 5; Molina, *Concordia liberi arbitrii cum gratiae donis* (Lisbon, 1588), disp. 26; 167–71.

38 *Concordia*, disp. 26; 170–1. This may be compared with Suaréz' opinion, that justification is to be attributed to grace rather than to the free will, despite the latter being a proximate cause of justification: *de gratia* v.xxxi.3–4; *Opera*, 8.544–5.

39 *Concordia*, disp. 47; 298.

40 *Concordia*, disp. 50; 329–30. Molina distinguishes this *scientia media* from *scientia visionis* (by which God knows realities) and *scientia simplicis intelligentiae* (by which God contemplates the realm of the unreal). The objects apprehended by the *scientia media* thus fall between the categories of the real and unreal – i.e., *futurabilia*, which exist only if certain preconditions are realised.

41 Molinism is paralleled at this point by Congruism, particularly associated with Roberto Bellarmine and Francisco de Suaréz: see F. Stegmüller, *Zur Gnadenlehre des jungen Suaréz* (Freiburg, 1933). This teaching should be distinguished from that of Gabriel Vásquez: see J. A. de Aldama, 'Un perecer inédito del P. Gabriel Vásquez sobre la doctrina agustiniana de la gracia eficaz', *EE* 23 (1949), 515–20.

42 Báñez, *Apologia*, I.xxiii.1; in V. Beltrán de Heredia, *Domingo Báñez y las controversias sobre la gracia: textos y documentos* (Madrid, 1968), 210–11.

43 The classic account of the congregation remains J. H. Serry, *Historia congregationum de auxiliis divinae gratiae* (Antwerp, 1709).

44 D. 1090.

45 For the history of the controversy, see L. Ceyssens, *Sources relatives aux débuts du jansénisme et de l'antijansénisme 1640–1643* (Paris, 1957); Abercrombie, *The Origins of Jansenism*. *Augustinus* is divided into three parts,

and reference will be made to the part by name, rather than number. The edition used in the present study is that published at Paris in 1641. For a convenient synopsis of the work in English, see Abercrombie, *The Origins of Jansenism*, 126–53.

46 *de gratia primi hominis*, 10–12; 51A–59A.

47 To all intents and purposes, Jansen's *adiutorium sine quo non* appears to correspond to the general medieval concept of *concursus generalis*.

48 *de gratia Christi salvatoris*, ii.5; 36bE.

49 *de gratia Christi salvatoris*, i-iii.

50 *de gratia Christi salvatoris*, iii.20; 161bC-D; 161bE-162aA.

51 *de gratia Christi salvatoris*, iii.20; 162aE.

52 *de gratia Christi salvatoris*, iii.20; 162bD.

53 This interpretation of Augustine goes back to Baius, and had been challenged by Suaréz: Suaréz, *de gratia*, 1.xxi.1; *Opera*, 1.468–9.

54 D. 1092–6. For the background, see L. Ceyssens, *La première Bulle contre Jansénius: sources relatives à son histoire (1644–53)* (2 vols: Rome, 1961–2).

55 D. 1351–1451. See further J. D. Thomas, *La querelle de l'Unigenitus* (Paris, 1950); J. A. G. Tans, *Pasquier Quesnel et les Pays-Bas* (Gronigen, 1960).

56 V. Martin, *Les Origines du Gallicanisme* (2 vols: Paris, 1939).

57 Most notably, *Die katholische Lehre von der Rechtfertigung und von der Gnade*, ed. Wilfried Joest (Lüneburg, 1954); Hans Küng, *Rechtfertigung: Die Lehre Karl Barths und eine katholische Besinnung* (Einsiedeln, 1957); Karl Rahner, 'Fragen der Kontroverstheologie über die Rechtfertigung', in *Schriften zur Theologie* IV (Einsiedeln, 1960), 237–71.

58 A study of sermons preached in seventeenth-century Spain on the theme of justification indicates the considerable difficulties encountered in explaining the Council's pronouncements on the matter to the laity: see H. D. Smith, *Preaching in the Spanish Golden Age: A Study in Some Preachers of the Reign of Philip III* (Oxford, 1978), especially 140–5.

§30

1 J. F. Davis, 'Lollardy and the Reformation in England', *ARG* 73 (1982), 217–37.

2 Thus Thomas More was quick to point out the difference between the eucharistic views of Barnes, Frith and the anonymous *Souper of the Lorde*: W. A. Clebsch, *England's Earliest Protestants 1520–35* (New Haven, 1964), 293. For the argument that the author of the *Souper* was George Joye, see W. D. J. Cargill Thompson, 'Who wrote the "Supper of the Lord"?', in *Studies in the Reformation: Luther to Hooker* (London, 1980), 83–93.

3 For a careful study of the decline in Luther's influence, see Basil Hall, 'The Early Rise and Gradual Decline of Lutheranism in England (1520–1600)' in *Reform and Reformation: England and the Continent c. 1500–c. 1750*, ed. Derek Baker (Oxford, 1979), 103–31.

4 Rupp, *English Protestant Tradition*, 161; Knox, *Doctrine of Faith*, 106–9.

5 His *Parable of the Wicked Mammon* (1528: incipit *That fayth the mother of all good workes iustifyeth us*) is generally thought to be based upon Luther's 1522 sermon for the ninth Sunday after Trinity: WA 10 III.283–92. Note the conclusions of Clebsch, *England's Earliest Protestants*, 153, on Tyndale's general conformity to Luther's positions. L. J. Trinterud, 'A Reappraisal of William Tyndale's Debt to Martin Luther', *ChH* 31 (1962), 24–45, argues that Tyndale owed more to humanism and the Rhineland Reformers than to Luther; this suggestion was clarified and criticised by Jens G. Møller, 'The Beginnings of Puritan Covenant Theology', *JEH* 14 (1963), 46–67.

6 e.g., see the *Prologue to Romans: Works*, 493–4, which emphasises that faith 'altereth a man, and changeth him into a new spiritual nature'. See further *Mammon: Works*, 53–5. In his later works, such as his *Exposition of Matthew V VI VII*, he appears to reproduce the basic features of the concept of the *imputatio iustitiae*.

7 His statement that, although the believer is righteous in Christ, he continues to be a sinner in fact, is based upon a proleptic understanding of justification: 'Bulwark against Rastell': *Workes*, 72.

8 See Knox, *Doctrine of Faith*, 43–51; 44. There is one isolated passage in which Frith refers to Christ's righteousness being 'reputed unto us for our own': *Workes*, 49. The parallelism between Adam's sin and Christ's righteousness is evidently constructed on the basis of Augustinian presuppositions, rather than those of later Lutheranism.

9 e.g., *Supplication* (1531), fol. liiir: 'the faith of Christ Jesus which is imputed unto them for justice'. For an incomplete list of the differences between the two editions, see W. D. J. Cargill Thompson, 'The Sixteenth Century Editions of *A Supplication unto King Henry VIII* by Robert Barnes D.D.', *Transactions of the Cambridge Bibliographical Society* 3 (1960), 133–42.

10 e.g., *Supplication* (1534); *Workes*, 242A: 'Wherefore we say with S. Paul, that faith only justifies *imputative*; that is, all the merits and goodness, grace and favour, and all that is in Christ, to our salvation, is imputed and reckoned unto us.'

11 George Joye, *Answer to Ashwell* (London, 1531), B3.

12 Rupp, *English Protestant Tradition*, 109–14. See further Jasper Ridley, *Thomas Cranmer* (Oxford, 1962), 113–15; Philip Hughes, *The Reformation in England* (3 vols: London, 5th edn, 1963), 1.348–55.

13 Hardwick, *Articles of Religion*, 250; Lloyd, *Formularies of Faith*, xxvi.

14 R. W. Dixon, *History of the Church of England* (6 vols: London, 3rd edn, 1895–1902) 1.415; Hughes, *Reformation in England*, 2.29 n. 2. It may also be noted that the scriptural citations (Romans 8.12 – note that Lloyd wrongly attributes it to the tenth chapter – and Matthew 19.17) in Article Five are taken from Melanchthon's 1535 *locus de bonis operibus*, which follows immediately after the *locus de gratia et de iustificatione*. Tyndale's definition of justification parallels Melanchthon's closely, but omits any reference to its forensic dimension: *Prologue to Romans: Works*, 508: 'By justifying, understand no other thing than to be recon-

ciled to God, and to be restored unto his favour, and to have thy sins forgiven thee.'

15 CR (Melanchthon) 21.421. See also §22.

16 Lloyd, *Formularies of Faith*, 209–10.

17 Lloyd, *Formularies of Faith*, 35.

18 See E. Burton, *Three Primers put forth in the Reign of Henry VIII* (Oxford, 1834): Rupp, *English Protestant Tradition*, 133.

19 Lloyd, *Formularies of Faith*, 364. For full text of the article, see 363–9.

20 The Gardiner–Somerset correspondence makes it clear that Cranmer was the author of this anonymous work: see John Foxe, *Acts and Monuments*, ed. J. Pratt (8 vols: London, 1877), 4.45–55. For the text of the *Homily*, see *The Two Books of Homilies appointed to be read in Churches* (Oxford, 1859), 24–35.

21 cf. *Homily*, 29.6–18, with the *locus de vocabulo gratiae* of the 1543 edition of the *Loci communes*, CR (Melanchthon) 21.755. See W. Fitzgerald, *Lectures on Ecclesiastical History* (2 vols; London, 1885), 2.214–5. Fitzgerald suggests that it is beyond doubt that Cranmer had Melanchthon's *locus* open before him as he wrote: however, as Cranmer began work on the *Homily* in 1539, and the Melanchthonian passage he cites is only to be found in editions of the *Loci* subsequent to 1543, he must be challenged on this point. Fitzgerald is, however, positively convincing in comparison with the ridiculous suggestion of R. C. Jenkins, *Pre-Tridentine Doctrine: A Review of the Commentary on the Scriptures of Thomas de Vio* (London, 1891), 70–2, that the *Homily* is dependent upon Cajetan. Both Cajetan and Cranmer represent refractions of Augustine's thought, and in so far as they share this common source, a certain degree of similarity is inevitable.

22 Cranmer: 'no man can fulfil the law, and therefore by the law all men are condemned' (*Homily*, 32.3–5); Melanchthon: 'nemo legem satisfaciet; lex accusat omnes' (CR 21.426).

23 *Homily*, 30.30–2.

24 See 'Notes on Justification', in *Works*, 2.203–8. Included among these patristic gobbets are such as: 'nos iustificari, hoc est, iustos fieri' (203); 'impius accepit Spiritum Dei et factus est iustus' (206). Note also the important reference to the 'continuation and increase' of justification (208). These texts appear to underlie passages such as *Homily*, 28.7–22.

25 Letter of Cranmer to Paul Fagius, dated 24 March 1549; *Original Letters relative to the English Reformation* (2 vols: Cambridge, 1846–7), 1.329. Peter Martyr arrived in 1547; Bucer and Fagius in 1549.

26 As noted by Hughes, *Reformation in England*, 2.97 n. 1.

27 Letter of 26 April 1549; *Original Letters*, 2.535–6.

28 *BSRK* 509.24–8 (left-hand column).

29 e.g., *BSLK* 174.34–44; 175.37–9. For the significance of these passages in relation to the doctrine of the *Apology* as a whole, see Pfnür, *Einig in der Rechtfertigungslehre*, 155–81.

30 *BSRK* 509.24–8 (right-hand column).

31 *BSRK* 509.20–4 (right-hand column).

32 *BSLK* 165.12–13.

33 *BSLK* 201.23. See also 200.25–6; 298.45; 299.29.

34 Hughes, *Reformation in England*, 3.16–47. All but six of the new bishops were Marian exiles; only one (Richard Cheney) was a Lutheran.

35 *Works*, 3.469–81; 483–547. For an analysis of these sermons, see Gibbs, 'Richard Hooker's *Via Media* Doctrine of Justification'.

36 *Works*, 3.486.

37 *Works*, 3.487–9.

38 *Works*, 3.507.

39 *Works*, 3.485–6; 531–2.

40 *Works*, 3.530.

41 *Works*, 3.515. Note the reference to man's passivity in his justification, 'working no more than dead and senseless matter, wood or stone or iron': *Works*, 3.531.

42 For a discussion of this paradox, see *Works*, 3.508.

43 Hooker is careful to exclude the doctrine of justification *propter fidem*: 'God doth justify the believing man, yet not for the worthiness of his belief, but for his worthiness which is believed' (*Works*, 3.538).

§31

1 See Charles F. Allison, *The Rise of Moralism: The Proclamation of the Gospel from Hooker to Baxter* (London, 1966); McGrath, 'Anglican Tradition on Justification'. For useful background material, see R. Buick Knox, 'Bishops in the Pulpit in the Seventeenth Century: Continuity amid Change', in *Reformation, Conformity and Dissent : Essays in Honour of Geoffrey Nuttall* (London, 1977), 92–114.

2 *BSRK*, 532.15–526.5. Cf. Philip Hughes, *The Reformation in England* (3 vols: London, 5th edn, 1963), 3.232–4. Barrett's sermon was sharply critical of Calvin, Beza, Bullinger and Peter Martyr.

3 Charles I appears to have elevated known Arminians, such as Richard Montagu, to the episcopacy largely on account of their anti-Puritan attitudes, thus occasioning the famous, and largely justified, jibe concerning the tenets of Arminianism:
   Q. What do the Arminians hold?
   A. All the best bishoprics and deaneries in England.

4 J. W. Packer, *The Transformation of Anglicanism 1643–1660* (Manchester, 1969), 26–8.

5 *A Practical Catechism*, 2nd edn (London, 1646), 9.

6 Packer, *Transformation of Anglicanism*, 53–6; 56. Cf. *BSRK* 523.3.

7 Thus H. C. Porter, *Reformation and Reaction in Tudor Cambridge* (Cambridge, 1958), 281.

8 But see James Ussher's more predestinarian views: *Works*, 11.203.

9 *Two Letters written by the Rt Rev. Thomas Barlow* (London, 1701).

10 *Two Letters*, 139. Cf. 102.

11 Ussher, *Works*, 13.250–1; 264; Hall, *Works*, 9.322; Jackson, *Works*, 5.118; Davenant, *Treatise on Justification*, 164–5; Cosin, *Works*, 2.49; Andrewes, *Works*, 5.104–26, especially 116–17.

12 *A Treatise of Justification* (London, 1639), 2.

13 See Allison, *Rise of Moralism*, 181–2.

14 Hammond, *Practical Catechism*, 78. Note also his criticism of the priority of justification over sanctification (78–83).

15 Forbes, *Considerationes*, 1.174; 204. His appeal to the support of Augustine is significant.

16 *Considerationes*, 1.216. Cf. McGrath, 'Anglican Tradition on Justification', 33–6.

17 See Allison, *Rise of Moralism*, 98–106.

18 *Considerationes*, 1.54.

19 See McGrath, 'Anglican Tradition on Justification', 33.

20 *Works*, 8.247–302; especially 284–90 (on the relation between Paul and James). See H. R. McAdoo, *The Structure of Caroline Moral Theology* (London, 1949); Allison, *Rise of Moralism*, 64–95; McGrath, 'Anglican Tradition on Justification', 38–9.

21 See Allison, *Rise of Moralism*, 118–37.

22 *Harmonia Apostolica*, 279–80.

23 Barlow, *Two Letters*, 82; Barrow, *Works*, 5.162; 168–70; Beveridge, *Works*, 7.292.

24 Bramhall, *Works*, 1.56; Sanderson, *Sermons*, 1.543.

25 Hooker, *Works*, 3.486.

26 Newman, *Lectures on Justification*, 400.

27 Newman, *Lectures on Justification*, 402.

28 Newman, *Lectures on Justification*, 400–1.

29 See Barrow, *Works*, 162–79.

§32

1 See C. H. and K. George, *The Protestant Mind of the English Reformation 1570–1640* (Princeton, 1961); J. F. H. New, *Anglican and Puritan. The Basis of Their Opposition 1558–1640* (London, 1964); Basil Hall, 'Puritanism: The Problems of Definition', in *Studies in Church History* II, ed., G. J. Cuming (London, 1965), 283–9b; C. H. George, 'Puritanism as History and Historiography', *Past and Present* (1968), 77–104; J. S. Coolidge, *The Pauline Renaissance in England: Puritanism and the Bible* (Oxford, 1970); J. Sears McGee, *The Godly Man in Stuart England: Anglicans, Puritans and the Two Tables* (New Haven, 1976); R. L. Greaves, *Society and Religion in Elizabethan England* (Minneapolis, 1981).

2 *Elizabethan Puritanism*, ed. L. J. Trinterud (New York, 1971), 6–7.

3 See J. van der Berg, 'Het puriteinse ethos en zijn bronnen', *Vox Theologica* 33 (1963), 161–71; 34 (1964), 1–8.

4 On the 'grey area' between Puritan and Separatist, see M. I. Tolmie, *The Triumph of the Saints: The Separate Churches of London 1616–1649* (Cambridge, 1977).

5 Hall, 'Puritanism', 296.

6 Hall, 'Puritanism', 288–9.

7 R. T. Kendall, *Calvin and English Calvinism to 1649* (Oxford, 1979), 8–9.

8 Tyndale, *Works*, 1.403. Cf. *Works*, 1.469: 'God hath made a covenant with us, to be merciful unto us, if we will be merciful one to another'; 2.90. For further references, see Trinterud, 'The Origins of Puritanism'; Møller, 'The Beginnings of Puritan Covenant Theology'; Clebsch, *England's Earliest Protestant*, 182–95.

9 Knewstub, *Lectures*, 5–6.

10 The 'chart' may be found in later editions: see *Works* (3 vols: Cambridge, 1608–9), 2.689 (printed facing the page). The chart is not contained in the 1590 or 1600 editions although its contents may be deduced from the work itself. For modern facsimiles, see H. C. Porter, *Puritanism in Tudor England* (London, 1970), 296–7; I. Breward, *The Work of William Perkins* (Abingdon, 1970),169.

11 *Workes*, 1.32.

12 *Workes*, 1.71.

13 See Kendall, *Calvin and English Calvinism*, 51–76.

14 *Workes*, 1.541. This 'practical syllogism' should be compared with the 'murtherer'-syllogism employed earlier: *Workes*, 1.529. Cf. *Workes*, 1.290; 2.322. The comparison with Richard Sibbes on this point is instructive: Kendall, *Calvin and English Calvinism*, 102–9.

15 Mosse, *Iustifying and Saving Faith*, 17. The distinction is further illustrated later: 29–35.

16 Clarke, *Saints Nosegay*, 242 (Spiritual Flower No. 688).

17 Clarke, *Saints Nosegay*, 53 (Spiritual Flower No. 134).

18 Kendall, *Calvin and English Calvinism*, 79–93.

19 *BSRK* 562.40–563.10; 563.23–9.

20 Kendall, *Calvin and English Calvinism*, 202–5.

21 *BSRK* 580.30–42.

22 *BSRK* 580.12–14.

23 *Works*, ed. Russell, 5.41–204.

24 *Works*, 5.145–59, especially 145.

25 *Works*, 5.284–90.

26 *Works*, 5.308. Owen's distinction between *impetration* and *application* should be noted: *Works*, 5.307–8.

27 *Works*, 5.320–1. Owen thus styles the Arminian Christ 'but a half-mediator' (323), in that he procures the end, but not the means thereto. Similarly, he ridicules the Arminian condition of salvation (i.e., faith) as an impossibility: it is 'as if a man should promise a blind man a thousand pounds upon condition that he will see' (323).

28 *Works*, 5.324.

29 Baxter, *Treatise of Justifying Righteousness*, 29; 88; 129–30.

30 Baxter, *Aphorisms on Justification*, 70.

31 *Defence of the True Sence*, 15.

32 *Imputatio fidei*, 3–4. Cf. 212.

33 e.g., John Eedes, *The Orthodox Doctrine concerning Justification* (London, 1642), 56–62; William Eyre, *Vindiciae Iustificationis Gratuitae* (London, 1654), 7; Thomas Gataker, *An Antidote against Error* (London, 1670), 37–8; Owen, *Works*, 11.214–15; 258–60.

34 Hooker, *Writings*, 152–86. Cf. Norman Pettit, *The Heart Prepared* (New Haven, 1966); Kendall, *Calvin and English Calvinism*, 125–38.

35 *Writings*, 160–2.

36 *The Soules Humiliation*, 170. Cf. *Unbeleevers Preparing* 1; 104; *The Soules Preparation*, 165. Note also the important statement to the effect that not every *saving* work is a *sanctifying* work: *Writings*, 145.

37 Cotton, *Gods Mercie mixed with his Iustice*, 10–12. See also Pettit, *The Heart Prepared*, 129–79; Kendall, *Calvin and English Calvinism*, 110–17; 167–83.

38 *Christ the Fountaine*, 40–1.

39 Pettit, *The Heart Prepared*, 137; Kendall, *Calvin and English Calvinism*, 169–77. Kendall indicates (170 n. 1) the reasons for supposing that Cotton arrived at his new insights while still in England.

40 *A Treatise of the Covenant of Grace*, 39–42.

41 A contemporary source which summarises the chief points of her teaching is E. Pagitt, *Heresiography* (London, 1662), 124–6. This work also provides a useful general summary of English Antinomianism (122), based on Thomas Gataker, *Antinomianism Discovered and Confuted* (London, 1642).

42 See Perry Miller, *The New England Mind: The Seventeenth Century* (New York, 1939); A. Simpson, *Puritanism in Old and New England* (Chicago, 1955).

43 See A. E. Dunning, *Congregationalists in America* (New York, 1894), 186–8; W. Walker, *Ten New England Leaders* (New York, 1901), 126–34; 244–7. The later defence of this 'Half-Way Covenant' by William Hart, Moses Hemmenway and Moses Mather is important: see W. Walker, *Creeds and Platforms of Congregationalism* (New York, 1893), 283–7.

44 See P. J. Tracy, *Jonathan Edwards, Pastor: Religion and Society in Eighteenth Century Northampton* (New York, 1979), 109–22, and references therein. For an excellent analysis of Edwards' reaction to Stoddardeanism, see John F. Jamieson, 'Jonathan Edwards' Change of Position on Stoddardeanism', *HThR* 74 (1981), 79–99.

45 For the emphasis upon justification by faith, characteristic of the period, see E. B. Lowrie, *The Shape of the Puritan Mind: The Thought of Samuel Willard* (New Haven, 1974); R. F. Lovelace, *The American Pietism of Cotton Mather: Origins of American Evangelicalism* (Grand Rapids, 1979), 73–109.

46 *Works*, 2.950b. For Samuel Willard's views on the covenant, see Lowrie, *Shape of the Puritan Mind*, 160–85. For the importance of the covenant-concept to Puritan theology in the period, see the classic study of Perry Miller, 'The Marrow of Puritan Divinity', in *Errand into the Wilderness* (Cambridge, Mass., 1956), 48–98.

47 On the federal doctrine of original sin, of particular importance in this respect, see H. S. Smith, *Changing Concepts of Original Sin: A Study in American Theology since 1750* (New York, 1955), 1–9.

48 *Works*, 2.983b.

49 See F. H. Forster, *A Genetic History of the New England Theology* (Chicago, 1907).

50 Hopkins, *The Wisdom of God in the Permission of Sin* (Boston, 1759).

51 K. Francke, 'The Beginning of Cotton Mather's Correspondence with August Hermann Franke', *Philological Quarterly* 5 (1926), 193–5. See also Lovelace, *Cotton Mather, passim*.

52 Mayhew, *Practical Discourses* (Boston, 1760), 5.

53 John Tucker, *Observations on the Doctrines and Uncharitableness of the Rev Mr Jonathan Parsons of Newbury* (Boston, 1757), 5.

54 e.g., William Balch, *The Apostles Paul and James Reconciled with Respect to Faith and Works* (Boston, 1743).

55 Samuel Webster, *Justification by the Free Grace of God* (Boston, 1765), 27. It will be obvious that this opened the Arminians to the charge that they were preaching justification by works – a charge which they vigorously denied: Lemuel Briant, *Some Friendly Remarks upon a Sermon Lately Preached at Braintree* (Boston, 1750), 10; Charles Chauncy, *Twelve Sermons* (Boston, 1765). 12; Jonathan Mayhew, *Striving to enter in at the Strait Gate* (Boston, 1761), 19–20.

§33

1 On the sense of the term 'High Church', see Owen Chadwick, *The Mind of the Oxford Movement* (London, 1960), 14–15.

2 Originally a letter to D. Parker, dated 16 April 1810, entitled 'On Justification': *Remains*, 1.281–317.

3 *Remains*, 1.308. Note the deliberate avoidance of the term 'imputation'. Cf. 1.298–9.

4 G. S. Faber's *Primitive Doctrine of Justification investigated* (London, 1837) attempted to disprove Knox on this point, while at the same time suggesting that Knox was Tridentine, rather than Anglican, in his personal view on justification.

5 For a useful introduction, see Thomas Sheridan, *Newman on Justification* (New York, 1967).

6 Newman, *Apologia pro vita sua* (London, 1964), 86. Note the statement that the 'essay on Justification' was 'aimed at the Lutheran dictum that justification by faith only was the cardinal doctrine of Christianity'.

7 C. S. Dessain, 'Cardinal Newman and the Eastern Tradition', *Downside Review* 94 (1976), 83–98.

8 *English Hymnal* No. 471; *Hymns Ancient and Modern Revised* No. 185. The hymn first appeared in 1865, as part of the *Dream of Gerontius*.

9 *Lectures on Justification*, 144. Cf. 150–1.

10 *Lectures on Justification*, 144.

11 *Lectures on Justification*, 149.

12 Newman here distances himself from Knox, who suggested that justification concerned being *made righteous*, and sanctification being *made holy*: Knox, *Remains*, 1.307–9.

13 *Lectures on Justification*, 154.

14 *Lectures on Justification*, 74. This also permits the earlier statement (63) to be understood correctly: 'justification and sanctification [are] in fact substantially one and the same thing; ... in order of ideas, viewed relatively to each other, justification followed upon sanctification.'

15 *Lectures on Justification*, 112.

16 *Lectures on Justification*, 263.

17 *Lectures on Justification*, 262.

18 *Lectures on Justification*, 275–6.

19 *Lectures on Justification*, 303.

20 *Lectures on Justification*, 343–404.

21 See Basil Hall, 'The Early Rise and Gradual Decline of Lutheranism in England (1520–1600)', in *Reform and Reformation: England and the Continent c. 1500–c. 1750*, ed. Derek Baker (Oxford, 1979), 103–31.

22 See McGrath, 'High Church Misrepresentation of Luther'. It is possible that Newman bases his evaluation of Luther upon the Tübingen Roman Catholic Johann Adam Möhler's *Symbolik* (1832). There is evidence to suggest that Newman read his work (in French translation) while preparing for his *Lectures*: Henry Tristram, 'J. A. Moehler et J. H. Newman et la renaissance catholique en Angleterre', *RSPhTh* 27 (1938), 184–204. It is known to have been in E. B. Pusey's library: Y. Brilioth, *The Anglican Revival* (London, 1933), 329 n. 2. There are certainly strong similarities between Newman and Möhler at points of importance – for example, in their common assertion that Luther excluded love, hope and obedience from justification. Möhler's criticism of Luther also underlies N. P. Williams' hostile and inaccurate assessment of the Reformer: *The Idea of the Fall and of Original Sin* (London, 1927), 427–31. Note especially the references to Möhler at 428 n. 1; 429 n. 3.

23 See M. Schloenbach, *Glaube als Geschenk Gottes* (Stuttgart, 1962) for documentation.

24 Luther, WA 40 I.41.2; Hooker, *Works*, 3.531.

25 WA 40 I.229.28–9.

26 *Lectures on Justification*, 148. Cf. 149: 'Whatever blessings in detail we ascribe to justification, are ascribed in Scripture to this sacred indwelling.'

27 *Lectures on Justification*, 300.

28 *Lectures on Justification*, 300–1.

29 Cf. *Luther's Works* (56 vols: St Louis, 1955–76), 26.265–6.

30 *Lectures on Justification*, 343 n. 1.

31 WA 40 I.239.31–240.2.

32 *Institutio*, III.iii.35. See §22 for further details.

33 *Lectures on Justification*, 154.

34 *Lectures on Justification*, 154.

35 *Remarks on Certain Passages*, 4.

36 An exception may be noted in the case of N. P. Williams' unpublished commentary on Romans (MS in library of Christ Church, Oxford). For a brief survey of its features, see A. E. McGrath, 'Justification; "Making Just" or "Declaring Just"?', *Churchman* 96 (1982), 44–52. A totally inept

account of the teaching of the Anglican Reformers on justification was given by A. H. Rees, *The Doctrine of Justification in the Anglican Reformers* (London, 1939), and convincingly refuted by E. G. Rupp, *English Protestant Tradition*, 172–85. An uncritical appraisal of Rees' work underlies the serious inaccuracies and misunderstandings which litter Gregory Dix's *Question of Anglican Orders: Letters to a Layman* (London, 1944), 21–8 (note especially the appeal to Rees: 27).

37 This is the somewhat simplistic approach adopted by Hans Küng (*Rechtfertigung: Die Lehre Karl Barths und eine katholische Besinnung*), who identifies Karl Barth as such a 'typical' theologian.

38 Once more, it is necessary to point out the deficiencies of Küng's study, which tends to adopt a Thomist interpretation of Trent, overlooking alternative interpretations less congenial to his attempt to harmonise Barth and Trent.

39 Thus the Council of Trent's explicit statement that there is only a single formal cause of justification is directed against Seripando's version of the mediating Regensburg theology: see §§27, 28.

Introduction to chapter 9

1 e.g., see Hans Baron, 'Towards a More Positive Evaluation of the Fifteenth Century Renaissance', *Journal of the History of Ideas* 4 (1943), 22–49; Karl Dannhauer, *The Renaissance: Medieval or Modern?* (Boston, 1959), 35–48; 64–75. For a careful evaluation of the 'Burckhardtian thesis' – that the Renaissance was the first-born among the sons of modern Europe – see Wallace K. Ferguson, *The Renaissance in Historical Thought: Five Centuries of Interpretation* (Boston, 1948), 195–252; 290–385.

2 See Ruprecht Paqué, *Das Pariser Nominalistenstatut: Zur Entstehung des Realitätsbegriff der neuzeitlichen Naturwissenschaft* (Berlin, 1970).

3 See Alister E. McGrath, *The Making of Modern German Christology: From the Enlightenment to Pannenberg* (Oxford, 1986), for a discussion.

4 e.g., see James Buchanan, *The Doctrine of Justification: An Outline of its History in the Church and of its Exposition from Scripture* (1867: reprinted London, 1961), 114–40.

5 Gerhard Ebeling, 'Luther und der Anbruch der Neuzeit', *ZThK* 69 (1972), 185–213.

6 The continuity between the late medieval period and the Reformation has been emphasised throughout the present study. For the specific case of Luther, see McGrath, *Luther's Theology of the Cross*, 72–128.

7 See the essay of Ernst Troeltsch, 'Renaissance und Reformation', in *Gesammelte Schriften* (4 vols: Tübingen, 1912–25), 4.261–96. The thesis of the medieval and non-modern character of the Reformation was developed at greater length – against Hegel and his disciples – in two of Troeltsch's more important works: *Vernunft und Offenbarung bei Johann Gerhard und Melanchthon: Untersuchungen zur Geschichte der altprotestantischen Theologie* (Göttingen, 1891); and *Die Bedeutung des Protestantismus für die Entstehung der modernen Welt* (München/Berlin, 1911). For a more

scholarly exposition of this point, see Heiko A. Oberman, *Forerunners of the Reformation: The Shape of Late Medieval Thought illustrated by Key Documents* (Philadelphia, 1981), 3–66. Oberman's later study *Werden und Wertung der Reformation* explores this theme in some depth.

8 Although Althaus, 'Gottes Gottheit als Sinn der Rechtfertigungslehre Luthers', emphasises the theocentric dimension of Luther's theology of justification, it must be noted that it is quite inadequate as a leading characteristic.

§34

1 For an introduction, see A. O. Dyson, 'Theological Legacies of the Enlightenment: England and Germany', in *England and Germany: Studies in Theological Diplomacy*, ed. S. W. Sykes (Frankfurt, 1982), 45–62. For the influence of Deism upon the *Aufklärung*, see G. Gawlick, 'Deismus als Grundzug der Religionsphilosophie der Aufklärung', in *Hermann Samuel Reimarus (1694–1768), ein 'bekannter Unbekannter' der Aufklärung* (Hamburg, 1973), 15–43.

For the Enlightenment in general, see the important studies of Paul Hazard, *La crise de la conscience européene (1680–1715)* (3 vols: Paris, 1935); *idem, La pensée européene au XVIIIᵉ siècle de Montesquieu à Lessing* (3 vols: Paris, 1946).

2 Herbert was treated as a precursor of Deism by its exponents: Blount's *Religio Laici* is clearly dependent upon an earlier draft of Herbert's work of the same name. See further M. Rossi, *La vita, le opere i tempi di Eduardo Herbert di Chirbury* (3 vols: Roma, 1947).

3 The Stoicism underlying the concept of *notitiae communes* derives from Cicero: see G. Gawlick, 'Cicero and the Enlightenment', *Studies on Voltaire and the Eighteenth Century* 25 (1963), 657–62. Rossi suggests an Aristotelian basis for Herbert's epistemology, but concedes the influence of Stoicism: Rossi, *Eduardo Chirbury*, 1.291.

4 Rossi, *Eduardo Chirbury*, 1.535 n. 1.

5 On this distinction see M. Schneckenburger, *Vorlesungen über die Lehrbegriffe der kleineren protestantischen Kirchenparteien* (Frankfurt, 1863), 22.

6 Toland, *Christianity not Mysterious*, ed. Gawlick, 58–63. See further F. Heinemann, 'John Toland and the Age of Reason', *Archiv für Philosophie* 4 (1950), 35–66.

7 Locke, *Reasonableness of Christianity: Works*, 7.6.

8 *Reasonableness of Christianity: Works*, 7.14. Cf. 7.112.

9 *Reasonableness of Christianity: Works*, 7.101; 110. Cf. Leslie Stephen, *History of English Thought in the Eighteenth Century* 3rd edn (2 vols: London, 1902), 1.95–6.

10 *Reasonableness of Christianity: Works*, 7.101–3.

11 *Reasonableness of Christianity: Works*, 7.105.

12 Locke treats the New Testament epistles as occasional writings, rather than as sources of fundamental Christian truths, being intended to strengthen Christians rather than proclaim basic truths to outsiders:

Reasonableness of Christianity: Works, 7.151-5. A further point which Locke emphasises is that only fundamentals – i.e., the belief that Jesus is the Christ, and repentance – can be necessary to salvation, on account of the obscurity which the Bible, as an ancient text, displays: see J. T. Moore, 'Locke's Analysis of Language and the Assent to Scripture', *Journal of the History of Ideas* 36 (1976), 707-14.

13 *Reasonableness of Christianity: Works*, 7.148.

14 On this work, see J. W. Yolton, *Locke and the Compass of Human Understanding* (Cambridge, 1970); R. I. Aaron, *John Locke* (Oxford, 1971); J. L. Mackie, *Problems from Locke* (Oxford, 1976); P. A. Schouls, *The Imposition of Method: A Study of Descartes and Locke* (Oxford, 1980), 149-85.

15 See H. R. McAdoo, *The Spirit of Anglicanism: A Survey of Anglican Theological Method in the Seventeenth Century* (London, 1965), 240-315.

16 See H. R. McAdoo, *The Structure of Caroline Moral Theology* (London, 1949).

17 *Essay*, II.23-25; ed. Nidditch, 117.24-118.31.

18 See L. Krüger, 'The Concept of Experience in John Locke', in *John Locke: Symposium Wolfenbüttel*, ed. R. Brandt (Berlin/New York, 1981), 74-89.

19 *Essay*, I.iv.17; 95.10-11. Cf. I.iv.9; I.iv.16; IV.x.1.

20 The question of how God's existence may be determined empirically is also significant: see M. R. Ayers, 'Mechanism, Superaddition and the Proof of God's Existence in Locke's *Essay*', *Philosophical Review* 90 (1981), 210-51.

21 *Essay*, IV.x.6; 621.6-8.

22 *Essay*, II.xxiii.33; 314.25-35. See also II.xxiii.35. It is important to note that Locke has avoided applying moral epithets (such as 'good' or 'righteous') to the 'Supreme Being' until this point.

23 *Essay*, II.xxiii.36; 315.34-6.

24 See the analysis of G. A. J. Rogers, 'Locke, Law and the Laws of Nature', in *Symposium Wolfenbüttel*, 146-62.

25 See G. Schedler, 'Hobbes on the Basis of Political Obligation', *Journal of the History of Philosophy* 15 (1977), 165-70. On the concept of 'contract' in Hobbes' theory of cession, see M. T. Delgano, 'Analysing Hobbes' Contract', *Proceedings of the Aristotelian Society* 76 (1975-6), 209-26.

26 Hobbes, *Leviathan* (London, 1651), II.xxvi.4; 138. For the concept of 'covenant' employed, see Delgano, 'Hobbes' Contract'; for the concept of the 'Law of Nature', see P. E. Moreau, 'Loi divine et loi naturelle selon Hobbes', *Reveue Internationale de Philosophie* 33 (1979), 443-51.

27 For the development of the theory of the state from Hobbes to Locke, see C. B. Macpherson, *The Political Theory of Possessive Individualism: Hobbes to Locke* (Oxford, 1962).

28 See D. P. Walker, *The Decline of Hell: Seventeenth-Century Discussions of Eternal Torment* (London, 1964). The chief argument advanced against the notion was that it appeared to serve no useful preservatory function.

29 *Christianity as Old as the Creation*, ed. Gawlick, 14-15. Gawlick suggests

that Tindal was the first to reverse the traditional relationship of morality and religion (17*): it seems to us that this development is implicit in the writings of Locke.

30 Chubb, *True Gospel of Jesus Christ*, in *Posthumous Works* (2 vols: London, 1748), 2.20. For a useful discussion of Chubb's doctrine of the work of Christ, see R. S. Franks, *The Work of Christ* (London, 1962), 485–91.

31 *Posthumous Works*, 2.18; 104–5; 140–1. Note that these correspond to the final three *notitiae communes*, as defined by Cherbury.

32 *Posthumous Works*, 2.55.

33 *Posthumous Works*, 2.32. Cf. 2.43–9; 112–20. For his critique of the doctrine of original sin, see 2.164.

34 *Posthumous Works*, 2.150.

35 *Posthumous Works*, 2.115–16.

36 Morgan, *The Moral Philosopher*, 1.439. Cf. 1.412.

37 *The Moral Philosopher*, 1.411–12.

38 *The Moral Philosopher*, 3.150.

39 See Franks, *The Work of Christ*, 492–7.

40 For the critique of the doctrine of original sin associated with the French Enlightenment, see Ernst Cassirer, *The Philosophy of the Enlightenment* (Boston, 1960), 137–60.

41 See Herbert Butterfield, 'England in the Eighteenth Century', in *A History of the Methodist Church in Great Britain*, eds. Rupert Davies and Gordon Rupp (4 vols: London, 1965–), 1.1–33. On the relation of John Wesley to German Pietism, see Jean Orcibal, 'The Theological Originality of John Wesley and Continental Spirituality', in *A History of the Methodist Church*, ed. Davies and Rupp, 1.81–111.

42 See A. C. McGiffert, *Protestant Thought before Kant* (London, 1919), 251. On the soteriologies of the *Aufklärung*, see F. C. Baur, *Die christliche Lehre von der Versöhnung in ihrer geschichtlichen Entwicklung* (Tübingen, 1838), 478–530; Baur, *Salus Christiana*, 111–79.

43 *Institutiones theologiae dogmaticae*, IV.iv.4; 956. Cf. IV.iv.12; 978; 'neminem nisi regenitum iustificari'.

44 *Institutiones theologiae dogmaticae*, IV.iv.4; 956. As Stolzenburg emphasises, both Budde and Pfaff presuppose that man is naturally capable of receiving grace without the necessity of *satisfactio Christi* (in the Orthodox sense): A. F. Stolzenburg, *Die Theologie des J. Fr. Buddeus und des Chr. M. Pfaff* (Berlin, 1926), 211.

45 *Institutiones theologiae*, 487. See further Stolzenburg, *Theologie*, 207–20.

46 *Elementa theologiae dogmaticae*, 819.

47 *Elementa theologiae dogmaticae*, 822.

48 'Ponendo scilicet tres salutis conditiones, conversionem, fidem, renovationem': *Elementa theologiae dogmaticae*, 713. Cf. 829: 'Nemo negat, pios motus antecedere iustificationem et adesse in actu iustificationis.' For similar views in the writings of a noted later *Aufklärer*, see Henke, *Lineamenta*, §116; 165–6. The theme is important in the preaching of the later *Aufklärung*: see R. Krause, *Die Predigt der späten deutschen Aufklärung* (Stuttgart, 1965).

49 Hobbes, *Leviathan*, II.xxvii; 161–7.

50 The impact of Hobbes' theory of punishment upon German theology was delayed through the influence of Leibniz' *Théodicée* (1710), in which he developed the view that the *civitas Dei*, the moral world, is an end in itself, rather than the means to some other end.

51 See Ritschl, *Justification and Reconciliation*, 337–41.

52 A similar critique of the concept of vindictive justice underlies the contemporary critique of the notion of eternal punishment, particularly in early eighteenth-century France: see Walker, *The Decline of Hell*, 40–51.

53 It is of interest to note that the most penetrating contemporary criticism of Dippel's views was due to the Wolffian I. G. Kanz. Unlike Dippel, who regarded the divine government of mankind as the means towards man's well-being, Kanz retained the Leibnizian concept of the *civitas Dei* as an end in itself. The establishment of moral order among mankind is thus an end in itself, rather than a means to an eudaemonistic end. Kanz is thus able to follow Leibniz in retaining the concept of the retributive justice of God, in addition to the purely natural punishment for sin which Dippel allowed.

54 *Der thätige Gehorsam*, 419–21. For a useful analysis, see Ritschl, *Justification and Reconciliation*, 346–55.; Baur, *Salus Christiana*, 132–44. Ritschl's suggestion that Töllner adopts an Abailardian understanding of the significance of the death of Christ rests upon his improper exposition of Abailard's soteriology: see R. E. Weingart, *The Logic of Divine Love* (Oxford, 1970), 120–50. In part, the success of Töllner's critique of the significance of the *obedientia activa Christi* was due to the astonishingly poor quality of his opponents. Thus J. A. Ernesti, finding himself obliged to concede that it was impossible to conceive of a man who was not under an obligation to obey the law, laboured under the misapprehension that the denial of the obligation of Christ's obedience to the law was equivalent to the denial of the humanity of Christ. For a consideration of some of the responses to Töllner, see I. A. Dorner, *History of the Development of the Doctrine of the Person of Christ* (5 vols: Edinburgh, 1863), 5.263–5.

55 *Der thätige Gehorsam*, 42. Cf. 631–2, especially 632: 'Ich stelle mich vor, daß Gott zur Begnadigung an sich niemals eine Genugthuung gefordert oder veranstaltet haben würde: und daß wir daher gar nicht auf dem rechten Wege sind, wenn wir sie als eine zur Begnadigung der Menschen nöthig befundne Veranstaltung betrachten.'

56 *Der thätige Gehorsam*, 685.

57 See his important essay 'Alle Erklärungsarten vom versöhnenden Tode Christi laufen auf Eins heraus', in *Theologische Untersuchungen*, 2.316–35.

58 *Glückseligkeitslehre*, 78.

59 *Glückseligkeitslehre*, 73.

60 cf. *Glückseligkeitslehre*, 83.

61 *Glückseligkeitslehre*, 93–162.

62 It is worth recalling Loofs' famous remark, 'Die Dogmengeschichte ist ein Kind der deutschen Aufklärungszeit': Friedrich Loofs, *Leitfaden zum Studium der Dogmengeschichte*, 4th edn (Halle, 1904), 1. The original

purpose of *Dogmengeschichte* was the *criticism* of dogma through an historical investigation of its origins, rather than a mere scientific documentation of its historical forms. This point is of particular importance in relation to our study, in that the early studies of the development of the doctrine of justification (such as those of F. C. Baur and A. B. Ritschl) were undertaken for polemical, rather than purely scholarly, motives.

63 *Glückseligkeitslehre*, 146. Note also his criticism of the Christological application of the concept of 'sacrifice': *Glückseligkeitslehre*, 288.
64 *Glückseligkeitslehre*, 149.
65 *Glückseligkeitslehre*, 130.
66 *Glückseligkeitslehre*, 161–2.
67 *Glückseligkeitslehre*, 162.
68 *Glückseligkeitslehre*, 180: 'Gott fordert so wenig, als irgends ein menschlicher Vater von schwachen unmündigen Kindern mehr als aufrichtigen Willen und treuen Gebrauch der vorhandnen Kräfte.'
69 See Baur, *Salus Christiana*, 134–8.
70 See McGrath, 'The Moral Theory of the Atonement'.
71 See Teller, *Religion der Vollkommnern*, 9–12; especially 12.
72 For further discussion of the Christology of the *Aufklärung*, see Alister E. McGrath, *The Making of Modern German Christology: From the Enlightenment to Pannenberg* (Oxford, 1986), 9–18.

§35

1 For the remarkable influence of Kant upon the nineteenth-century Göttingen theological faculty, and particularly Albrecht Ritschl, see J. Meyer, 'Geschichte der Göttinger theologischen Fakultät 1737–1937', *Zeitschrift für niedersächsische Kirchengeschichte* 42 (1937), 7–107; P. Wrzecionko, *Die philosophischen Wurzeln der Theologie Albrecht Ritschls: Ein Beitrag zum Problem des Verhältnisses von Theologie und Philosophie im 19. Jahrhundert* (Berlin, 1964).
2 See Ritschl's careful analysis of Kant's significance in this respect: *Justification and Reconciliation*, 320–86.
3 See McGrath, 'The Moral Theory of the Atonement'.
4 The brilliant study of A. Schweitzer, *Die Religionphilosophie Kants in der Kritik der reinen Vernunft bis zur Religion innherhalb der Grenzen der bloßen Vernunft* (Freiburg, 1899), is still invaluable. See further W. Reinhart, *Über das Verhältnis von Sittlichkeit und Religion bei Kant* (Bern, 1927); A. Messer, *Kommentar zu Kants ethischen und religionsphilosophischen Hauptschriften* (Leipzig, 1929); and especially the richly documented study of J. Bohatec, *Die Religionsphilosophie Kants in der 'Religion innherhalb der Grenzen der bloßen Vernunft'* (Hildesheim, 1966). The best study of the question of the translation of human finitude from the cognitive to the moral realm remains G. Krüger, *Philosophie und Moral in der Kantischen Kritik* (Tübingen, 1931).
5 *Schriften*, 6.170.15–19.

6 See the classic study of A. Döring, 'Kants Lehre vom höchsten Gut', *Kantstudien* 4 (1898), 94–101. The more recent studies of J. R. Silber should be noted, especially his essay 'The Importance of the Highest Good in Kant's Ethics', *Ethics* 73 (1963), 179–97.

7 For a useful introduction to this concept, see E. L. Fackenheim, 'Kant and Radical Evil', *University of Toronto Quarterly* 23 (1953), 339–52.

8 See the argument of H. J. Paton, *The Categorical Imperative* (London, 1946).

9 *Schriften*, 6.75.1–76.6 (our italics). For the background to this remarkable statement, see *Werke*, 6.62.14–66.18. Elsewhere in this work, Kant asserts that a lenient judge who relaxes the moral law represents a contradiction in terms: *Werke*, 6.141.9–142.3. The apparent discrepancy between such statements is not discussed.

10 *Schriften*, 6.117.14–15.

11 *Schriften*, 6.120.10–16.

12 The first difficulty concerns the relationship between moral acts and the moral disposition, and forces Kant to discuss how God can accept a good moral disposition as equivalent to perfectly good moral acts: *Schriften*, 6.66.21–67.16. The second difficulty concerns how an individual may know with certainty that his new disposition is, in fact, good: *Schriften*, 6.67.17–71.20.

13 *Schriften*, 6.71.21–78.2.

14 *Schriften*, 6.74.16–17.

15 For the argument, see *Schriften*, 6.74.1–75.1.

16 *Schriften*, 6.183.37–184.3.

17 For the influence of Kant upon contemporary discussion of the theology of reconciliation, see J. H. Tieftrunk, *Censur des christlichen Lehrebegriffs nach den Prinzipien der Religionskritik* (3 vols: Berlin, 1791–95) (the first volume of which appeared in a second edition in 1796). Note the explicit reference to the theological significance of radical evil (e.g., 3.122), and the concept of grace as *die Ergänzung unseres Unvermögens zum Übergange aus dem Bösen zum Guten* (2.228).

18 For further details, see Jack Forstman, *A Romantic Triangle: Schleiermacher and Early German Romanticism* (Missoula, Mont., 1977). On 'Romanticism' in general, see F. Schulz, 'Romantik und Romantiker als literarhistorische Terminologien und Begriffsbildungen', *Deutsche Vierteljahrschrift für Literaturwissenschaft und Geistesgeschichte* 2 (1924), 349–66; B. M. G. Reardon, *Religion in the Age of Romanticism* (Cambridge, 1985), *passim*. On the rôle of *Gefühl* in Schleiermacher's theology, see W. Schutz, 'Schleiermachers Theorie des Gefühls und ihre religiöse Bedeutung', *ZThK* (1956), 75–103; F. W. Graf, 'Ursprüngliches Gefühl unmittelbarer Koinzidenz des Differenten: Zur Modifikation des Religionsbegriffs in der verschiedenen Auflagen von Schleiermachers "Reden über Religion"', *ZThK* 75 (1978), 147–86.

19 *Der christliche Glaube*, §33, 3; 1.174–6.

20 *Der christliche Glaube*, §28, 2; 1.154–6.

21 *Der christliche Glaube*, §3, 2–4; 1.7–13.

22 *Der christliche Glaube*, §15, 1; 1.99–100. It should be noted that Schleiermacher emphasises the communal dimension of such experience, and does not lapse into a form of solipsism: for Schleiermacher, Christian faith is essentially and primarily faith in Christ as grounded in the community of faith. See further D. Offermann, *Schleiermachers Einleitung in die Glaubenslehre* (Berlin, 1969), 293–321.

23 See Graß, 'Die durch Jesum von Nazareth vollbrachte Erlösung', for an excellent analysis. Schleiermacher's definition of Christianity is significant in this respect, in that it makes explicit that the distinguishing feature of Christianity lies in the total subordination of its content to the redemption accomplished by Jesus of Nazareth: *Der christliche Glaube*, §11 (title); 1.67.

24 *Der christliche Glaube*, §4, 4; 1.20–2. Cf. F. Beisser, *Schleiermachers Lehre von Gott* (Göttingen, 1970), 57–68; Offermann, *Einleitung*, 47–65.

25 *Der christliche Glaube*, §94, 1–3; 2.40–5. On the use of the term *Urbild*, see P. Seifert, *Die Theologie des jungen Schleiermacher* (Gütersloh, 1960), 141–2.

26 *Der christliche Glaube*, §106, 1; 2.162.

27 *Der christliche Glaube*, §102, 1; 2.112–13. Schleiermacher notes the traditional interpretation of the *munus Christi triplex*, as prophet, priest and king, and argues that any attempt to reduce Christ to a single one of these 'offices' results in serious distortion. His (inaccurate) criticism of the Roman Catholic position is not relevant to our purpose.

28 *Der christliche Glaube*, §100, 3; 2.101.

29 *Der christliche Glaube*, §100, 3; 2.101.

30 See H. Pieter, *Theologische Ideologiekritik: Die praktische Konsequenzen der Rechtfertigungslehre bei Schleiermacher* (Göttingen, 1977).

31 *Der christliche Glaube*, §107, 2; 2.167–8.

32 *Der christliche Glaube*, §109, 4; 2.201. But note the emphatic rejection of the suggestion that faith is the instrumental cause of justification: §109, 4; 2.202.

33 *Der christliche Glaube*, §107, 1; 2.165–7.

34 *Der christliche Glaube*, §70; 1.376 '[eine] aufzuhebende vollkommne Unfähigkeit zum Guten'.

35 *Der christliche Glaube*, §71, 3; 1.386–8. Note how Schleiermacher thus correlates the first consciousness of sin with the first presentiment of redemption.

36 *Der christliche Glaube*, §22, 1–3; 1.124–9. See further K.-M. Beckmann, *Der Begriff der Häresie bei Schleiermacher* (München, 1959), 36–62. For consideration of the four heresies in more detail, see 85–114.

37 *Der christliche Glaube*, §22, 2; 1.125.

38 *Der christliche Glaube*, §22, 2; 1.125.

39 *Der christliche Glaube*, §109, 4; 2.201.

40 *Der christliche Glaube*, §84, 3; 1.471.

41 *Der christliche Glaube*, §84, 3; 1.470.

42 *Der christliche Glaube*, §84, 3; 1.471–3.

43 *Der christliche Glaube*, §84, 1; 1.465–6.

44 *Der christliche Glaube*, §84, 1; 1.466–7.
45 *Der christliche Glaube*, §84. 1; 1.467.

§36

1 See Alister E. McGrath, *The Making of Modern German Christology* (Oxford, 1986), 32–52 for details. Of particular importance is F. C. Baur's critique of Schleiermacher's inference of the Christ-event from the collective Christian consciousness: 38–9.

2 F. C. Baur, *Die christliche Lehre von der Versöhnung in ihrer geschichtlichen Entwicklung* (Tübingen, 1838), 748. It may be noted that Baur minimised the distinction between the soteriologies of the *Aufklärung* and both Kant and Schleiermacher, presumably to achieve consistency with his Hegelian theory of historical development.

3 Ritschl, *Justification and Reconciliation*, §76; 605.

4 The third edition of this work (1888) has been used in the present study: for the differences between the various editions, see C. Fabricius, *Die Entwicklung in Albrecht Ritschls Theologie von 1874 bis 1889 nach der verschiedene Auflagen seiner Hauptwerke dargestellt und beurteilt* (Tübingen, 1909).

5 *Rechtfertigung und Versöhnung*, §27; 189–90.

6 *Rechtfertigung und Versöhnung*, §27; 185.

7 *Rechtfertigung und Versöhnung*, §28; 195–200.

8 *Loci communes* (1521), preface. It should, of course, be noted that Melanchthon was not defining the basis of a theological programme with this statement, but merely explaining the omission of a *locus* concerning Christology from this work, which was primarily concerned with soteriology. Melanchthon's theological criticisms were directed against the medieval soteriologies, not the Christologies of the period. In subsequent editions, in which a Christological *locus* is included, this dictum is omitted.

9 *Rechtfertigung und Versöhnung*, (Bonn, 1st edn, 1874) §44; 343: 'Wir erkennen nämlich die Art und die Eigenschaften, d.h. die Bestimmtheit des Seins, nur an dem Wirken eines Dinges auf uns, und wir denken die Art und den Umfang seines Wirkens auf uns als sein Wesen.'

10 *Justification and Reconciliation*, §1; 1.

11 See Hermann Timm, *Theorie und Praxis in der Theologie Albrecht Ritschls und Wilhelm Herrmanns* (Gütersloh, 1967); James Richmond, *Ritschl: A Reappraisal* (London, 1978), 124–67.

12 *Rechtfertigung und Versöhnung*, §16; 83. The other two definitions of justification offered by Ritschl represent an extension of this basic definition.

13 See Schäfer, 'Rechtfertigungslehre bei Ritschl und Kähler', 69–70.

14 *WA* 2.722.24–5.

15 *Rechtfertigung und Versöhnung*, §56; 517.

16 *Rechtfertigung und Versöhnung*, §31; 58–9.

17 *Rechtfertigung und Versöhnung*, §15; 72.

18 *Rechtfertigung und Versöhnung*, §15; 75–7.
19 See W. von Loewenich, *Luther und der Neuprotestantismus* (Witten, 1963), 105; Schäfer, 'Rechtfertigungslehre bei Ritschl und Kälher', 73–4.
20 *Rechtfertigung und Versöhnung*, §1; 11. For a helpful analysis of this structure, see G. Hök, *Die elliptische Theologie Albrecht Ritschls nach Ursprung und innerem Zusammenhang* (Uppsala, 1941).
21 See Fabricius, *Entwicklung in Albrecht Ritschls Theologie*, 75–88.
22 *Rechtfertigung und Versöhnung*, §16; 78.
23 Ritschl has clearly misunderstood the theological significance of the concept of *gratia gratum faciens* within the context of Roman Catholic theologies of justification: *Rechtfertigung und Versöhnung*, §16; 78. His criticisms directed against the *Aufklärung* are considerably more accurate.
24 *Rechtfertigung und Versöhnung*, §16; 77–83, especially 82–3. Note particularly Ritschl's criticism of Pietism, which would be developed in his *Geschichte des Pietismus* (3 vols: Bonn, 1880–6).
25 *Rechtfertigung und Versöhnung*, §17; 90.
26 For a discussion of Grotius, see R. S. Franks, *The Work of Christ* (London, 1962), 389–409. The point with which Ritschl is concerned is developed in A. E. McGrath, 'Justice and Justification: Semantic and Juristic Aspects of the Christian Doctrine of Justification', *SJTh* 35 (1982), 403–18, *in fine*.
27 *Rechtfertigung und Versöhnung*, §17; 84.
28 *Rechtfertigung und Versöhnung*, §17; 86.
29 *Rechtfertigung und Versöhnung*, §17; 87–9.
30 *Rechtfertigung und Versöhnung*, §17; 89–90.
31 See C. Walther, 'Der Reich-Gottes-Begriff in der Theologie Richard Rothes und Albrecht Ritschls', *KuD* 2 (1956), 115–38; R. Schäfer, 'Das Reich Gottes bei Albrecht Ritschl und Johannes Weiß', *ZThK* (1964), 68–88. The older study of R. Wegener, *Albrecht Ritschls Idee des Reich Gottes* (Leipzig, 1897), is intensely hostile.
32 Schäfer, 'Das Reich Gottes', 82–5.
33 Some earlier commentators suggested that Ritschl confuses the abstract concept of the destiny of the universe with that of God: see James Orr, *The Ritschlian Theology and the Evangelical Faith* (London, 1897), 255–6; A. E. Garvey, *The Ritschlian Theology* (Edinburgh, 1902), 237–63.
34 *Unterricht in der christlichen Religion* (Bonn, 1875), §14. Cf. *Rechtfertigung und Versöhnung*, §37; 284.
35 *Unterricht in der christlichen Religion*, §16.
36 Particular attention should be paid to §§14 and 15 of the second volume of *Rechtfertigung und Versöhnung* (Bonn, 1874). Note particularly the reference to the study of Ludwig Diestel, 'Die Idee der Gerechtigkeit, vorzüglich im Alten Testament, biblisch-theologisch dargestellt', *Jahrbuch für deutsche Theologie* 5 (1860), 173–204: *Rechtfertigung und Versöhnung* II, §14; 102 n. 1.
37 cf. *WA* 2.504.25: 'iustitia Dei in scripturis fere semper pro fide et gratia accipitur'.
38 *Rechtfertigung und Versöhnung*, §1; 5.

39 Note the question raised by Martin Kähler, *Zur Lehre von der Versöhnung* (Leipzig, 1898), 337: 'Hat Christus bloß irrige Ansichten über eine unwandelbare Sachlage berichtigt, oder ist er der Begründer einer veränderten Sachlage?' For the Christology of Ritschl and Harnack, of relevance here, see Alister E. McGrath, *The Making of Modern German Christology: From the Enlightenment to Pannenberg* (Oxford, 1986), 53–68.

40 See Schäfer, 'Rechtfertigungslehre bei Ritschl und Kähler', 77–85.

41 See McGrath, *The Making of Modern German Christology*, 69–93.

§37

1 See W. Pressel, *Die Kriegspredigt 1914–1918 in der evangelischen Kirche Deutschlands* (Göttingen, 1967); K. Hammer, *Deutsche Kriegstheologie (1870–1918)* (München, 1971).

2 The 'Manifesto of the Intellectuals' is particularly significant in this respect: see W. Härle, 'Der Aufruf der 93 Intellektuellen und Karl Barths Bruch mit der liberalen Theologie', *ZThK* 72 (1975), 207–24.

3 Karl Holl, 'Was verstand Luther unter Religion?', in *Gesammelte Aufsätze zur Kirchengeschichte* (3 vols: Tübingen, 1928), I.1–110.

4 'Die Gerechtigkeit Gottes', in *Das Wort Gottes und die Theologie*, 5–17.

5 'Die Gerechtigkeit Gottes', 5.

6 'Die Gerechtigkeit Gottes', 7.

7 'Die Gerechtigkeit Gottes', 10.

8 'Die Gerechtigkeit Gottes', 11.

9 'Die Gerechtigkeit Gottes', 11–12.

10 For some useful reflections upon the impact of the *Rechtswillkür* of The Third Reich upon Protestant understanding of law, see Ernst Wolf, 'Zum protestantischen Rechtsdenken', in *Peregrinatio* II: *Studien zur reformatorischen Theologie, zum Kirchenrecht und zur Sozialethik* (München, 1965), 191–206.

11 'Die Gerechtigkeit Gottes', 12–13.

12 'Die Gerechtigkeit Gottes', 13.

13 'Die Gerechtigkeit Gottes', 13.

14 'Die Gerechtigkeit Gottes', 14.

15 'Die Gerechtigkeit Gottes', 15.

16 See Althaus, 'Gottes Gottheit als Sinn der Rechtfertigungslehre Luthers'.

17 *Kirchliche Dogmatik*, IV/1 §61, 1; 573–89. On Barth's doctrine of justification in general, see Küng, *Rechtfertigung*; G. C. Berkouwer, *The Triumph of Grace in the Theology of Karl Barth* (London, 1956); McGrath, 'Justification: Barth, Trent and Küng'.

18 *Kirchliche Dogmatik*, IV/1 §61, 1; 581. See McGrath, 'Karl Barth and the Articulus Iustificationis'.

19 *WA* 39 1.205.2–5. Barth refers to this dictum: *Kirchliche Dogmatik*, IV/1 §61, 1; 582.

20 Wolf, 'Die Rechtfertigungslehre als Mitte und Grenze reformatorischer Theologie', 14. The reference to the *subjectum theologiae* derives from *WA* 40 II.328.17–21: 'Theologiae proprium subiectum est homo peccati reus

ac perditus et Deus iustificans ac salvator hominis peccatoris. Quicquid extra hoc subiectum in theologia queritur aut disputatur, est error et venenum.'

21 Thus Luther's celebrated distinction between *Deus absconditus* and *Deus revelatus* arises within the context of his soteriology: see H. Bandt, *Luthers Lehre vom verborgenen Gott: Eine Untersuchung zu dem offenbarungsgeschichtlichen Ansatz seiner Theologie* (Berlin, 1958). Note the reference to Barth in the preface.

22 Note the reference at *Kirchliche Dogmatik*, IV/1 §61, 1; 581.

23 *Kirchliche Dogmatik*, IV/1 §61, 1; 583: 'Man tut aber in der Theologie gut, über die Bedürfnisse und Notwendigkeiten des Tages hinaus immer auch auf weitere Sicht zu denken, sich in allem noch so berechtigten Reagieren Maß zu auferlegen, sich der Grenzen der jeweils herrschenden "Anliegen" (mögen diese noch so echt und begründet sein!) bewußt zu bleiben.' Perhaps Barth has forgotten that his own theology is essentially a reaction against a particular theological position (that of the liberal school), and might therefore be subject to precisely the same criticism.

24 *Kirchliche Dogmatik*, IV/1 §61, 1; 583.

25 See M. F. Wiles, *The Making of Christian Doctrine: A Study in the Principles of Early Doctrinal Development* (Cambridge, 1978), 94–112.

26 *Kirchliche Dogmatik*, IV/1 §61, 1; 583. Cf. *Kirchliche Dogmatik*, IV/1 §61, 1; 578.

27 *Kirchliche Dogmatik*, IV/1 §61, 1; 584. Note also Barth's suggestion that a preoccupation with the question of how a gracious God may be found leads to a 'certain narcissism': *Kirchliche Dogmatik*, IV/1 §61, 1; 588: 'Die Frage: Wie kriege ich einen gnädigen Gott? in höchsten Ehren! Sie ist aber dem Protestantismus – jedenfalls dem europäischen und inbesondere dem deutschen Protestantismus – allzu lange Anlaß und Versuchung gewesen, einem gewissen Narzismus zu huldigen und gerade nach der nun zuletzt angedeuteten Seite auf der Stelle zu treten.' More generally, see Eberhard Leppin, 'Luthers Frage nach dem gnädigen Gott – heute', *ZThK* 61 (1964), 89–102.

28 For a comparison of the liberals, Brunner and Barth on this point, see Alister E. McGrath, *The Making of Modern German Christology: From the Enlightenment to Pannenberg* (Oxford, 1986), 105–6.

29 See the analysis of Hans Urs von Balthasar, *Karl Barth: Darstellung und Deutung seiner Theologie* (Köln, 1961), 210, who argues that Schleiermacher (as a typical representative of this school) determines Barth's theological concerns and methods as 'der Prägstock, der ein nicht mehr auszulöschendes Zeichen aufdrückt, die Form, aus der man bei aller materiellen Entgegensetzung, sich nicht mehr befreit'.

30 Holl, 'Was verstand Luther unter Religion?'. Holl appears to treat Luther's doctrine of justification as an aspect of his *Gewissensreligion*.

31 On this theme in Luther's theology, see G. Aulén, 'Die drei Haupttypen des christlichen Versöhnungslehre', *ZSTh* 7 (1930), 301–38; M. Leinhard, *Luther témoin de Jésus Christ* (Paris, 1968).

32 A monologue which von Balthasar derides as 'ein gespenstischer Spuk ohne Wirklichkeit': von Balthasar, *Karl Barth*, 225–6; 380.

33 See the important essay of Jacques de Senarclens, 'La concentration christologique', in *Antwort: Karl Barth zum 70. Geburtstag* (Zürich, 1956), 190–207.

34 Karl Barth, *Die protestantische Theologie im 19. Kahrhundert* (Zürich, 1952), 375–7.

35 On this, and especially Barth's concept of *das Nichtige*, see Wolf Krötke, *Sünde und Nichtiges bei Karl Barth* (Berlin, 1971).

36 See Alister E. McGrath, 'From the Reformation to the Enlightenment', in *The Science of Theology*, ed. P. D. L. Avis (London, 1986), for further details.

37 We first demonstrated this point recently: McGrath, 'Karl Barth als Aufklärer?'. Cf. G. Ebeling, *Lutherstudien* III (Tübingen, 1985), 492–573.

38 Barth, *Die protestantische Theologie*, 16–21.

39 *Kirchliche Dogmatik*, IV/1 §57, 1; 16: 'Wir müssens uns jetzt vergegenwärtigen, daß die christliche Botschaft in ihrer Mitte keinen Begriff und keine Idee ausspricht und auch nicht von einer anonymen, in Begriffen und Ideen als Wahrheit und Wirklichkeit aufzufangenden Geschichte Bericht erstattet ... Aber eben von dieser Geschichte und ihrer inkludierenden Kraft und Bedeutung berichtet sie in der Weise, daß sie einen Namen ausspricht ... Sie können gerade nur der Umschreibung dieses Namens dienen: des Namens Jesu Christi.' See further H. J. Iwand, 'Vom Primat der Christologie', in *Antwort: Karl Barth zum 70. Geburtstag* (Zürich, 1956), 172–89. S. W. Sykes, 'Barth on the Centre of Theology', in *Karl Barth: Studies of his Theological Method* (Oxford, 1979), 17–54. For Barth's Christology, see McGrath, *The Making of Modern German Christology*, 94–126.

40 See H. Vogel, 'Praedestinatio gemina: Die Lehre von der ewigen Gnadenwahl', in *Theologische Aufsätze: Karl Barth zum 50. Geburtstag* (München, 1936), 222–42; Konrad Stock, *Anthropologie der Verheißung: Karl Barths Lehre vom Menschen als dogmatisches Problem* (München, 1980), 65–72.

41 *Kirchliche Dogmatik*, II/2 §33, 2; 176–8.

42 *Kirchliche Dogmatik*, II/2 §33, 2; 181.

43 *Kirchliche Dogmatik*, II/2 §33, 2; 183: 'Prädestination heißt: der von Gott von Ewigkeit her beschlossene Freispruch des Menschen von der Verwerfung zu Gottes eigenen Ungusten, der Freispruch des Menschen, in welchem Gott sich selbst ... zum Verworfenen an Stelle des Freigesprochenen bestimmt.'

44 *Kirchliche Dogmatik*, IV/1 §57, 3; 72–3: 'Gottes Gnade triumphiert also – und das ist das Geschehen der Erfüllung des Bundes in Jesus Christus – über den Menschen und seine Sünde. Aber sie bekommt und hat nun den Charakter jenes "Dennoch" und "Trotzdem". Sie triumphiert nun – mitten im Gegensatz des Menschen zu ihr – erst recht wunderbar, einseitig, selbstherrlich.'

45 *Kirchliche Dogmatik*, IV/1 §59, 2; 252.

46 *Kirchliche Dogmatik*, IV/1 §60, 1; 458.

47 *Kirchliche Dogmatik*, III/2 §43, 2; 43: 'Die Lehre vom *liberum arbitrium* des sündigen Menschen ist ein Spottgebilde, das in alle Winde verwehen muß, wenn es von Erkenntnis der Güte Gottes auch nur von Ferne berührt wird.'

48 *Kirchliche Dogmatik*, III/2 §43, 2; 31: 'jene Verkehrtheit und Verderbnis ist radikal und total'. Cf. Stock, *Anthropologie der Verheißung*, 102–11.

49 *Kirchliche Dogmatik*, IV/1 §61, 4; 679–718, especially 701.

50 *Kirchliche Dogmatik*, II/2 §33, 2; 183: 'und heißt Prädestination Nicht-Verwerfung des Menschen'.

51 e.g., Berkouwer, *Triumph of Grace*, 262–96.

52 *Kirchliche Dogmatik*, IV/1 §60, 1; 410, where the following thesis is established: 'Daß der Mensch der Mensch der Sünde ist, was seine Sünde ist und was sie für ihn bedeutet, das wird erkannt, indem Jesus Christus erkannt wird, nur so, so wirklich'.

53 *Kirchliche Dogmatik*, IV/1 §61, 1; 574–5 (our italics).

54 *Kirchliche Dogmatik*, IV/1 §60, 1; 578.

55 E. Brunner, *Dogmatik* I: *Die christliche Lehre von Gott* (Zürich, 1946), 375–9. See further E. Buess, 'Zur Prädestinationslehre Karl Barths', in *Heilsgeschehen und Welt: Theologische Traktate* I (Göttingen, 1965), 77–132; Stock, *Anthropologie der Verheißung*, 44–61.

56 M. Kähler, *Zur Lehre von der Versöhnung* (Leipzig, 1898), 337.

57 For further discussion, see McGrath, 'Karl Barth als Aufklärer?', 280–3.

§38

1 The question of how it is possible for God to justify the sinner was, of course, by far the more important, raising questions concerning the nature of the 'righteousness of God', the work of Christ, and such. The question of the nature of justification, once settled by Augustine, only became an issue once more at the time of the Reformation itself.

2 See Jürgen Moltmann, 'Justification and New Creation', in *The Future of Creation* (London, 1979), 149–71, especially 151–2; 157–64.

3 See Walter Kern, 'Atheismus – Christentum – emanzipierte Gesellschaft', *ZKTh* 91 (1969), 289–321. Cf. C. Villa-Vicencio, 'Protestantism, Modernity and Justification by Faith', *SJTh* 38 (1985), 369–82. Subilia notes that contemporary interest lies in the question of the justification of *God*, rather than of man: *La giustificazione per fede*, 343–51.

4 See Eberhard Leppin, 'Luthers Frage nach dem gnädigen Gott – heute', *ZThK* 61 (1964), 89–102.

5 The trend is well illustrated by the first four statements of the document *Justification Today*, issued by the Helsinki Assembly of the Lutheran World Federation (1963): see "Justification Today": Document 75 – Assembly and Final Versions', *Lutheran World* 12/1 Supplement (1965), 1–11. On the background to this document, see Peter Kjeseth and Paul Hoffmann, 'Document 75', *Lutheran World* 11 (1964), 83–6. For further comment, see Albrecht Peters, 'Systematische Besinnung zu einer Neuinterpretation der reformatorischen Rechtfertigungslehre', in *Rechtfertigung im neuzeitlichen Lebenszusammenhang: Studien zur Neuinterpretation*

der Rechtfertigungslehre, ed. W. Lohff and C. Walther (Gütersloh, 1974), 107–25.

6 T. Langan, *The Meaning of Heidegger: A Critical Study of an Existentialist Phenomenology* (London, 1959); A. Chapell, *L'Ontologie phénoménologique de Heidegger: un commentaire de 'Sein und Zeit'* (Paris, 1962). On Heidegger's divergence from Husserl at points, see J. McGinley, 'Heidegger's Concern for the Lived-World in his Dasein Analysis', *Philosophy Today* 16 (1972), 92–116.

7 Heidegger, *Sein und Zeit* (Tübingen, 1927), 41–2.

8 See H. Diem, *Die Existenzdialektik von Sören Kierkegaard* (Zürich, 1950); K. E. Lögstrup, *Kierkegaarde und Heideggers Existenzanalyse und ihr Verhältnis zur Verkündigung* (Berlin, 1950).

9 See Jean Beaufret, 'Heidegger et la théologie', in *Heidegger et la question de Dieu*, ed. R. Kearny and J. S. O'Leary (Paris, 1980), 19–36.

10 See J. A. Macquarrie, *An Existentialist Theology* (London, 1973), 29–105; 127–49, for an excellent analysis.

11 *Sein und Zeit*, 177.

12 *Sein und Zeit*, 179. Cf. Macquarrie, *Existentialist Theology*, 78–97.

13 R. Lorenz, *Die unvollendete Befreiung vom Nominalismus: Martin Luther und die Grenzen hermeneutischer Theologie bei Gerhard Ebeling* (Gütersloh, 1973), 131–44. A similar point is made by H. Blumenberg, *Die Legitimät der Neuzeit* (Frankfurt, 1966).

14 See G. Ebeling, 'Gewißheit und Zweifel: Die Situation des Glaubens im Zeitalter nach Luther und Descartes', *ZThK* 64 (1967), 282–324.

15 On this, see Alister E. McGrath, *The Making of Modern German Christology: from the Enlightenment to Pannenberg* (Oxford, 1986), 127–43.

16 Bultmann, *Glauben und Verstehen* (4 vols: Tübingen, 1964–5), 2.111.

17 Gerhardt Kuhlmann, 'Zum theologischen Problem der Existenz: Fragen an Rudolf Bultmann', *ZThK* 10 (1929), 28–57.

18 Bultmann, 'Die Geschichtlichkeit des Daseins und der Glaube: Antwort an Gerhardt Kuhlmann', *ZThK* 11 (1930), 339–64.

19 The original essay, 'Rechtfertigung und Zweifel', was published in the 1924 *Vorträge der theologischen Konferenz zu Gießen*. Cf. Tillich, *The Protestant Era* (London, 1951), xxix.

20 For what follows, see 'The Protestant Message and the Man of Today', in *The Protestant Era*, 189–204.

21 See John P. Clayton, *The Concept of Correlation: Paul Tillich and the Possibility of a Mediating Theology* (Berlin, 1980).

22 See Tillich, 'You are Accepted', in *The Shaking of the Foundations* (New York, 1948), 153–63. Despite the verbal parallels with the concept of *acceptatio Dei*, it is difficult to see quite how Tillich understands man to be accepted *by* God.

23 Ebeling, *Dogmatik des christlichen Glaubens* (3 vols: Tübingen, 1979), 3.205–6, 218. On the concept of 'relational ontology', which underlies Ebeling's statements, see Miikka Ruokanen, *Hermeneutics as an Ecumenical Method in the Theology of Gerhard Ebeling* (Helsinki, 1982), 72–100.

24 *Dogmatik des christlichen Glaubens*, 3.195–200.

25 For the relation of anthropology, the Word of God, and justification according to Eberhard Jüngel, see J. B. Webster, *Eberhard Jüngel: An Introduction to His Theology* (Cambridge, 1986), 93–103.

26 See J. M. Robinson, *A New Quest of the Historical Jesus* (London, 1959); McGrath, *The Making of Modern German Christology*, 161–85.

27 The contribution of Eberhard Jüngel is particularly significant: Jüngel, *Paulus und Jesus: Eine Untersuchung zur Präzisierung der Frage nach dem Ursprung der Christologie* (Tübingen, 1962).

28 McGrath, 'Justification and Christology'; *idem*, 'Der articulus iustificationis als axiomatischer Grundsatz des christlichen Glaubens'.

29 Most significant to date is the agreement between Lutherans and Catholics in the United States: see 'Justification by Faith', *Origins* 13/17 (1983), 277–304. A similar agreement between Anglicans and Catholics is expected to be announced in 1986.

30 If any period may be said to demonstrate continuity in development, it is the medieval period: the initial formulation of, and subsequent critique of, the necessary rôle of created grace in justification is an excellent example of continuous development.

31 If the Anselmian motto *fides quaerens intellectum* is accepted, and taken to imply the priority of faith over understanding, it will be clear that the manner by which faith comes about is prior to subsequent reflection upon that faith. In that the doctrine of justification is primarily concerned with the origin of faith, as *fides ex auditu*, it clearly assumes an implicit rôle in theological reflection. For an analysis, see McGrath, 'Justification and Christology'; *idem*, 'Der articulus iustificationis als axiomatischer Grundsatz des christlichen Glaubens'.

32 Goethe, *Faust* I. Teil, 682–3.

Bibliography

1. Primary Literature

a. Collected Works

Hardwick, C., *A History of the Articles of Religion*, 3rd edn (London, 1890)
Lloyd, C., *Formularies of Faith put forth by Authority during the Reign of Henry VIII* (Oxford, 1825)
Müller, E. F. K., *Die Bekenntnisschriften der reformierten Kirche* (Leipzig, 1903)
   Die Bekenntnisschriften der evangelisch-lutherischen Kirche (Göttingen, 1952)
   Concilium Tridentinum diarorum, actorum, epistularum, tractatuum nova collectio, ed. Societas Goeresiana (Freiburg, 1901–)

b. Individual Authors

Alsted, Johann Heinrich, *Theologia scholastica didactica* (Hanover, 1618)
Andrewes, Launcelot, *Works* (11 vols: London, 1841–52)
Arminius, Jakobus, *Works* (3 vols: London, 1825–75)
Baius, Michel, *Opera* (Cologne, 1696)
Barlow, Thomas, *Two Letters written by the Rt Rev. Thomas Barlow* (London, 1701)
Barrow, Isaac, *Theological Works*, ed. A. Napier (9 vols: Cambridge, 1859)
Barth, Karl, *Das Wort Gottes und die Theologie* (München, 1925)
   Kirchliche Dogmatik (Zürich, 1932–68)
Baxter, Richard, *Aphorisms on Justification* (London, 1649)
   A Treatise of Justifying Righteousness (London, 1676)
(Benedetto da Mantova, Dom?) *Trattato utilissimo di Giesu Cristo crocifisso verso i Cristiani*, ed. Salvatore Caponetto (Firenze, 1972)
Beveridge, William, *Theological Works* (12 vols: Oxford, 1844–8)
Beza, Theodore, *Tractationes theologicae*, 2nd edn (Geneva, 1632)
Bramhall, John, *Works* (5 vols: Oxford, 1842–5)
Brochmand, Jesper Rasmussen, *Universae theologiae systema* (Ulm, 1638)
Bucanus, Guillaume, *Institutiones theologicae* (n.p., 1604)

251

Bibliography

Bucer, Martin, *Praelectiones in epistolam ad Ephesios* (Basel, 1561)
  Metaphrasis et enarratio in epistolam ad Romanos (Basel, 1562)
Budde, Johann Franz, *Institutiones theologiae dogmaticae* (Jena, 1723)
Bull, George, *Harmonia Apostolica* (London, 1842)
Bullinger, Heinrich, *Sermonum decades quinque* (Zürich, 1552)
  De gratia Dei iustificante (Zürich, 1554)
Burmann, Franz, *Synopsis theologiae* (Amsterdam, 1699)
Calov, Abraham, *Systema locorum theologicorum* (Wittenberg, 1655)
Calvin, John, *Opera omnia quae supersunt* (59 vols: Brunswick, 1863–1900)
  Opera selecta, ed. P. Barth and W. Niesel (5 vols: München, 1926–36)
Chemnitz, Martin, *Loci theologici* (3 vols: Frankfurt, 1599)
  Examinis Concilii Tridentini (Frankfurt, 1646)
Clarke, Samuel, *The Saints Nosegay, or, 741 Spiritual Flowers* (London, 1642)
Cocceius, Johannes, *Summa theologiae* (Amsterdam, 1665)
  Opera (8 vols: Amsterdam, 1673–5)
Contarini, Gasparo, *Regesten und Briefen* ed. F. Dittrich (Braunsberg, 1881)
  Gegenreformatorische Schriften 1530–42 (Aschendorf, 1923)
Cosin, John, *Works* (5 vols: Oxford, 1843–55)
Cotton, John, *Gods Mercie mixed with his Iustice* (London, 1641)
  Christ the Fountaine of Life (London, 1651)
  A Treatise of the Covenant of Grace (London, 1659)
Cranmer, Thomas, *Works* (2 vols: Cambridge, 1844–6)
Davenant, John, *A Treatise on Justification, or the 'Disputatio de Iustitia Habituali et Actuali'* (London, 1844)
Downham, George, *A Treatise of Justification* (London, 1639)
Edwards, Jonathan, *Five Discourses on Justification by Faith* (Boston, 1738)
  Works, ed. E. Hickman (2 vols: Edinburgh, 1974)
Erasmus, Desiderius, *Novum instrumentum omne* (Basel, 1516)
  Opera omnia, ed. J. Leclerc (Leiden, 1703–6)
Fisher, John, *Opera* (Würzburg, 1597)
  English Works, ed. J. E. B. Mayor (EETS Extra Series 27: London, 1876)
Forbes, William, *Considerationes modestae et pacificae* (2 vols: London, 1850–6)
Frith, John, *Whole Workes* (London, 1573)
Gerhard, Johann, *Loci communes*, ed. Cotta (10 vols: Tübingen, 1768)
Goodwin, John, *Imputatio fidei; or A Treatise of Justification* (London, 1615)
Gropper, Johann, *Enchiridion Christianae Institutiones* (Cologne, 1536)
Hafenreffer, Matthias, *Loci theologici* (Tübingen, 1603)
Hall, Joseph, *Works* (12 vols: Oxford, 1837–9)
Hammond, Henry, *A Practical Catechism* (London, 1847)
Heidegger, Johann Heinrich, *Medulla theologiae Christianae* (Zürich, 1616)
Henke, Heinrich Philipp Konrad, *Lineamenta institutionum fidei Christianae* (Helmstedt, 1793)
Hooker, Richard, *Works*, ed. J. Keble, 3rd edn (3 vols: Oxford, 1845)
Hooker, Thomas, *The Soules Preparation for Christ* (London, 1632)
  The Unbeleevers Preparing for Christ (London, 1638)
  The Soules Humiliation (London, 1638)

Bibliography

Thomas Hooker: Writings in England and Holland 1626–33 (Harvard Theological Studies 28: Cambridge, Mass. 1975)

Hutter, Leonhard, *Compendium locorum theologicorum* (Wittenberg, 1652)

Jackson, Thomas, *Works* (12 vols: Oxford, 1844)

Jansenius, Cornelius, *Augustinus* (Paris, 1641)

Kant, Immanuel, *Gesammelte Schriften* (22 vols: Berlin, 1902–42)

Knewstub, John, *Lectures upon the Twentieth Chapter of Exodus* (London, 1577)

Knox, Alexander, *Remains*, ed. J. H. Newman, 2nd edn (4 vols: London, 1836–7)

Koenig, Johann Friedrich, *Theologia positiva acroamatica*, 11th edn (Rostok/Leipzig, 1703)

Locke, John, *Reasonableness of Christianity*, in *Works* VII (London, 1823), 1–158

Essay concerning Human Understanding, ed. P. H. Nidditch (Oxford, 1975)

Luther, Martin, *Kritische Gesamtausgabe* (Weimar, 1883)

Maresius, Samuel, *Collegium theologicum* (Geneva, 1662)

Mastricht, Peter van, *Theoretico-practica theologia* (Rhenum/Amsterdam, 1725)

Melanchthon, Philip, *Opera omnia quae supersunt* (28 vols: Brunswick, 1834–60)

Werke in Auswahl, ed. R. Stupperich (8 vols: Gütersloh, 1951–   )

Molina, Luis de, *Concordia liberii arbitrii cum gratiae donis* (Lisbon, 1588)

Morgan, Thomas, *The Moral Philosopher* (3 vols: London, 1738–40)

Mosheim, Lorenz vom, *Elementa theologiae dogmaticae* (Nürnburg, 1758)

Mosse, Miles, *Iustifying and Saving Faith distinguished from the Faith of the Devils* (Cambridge, 1614)

Musculus, Wolfgang, *Loci communes sacrae theologiae* (Basel, 1561)

Newman, John Henry, *Remarks on Certain Passages in the Thirty-Nine Articles* (Tract 90: Oxford, 1841)

Lectures on the Doctrine of Justification, 3rd edn (London/Cambridge, 1874)

Owen, John, *Works*, ed. T. Russell (21 vols: London, 1826)

Perkins, William, *Workes* (3 vols: Cambridge, 1608–9)

Petavius, Dionysius, *Opus de theologicus dogmatibus* (3 vols: Antwerp, 1700)

Pfaff, Christoph Matthaeus, *Institutiones theologiae dogmaticae et moralis* (Tübingen, 1720)

Polanus a Polansdorf, Amandus, *Syntagma theologiae Christianae* (Geneva, 1612)

Quenstedt, Johannes Andreas, *Theologia didactico-polemica* (Wittenberg, 1685)

Rijssen, Leonhard van, *Compendium theologiae didactico elencticae* (Amsterdam, 1695)

Ritschl, A. B., *Die christliche Lehre von der Rechtfertigung und Versöhnung.* III. *Die positive Entwickelung der Lehre*, 3rd edn (Bonn, 1888)

Sanderson, Robert, *Sermons*, ed. P. Montgomery (2 vols: London, 1841)

Scherzer, J. A., *Breviculus theologicus*, 3rd edn (Leipzig, 1680)

Bibliography

Schleiermacher, F. D. E., *Der christliche Glaube*, 4th edn (2 vols: Berlin, 1842–3)

Sharp, John, *Breviculus theologicus*, 3rd edn (Leipzig, 1680)

Soto, Domingo de, *De natura et gratia* (Paris, 1549)

In epistolam ad Romanos commentarii (Antwerp, 1550)

Stapleton, Thomas, *Opera* (4 vols: Paris, 1620)

Steinbart, Gotthelf Samuel, *System der reinen Philosophie oder Glückseligkeitslehre des Christenthums* (Züllichau, 1778)

Suarez, Francisco de, *Opera omnis* (28 vols: Paris, 1856–78)

Taylor, Jeremy, *Works*, ed. C. P. Eden (10 vols: London, 1847–54)

Teller, Wilhelm Abraham, *Die Religion der Vollkommnern* (Berlin, 1792)

Tindal, Matthew, *Christianity as Old as the Creation*, ed. G. Gawlick (Stuttgart, 1968)

Töllner, Johann Gottlieb, *Der thätige Gehorsam Christi untersucht* (Breslau, 1768)

Theologische Untersuchungen (2 vols: Riga, 1772–4)

Toland, John, *Christianity not Mysterious*, ed. G. Gawlick (Stuttgart, 1964)

Turrettini, Franciscus, *Institutio theologiae elencticae* (Geneva, 1688)

Tyndale, William, *Works* (3 vols: Cambridge, 1848)

Ussher, James, *Whole Works*, ed. C. R. Elrington and J. H. Todd (17 vols: Dublin/London, 1847–64)

Valdès, Juan de, *Diálogo de doctrina Cristiana*, ed. B. F. Stockwell (México, 1946)

Los ciento diez divinas consideraciones, ed. J. I. T. Idígoras (Salamanca, 1975)

Vega, Andres de, *Opusculum de iustificatione* (Venice, 1546)

De iustificatione doctrina universa (Cologne, 1572)

Walker, George, *A Defence of the True Sense and Meaning of the Words of the Holy Apostle: Rom. 4 ver. 3.5.9* (London, 1641)

Wendelin, Friedrich, *Christianae theologiae libri II* (Amsterdam, 1646)

Wesley, John, *Works* (14 vols: London, 1829–31)

Standard Sermons (2 vols: London, 1921)

Wollebius, Johannes, *Christianae theologiae compendium* (Amsterdam, 1637)

Zwingli, Huldrych, *Sämtliche Werke* (Zürich, 1905–)

2. Secondary Literature

Abercrombie, N., *The Origins of Jansenism* (Oxford, 1936)

Alfaro, J., 'Sobrenatural y pecado original en Bayo', *RET* 12 (1952), 3–76

Althaus, P., 'Gottes Gottheit als Sinn der Rechtfertigungslehre Luthers', *Luther Jahrbuch* 13 (1931), 1–28

Armstrong, B. G., *Calvinism and the Amyraut Heresy: Protestant Scholasticism and Humanism in Seventeenth-Century France* (Madison, 1969)

Baur, J., *Salus Christiana: Die Rechtfertigungslehre in der Geschichte des christlichen Heilsverständnisses* (Gütersloh, 1968)

Bavaud, G., 'La doctrine de la justification d'après Saint Augustin et la Réforme', *REAug* 5 (1959), 21–32

Bibliography

'La doctrine de la justification d'après Calvin et le Concile de Trent', *Verbum Caro* 22 (1968), 83–92

Becker, K. J., *Die Rechtfertigungslehre nach Domingo de Soto: Das Denken eines Konzilsteilnehmers vor, in und nach Trient* (Rom, 1967)

Beltrán de Heredia, V., 'Controversia de certitudine gratiae entre Domingo de Soto y Ambrosio Catarino', *Ciencia Tomista* 62 (1941), 33–62

Bizer, E., *Theologie der Verheißung: Studien zur theologische Entwicklung des jungen Melanchthon 1519–1524* (Neukirchen, 1964)

Fides ex auditu: Eine Untersuchung über die Entdeckung der Gerechtigkeit Gottes durch Martin Luther, 3rd edn (Neukirchen, 1966)

Boisset, J., 'Justification et sanctification chez Calvin', in *Calvinus Theologus: Die Referate des Congrés Européen de recherches Calviniennes*, ed. W. H. Neuser (Neukirchen, 1976), 131–48

Bornkamm, H., 'Zur Frage der Iustitia Dei beim jungen Luther', *ARG* 52 (1961), 16–29; 53 (1962), 1–60

Braunisch, R., *Die Theologie der Rechtfertigung im 'Enchiridion' (1538) des Johannes Gropper: Sein kritischer Dialog mit Philipp Melanchthon* (Münster, 1974)

Brunner, P., 'Die Rechtfertigungslehre des Konzils von Trient', in *Pro veritate: Eine theologischer Dialog* (Münster/Kassel, 1963), 59–96

Buuck, F., 'Zum Rechtfertigungsdekret' in *Das Weltkonzil von Trient*, ed. G. Schreiber, 117–43

Dalmau, J. M., 'La teología de la disposición a la justificación en vísperas de la revolucíon protestante', *RET* 6 (1946), 249–75

Fock, O., *Der Socianismus nach seiner Stellung* (Kiel, 1847)

Gibbs, Lee W., 'Richard Hooker's *Via Media* Doctrine of Justification', *HThR* 74 (1981), 211–20

Göhler, A., *Calvins Lehre von der Heiligung* (München, 1934)

Gonzáles Rivas, S., 'Los teólogos salmantinos y el decreto de la justificación', *EE* 21 (1947), 147–70

Grane, L., *Contra Gabrielem: Luthers Auseinandersetzung mit Gabriel Biel in der Disputatio contra scholasticam theologiam 1517* (Gyldenhal, 1962)

'Gregor von Rimini und Luthers Leipziger Disputation', *StTh* 22 (1968), 29–49

'Augustins "Expositio quarumdam propositionum ex Epistola ad Romanos" in Luthers Römerbriefvorlesung', *ZThK* 69 (1972), 304–30

Graß, H., 'Die durch Jesum von Nazareth vollbrachte Erlösung: Ein Beitrag zur Erlösungslehre Schleiermachers', in *Denkender Glaube: Festschrift für Carl Heinz Ratschow* (Berlin/New York, 1976), 152–69

Greschat, M., *Melanchthon neben Luther: Studien zur Gestalt der Rechtfertigungslehre zwischen 1528 und 1537* (Witten, 1965)

Guérard des Lauriers, M. L., 'Saint Augustin et la question de la certitude de la grâce au Concile de Trente', *Augustinus Magister* (Paris, 1954), 2.1057–69

Gyllenkrok, A., *Rechtfertigung und Heiligung in der frühen evangelischen Theologie Luthers* (Uppsala, 1952)

Hefner, J., *Die Entstehungsgeschichte des Trienter Rechtfertigungsdekretes: Ein Beitrag zur Geschichte des Reformationszeitalters* (Paderborn, 1939)

Bibliography

Hermann, R., *Luthers These 'Gerecht und Sünder zugleich': Eine systematische Untersuchung* (Darmstadt, 1960)

Heynck, V., 'Untersuchungen über die Reuelehre der tridentinischen Zeit', *FS* 29 (142), 25–44; 120–50; 30 (1943), 53–73

'A Controversy at the Council of Trent concerning the Doctrine of Duns Scotus', *FcS* 9 (1949), 181–258

'Der Anteil des Konzilstheologen Andreas de Vega O.F.M. an dem ersten amtlichen Entwurf des Trienter Rechtfertigungsdekretes', *FS* 33 (1951), 49–81

'Zum Problem der unvollkommenen Reue auf dem Konzil von Trient', in *Das Weltkonzil von Trient*, ed. G. Schreiber, 231–80

'Zur Kontroverse über die Gnadengewissheit auf dem Konzil von Trient', *FS* 37 (1955) 1–17; 161–88

'Die Bedeutung von "mereri" und "promereri" bei dem Konzilstheologen Andreas de Vega', *FS* 50 (1968), 224–38

Hirsch, E., *Die Theologie des Andreas Osiander und ihre geschichtlichen Voraussetzungen* (Göttingen, 1919)

Holfelder, H. H., *Tentatio et consolatio: Studien zu Bugenhagens Interpretatio in librum psalmorum* (Berlin/New York, 1974)

Solus Christus: Die Ausbildung von Bugenhagens Rechtfertigungslehre in der Paulusauslegung (1524/25) und ihre Bedeutung für die theologische Argumentation im Sendbrief 'Von dem christlichen Glauben' (Tübingen, 1981)

Holl, K., *Gesammelte Aufsätze zur Kirchengeschichte* (3 vols: Tübingen, 1928)

Horn, S., *Glaube und Rechtfertigung nach dem Konzilstheologer Andrés de Vega* (Paderborn, 1972)

Hünermann, F., *Wesen und Notwendigkeit der aktuellen Gnade nach dem Konzil von Trient* (Paderborn, 1926)

Huthmacher, H., 'La certitude de la grâce au Councile de Trente', *Nouvelle Revue Théologique* 60 (1933), 213–26

Jansen, F.-X., *Baius et la Baïanisme* (Louvain, 1927)

Jedin, H., *Kardinal Contarini als Kontroverstheologe* (Münster, 1949)

Geschichte des Konzils von Trient (4 vols: Freiburg, 1951–75)

Joest, W., 'Die tridentinische Rechtfertigungslehre', *KuD* 9 (1963), 41–59

Kähler, E., *Karlstadt und Augustin: Der Kommentar des Andreas Bodenstein von Karlstadt zu Augustins Schrift De spiritu et litera* (Halle, 1952)

Kaiser, A., *Natur und Gnade im Urstand: Eine Untersuchung der Kontroverse zwischen Michael Baius und Johannes Martinez de Ripaldi* (München, 1965)

Knox, D. B., *The Doctrine of Faith in the Reign of Henry VIII* (London, 1961)

Kolb, R., *Nikolaus von Amsdorf: Popular Polemics in the Preservation of Luther's Legacy* (Nieuwkoop, 1978)

Kriechbaum, F., *Grundzüge der Theologie Karlstadts: Eine systematische Studie zur Erhellung der Theologie Andreas von Karlstadts* (Hamburg, 1967)

Krüger, F., *Bucer und Erasmus: Eine Untersuchung zum Einfluß des Erasmus auf die Theologie Martin Bucers* (Wiesbaden, 1970)

Bibliography

Küng, H., *Rechtfertigung: Die Lehre Karl Barths und eine katholische Besin-nung* (Einsiedeln, 1957)

Laplanche, F., *Orthodoxie et prédication: l'oeuvre d'Amyraut et la querelle de la grâce universelle* (Paris, 1965)

Lennerz, J., 'Voten auf dem Trienter Konzil über die Rechtfertigung', *Gregorianum* 15 (1934), 577–88

Loewenich, W. von., *Von Augustin zu Luther* (Witten, 1959)

Duplex Iustitia: Luthers Stellung zu einer Unionsformel des 16. Jahrhunderts (Wiesbaden, 1972)

Logan, E. M. T., 'Grace and Justification: Some Italian Views on the 16th and early 17th centuries', *JEH* 20 (1969), 67–78

Loofs, F., 'Der articulus stantis et cadentis ecclesiae', *Theologische Studien und Kritiken* 90 (1917), 323–400

McGrath, A. E., 'Justification: Barth, Trent and Küng', *SJTh* 34 (1981), 517–29

'Humanist Elements in the Early Reformed Doctrine of Justification', *ARG* 73 (1982), 5–30

'Mira et nova diffinitio iustitiae: Luther and Scholastic Doctrines of Justification', *ARG* 74 (1983), 37–60

'John Henry Newman's "Lectures on Justification": The High Church Misrepresentation of Luther', *Churchman* 97 (1983), 112–22

'Karl Barth and the Articulus Iustificationis: The Significance of His Critique of Ernst Wolf within the Context of His Theological Method', *Theologische Zeitschrift* 39 (1983), 349–61

'ARCIC II and Justification: Some Difficulties and Obscurities relating to Anglican and Roman Catholic Teaching on Justification', *Anvil* 1 (1984), 27–42

'Der articulus iustificationis als axiomatischer Grundsatz des christlichen Glaubens', *ZThK* 81 (1984), 273–83

'The Emergence of the Anglican Tradition on Justification', *Churchman* 98 (1984), 28–43

'Karl Barth als Aufklärer? Der Zusammenhang seiner Lehre vom Werke Christi mit der Erwählungslehre', *KuD* 30 (1984), 273–83

'Justification and Christology: The Axiomatic Correlation between the Proclaimed Christ and the Historical Jesus', *Modern Theology* 1 (1984–5), 45–54

'The Moral Theory of the Atonement: An Historical and Theological Critique', *SJTh* 38 (1985), 205–20

Luther's Theology of the Cross: Martin Luther's Theological Breakthrough (Oxford, 1985)

'John Calvin and Late Medieval Thought: A Study in Late Medieval Influences upon Calvin's Theological Thought', *ARG* 77 (1986)

McSorley, H. J., *Luther – Right or Wrong? An Ecumenical-theological Study of Luther's Major Work, The Bondage of the Will* (New York/Minneapolis, 1969)

Modalsi, O., *Das Gericht nach den Werken: Ein Beitrag zu Luthers Lehre vom Gesetz* (Göttingen, 1963)

Bibliography

Moltmann, G., 'Prädestination und Heilsgeschichte bei Moyse Amyraut', *ZKG* 65 (1954), 270–303

Müller, J., *Die Rechtfertigungslehre nominalistischer Reformationsgegner: Bartholomäus Arnoldi von Usingen und Kaspar Schatzgeyer über Erbsünde, erste Rechtfertigung und Taufe* (Breslau, 1940)

Niesel, W., 'Calvin wider Osianders Rechtfertigungslehre', *ZKG* 46 (1982), 410–30

Nygren, A., 'Simul iustus et peccator bei Augustin und Luther', *ZSTh* 16 (1940), 364–79

Oberman, H. A., 'Das tridentinische Rechtfertigungsdekret im Lichte spätmittelalterlicher Theologie', *ZThK* 61 (1964), 251–82

'"Iustitia Christi" and "Iustitia Dei": Luther and the Scholastic Doctrines of Justification', *HThR* 59 (1966), 1–26

Olazarán, J., *Documentos inéditos tridentinos sobre la justificación* (Madrid, 1957)

Oltra, M., *Die Gewissheit des Gnadenstandes bei Andres de Vega: Ein Beitrag zum Verständnis des Trienter Rechtfertigungsdekretes* (Düsseldorf, 1941)

Pas, P., 'La doctrine de la double justice au Councile de Trente', *EThL* 30 (1954), 5–53

Peters, A., *Glaube und Werk: Luthers Rechtfertigungslehre im Lichte der heiligen Schrift*, 2nd edn (Berlin/Hamburg, 1967)

Pfnür, V., *Einig in der Rechtfertigungslehre? Die Rechtfertigungslehre der Confessio Augustana (1530) und die Stellungnahme der katholischen Kontroverstheologie zwischen 1530 und 1535* (Wiesbaden, 1970)

Philips, G., 'La justification luthérienne et la Concile de Trente', *EThL* 47 (1971), 340–58

Rich, A., *Die Anfänge der Theologie Huldrych Zwinglis* (Zürich, 1949)

Ritschl, A. B., *The Christian Doctrine of Justification and Reconciliation* (Edinburgh, 1871)

Rückert, H., *Die Rechtfertigungslehre auf dem Tridentinischen Konzil* (Bonn, 1925)

'Promereri: Eine Studie zum tridentinischen Rechtfertigungsdekret als Antwort an H. A. Oberman', *ZThK* 68 (1971), 162–94

Rupp, E. G., *The Righteousness of God: Luther Studies* (London, 1953)

Studies in the Making of the English Protestant Tradition (Cambridge, 1966)

Sagúes, J., 'Un libro pretridentino de Andrés de Vega sobre la justificación, *EE* 20 (1946), 175–209

Santoro, S., 'La giustificazione in Giovanni Antonio Delfini, teologo del Concilio di Trento', *Miscellanea Franciscana* 40 (1940), 1–27

Schäfer, R., 'Die Rechtfertigungslehre bei Ritschl und Kähler', *ZThK* 62 (1965), 66–85

Schierse, F. J., 'Das Trienterkonzil und die Frage nach der christliche Gewissheit', in *Das Weltkonzil von Trient*, ed. G. Schreiber, 145–67

Schreiber, G. (ed.), *Das Weltkonzil von Trient: Sein Werden und Wirken* (2 vols: Freiburg, 1951)

Schrenk, G., *Gottesreich und Bund im älteren Protestantismus* (Darmstadt, 1967)

Bibliography

Schwarz, R., *Fides, spes und caritas beim jungen Luther, unter besonderer Berücksichtigung der mittelalterlichen Tradition* (Berlin, 1962)

Serry, J. H., *Historia congregationis de auxiliis* (Louvain, 1700)

Seybold, M., *Glaube und Rechtfertigung bei Thomas Stapleton* (Paderborn, 1967)

Sider, R. J., *Andreas Bodenstein von Karlstadt: The Development of his Thought 1517–1525* (Leiden, 1974)

Stadtland, T., *Rechtfertigung und Heiligung bei Calvin* (Neukirchen, 1972)

Staedtke, J., *Die Theologie des jungen Bullinger* (Zürich, 1962)

Stakemeier, A., *Das Konzil von Trient über die Heilsgewissheit* (Heidelberg, 1949)

Stakemeier, E., 'Die theologischen Schulen auf dem Trienter Konzil während der Rechtfertigungsverhandlung', *Theologisches Quartalschrift* 117 (1936), 188–207; 322–50; 446–504

Der Kampf um Augustin: Augustinus und die Augustiner auf dem Tridentinum (Paderborn, 1937)

Stegmüller, F., *Francisco de Vitoria y la doctrina de gracia en la escuela salmantina* (Barcelona, 1934)

Stupperich, R., 'Der Ursprung des Regensburger Buches von 1541 und seine Rechtfertigungslehre', *ARG* 36 (1939), 88–116

Tellechea, I., 'El articulus de iustificatione de Fray Bartolomeo de Carranza', *RET* 15 (1955), 563–635

Van't Spijker, W., 'Prädestination bei Bucer und Calvin', in *Calvinus Theologus*, ed. W. Neuser (Neukirchen, 1976), 85–111

Vignaux, P., 'Sur Luther et Ockham', *FS* 32 (1950), 21–30

Villalmonte, A. de, 'Andrés de Vega y el processo de la justificación según el Concilio Tridentina', *RET* 5 (1945), 311–74

Vogelsang, E., *Die Anfänge von Luthers Christologie nach der ersten Psalmenvorlesung* (Berlin/Leipzig, 1929)

Walz, A., 'La giustificazione tridentina', *Angelicum* 28 (1951), 97–138

Wolf, E., 'Die Rechtfertigungslehre als Mitte und Grenze reformatorischer Theologie', in *Peregrinatio* II: *Studien zur reformatorischen Theologie, zum Kirchenrecht und zur Sozialethik* (München, 1965), 11–21

Xiberta, B., 'La causa meritoria de la justificación en las controversias pretridentinas', *RET* 5 (1945), 87–106

Index of names

260

Index of names

Index of subjects

Index of subjects

21710